discover
JAPAN

CHRIS ROWTHORN
ANDREW BENDER, MATTHEW D FIRESTONE,
TIMOTHY N HORNYAK, BENEDICT WALKER,
PAUL WARHAM, WENDY YANAGIHARA

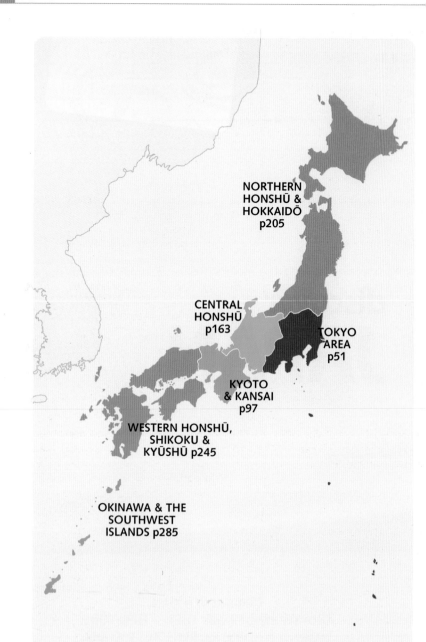

NORTHERN HONSHŪ & HOKKAIDŌ p205

CENTRAL HONSHŪ p163

TOKYO AREA p51

KYOTO & KANSAI p97

WESTERN HONSHŪ, SHIKOKU & KYŪSHŪ p245

OKINAWA & THE SOUTHWEST ISLANDS p285

DISCOVER JAPAN

Tokyo Area (p51) Japan's frenetic capital is surrounded by attractions including Mt Fuji, Nikkō, Kamakura and the Ogasawara-shotō island group.

Kyoto & Kansai (p97) Japan's cultural capital, Kyoto, is a must-see attraction; the Kansai region contains many first-rate sights such as Nara and Kōya-san.

Central Honshū (p163) Central Honshū is home to the Japan Alps and several historic cities including Kanazawa, Takayama and Matsumoto.

Northern Honshū & Hokkaidō (p205) Honshū's seldom-visited north offers good hiking and historic towns; Hokkaidō features incredible skiing, driving and outdoor adventures.

Western Honshū, Shikoku & Kyūshū (p245) Western Honshū and the adjoining islands of Shikoku and Kyūshū boast history, coastal scenery and outdoor attractions.

Okinawa & the Southwest Islands (p285) Japan's Southwest Islands offer excellent beaches, hiking, snorkelling, diving and a unique culture that's not quite Japanese.

⇲ CONTENTS

RICHARD CUMMINS

Japanese bonsai

NORTHERN
HONSHŪ &
HOKKAIDŌ
p205

WESTERN
HONSHŪ,
SHIKOKU
& KYŪSHŪ
p245

CENTRAL
HONSHŪ
p163

TOKYO
AREA
p51

KYOTO
& KANSAI
p97

OKINAWA & THE
SOUTHWEST
ISLANDS p285

CHINA

RUSSIA

Inset

See Main Map

YAKUSHIMA p297

Head into moss-covered forests to find the 3000-year-old tree, Jōmon-sugi

Tanegashima

Yakushima

Tokara-shotō

Kagoshima ●
KYŪSHŪ

EAST CHINA SEA

Amami-shotō
● Naze

IRIOMOTE-JIMA p316

Dive with mantas, snorkel on pristine reefs and kayak up jungle rivers

Nansei-shotō
Nago ● Okinawa-hontō
● Okinawa City
● NAHA

SEA OF JAPAN

Miyako-shotō
● Hirara

Iriomote-jima ● Ishigaki
Yaeyama-shotō

0 — 200 km
0 — 120 miles

✪ Pyongyang

NORTH KOREA

SEOUL ✪

SOUTH KOREA

TAKAYAMA p176

This town is both a gateway to the Japan Alps and a fascinating historical destination

KYOTO p110

Find the Japan of your imagination in the nation's culture capital

Noto-hantō

HIROSHIMA p256

Learn the tragic history of this city and marvel at its recovery

Oki-shotō

TOYAMA ●

KANAZAWA ●

FUKUI ● Takayam

MATSUE TOTTORI
Izumo ● ●

HONSHŪ

Hamada *San-yō* OKAYAMA Himeji

GIFU

KANSAI

KYOTO ● NAGO
Nara ● TSU

Hagi *Shinkansen*

Tsu-shima

Shimonoseki ● **HIROSHIMA**

KŌBE ● ● OSAKA

TAKAMATSU ● WAKAYAMA

FUKUOKA (HAKATA) ●

Kitakyūshū ● **MATSUYAMA**

TOKUSHIMA

Kansai International Airport

Beppu
● Oita
● Usuki

SHIKOKU KŌCHI ●

Shingū

Gotō-rettō

Nagasaki ●
KUMAMOTO

Aso-san ▲

NARA p151

Check out Japan's first permanent capital which boasts eight World Heritage sites

Amakusa-shotō
● Yatsushiro
Kagoshima Shinkansen
KYŪSHŪ

● MIYAZAKI

See Inset

KAGOSHIMA ●

PACIFIC OCEAN

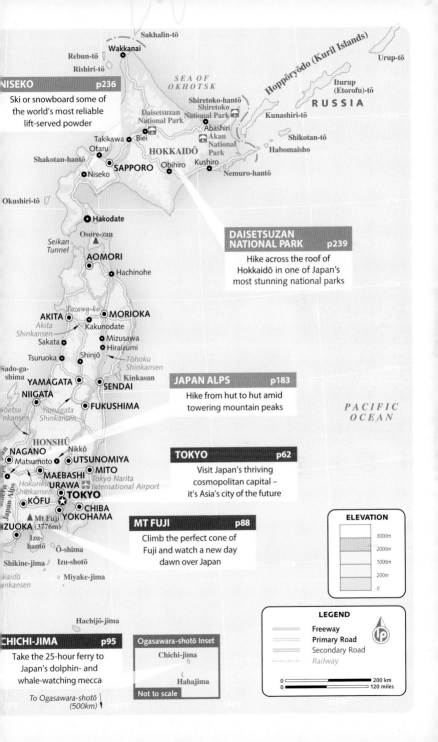

NISEKO   p236

Ski or snowboard some of the world's most reliable lift-served powder

DAISETSUZAN NATIONAL PARK   p239

Hike across the roof of Hokkaidō in one of Japan's most stunning national parks

JAPAN ALPS   p183

Hike from hut to hut amid towering mountain peaks

TOKYO   p62

Visit Japan's thriving cosmopolitan capital – it's Asia's city of the future

MT FUJI   p88

Climb the perfect cone of Fuji and watch a new day dawn over Japan

CHICHI-JIMA   p95

Take the 25-hour ferry to Japan's dolphin- and whale-watching mecca

To Ogasawara-shotō (500km)

Ogasawara-shotō Inset

Chichi-jima

Hahajima

Not to scale

ELEVATION

3000m
2000m
1000m
200m
0

LEGEND

Freeway
Primary Road
Secondary Road
Railway

0   200 km
0   120 miles

Sakhalin-tō
Wakkanai
Rebun-tō
Rishiri-tō

Hoppōryōdo (Kuril Islands)
Urup-tō

SEA OF OKHOTSK

Shiretoko-hantō
Shiretoko National Park
Daisetsuzan National Park
Abashiri
Akan National Park

RUSSIA

Iturup (Etorofu)-tō

Kunashiri-tō
Shikotan-tō
Habomaisho

Takikawa
Biei
Otaru
Shakotan-hantō
SAPPORO
Obihiro
Kushiro
Niseko
Kushiro
Nemuro-hantō

HOKKAIDŌ

Okushiri-tō

Hakodate
Osore-zan

Seikan Tunnel

AOMORI
Hachinohe

Tazawa-ko
AKITA
MORIOKA
Akita Shinkansen
Kakunodate
Sakata
Mizusawa
Hiraizumi
Tsuruoka
Shinjō
Tōhoku Shinkansen

Sado-ga-shima
YAMAGATA
Kinkasan
SENDAI
NIIGATA
Yamagata Shinkansen
FUKUSHIMA

Jōetsu Shinkansen

HONSHŪ
NAGANO
Nikkō
Matsumoto
UTSUNOMIYA
MAEBASHI
MITO
Hokuriku Shinkansen
URAWA
Tokyo Narita International Airport
KŌFU
TOKYO
Japan Alps
YOKOHAMA
CHIBA
ZUOKA (3776m)
Mt Fuji
Izu-hantō
Ō-shima
Shikine-jima
Izu-shotō
kaidō nkansen
Miyake-jima

PACIFIC OCEAN

Hachijō-jima

↘ THIS IS JAPAN

Japan is a world apart – a wonderful little planet floating off the coast of China. It is a kind of cultural Galapagos, a place where a unique civilisation was allowed to grow and unfold on its own, unmolested by invading powers.

Even today, the world struggles to categorise Japan: is it the world's most advanced technological civilisation, or a bastion of traditional Asian culture? Has the country become just another outpost of the West, or is there something decidedly Eastern lurking under the veneer of its familiar modernity? There are no easy answers, but there is plenty of pleasure to be had in looking for them.

First and foremost, Japan is a place of delicious contrasts: ancient temples and futuristic cities; mist-shrouded hills and lightning-fast bullet trains; kimono-clad geisha and suit-clad businesspeople; quaint thatch-roofed villages and pulsating neon urban

jungles. This peculiar synthesis of the modern and the traditional is one of the things that makes travel in Japan such a fascinating experience.

Japan is arguably the easiest country in Asia in which to travel; while English may not be as widely spoken as in places such as Singapore, the country's brilliant infrastructure, first-class public transport system and friendly people make travelling here a breeze. Despite having all the developed-world conveniences (and then some), Japan offers regular doses of exoticism and wonder. Best of all, Japan is one of the cheapest countries in the developed world and no country on earth offers as much bang for the buck. All told, Japan is an eminently rewarding travel destination.

'ancient temples and futuristic cities; mist-shrouded hills and lightning-fast bullet trains'

1

☝ KYOTO'S TEMPLES & GARDENS

From the riotous colours of Kiyomizu-dera (p121) to the shining apparition
that is Kinkaku-ji (p126), Kyoto is home to the most beautiful temples in all
of Japan, and most of them are surrounded by sublime gardens. With 1600
to choose from, exploring them all is a life's work.

Chris Rowthorn, Lonely Planet Author, Japan

⇘ FOOD IN JAPAN

People simply love to eat in Japan. No wonder, since Japanese cuisine delivers an eye-popping variety of options that delight your tastebuds. Popular Japanese dishes include *gyōza*, tempura, *rāmen*, *soba*, *yakitori*, sukiyaki, *okonomiyaki, shabu-shabu* and, of course, sushi. For a foodie adventure, head to the basement of any department store. (See p326.)

Melissa Randall, Traveller, USA

⇘ ONSEN

Making my way through the steam and other naked bodies, I pad self-consciously to the stone pool. Am I doing this right? Is that girl looking at me? My inhibitions, however, soon melt as I touch the water. Snow falls gently on our reddened faces, and a little Japanese boy squeals in delight. (See p350.)

Stephanie Ong, Traveller, Australia

1 IZZET KERIBAR; 2 GREG ELMS; 3 JOHN ASHBURNE

1 Torii at Fushimi-Inari Taisha (p129), Kyoto; 2 Prawn tempura and udon (p331); 3 Traditional onsen (p348)

⬉ TSUKIJI FISH MARKET

I'm not awake yet, really, since it's before dawn. But the action at Tokyo's Tsukiji Fish Market (p66) wakes me up right quick. Motorised carts, loaded with produce and enormous frozen tuna, zip by. This is where fresh seafood of every variety appears before being shipped to the city's restaurants and shops.

Wendy Yanagihara, Lonely Planet Author, USA

⬉ TRADITIONAL RYOKAN

Staying at a ryokan is a must. Classic ryokan, often in secluded rural areas and made from wood, are the best. One of my favourites is Hōshi Onsen Chōjūkan (p87) in Gunma-ken. Its legendary bathhouse is over 100 years old, with deep chestnut-wood tubs, arched windows and mixed bathing.

Timothy N Hornyak, Lonely Planet Author, Japan

◥ TŌDAI-JI

Nothing can prepare you for your first glimpse of the Daibutsu at the temple of Tōdai-ji (p154) in Nara. This 'Cosmic Buddha' towers over you and fills the space with a palpable feeling of energy. It takes a few moments to recover your senses and start exploring the hall.

Chris Rowthorn, Lonely Planet Author, Japan

6

4 GREG ELMS; 5 DAVID KLEYN/ALAMY; 6 ULANA SWITUCHA/ALAMY

4 Tuna at Tsukiji Fish Market (p66), Tokyo; 5 Onsen at a traditional ryokan (p350); 6 Daibutsu (p155) at Tōdai-ji, Nara

⤵ HIKING IN THE ALPS

The long traverse over the northern Japan Alps from Kamikōchi (p183) to Tsurugi-dake (the northern terminus of the route) is world-class. If you've got a strong back, you can take a backpack and camp it; if not, you can stay in the excellent mountain huts.

7

PEACE MEMORIAL PARK

At Hiroshima's Peace Memorial Park (p257), a Japanese man sat by me. Hearing his first-hand account of the day of the bomb – he lost his father, who worked in the city centre, and his younger brother, who was one of many schoolchildren clearing fire zones – is one of my most valued experiences.

Angela Tinson, Lonely Planet Staff

OKU-NO-IN

Far from the bustle of Tokyo, this Buddhist cemetery-temple (p158) in the Kōya-san monastic complex is filled with beautiful, old moss-covered tombstones in an eerily misty cedar forest – it's possibly the most peaceful place on earth. Spend a couple of hours wandering before finishing the day with a vegetarian meal served in a Japanese-style tatami room at your temple lodging.

Angela Tinson, Lonely Planet Staff

7 JUDY BOARD/ALAMY; 8 LOU JONES; 9 FRANK CARTER

7 Hikers in the Japan Alps (p183); 8 Paper cranes at Peace Memorial Park (p257), Hiroshima; 9 Oku-no-in (p158), Kōya-san

⬎ SUMŌ

10

Even from the cheap seats, the sumō tournaments (p80) are riveting: the wrestler's elegant rituals of scattering handfuls of salt before him in the ring, squatting and retreating, staring his opponent down. Each short match culminates in both wrestlers leaping forth in a burst of energy.

Wendy Yanagihara, Lonely Planet Author, USA

⬎ MT FUJI

11

At the end of my six-week, 10,000km motor-cycle tour of Japan I came around the corner and saw the majestic summit of Mt Fuji (p88) seemingly suspended above the landscape. The sun had set but the snow-covered peak was still bathed in light. It took my breath away.

Brock Goss, Traveller, USA

⬎ HANAMI

If you want to lose any image you have of the Japanese as formal and reserved people, come to Japan during the cherry-blossom season (p47) and attend one of their famous *hanami* (blossom viewing) parties. The sake and beer flow, the portable karaoke systems come out and all inhibitions are cast off.

⬎ OGASAWARA-SHOTŌ

The 25-hour ferry ride from Tokyo down to the isolated islands of Ogasawara-shotō (p95) is the most unusual and rewarding trip you can take in Japan. It's another world, and few non-Japanese make the trip (although it was originally settled by New England whalers).

10 RICHARD I'ANSON; 11 BOB CHARLTON; 12 JOHN BANAGAN; 13 BOB CHARLTON

10 Sumō wrestlers (p80); 11 Mt Fuji (p88); 12 Cherry blossoms near the Imperial Palace (p63), Tokyo; 13 Chichi-jima, Ogasawara-shotō (p95)

14

⤵ SHOPPING IN TOKYO

We're going right out on a limb and declaring Tokyo the world's best shopping city – if you can't buy it here, it probably doesn't exist. From the ultrachic fashion emporia of **Omote-sandō** (p70) in Harajuku to the seething electronics kasbah of **Akihabara** (p63), this city is a shoppers paradise.

⬎ SKIING

Skiing Hakuba (p189) was one of the most amazing experiences of our lives. Incredible accommodation, awesome slopes and snow, and the friendliest people ever. To come down those pristine white slopes, only you and your partner, hearing only wind beneath your skis – what an exhilarating adventure.

Mary Nemarich, Traveller, Australia

15

14 RACHEL LEWIS; 15 BLEND IMAGES/ALAMY

14 Shibuya (p71), Tokyo; 15 Downhill skiing (p354)

⬋ OSAKA AQUARIUM

Ride the vertiginous escalator to the entrance of Osaka's aquarium (p148), one of the world's largest, for all things weird and wonderful. Cruising around the 9m-deep cylinder tank at the heart of the building is the famous whale shark, Kai-Kun. Kids squeal in delight and the cameras come out.

Kate Morgan, Lonely Planet Staff

16

17

◢ GINKAKU-JI

At the north end of Kyoto's Tetsugaku-no-michi (Path of Philosophy), Ginkaku-ji (p126) is eye-wateringly lovely. The main hall overlooks a perfect little pond. Paths snake through the garden and up the hills to a point where you can gaze across the city. Come as early as possible to escape the crowds.

◢ DIVING WITH MANTA RAYS

18

There are few places on earth where you can regularly dive with mantas. One such place is off the west coast of the island of Ishigaki (p314), in the Yaeyama-shotō island group of Okinawa-ken, in Japan's southwest islands. If you come here between April and November, you can usually count on a sighting.

16 DAVID PEARSON/ALAMY; 17 JOHN ELK III; 18 MICHAEL AW

16 Giant crabs at Osaka Aquarium (p148); 17 Garden at Ginkaku-ji (p126), Kyoto; 18 Manta ray (p314)

JAPAN'S TOP 25 EXPERIENCES

⤵ NISHIKI MARKET

This covered market (p115) in downtown Kyoto is a great place to check out all the weird and wonderful things that go into the Japanese food you've been eating. It's also a great place to snack-track: pick up some *senbei* (rice crackers), skewers of cooked chicken or fish and a fresh fruit juice.

19

20

⤡ ARASHIYAMA BAMBOO GROVE

Walking through the Arashiyama bamboo grove (p127) in Kyoto I had the sense of something spiritual. The tall swaying trunks made me look up into the sky and I realised how lucky I was to be standing among these life-giving ancient trees.

Maria Mitsos, Traveller, Australia

19 PETER PTSCHELINZEW; 20 GREG ELMS

19 Pickled vegetables at Nishiki Market (p115), Kyoto; 20 Arashiyama bamboo grove (p127), Kyoto

⇘ KAMIKŌCHI

21

For the classic view of the Japan Alps, head to Kamikōchi (p183) in Central Honshū. It's an alpine sanctuary surrounded by mountains on all sides (a river snakes out via a narrow canyon). Do some gentle hikes along the banks of the Azusa-gawa or grab your pack and climb up to the high peaks.

⇘ SHINKANSEN

Transport is rarely worth calling a highlight in its own right, but Japan's shinkansen (p378) are way beyond ordinary transport. These **22** 'bullet trains' are like earthbound jetliners. Comfortable, fast, quiet and clean, *shinkansen* make it easy to cover huge distances on the main island of Japan in surprisingly little time.

⤷ YAKUSHIMA

If you like hiking, soaking in onsen and swimming off good sand beaches, Yakushima (p297) is the island for you. An easy ferry trip from the main island of Kyūshū, Yakushima is famous for its craggy mountain peaks, ancient *yaku-sugi* (cedar trees) and onsen built into the rocks overlooking the Pacific Ocean.

23

24

⤷ DAISETSUZAN

Hikers take note: there is some world-class hiking on Japan's northern island of Hokkaidō. The competition is stiff, but the island's best hiking can be found in Daisetsuzan National Park (p239). The multiday traverse of this rugged massif is one of Japan's great treks.

21 MARTIN MOOS; 22 RACHEL LEWIS; 23 CHRIS WILLSON/ALAMY; 24 JEFF CANTARUTTI

21 View to Nishi Hotaka-dake (p186), Japan Alps; 22 *Shinkansen* (bullet train; p378); 23 Yudomari Onsen (p299), Yakushima; 24 View to Asahi-dake (p241), Daisetsuzan National Park

⬎ IRIOMOTE-JIMA

Way down in Japan's southwest island chain, the island of Iriomote-jima
(p316) is one of Japan's great natural attractions. It's covered with intact
subtropical jungle and mangrove swamps and fringed with healthy and
colourful coral reefs. There's minimal tourist infrastructure and that's all
for the best.

25

MASON FLORENCE

River kayaking, Iriomote-jima (p316)

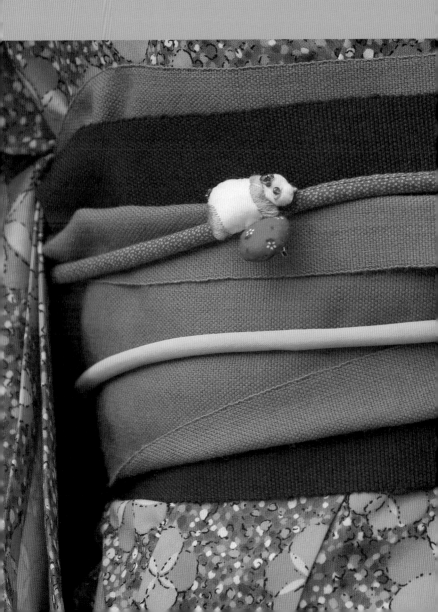

JUST THE HIGHLIGHTS

FIVE DAYS TOKYO TO KYOTO

The Tokyo–Kyoto route is the classic Japan route and the best way to get a quick taste of the country. Spend a few days in Tokyo sampling modern Japan, then jump on the *shinkansen* (bullet train) and head to Kyoto to experience traditional Japan. Easy day trips out of each city allow glimpses of the Japanese countryside.

❶ TOKYO

Start your Japan adventure in Tokyo. We recommend concentrating on the modern side of Japan in Tokyo, since you'll see the traditional side of Japan in Kyoto. That said, you can't miss Meiji-jingū (p70) and Sensō-ji (p69), the city's main Shintō shrine and Buddhist temple, respectively. The next day, take advantage of your jet lag and wake up early to visit the famous Tsukiji Fish Market (p66). You'll have most of the day left after the market, so you can check out the elite shopping district of Ginza (p66), the electronics bazaar of Akihabara (p63) or the frenetic urban centres of Shibuya (p71) or Shinjuku (p69), both of which look incredible by night.

❷ NIKKŌ

For a break from the frenetic intensity of Tokyo, take a day trip to Nikkō (p82). About two hours north of Tokyo by express train, this ornately decorated shrine and temple complex is one of the most incredible sights in Japan.

BRENT WINEBRENNER

Signage to a market in Ueno (p67), Tokyo

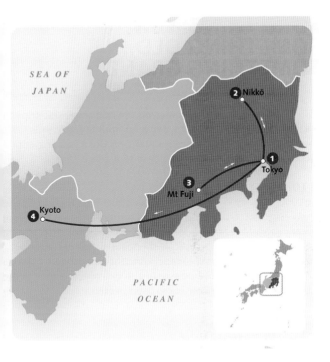

❸ MT FUJI

Mt Fuji (p88) is occasionally visible from the skyscrapers of downtown Tokyo, but nothing compares to the view of the mountain from the villages around its base. Take a bus from Shinjuku to Kawaguchi-ko (p91) for a truly awe-inspiring view of the mountain (but don't bother going unless the weather is really clear – ask the folks at your lodgings to check the local forecast).

❹ KYOTO

After exploring the Tokyo area, hop on the bullet train for the 2½-hour trip to Kyoto (p110). We recommend spending your first day in the Southern Higashiyama district (p119). This is the thickest concentration of first-rate sights in the entire country: Kiyomizu-dera (p121), Maruyama-kōen (p122), Chion-in (p123) and Shōren-in (p125). The next day hit the Northern Higashiyama district (p123), walking from Nanzen-ji (p123) to Ginkaku-ji (p126) via the Tetsugaku-no-michi (Path of Philosophy; p126). Round out your visit with a look at Nishiki Market (p115) and be sure to spend one of your evenings exploring the Gion entertainment area (p122), which looks magical in the evening.

SOMETHING NEW, SOMETHING OLD, SOMETHING GRAND

TEN DAYS TOKYO TO NARA

With 10 days to spend in Japan, you can add some side trips to the usual Tokyo–Kyoto route. Between April to October, a few days in the Japan Alps are recommended. Once you arrive in Kyoto, you can use the city as a base to explore Kansai.

❶ TOKYO

Start your journey in Tokyo (p62). Check out Meiji-jingū (p70) and Sensō-ji (p69), the city's main spiritual centres. The next day, wake up early to visit the famous Tsukiji Fish Market (p66). After visiting the market, check out the upscale shopping district of Ginza (p66), the techie-geek heaven of Akihabara (p63) or hypermodern Shibuya (p71) and Shinjuku (p69). Be sure to visit one of these areas in the evening to enjoy that classic Tokyo neon ambience.

❷ TAKAYAMA

Take a *shinkansen* to Nagoya and switch to an express train to Takayama (p176), the gateway to the Japan Alps. Spend a day exploring Takayama, checking out the preserved wooden houses in Sanmachi-suji (p177); the Takayama Yatai Kaikan (p178), which houses the festival floats used in the Takayama Matsuri (p179); and Hida-no-Sato (p179), a collection of thatched-roof houses from the region. Then head into the Alps for some hiking. Kamikōchi (p183) is close by and makes the best base, but you can also head up to the Tateyama-Murodo area (p193).

GREG ELMS

Customers behind patterned shop window in Aoyama (p70), Tokyo

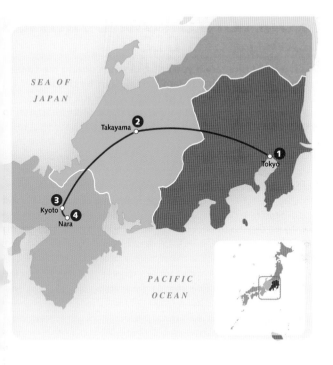

❸ KYOTO

Take an express train to Nagoya and jump on the *shinkansen* to Kyoto (p110). Spend your first day in the Southern Higashiyama district (p119) checking out some of Japan's most amazing sights: Kiyomizu-dera (p121), Maruyama-kōen (p122), Chion-in (p123) and Shōren-in (p125). The next day, visit the Northern Higashiyama district (p123), walking from Nanzen-ji (p123) to Ginkaku-ji (p126) via the Tetsugaku-no-michi (Path of Philosophy; p126). Spend one day downtown exploring Nishiki Market (p115) and the nearby shopping streets. Spend at least one evening strolling the Gion entertainment area (p122), and if you're lucky, you might catch sight of a geisha.

❹ NARA

Japan's first permanent capital, Nara (p151) is only about half an hour away from Kyoto by express train. It contains a fine selection of first-rate sights, most of which are clustered together within a beautiful park, Nara-kōen (p153). Must-see attractions here include Tōdai-ji (p154), a temple famous for its enormous Daibutsu (Great Buddha) and Kasuga Taisha (p155), an ancient Shintō shrine.

FROM TOKYO TO THE TROPICS

TWO WEEKS TOKYO TO IRIOMOTE-JIMA

This is a great itinerary if you arrive in Japan during the cooler months (late September to late March). Start by checking out the must-see attractions of Tokyo and Kyoto, then head southwest to Hiroshima, Miyajima and the wonderful islands of Okinawa.

❶ TOKYO

Start your journey in Tokyo (p62). Check out Meiji-jingū (p70) and Sensō-ji (p69), and wake up early one morning to visit the famous Tsukiji Fish Market (p66). Spend the rest of your time in the capital exploring Ginza (p66), Akihabara (p63), Shibuya (p71) and Shinjuku (p69).

❷ KYOTO

Take a *shinkansen* to Kyoto (p110) and spend one day exploring the Southern Higashiyama district (p119) where you'll find Kiyomizu-dera (p121), Maruyama-kōen (p122), Chion-in (p123) and Shōren-in (p125). The next day, visit the Northern Higashiyama district (p123), walking from Nanzen-ji (p123) to Ginkaku-ji (p126) via the Tetsugaku-no-michi (Path of Philosophy; p126). Spend another day exploring Nishiki Market (p115) and an evening strolling around the Gion entertainment area (p122). If you've got an extra day, take a day trip to nearby Nara (p151).

Traditionally attired man at Sensō-ji (p69), Tokyo

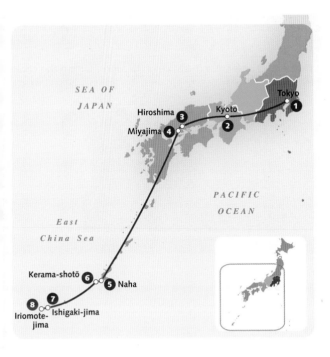

❸ HIROSHIMA

From Kyoto, head west on the *shinkansen* to Hiroshima (p256), where you can learn about the tragic events of 1945 in the Peace Memorial Park (p257). While you're in Hiroshima, be sure to sample the city's famous *okonomiyaki* (savoury pancakes) and oysters (p260).

❹ MIYAJIMA

From Hiroshima, head to the nearby island of Miyajima (p262) to visit one of Japan's most iconic sights, the 'floating torii' (Shintō shrine gate) at Itsukushima-jinja (p263). After taking a few snaps, climb Misen (p263), the island's peak, to get some great Inland Sea views.

❺ NAHA

The next day, return to Hiroshima, jump on the *shinkansen* and take it south to the city of Fukuoka (Kyūshū), where you can catch a plane south to the city of Naha (p304) on the main island of Okinawa-hontō. Spend a day or two exploring Naha. Highlights here include the castle Shuri-jō (p305) and funky market streets (p304). Next day, rent a car and explore the WWII sites and the Memorial Peace Park (p309) in the south of the island, or the beaches and bays to the north of the city.

JAPAN'S TOP ITINERARIES

FROM TOKYO TO THE TROPICS

GREG ELMS

Maiko (apprentice geisha) on Shimbashi (p123), Kyoto

❻ KERAMA-SHOTŌ

After exploring the Naha area, it's time for some fun in the sun. Take a ferry from Naha to Aka-jima (p310) or Zamami-jima (p310) in the nearby Kerama-shotō (p310).

❼ ISHIGAKI-JIMA

For nature lovers, the final leg of this trip may well be the most memorable. Hop a quick flight from Naha down to the island of Ishigaki-jima (p311). If you're there between April and November and you've got a diving certificate, you can dive with the manta rays off the island's west coast.

❽ IRIOMOTE-JIMA

Finally, hop aboard a ferry for the short trip over to the adjoining island of Iriomote-jima (p316). This island is Japan's last frontier – one of the only places in the entire country which has not been permanently altered by human activity. It's covered with healthy subtropical jungle and fringed with colourful and healthy coral reefs. You can trek to waterfalls, take boat journeys up the island's rivers and snorkel over incredible coral gardens. When you arrive back in Tokyo for your flight home, you'll find it hard to believe that you're still in the same country.

↘ PLANNING YOUR TRIP

JAPAN'S BEST...

⬐ TEMPLES

- **Tōdai-ji** (p154) The Daibutsu (Great Buddha) at this Nara temple is Japan's most awesome sight.
- **Nanzen-ji** (p123) Zen perfection tucked at the base of Kyoto's Higashiyama mountains. Don't miss the subtemples nearby.
- **Sensō-ji** (p69) Tokyo's bustling spiritual centre is one of the capital's must-see sights. It's a great insight into popular religion in Japan.
- **Kiyomizu-dera** (p121) Gaudy colours and a holy spring draw the crowds to this ancient Kyoto temple. The cherry-blossom illuminations here in April are otherworldly.

⬐ GARDENS

- **Ryōan-ji** (p127) The 15 rocks at this Kyoto Zen garden have been mystifying people for centuries – take a seat and ponder the riddle.

- **Isui-en** (p154) There's almost always something blooming at this brilliant Nara garden.
- **Kenroku-en** (p197) This famed garden is Kanazawa's top draw.
- **Ōkōchi Sansō** (p128) Don't visit this garden if you suffer from home and garden envy! Even God is jealous of this house.

⬐ ONSEN

- **Takaragawa Onsen** (p87) Two hours from Tokyo in Gunma-ken, these riverside onsen (hot springs) are worth the trip.
- **Kinosaki** (p145) This onsen town in northern Kansai is the classic Japanese onsen resort. Don a *yukata* (light cotton kimono) and stroll from bath to bath.
- **Hirauchi Kaichū Onsen** (p298) You'll have to time the tide right to enter this heavenly onsen on Yakushima.

かくるね……
好きだよ兄さん

DIGI：F@N特典
描き下ろしテレホンカード

ANTHONY PLUMMER

Manga advertising sign, Akihabara (p63), Tokyo

- **Dōgo Onsen** (p270) This Shikoku onsen has oodles of old-Japan atmosphere.

PLACES TO HIKE

- **Japan Alps** (p183) Go hut to hut across the roof of Japan.
- **Yakushima** (p297) Hike among ancient trees and soaring peaks on this southwest island.
- **Daisetsuzan** (p239) Wild and rugged hiking draws hikers to Hokkaidō's 'Big Snow Mountain'.
- **Aso-san** (p279) Hike amid semiactive volcanoes in Kyūshū's brilliant national park.

BEACHES

- **Nishibama Beach** (p310) A short ferry ride from the main island of Okinawa brings you to this perfect beach.
- **Furuzamami Beach** (p310) A short boat ride from Nishibama is this Kerama classic.
- **Nagata Inaka-hama** (p300) Take a break from hiking on Yakushima to swim at this excellent beach.
- **Hoshisuna-no-hama** (p316) The coral at this Iriomote-jima beach is a snorkeller's playground.

FESTIVALS

- **Sapporo Yuki Matsuri** (p213) February fun in Hokkaidō: snow, ice and plenty of sake.
- **Earth Celebration** (p226) Listen to the drums of August on faraway Sado-ga-shima, Northern Honshū.

- **Gion Matsuri** (p131) Held in July in Kyoto, this is Japan's most famous festival. The highlight is a parade of enormous wooden floats through the streets of downtown Kyoto.
- **Kurama-no-hi Matsuri** (p132) The tiny hamlet of Kurama, in the hills north of Kyoto, comes alive with burning torches in this incredible October festival.

MARKETS & SHOPPING DISTRICTS

- **Tsukiji Fish Market** (p66) Tokyo's sprawling fish market is the biggest on earth. It's arguably the world's most incredible food market.
- **Nishiki Market** (p115) Kyoto's traditional food market is among the city's most interesting sights.
- **Akihabara** (p63) Tokyo's electronics district has to be seen to be believed.
- **Daichi Makishi Kōsetsu Ichiba** (p304) Retro is the word at this Naha (Okinawa) market.

PLACES TO STAY

- **Tawaraya** (p134) This Kyoto ryokan is the best in all Japan.
- **Park Hyatt Tokyo** (p75) A castle in the sky above Tokyo's Shinjuku district.
- **Nishimuraya Honkan** (p145) An elegant ryokan in the onsen resort town of Kinosaki, northern Kansai.
- **Hyatt Regency Kyoto** (p134) Creature comforts and smooth service make this Kyoto's top hotel.

PLANNING YOUR TRIP

THINGS YOU NEED TO KNOW

 # THINGS YOU NEED TO KNOW

AT A GLANCE

- **ATMs** In post offices and some convenience stores; simple withdrawals generally possible; 'charging cash' on a credit card usually not possible
- **Bargaining** Only in flea markets
- **Credit cards** Visa and MasterCard widely accepted, others less so
- **Currency** Yen (¥)
- **Language** English spoken in most hotels, limited English elsewhere
- **Tipping** Not necessary
- **Visas** Most visitors receive short-stay visas on arrival

ACCOMMODATION

- **Guesthouses** Travellers' accommodation found in tourist spots.
- **Hotels** Luxury and business hotels in cities, business hotels in towns.
- **Ryokan** Traditional Japanese inns across the country, in a variety of budget ranges.

ADVANCE PLANNING

- **Japan Rail Pass** This pass, which is only available for purchase outside of Japan (see p379), can save you a lot of money if you are planning to travel extensively by rail within Japan.
- **Reservations** Make accommodation reservations several months in advance if you are travelling in cherry-blossom season (March and April) and the autumn-foliage season in Honshū (October and November).

BE FOREWARNED

- **Crowds** Kyoto and Nara can be very crowded in cherry-blossom season (late March to early April).
- **Heat** Most of Japan is very hot and humid in July and August.
- **New Year's Holiday** Most businesses and many sights shut down from 27 December to 4 January.
- **Typhoons** These strike Okinawa, the Southwest Islands and the Ogasawara-shotō between July and October.

COSTS

- **US$100 per day** Simple guesthouses and cheap business hotels, meals in simple restaurants, local transport.
- **US$100 to US$200 per day** Business hotels and budget ryokan, great restaurants, a taxi ride or two.
- **More than US$300 per day** Luxury hotels and ryokan, great restaurants, taxis.

EMERGENCY NUMBERS

- **Ambulance & Fire** ☎ 119
- **Police** ☎ 110

GETTING AROUND

- **Air** Japan's domestic air system is efficient, reasonably priced and comfortable (see p374).
- **Buses** Long-distance and local buses are widely available and comfortable (see p376).

- **Ferries** These serve Okinawa and the Southwest Islands, the Inland Sea and the Ogasawara-shotō.
- **Taxis** These are found everywhere and can be cheap for groups, especially in Kyoto.
- **Trains** Japan has one of the best train systems in the world, including the famous *shinkansen* (bullet trains; see p378).

GETTING THERE & AWAY

- **Air** Japan is well served by international air connections; fly into Tokyo's Narita International Airport or Kansai International Airport.

TECH STUFF

- **Computers and internet** Many hotels and guesthouses have internet access; wi-fi is only found in bigger cities; internet cafes can be found in cities (see p366).
- **Mobile (cell) phones** Japan uses G3 phones (if your phone is not G3 it will not work in Japan); rental mobile phones are widely available and cheap (see p370).
- **Plugs and voltage** Japan's electricity is 100V AC; most foreign electrical appliances and computers work with this current; Japanese sockets accept flat two-pin plugs (identical to North American sockets, but without the third ground pin); transformers and adaptors are available at electronics shop in cities.

TRAVEL SEASONS

- **High season** In late April and early May (Golden Week), mid-August (Obon holiday) and at Christmas and New Year international flights are more expensive, and

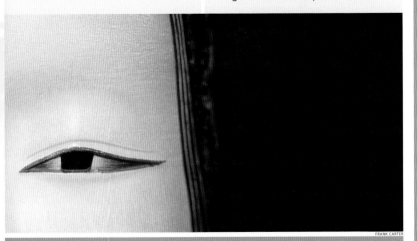

FRANK CARTER

Deatail of a *nō* (classical Japanese drama) mask

PLANNING YOUR TRIP

THINGS YOU NEED TO KNOW

transport and accommodation can
be crowded. April and November
(cherry-blossom and autumn-
foliage season, respectively) can
be busy, particularly in Kyoto.
- **Low season** Other than Christmas and New Year period, winter
(December to March) tends to
be very quiet in Japan and travel
bargains can usually be had.

WHAT TO BRING

- **International licence** If you plan
to rent a car in Japan, get an
international licence from your
country's automobile association
(see p377).
- **Japan Rail Pass** You must purchase this pass before arriving in
Japan (see p379).
- **Slip-on shoes** You'll be taking
off your shoes a lot, especially in
Kyoto.

WHEN TO GO

- **Spring (March to June)** Warm,
with cherry blossoms in March
and April, rain in June
- **Summer (July and August)** Hot
and humid (except for Hokkaidō)
- **Autumn (September to November)** Sunny and pleasant with
foliage in November
- **Winter (December to February)**
Cool (southern Japan) or cold
(northern Japan)

BRENT WINEBRENNER

Buddhist monk with alms bowl, Ueno (p67), Tokyo

GET INSPIRED

BOOKS

- The Roads to Sata (nonfiction; 1985; Alan Booth) An account of a four-month walk from Hokkaidō to Kyūshū.
- Looking for the Lost: Journeys Through a Vanishing Japan (nonfiction; 1990; Alan Booth) Another account of walks in rural Japan.
- Inventing Japan (nonfiction; 1989; Ian Buruma) A brief but riveting account of Japan from the opening of the country to prewar militarisation.
- Memoirs of a Geisha (fiction; 1997; Arthur Golden) The classic tale of a Kyoto geisha.
- Lost Japan (nonfiction; 1996; Alex Kerr) A clear-eyed look at the state of modern Japan by one of the ultimate Japan insiders.

FILMS

- Tampopo (1987) Itami Jūzō's film about *rāmen*, (egg noodles) is told in the manner of a spaghetti Western.
- Osōshiki (The Funeral; 1987) A penetrating look at Japanese society through the lens of a funeral – a classic from Itami Jūzō.
- Lost in Translation (2003) Sofia Coppola's Tokyo story of emotional near misses is a great pre-trip look at Japan.
- My Neighbor Totoro (1988) This touching children's story is the perfect introduction to the work of Miyazaki Hayao, the master of Japanese anime.

MUSIC

- The New Best of Shoukichi Kina & Champloose (Shoukichi Kina & Champloose) A mix of mellow and upbeat Okinawan-style music. Good stuff for the plane ride over.
- Okinawa Jyoka (Tokiko Kato) Mellow tunes with an Okinawan vibe.
- Hainumikaze (Moto Chitose) Female vocalist Moto Chitose's album is head and shoulders above the standard J-pop offerings.
- The Folk Crusaders New Best (The Folk Crusaders) Nostalgic Japanese folk music from the '60s. This album contains the superb 'Kanashikute Yarikirenai'.

WEBSITES

- Hyperdia Japan (www.hyperdia .com/cgi-english/hyperWeb.cgi) Get Japan transport information (fares, times etc) in English.
- Japan National Tourism Organization (JNTO; www.jnto.go.jp) Great information on all aspects of travel in Japan.
- Japan Ministry of Foreign Affairs (MOFA; www.mofa.go.jp) Useful visa info and embassy/consulate locations under the 'Visa' tab.
- Japan Rail (www.japanrail.com) Information on rail travel in Japan, with details on the Japan Rail Pass.
- Kōchi University Weather Home Page (http://weather.is.kochi-u .ac.jp/index-e.html) Satellite images updated several times a day – very useful during typhoon season (August to October).

PLANNING YOUR TRIP

CALENDAR

CALENDAR

JAN FEB MAR APR

BRENT WINEBRENNER

Autumn foliage (p49)

↘ JANUARY

SHŌGATSU

New Year's is one of the most important celebrations in Japan. The central ritual, *hatsu-mōde,* involves the first visit to the local shrine to pray for health, happiness and prosperity during the coming year. Festivities run from 31 December to 3 January.

↘ FEBRUARY

SETSUBUN MATSURI

To celebrate the end of winter (3 or 4 February; one day before the start of spring according to the Japanese lunar calendar) and to drive out evil spirits, the Japanese throw roasted beans while chanting '*oni wa soto, fuku wa uchi*' (out with the demons, in with good luck). Events are often

held at local shrines with characters dressed as devils, who act as good targets for beans.

SAPPORO YUKI MATSURI

Check out the incredible ice sculptures, take a ride down an ice slide and then sample some of Sapporo's famous seafood and hospitality at Japan's premier winter festival; see p231.

↘ MARCH–APRIL

PLUM-BLOSSOM VIEWING

Not as famous as the cherries, but quite lovely in their own right, Japan's plum trees bloom from late February into March. Strolling among the plum orchards at places such as the Kyoto Imperial Palace Park (p117) is a fine way to spend an early spring day in Japan.

| MAY | JUN | JUL | AUG | SEP | OCT | NOV | DEC |

CHERRY BLOSSOM VIEWING

Japan's famous cherry blossoms burst into bloom in the early spring, starting in February in Kyūshū and generally peaking in Honshū in late March or early April. Their moment of glory is brief, generally lasting only a week. Famous spots include Kyoto's Maruyama-kōen (p122) and Tokyo's Ueno-kōen (p67).

TAKAYAMA MATSURI: SANNŌ MATSURI

The Takayama Matsuri (p179) is one of Japan's most impressive festivals – a mountain counterpart to Kyoto's famous Gion Matsuri (right). The festival is held twice a year. The spring festival, known as the Sannō Matsuri, is held on 14 and 15 April, while the fall festival, known as the Hachiman Matsuri, is held on 9 and 10 October.

FRANK CARTER

Stall at Gion Matsuri

⬎ MAY

GOLDEN WEEK

Golden Week takes in Shōwa-no-hi (Shōwa Emperor's Day; 29 April), Kempō Kinem-bi (Constitution Day; 3 May), Midori-no-hi (Green Day; 4 May) and Kodomo-no-hi (Children's Day; 5 May). Transport and lodging in popular holiday areas are often booked solid during this time.

⬎ JULY

GION MATSURI   17 JUL

The mother of all Japanese festivals: huge floats are pulled through the streets of Kyoto by teams of chanting citizens. On the three evenings preceding the parade, people stroll through Shijō-dōri dressed in beautiful *yukata* (light cotton kimono); see p131.

FRANK CARTER

Geisha at Setsubun Matsuri

PLANNING YOUR TRIP

CALENDAR

CALENDAR

| JAN | FEB | MAR | APR |

TENJIN MATSURI

The city of Osaka comes alive on 24 and 25 July during this raucous mid-summer festival. On the evening of the second day, people wearing *yukata* gather around Osaka Temman-gū and along the banks of the O-kawa to watch festival floats and fireworks; see p148.

◼ AUGUST

O-BON (FESTIVAL OF THE DEAD)

According to Buddhist tradition, mid-August is a time when ancestors return to earth. Across Japan, lanterns are lit and floated on rivers, lakes or the sea to signify the return of the departed to the underworld.

DAIMON-JI GOZAN

OKURIBI   16 AUG

Commonly known as Daimon-ji Yaki, this is part of the summer O-Bon festival. Huge kanji (Chinese characters) and symbols are burned on five mountains around the city of Kyoto.

SUMMER FIREWORKS FESTIVALS

Cities and towns across Japan hold spectacular summer fireworks festivals throughout August. You'll be amazed at the quality and duration of some of these incredible displays.

EARTH CELEBRATION

The island of Sado-ga-shima, off the coast of Northern Honshū, is the scene of this internationally famous festival of dance, art and music (see p226). Attention is centred on performances

JUDY BELLAH

Sweet rice cakes, traditionally served at Shōgatsu (p46)

Shichi-go-san
MARK HEMMINGS

PLANNING YOUR TRIP

CALENDAR

TAKAYAMA MATSURI: HACHIMAN MATSURI
The autumn version of the famous Takayama Matsuri takes place on 9 and 10 October (see p179).

KURAMA-NO-HI MATSURI   22 OCT
Huge flaming torches are carried through the streets of the tiny hamlet of Kurama in the mountains north of Kyoto. This is one of Japan's more primeval festivals; see p132.

◥ NOVEMBER

SHICHI-GO-SAN   15 NOV
Also known as the 7-5-3 Festival, this event is in honour of girls who are aged three and seven and boys who are aged five. Children are dressed in their finest clothes and taken to shrines or temples, where prayers are offered for good fortune.

by the island's famous taiko (Japanese drum) group. This is a must-see if you find yourself in Northern Honshū in the third week of August.

◥ SEPTEMBER–OCTOBER

AUTUMN FOLIAGE
Japan's autumn foliage rivals the more famous cherry blossoms for beauty and it's much easier to catch; while the cherries bloom for only about a week in most areas, the fall colours last over a month. Up in the Japan Alps and Hokkaidō the foliage peaks in September. In most parts of Honshū you can catch the colours in October and November.

◥ DECEMBER

BŌNENKAI
Literally 'forget the year parties', these raucous celebrations are held from mid- to late December across Japan to ring out the old year and get ready for the new one. If you visit a Japanese izakaya (pub-eatery) or bar during this time, you're likely to get swept up in the madness.

Shinjuku Station, Tokyo

GREG ELMS

TOKYO AREA

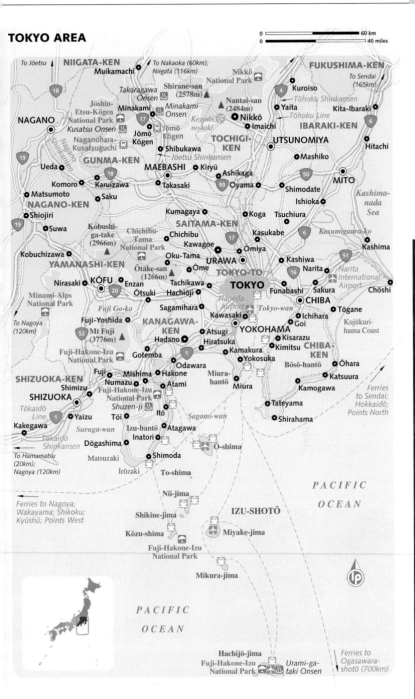

HIGHLIGHTS

1 | TSUKIJI FISH MARKET

BY KONO KIYOMI, TOKYO RESIDENT & PROFESSIONAL GUIDE

Tsukiji Fish Market has been called 'Tokyo's Kitchen' and it's one of the most exciting spots in the city. You can't imagine such organised chaos taking place inside this advanced modern city. It's a great window into how food is brought to your table, and where else can you see a 300kg fish in a market?

↘ KONO KIYOMI'S DON'T MISS LIST

❶ EXPLORING THE MARKET

The famous tuna auction takes place around 5am, but you don't have to go that early to enjoy the other parts of the market. If you make it by 9am or so, you'll see plenty of stalls open. Just wander the alleyways and check out all the weird and wonderful things for sale.

❷ SUSHI ZANMAI

I often go to the restaurant **Sushi Zanmai** (p77) in the outer market. It serves sushi on a conveyer belt and it's the freshest fish just brought from the market. The colours of plates tell the price of sushi, so it's easy to pick whatever appeals to you.

❸ HAMA-RIKYŪ-TEIEN

If you walk for seven minutes west from the market, you'll find a traditional stone wall to your left. This is the wall of the garden **Hama-Rikyū-Teien** (p66), which used to be the Shōgun's villa in the 17th century. Go inside and take a pleasant stroll among the greenery.

Clockwise from top: Octopus on ice; Octopus seller; Frozen tuna; Cut salmon; Market sushi stall

TOKYO AREA

HIGHLIGHTS

❹ NAMIYOKE-JINJA

One of the market's hidden treasures is Namiyoke-jinja, a shrine located south of the outer market and east of the inner market – look for the torii (shrine gate). On the left side of the shrine you'll find small gravestones. These are dedicated to fish, shrimp and eggs to give thanks for their role in Japanese food. You can get a sense of the Japanese appreciation of seafood here.

❺ DENTSU OBSERVATORY

Another secret spot is the free observatory on the 46th floor of the Dentsu building, across from the market. You can take an elevator from the B1 floor straight up to the 46th floor for free. From the observatory you can look down on Tsukiji Fish Market and Hama-Rikyū-Teien, as well as the Sumidagawa, Tokyo Bay, the Rainbow Bridge and the man-made island of Odaiba.

❱ THINGS YOU NEED TO KNOW

Days off Tsukiji Fish Market is closed on the second and fourth Wednesdays of most months, as well as Sundays and public holidays **Warning** Watch out for the electric carts that prowl the market **See our author's review on p66**

HIGHLIGHTS

2 | ASAKUSA AREA

BY TAKAHASHI MICHIKO, TOKYO RESIDENT & PROFESSIONAL GUIDE

Asakusa preserves a traditional downtown atmosphere. If you imagine Tokyo as a buttoned-down hypermodern city, you should visit Asakusa to enjoy its down-to-earth culture and warm-hearted hospitality. There are many annual events, but it doesn't really matter when you go, because Asakusa always has a festive atmosphere.

⤴ TAKAHASHI MICHIKO'S DON'T MISS LIST

❶ SENSŌ-JI

Sensō-ji (p69) is the main temple in Asakusa. The incense-filled main hall is always busy with worshippers. In front of the gold-plated altar, you will often see the monks chanting sutras. The solemn atmosphere puts my mind at ease. While you're here, take an *omikuji* (paper fortune); whether it's a good one or a bad one, it's fun to try. The fortunes are written in both English and Japanese here. If you get a bad one, you can tie it up and let the wind blow the bad fortune away.

❷ NAKAMISE-DŌRI

Nakamise-dōri shopping arcade is the main approach to Sensō-ji. Nearly 100 shops lining the street here attract crowds of visitors from inside and outside of Japan. You will find many traditional goods such as fans, Japanese paper crafts, *ukiyo-e* (wood-block prints), fake swords, kimono, freshly blended Japanese spices and traditional cosmetics made from a bird's droppings. There are goods to tempt bargain hunters and connoisseurs alike.

Clockwise from top: Sensō-ji (p69); Outdoor dining; Plastic food models; Traditional paper fans; Tying an *omikuji* (paper fortune)

TOKYO AREA

HIGHLIGHTS

❸ WATCHING THE WORSHIPPERS

One of the most interesting things to do at Sensō-ji is to watch the throngs of worshippers from all over Japan pray in and around the main hall. The giant incense urn in front of the hall is always surrounded by people waving the smoke over themselves to ensure good luck. This place gives you a real insight into popular folk religion in Japan.

❹ KAPPABASHI

Kappabashi is located just west of Asakusa. It's Tokyo's main wholesale district for kitchenware and restaurant equipment. A wide variety of items such as crockery, lacquerware, shop curtains and tablecloths are on sale here. You can also find some of the best Japanese kitchen knives here, and the plastic food models on display are a treat for the eye.

↘ THINGS YOU NEED TO KNOW

Ways to get there from downtown Take the Ginza subway line to Asakusa Station **Be warned** The Sensō-ji area can get crowded during holiday periods **See our author's review on p68**

HIGHLIGHTS

3

⬑ TOKYO NATIONAL MUSEUM

If you only see one museum in Tokyo, make it the **national museum** (p68). This is the best place in all of Japan to get a full overview of the main currents in Japanese art: lacquerware, textiles, painting, metalwork (including swords) and pottery. It's also a chance to learn the history of Japanese art. And don't miss the adjoining Hall of Hōryū-ji Treasures – both the building and the collection are first rate.

4

⬑ MEIJI-JINGŪ

For a break from Tokyo's seemingly endless concrete and neon, head to **Meiji-jingū** (p70). Sitting amid a rolling expanse of forest, this shrine serves as a retreat for harried Tokyoites. A walk down any of the tree-lined avenues is the perfect way to spend a few peaceful hours. Buy an *omikuji* at the shrine to check your luck and keep your eyes peeled for a traditional Japanese wedding.

TOKYO AREA

HIGHLIGHTS

↘ SHIBUYA

Shibuya (p71) is Tokyo at its most Tokyo-esque: throngs of people, huge neon signs, busy overhead train lines and an almost infinite number of shops and restaurants. If you've seen *Lost in Translation*, you've seen Shibuya: many of the city scenes were shot here. The people-watching here is the best anywhere.

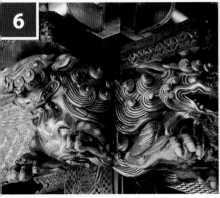

↘ NIKKŌ

In a country where the default colour for temples is bare wood, **Nikkō** (p82) stands out like a peacock among pigeons. This shrine-temple complex three hours north of Tokyo is the closest Japan has ever got to the riotous exuberance of rococo. Nikkō vies with Kamakura as the Tokyo area's most rewarding day trip.

↘ KAMAKURA

Only about an hour away from Tokyo by express train, **Kamakura** (p92) feels like a different world. This seaside collection of temples and shrines, and one giant bronze Buddha statue, makes a fine day trip out of the city and is an absolute must if you don't have the time to make it to Kyoto.

3 GREG ELMS; 4 ANTHONY PLUMMER; 5 BRENT WINEBRENNER; 6 & 7 MARTIN MOOS

3 Seventh-century bodhisattva statue, Tokyo National Museum (p68); 4 Torii at Meiji-Jingū (p70); 5 Shibuya (p71); 6 Detail of carved lions at Taiyūin-byō (p86); 7 Kamakura Daibutsu (p94)

TOKYO AREA

THE BEST

THE BEST...

⤵ EXPERIENCES

- **Walking across Shibuya Crossing** (p71) When the lights turn green here, a human tide steps off the curb.
- **The view from the Tokyo Metropolitan Government Offices** (p69) There's no finer view of the city.
- **The ferry ride to the Ogasawara-shotō** (p95) The 25-hour ferry ride down to these semitropical islands is the greatest adventure to be had in Japan.

⤵ PLACES TO STAY

- **Park Hyatt Tokyo** (p75) An oasis of calm and beauty in the sky above Tokyo.
- **Conrad Tokyo** (p74) The view over Tokyo Bay alone is worth the price of admission.

- **Grand Hyatt Tokyo** (p76) The Grand Hyatt combines the luxury of a Hyatt with a great location on the doorstep of Roppongi.

⤵ PLACES TO SHOP

- **Ginza** (p66) Head to Ginza to check out where the old money shops.
- **Akihabara** (p63) The world's largest collection of electronics shops.
- **Harajuku & Aoyama** (p70) This is the closest Japan will ever get to Paris.

⤵ ESCAPES

- **Nikkō** (p82) Towering trees and ancient shrines.
- **Kamakura** (p92) Seaside temples and a giant Buddha.
- **Mt Fuji** (p88) Japan's most iconic sight.

LEFT: GREG ELMS; RIGHT: ANTHONY PLUMMER

Left: Neon facade in Shinjuku (p69), Tokyo; Right: Shop windows in Harajuku (p70), Tokyo

THINGS YOU NEED TO KNOW

⬎ VITAL STATISTICS

- **Population** Tokyo 12.56 million
- **Area codes** Tokyo ☎ 03, Nikkō ☎ 0288, Kamakura ☎ 0467
- **Best times to visit** Cherry-blossom season (early April), autumn (late October to early December)

⬎ NEIGHBOURHOODS IN A NUTSHELL

- **Tokyo Station area** (p63) The gateway to the city and a good place to be based if you want easy access to transport.
- **Ginza** (p66) Tokyo's old-school luxury shopping district is a great place to be based.
- **Uneo** (p67) Tokyo's museum district, with a fine park and Shintō shrine.
- **Asakusa** (p68) A retro entertainment district that is home to the city's most important Buddhist temple.
- **Shinjuku** (p69) The east side here is all restaurants, shops and entertainment, while the west side is hotels and government buildings.
- **Harajuku & Aoyama** (p70) Tokyo's capital of chic shopping and European-style restaurants.
- **Shibuya** (p71) This shopping hub is the heart of Japan's youth culture.

⬎ RESOURCES

- **JNTO Tourist Information Center** (p62) The best English-speaking TIC in the city.

- **Tokyo Journal** Check out the Citysource section for listings of events happening while you are in town. Available at most big bookstores.
- **Metropolis** This free English-language magazine is another good source of info. Available at big bookstores and other foreigner-friendly businesses.

⬎ EMERGENCY NUMBERS

- **Ambulance & Fire** ☎ 119
- **Police** ☎ 110

⬎ GETTING AROUND

- **Walk** around the urban hubs of Tokyo.
- **Taxi** only if you miss the last train.
- **Subway** around all parts of the city.
- **JR Yamanote loop line** from one Tokyo hub to the next.
- **Private train lines** are for day trips to places such as Nikkō and Kamakura.

⬎ BE FOREWARNED

- **Rush hour** (7am to 9am and 4.30pm to 7pm) means huge crowds on subways and trains in and around Tokyo.
- **Summer** (July and August) can be very hot and humid in Tokyo.

TOKYO AREA

THINGS YOU NEED TO KNOW

TOKYO AREA

DISCOVER THE TOKYO AREA

DISCOVER THE TOKYO AREA

The heart of the Japanese economic miracle, Tokyo is a sprawling vortex of energy. Peopled with impossibly chic residents hurrying from one appointment to the next via a hyperefficient subway system, Tokyo is an easy peek into the future of the human race. Unlike most other cities, Tokyo doesn't really have a centre. Indeed, it's almost better not to think of Tokyo as one city at all, but as a collection of separate cities connected by the JR Yamanote loop line. And each of these 'cities' has its own distinct character, from funky old Ueno to ultramodern Shinjuku with its towering skyscrapers and endless department stores.

Within day-trip range of Tokyo, you'll find some of Japan's most compelling sights, including the colourful temple/shrine complex of Nikkō, the perfect summit cone of Mt Fuji, and the seaside town of Kamakura, with its awesome Daibutsu (Great Buddha) statue. And then there's the Ogasawara-shotō, a pristine island group 1000km out in the Pacific that's officially part of Tokyo.

TOKYO 東京
☎ 03 / pop 12.56 million

ORIENTATION

Tokyo is a vast conurbation spreading out across the Kantō Plain from Tokyo Bay (Tokyo-wan). Nearly everything of interest to visitors lies on or near the JR Yamanote line, the rail loop that circles central Tokyo. Areas not on the Yamanote line – such as Roppongi, Tsukiji and Asakusa – are nonetheless within easy reach, as the central city is criss-crossed by Tokyo's excellent subway system.

MAPS

We strongly recommend you pick up a free copy of the excellent *Tourist Map of Tokyo* from one of the tourist information centres (TICs – see right); along with detailed insets of Tokyo's major neighbourhoods, it also includes subway and rail maps.

Tokyo's train and subway lines are much easier to navigate with the free, colour-coded *Tokyo Metro Guide* map.

It's available at subway stations and TICs around town.

INFORMATION
BOOKSHOPS

Kinokuniya Shinjuku-dōri (Map p70; ☎ 3354-0131; 3-17-7 Shinjuku, Shinjuku-ku; ☻ 10am-9pm; ⏺ JR Yamanote line to Shinjuku, east exit); Takashimaya (Map p70; ☎ 5361-3301; Annexe Bldg, Takashimaya Times Sq, 5-24-2 Sendagaya, Shibuya-ku; ☻ 10am-8pm Sun-Fri, 10am-8.30pm Sat; ⏺ JR Yamanote line to Shinjuku, new south exit) Kinokuniya's Takashimaya Times Sq branch has one of Tokyo's largest selections of English-language books on the 6th floor.

TOURIST INFORMATION

The Japan National Tourism Organization (JNTO) runs two **tourist information centres** (TIC; ☎ 0476-303-383, 0476-345-877; ☻ 8am-8pm) on the arrival floors of both terminals at Narita airport.

JNTO Tourist Information Center (TIC; Map p66; ☎ 3201-3331; www.jnto.go.jp; 10th fl,

Kōtsu Kaikan Bldg, 2-10-1 Yūrakuchō, Chiyoda-ku; 9am-5pm; JR Yamanote line to Yūrakuchō) The main JNTO-operated TIC is just outside Yūrakuchō Station. It has the most comprehensive information on travel in Tokyo and Japan, and is an essential port of call. The Kōtsu Kaikan Building is just opposite the station as you exit to the right.

Tokyo Tourist Information Center Map p70; 5321-3077; 1st fl, Tokyo Metropolian Government Bldg No 1, 2-8-1 Nishi-Shinjuku, Shinjuku-ku; 9.30am-6.30pm; Toei Ōedo line to Tochōmae, exit A4) A good place to buy a Grutt Pass (¥2000) that saves on admission fees to museums and zoos.

SIGHTS
KANDA & TOKYO STATION
神田・東京駅
IMPERIAL PALACE 皇居
The Imperial Palace (Kōkyo; Map pp64-5) occupies the site of the castle Edo-jō, from which the Tokugawa shōgunate ruled Japan. In its heyday the castle was the largest in the world, though little remains of it today apart from the moat and walls. The present palace, completed in 1968, replaced the palace built in 1888 that was destroyed during WWII.

As it's the home of Japan's emperor and imperial family, the palace is closed to the public for all but two days of the year, 2 January and 23 December (the emperor's birthday). Though you can't enter the palace itself, you can wander around its outskirts and visit the gardens.

It's an easy walk from Tokyo Station, or from Hibiya or Nijū-bashi-mae subway stations, to Nijū-bashi. Crossing Babasaki Moat and the expansive Imperial Palace Plaza (Kōkyo-mae Hiroba), you'll arrive at a vantage point that gives a picture-postcard view of the palace peeking over its fortifications, behind Nijū-bashi.

AKIHABARA 秋葉原
Akihabara (Map pp64-5) began its evolution into 'Denki-gai' (Electric Town) post-WWII, when the area around the station became a black market for radio parts. In more recent decades, Akihabara has been

LEFT: GREG ELMS; RIGHT: RICHARD I'ANSON

Left: Bar in Shinjuku (p69); Right: Fluorescent lights for sale in Akihabara

GREATER TOKYO

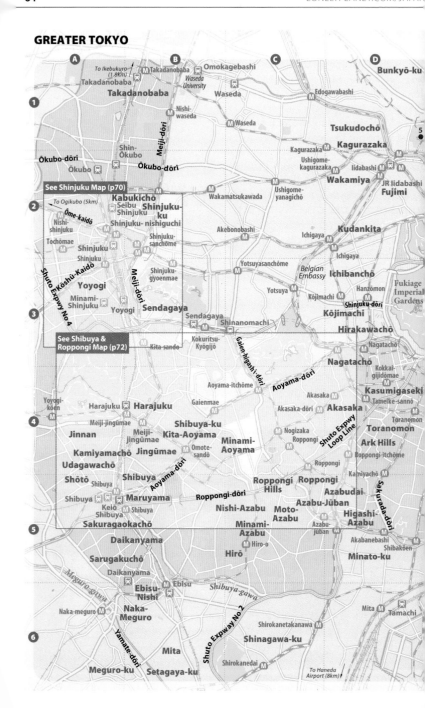

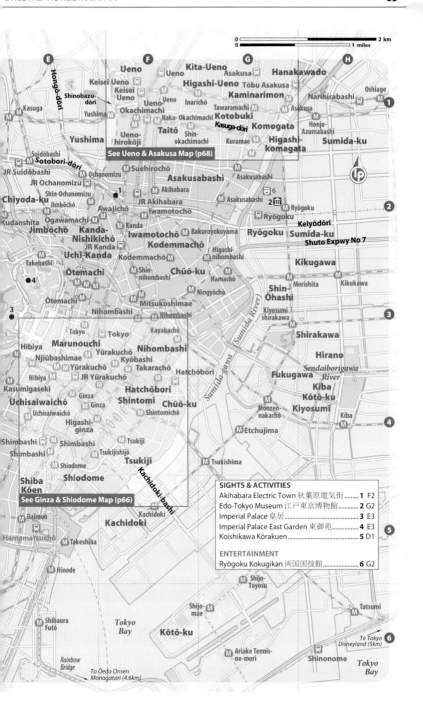

0 — 2 km
0 — 1 miles

E

Hongō-dōri

Kasuga

Shinobazu-dōri

Suidōbashi
Sotobori-dōri
JR Suidōbashi
JR Ochanomizu
Chiyoda-ku
Shin-Ochanomizu
Jimbōchō
Kudanshita
Ogawamachi
Jimbōchō
Kanda-
Nishikichō
Uchi-Kanda
JR Kanda
Takebashi
Ōtemachi
4
Ōtemachi

F

Ueno
Keisei Ueno
Keisei
Ueno
Ueno-
Okachimachi
Ueno
Naka-Okachimachi
Yushima
Ueno-
hirokōji
Taitō
Shin-
okachimachi

See Ueno & Asakusa Map (p68)

Ochanomizu
Suehirochō
Akihabara
JR Akihabara
Awajichō
Kanda
Iwamotochō
Kodemmachō
Shin-
nihombashi

G

Ueno
Kita-Ueno
Asakusa
Higashi-Ueno
Tōbu Asakusa
Kaminarimon
Inarichō
Tawaramachi
Kotobuki
Kasuga-dōri
Komogata
Kuramae

Asakusabashi
Asakusabashi
Asakusabashi
Iwamotochō
Bakuroyokoyama
Higashi-
nihombashi

H

Hanakawado
Narihirabashi
Oshiage
Asakusa
Honjo-
Azumabashi
Higashi-
komagata
Sumida-ku

6
2
Ryōgoku
Ryōgoku
Keiyōdōri
Ryōgoku Sumida-ku
Shuto Expwy No 7
Kikugawa

Yushima

Yushima

Chūō-ku

Shin-
nihombashi
Hamachō
Ningyōchō

Shin-
Ōhashi
Morishita
Kikukawa

Kodemmachō

Mitsukoshimae
Nihombashi
Nihombashi

Kiyosumi
shirakawa

Shirakawa

Tokyo
Tokyo
Kayabachō
Hibiya
Marunouchi
Nijūbashimae
Yūrakuchō
Kyōbashi
Hibiya
Yūrakuchō
JR Yūrakuchō
Kasumigaseki
Ginza
Ginza
Uchisaiwaichō
Uchisaiwaichō
Higashi-
ginza
Shimbashi
Shimbashi
Shimbashi
Shiodome
Shiba
Kōen
Shiodome

See Ginza & Shiodome Map (p66)

Nihombashi
Takarachō
Hatchōbori

Hatchōbori
Shintomi
Shintomichō
Chūō-ku

Tsukiji
Tsukijishijō
Tsukiji

Sumida-gawa

Kiyosumi
shirakawa

Hirano
Sendaiborigawa
River
Fukugawa
Kiba
Kōtō-ku
Kiyosumi
Kiba

Monzen-
nakachō
Etchujima

Tsukishima

Kachidoki-bashi

Daimon

Hamamatsuchō

Hinode

Shibaura
Futō

Takeshiba

Kachidoki

Kachidoki

Shijo-
mae

Shijin-
Toyosu

Tatsumi

Rainbow
Bridge

To Ōedo Onsen
Monogatari (4.6km)

Tokyo
Bay

Kōtō-ku

Ariake Tennis-
no-mori

To Tokyo
Disneyland (5km)

Shinonome
Tokyo
Bay

SIGHTS & ACTIVITIES
Akihabara Electric Town 秋葉原電気街........ **1** F2
Edo-Tokyo Museum 江戸東京博物館............ **2** G2
Imperial Palace 皇居.. **3** E3
Imperial Palace East Garden 東御苑............ **4** E3
Koishikawa Kōrakuen.. **5** D1

ENTERTAINMENT
Ryōgoku Kokugikan 両国国技館...................... **6** G2

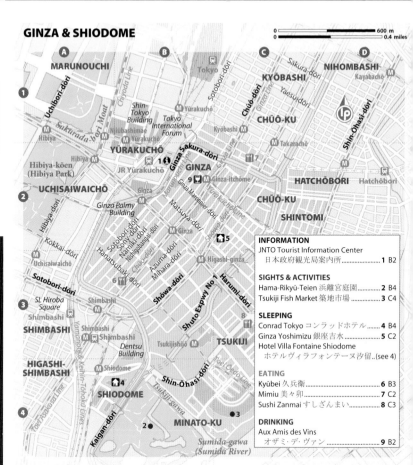

GINZA & SHIODOME

0 600 m
0 0.4 miles

INFORMATION
JNTO Tourist Information Center
日本政府観光局案内所.........................1 B2

SIGHTS & ACTIVITIES
Hama-Rikyū-Teien 浜離宮庭園..............2 B4
Tsukiji Fish Market 築地市場 3 C4

SLEEPING
Conrad Tokyo コンラッドホテル 4 B4
Ginza Yoshimizu 銀座吉水 5 C2
Hotel Villa Fontaine Shiodome
ホテルヴィラフォンテーヌ汐留..(see 4)

EATING
Kyūbei 久兵衛..6 B3
Mimiu 美々卯..7 C2
Sushi Zanmai すしざんまい...................8 C3

DRINKING
Aux Amis des Vins
オザミ・デ・ヴァン 9 B2

widely known as *the* place to hunt for bargains on new and used electronics.

GINZA & SHIODOME
銀座・汐留
GINZA 銀座
Ginza is Tokyo's answer to NYC's Fifth Ave. Back in the 1870s Ginza was one of the first areas to modernise, featuring a large number of novel (for Tokyoites of that era) Western-style brick buildings. Ginza was also home to Tokyo's first department stores, gas lamps and other harbingers of the modern world.

HAMA-RIKYŪ-TEIEN 浜離宮庭園
Arguably the loveliest garden in central Tokyo, **Hama-Rikyū-Teien** (Detached Palace Garden; Map p66; ☎ 3541-0200; admission ¥300; ⏰ 9am-5pm; 🚇 Toei Ōedo line to Tsukiji-Shijō, exit A2) is incongruously surrounded by gleaming high-rises at the edge of Tokyo Bay. Walk the garden paths along tide-fed ponds for a little peace.

TSUKIJI FISH MARKET 築地市場
Tsukiji Fish Market (Map p66; ☎ 3541-2640; www.tsukiji-market.or.jp; 5-2 Tsukiji, Chūō-ku; ⏰ closed 2nd & 4th Wed most months, Sun & public

holidays; 🚇 Toei Ōedo line to Tsukiji-Shijō, exits A1 & A2) is the world's biggest seafood market. The day begins very early, with the arrival of the catch and its early-morning wholesale auctioning.

To get to the climate-controlled auction hall, head into the main entrance of the market hall and go through to the back. You can get an English guide at the market entrance. The rest of the market is open to the public and is at its best before 8am.

UENO 上野
UENO-KŌEN 上野公園

Ueno Hill was the site of a last-ditch defence of the Tokugawa shōgunate by about 2000 Tokugawa loyalists in 1868. They were duly dispatched by the Imperial Army, and the new Meiji government decreed that Ueno Hill would be transformed into Tokyo's first public park. Today, **Ueno-kōen** (Map p68; 🚇 JR Yamanote line to Ueno, Park exit) may not be the sexiest of Tokyo's parks, but it certainly

KRZYSZTOF DYDYNSKI

Imperial Palace East Garden

⬎ IF YOU LIKE...

If you like the garden at **Hama-Rikyū-Teien** (opposite), we think you'll like these other Tokyo gardens and parks:

- **Imperial Palace East Garden** (Map pp64–5; Kōkyo Higashi-gyoen; ☎ 3213-2050; admission free; ⏰ 9am–4pm Nov–Feb, to 4.30pm Mar–Apr & Sep–Oct, to 5pm May–Aug, closed Mon & Fri; Ⓜ Chiyoda, Marunouchi & Tōzai lines to Ōtemachi, exit C10) This is a great place for a stroll right in the centre of Tokyo.

- **Koishikawa Kōrakuen** (Map pp64–5; ☎ 3811-3015; 1-6-6 Kōraku, Bunkyō-ku; admission ¥300; ⏰ 9am–5pm; Ⓜ Marunouchi line to Kōrakuen) This has to be one of the least-visited (by foreigners at least) and best gardens in Tokyo. A stroll-garden with a strong Chinese influence, it was established in the mid-17th century.

- **Shinjuku-gyoen** (Map p70; ☎ 3350-0151; Naitochō, Shinjuku-ku; adult/child under 15/child under 6 ¥200/50/free; ⏰ 9am–4.30pm Tue–Sun; Ⓜ Marunouchi line to Shinjuku-gyoenmae, exit 1) At 57.6 hectares, this is one of Tokyo's largest parks. It dates back to 1906 and was designed as a European-style park, though it also has a Japanese garden, a hothouse containing tropical plants and a pond with giant carp.

packs a bigger cultural punch than any others. Across the street from the park exit is a large map showing the layout of the park and museum complex.

The park is famous as Tokyo's most popular site for *hanami* (blossom-viewing) in early to mid-April – which isn't to say it's the *best* place: Shinjuku-gyoen (opposite) is an altogether quieter *hanami* spot).

TOKYO NATIONAL MUSEUM 東京国立博物館

The **Tokyo National Museum** (Tokyo Kokuritsu Hakubutsukan; Map p68; ☎ 3822-1111; www.tnm.jp; 13-9 Ueno-kōen, Taitō-ku; adult/student ¥600/400; ⏰ 9.30am-5pm Tue-Sun Oct-Mar, to 8pm Fri, to 6pm Sat & Sun Apr-Sep; ⓡ JR Yamanote line to Ueno, Park exit) is the one museum in Tokyo worth a spot on your itinerary. It is Japan's largest, housing 87,000 items, and also has the world's largest collection of Japanese

art. Only a portion of the museum's works is displayed at any one time.

TŌSHŌGŪ 東照宮

This **shrine** (Map p68; ☎ 3822-3455; 9-88 Ueno-kōen, Taitō-ku; admission ¥200; ⏰ 9am-4.30pm Dec-Feb, to 5.30pm Mar-Nov; ⓡ JR Yamanote line to Ueno, Shinobazu exit), like its counterpart in Nikkō, is dedicated to Tokugawa Ieyasu, who unified Japan. The shrine, resplendent in gold leaf and ornate details, dates from 1651 and is one of the few extant early-Edo structures, having fortuitously survived Tokyo's innumerable disasters.

ASAKUSA 浅草

Long considered the heart of old Shitamachi, Asakusa is an interesting, compact neighbourhood to explore on foot. Asakusa's main attraction is the temple Sensō-ji, also known as Asakusa

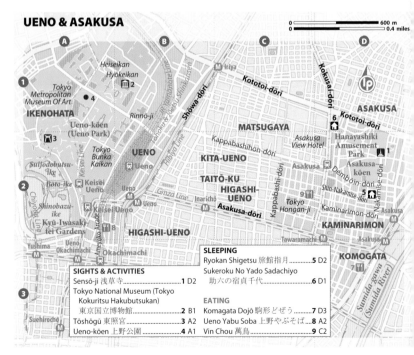

UENO & ASAKUSA

0 — 600 m
0 — 0.4 miles

SIGHTS & ACTIVITIES
Sensō-ji 浅草寺.............................1 D2
Tokyo National Museum (Tokyo Kokuritsu Hakubutsukan)
　東京国立博物館.........................2 B1
Tōshōgū 東照宮............................3 A2
Ueno-kōen 上野公園......................4 A1

SLEEPING
Ryokan Shigetsu 旅館指月..............5 D2
Sukeroku No Yado Sadachiyo
　助六の宿貞千代.........................6 D1

EATING
Komagata Dojō 駒形どぜう...........7 D3
Ueno Yabu Soba 上野やぶそば....8 A2
Vin Chou 萬鳥.............................9 C2

Restaurant in Shinjuku
GREG ELMS

Kannon-dō. In Edo times, Asakusa was a halfway stop between the city and its most infamous pleasure district, Yoshiwara. Eventually Asakusa developed into a pleasure quarter in its own right, becoming the centre for that most loved of Edo entertainments, kabuki. In the shadow of Sensō-ji a fairground spirit prevailed and a range of secular establishments thrived, from kabuki theatres to brothels.

SENSŌ-JI 浅草寺

This **temple** (Map p68; ☎ 3842-0181; 2-3-1 Asakusa, Taitō-ku; admission free; ⏰ 24hr; 🚇 Ginza or Toei Asakusa lines to Asakusa, exits 1 & A5) enshrines a golden image of Kannon (the Buddhist Goddess of Mercy), which, according to legend, was miraculously fished out of the nearby Sumida-gawa by two fishermen in AD 628. The image has remained on the spot ever since, through successive rebuildings of the temple; the present structure dates from 1950.

SHINJUKU 新宿

Here in Shinjuku, much of what makes Tokyo tick is crammed into one busy district: upscale department stores, anachronistic stand-up bars, buttoned-up government offices, swarming crowds, streetside video screens, hostess clubs, shyly tucked-away shrines and soaring skyscrapers.

Shinjuku's east side is a great one-stop mash-up of trashy low culture, sedate department stores and one of the city's best cherry- blossom viewing spots, Shinjuku-gyoen.

Shinjuku's west side is mainly administrative, with its attractions mainly centred around the gleaming building interiors and the observation floors of the towering Tokyo Metropolitan Government Offices.

TOKYO METROPOLITAN GOVERNMENT OFFICES 東京都庁

These city **offices** (Tokyo Tochō; Map p70; ☎ 5321-1111; 2-8-1 Nishi-Shinjuku, Shinjuku-ku; admission free; ⏰ observatories 9.30am-11pm Tue-Sun, North Tower closed 2nd & 4th Mon, South Tower closed 1st & 3rd Tue; 🚇 Toei Ōedo line to Tochōmae, exits A3 & A4) occupy two adjoining buildings worth visiting for their stunning architecture and for the

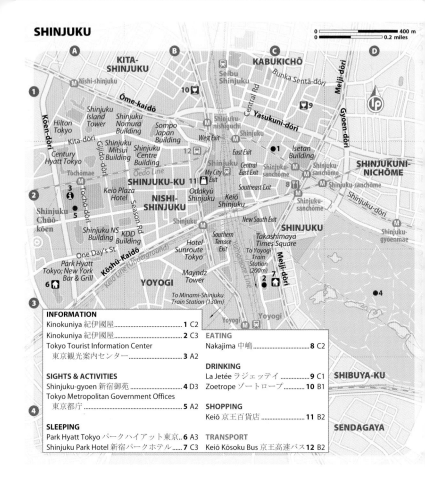

SHINJUKU

great views from the **twin observation floors**. On really clear days, you might even spot Mt Fuji to the west. To reach the observation floors, take one of the two 1st-floor lifts.

HARAJUKU & AOYAMA
原宿・青山

Harajuku and Aoyama (Map p72) are where Tokyoites come to be spendy and trendy. They're enjoyable areas to stroll and watch locals in contented consumer mode. **Takeshita-dōri** buzzes with teeny-boppers shopping for hilariously mis-translated T-shirts and fishnet stockings; tree-lined **Omote-sandō**, with its alfresco cafes, is still the closest Tokyo gets to Paris; and the bistro alleys of Aoyama harbour some of the best international cuisine in town.

MEIJI-JINGŪ 明治神宮

Completed in 1920, the **shrine (Map p72; ☎ 3379-5511; www.meijijingu.or.jp; 1-1 Yoyogi Kamizonochō, Shibuya-ku; admission free; ☀ dawn-dusk; ⓡ JR Yamanote line to Harajuku, Omote-sandō exit)** was built in memory of Emperor Meiji and Empress Shōken, under whose rule

Japan ended its long isolation from the outside world. Unfortunately, like much else in Tokyo, the shrine was destroyed in WWII bombing. Rebuilding was completed in 1958.

SHIBUYA 渋谷
Shibuya Crossing (Map p72) is probably one of the world's most visually famous four-way intersections, where the green light given to pedestrians releases a timed surge of humanity. Mostly of interest as a stupendous youth-oriented shopping district and people-watching hotspot, the goods for sale and energy of Shibuya offer glimpses into the desires and psyche of a certain generation. Especially on weekends, you might get the feeling that the jammed streets are populated solely by fashionable under-25s.

ROPPONGI & AKASAKA
六本木・赤坂
Roppongi has undergone a renaissance over the last several years, with monumental development changing the urban landscape as well as elevating its respectability quotient. While Roppongi is still the pulsating centre of wild nightlife, it now also claims bragging rights to world-class restaurants, a trio of superb museums collectively making up the **Roppongi Art Triangle** and even some green oases.

ODAIBA & TOKYO BAY
お台場・東京湾
Built on reclaimed land in Tokyo Bay, the island of Odaiba stands as another reminder that Tokyo is a waterfront city. Aside from the whole fake-island angle, Odaiba has loads of oddities that trump the views of Tokyo across the bay – including bizarre architecture, a petite Statue of Liberty, and an onsen (hot spring) dressed up as an ersatz Edo-era town.

Get to Odaiba on the driverless Yurikamome monorail, which departs from Shimbashi Station, and get around the island on the free shuttle than runs from 11am to 8pm.

Crowd of shoppers, Omote-Sandō

BRENT WINEBRENNER

SHIBUYA & ROPPONGI

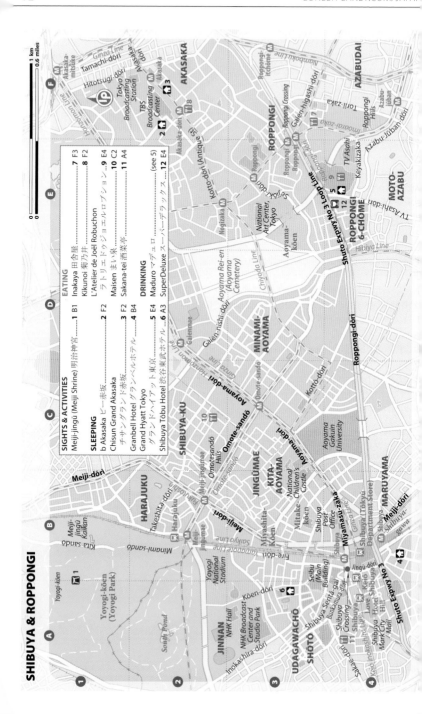

ŌEDO ONSEN MONOGATARI 大江戸温泉物語

Modelled on an old Edo town, this **onsen** (off Map pp64-5; ☎ 5500-1126; www.ooedoonsen.jp/higaeri/english; 2-57 Aomi, Kōtō-ku; adult/child ¥2900/1600; ☻ 11am-9am, last entry at 7am; ☒ Yurikamome line to Telecom Center) pipes in natural mineral water from 1400m beneath Tokyo Bay. Though it sounds hokey, the place is attractively designed, with lovely mixed-gender (*yukata* – light cotton kimono – required) outdoor pools, traditional baths and spa treatments.

ELSEWHERE IN TOKYO
TOKYO DISNEYLAND 東京ディズニーランド

This **amusement park** (off Map pp64-5; ☎ 045-683-3777; www.tokyodisneyresort.co.jp; 1-1 Maihama, Urayasu-shi, Chiba; 1-day ticket adult/youth/child ¥5800/5000/3900; ☻ varies; ☒ JR Keiyō line to Maihama) is a near-perfect replica of the original in Anaheim, California, but it has the added attraction of a sister park called Tokyo DisneySea, which is aimed at adults. The resort is open year-round except for about a dozen days a year (most of them in January), and opening hours vary seasonally, so check the website before heading out.

KAGURAZAKA WALKING TOUR

Mention Kagurazaka to a Tokyoite, and it will likely conjure visions of geisha turning down cobbled alleys to tucked-away *ryōtei* (traditional Japanese restaurants). That romantic mood still pervades, surprisingly, in a city known for its hypermodernity and blasé ease with demolition.

To get there, hop the Tōzai line to Kagurazaka Station. From exit 1, turn left and you'll be at the top of Kagurazaka-dōri, a small one-way street leading downhill. Make another immediate left at the

KAGURAZAKA WALKING TOUR

stoplight, and at the end of the alley lies the small shrine, **Akagi-jinja** (赤城神社; **1**). Kagurazaka's most famous feature is its mazelike *kakurembo-yokochō* (hide-and-seek alleys; **2**). Enter the alleys with a right turn at the shrine entrance, to find a wealth of tiny bars (some barely big enough to fit two or three patrons), expat-run French cafes and Italian restaurants, and small homes fronted by bonsai. Make your way up to the peaceful grounds of **Tsukudo Hachiman shrine** (筑土八幡神社; **3**), with the oldest torii in Shinjuku-ku.

Roaming back to Kagurazaka-dōri, where the slope below Ōkubo-dōri is lined with family-run groceries and noisy pachinko parlours, have a look at the shrine **Zenkoku-ji** (善国寺; **4**), also known as Bishamonten, for its statue of the military god housed in one of its halls. Head down the hill, to browse the parasols, *geta* (wooden sandals) and other kimono-appropriate accessories at **Sukeroku** (**5**; 助六; ☎ 3260-0015; www.bolanet.ne.jp/sukeroku, in Japanese; 3-6 Kagurazaka, Shinjuku-ku; ☻ 10.30am-8.30pm). Then stop for an azuki-bean or custard-filled Peko-yaki (grilled pastry shaped like the shop mascot,

TOKYO AREA

TOKYO

Portrait of a kabuki villain, Edo-Tokyo Museum

↘ EDO-TOKYO MUSEUM

This museum is a gem, with a replica of Nihombashi (the bridge that is the namesake of today's Tokyo neighbourhood) dividing this display of re-creations of Edo-period and Meiji-period Tokyo. Exhibits range from examples of actual Edo infrastructure – a wooden sewage pipe, for one – to exquisite scale models of markets and shops, including such meticulous details as period costumes and stray cats scavenging fish scraps.

Things you need to know: Map pp64-5; ☎ 3626-9974; www.edo-tokyo-museum.or.jp; 1-4-1 Yokoami, Sumida-ku; adult/child ¥600/free, student ¥300-450; ⏱ 9.30am-5.30pm Tue-Fri & Sun, to 7.30pm Sat; ♿ ♿ ; 🚃 JR Sōbu line to Ryōgoku, west exit or Toei Ōedo line to Ryōgoku, exit A4

Peko-chan) at **Fujiya** (6; 不二家; ☎ 3269-1526; 1-12 Kagurazaka, Shinjuku-ku; ⏱ 10am-9.30pm Mon-Fri, to 8pm Sat).

Alternatively, work up an appetite by renting a rowboat at **Canal Café** (7; カナルカフェ; ☎ 3260-8068; 1-9 Kagurazaka, Shinjuku-ku; per 30min ¥500; ⏱ 11.30am-dusk) on the canal, and end with a drink here. Or, backtrack up Kagurazaka-dōri, turn-

ing left at the first alley, for an *izakaya* (pub-eatery) dinner at **Seigetsu** (8; 霽月; ☎ 3269-4320; 2nd fl, 6-77-1 Kagurazaka, Shinjuku-ku; ⏱ 5-11pm) down the alley next to the Family Mart convenience store. Retrace your steps to Kagurazaka Station, or return via Iidabashi Station adjacent to the canal.

SLEEPING

GINZA & SHIODOME
銀座・汐留

Hotel Villa Fontaine Shiodome (Map p66; ☎ 3569-2220; fax 3569-2221; www.hvf.jp; 1-9-2 Higashi-Shimbashi, Minato-ku; s/d/tw from ¥10,000/14,000/18,000; ℗ ✕ 🖳 ; 🚃 Toei Ōedo line to Shiodome, exit 10) This place is a superb midrange deal with an upscale feel. Lighting in lobby areas is dim and subtly spooky, but the rooms are comfortable and modern, with internet-TV and high-speed local area network (LAN).

Ginza Yoshimizu (Map p66; ☎ 3248-4432; www.yoshimizu.com; 3-11-3 Ginza, Chūō-ku; s/tw/tr ¥17,000/27,500/31,800; 🚃 Hibiya & Toei Asakusa lines to Higashi-Ginza, exits 3 & A7) Stepping through the bamboo doors of the Yoshimizu means leaving behind TVs, phones, internet access and city din in favour of more natural living. This elegantly simple ryokan features earth walls, bamboo and tatami flooring, organic cotton bedding and a *sentō* (public bath) made from immaculate granite and *hinoki* (Japanese cypress).

Conrad Tokyo (Map p66; ☎ 6388-8000; fax 6388-8001; www.conradtokyo.co.jp; 1-9-1 Higashi-Shimbashi, Minato-ku; s/d from ¥74,000/79,000; ✕ 🖳 🛄 ♿ ; 🚃 Toei Ōedo line to Shiodome, exit 10) It's big. Whether you choose city or garden views, you'll find varnished hardwoods and cushy elegance. Enormous bathrooms boast rainshower fixtures, freestanding tubs, Shiseido amenities and floor-to-ceiling glass walls facing the windows.

ASAKUSA 浅草

Ryokan Shigetsu (Map p68; ☎ 3843-2345; fax 3843-2348; www.shigetsu.com; 1-31-11 Asakusa, Taitō-ku; Western-style s/tw ¥7665/14,900, Japanese-style s/d from ¥9450/17,200; ✂ 🖳; 🚇 Ginza & Toei Asakusa lines to Asakusa, exits 1 & 2) This ryokan is a gorgeous oasis of Japanese hospitality, just off Nakamise-dōri. Most rooms have bathrooms, but bathing in the *sentō* is a must – both the black granite bath and the *hinoki* one have unique, stunning views.

Sukeroku No Yado Sadachiyo (Map p68; ☎ 3842-6431; fax 3842-6433; www.sadachiyo.co .jp; 2-20-1 Asakusa, Taitō-ku; s/d from ¥14,100/19,400; 🚇 Ginza line to Tawaramachi, exit 3 or Tsukuba Express to Asakusa, exit A1) Another traditionally elegant spot, just far enough removed from bustling Nakamise-dōri, the Sadachiyo features rooms of *shōji* (movable screens) and tatami, each with a Western-style bath.

SHINJUKU 新宿

Shinjuku Park Hotel (Map p70; ☎ 3356-0241; fax 3352-2733; www.shinjukuparkhotel.co.jp; 5-27-9 Sendagaya, Shibuya-ku; s/tw from ¥7900/14,000, Japanese-style r ¥24,800; 🅿 ✂ 🖳; 🚇 JR Yamanote line to Shinjuku, new south exit) Just south of Takashimaya Times Sq, this pleasant business hotel has larger rooms than most.

Park Hyatt Tokyo (Map p70; ☎ 5322-1234; fax 5322-1288; www.tokyo.park.hyatt .com; 3-7-1-2 Nishi-Shinjuku, Shinjuku-ku; r/ste from ¥55,650/68,250; ✂ 🖳; 🚇 JR Yamanote line to Shinjuku, south exit) Views here are legendarily stunning, day and night, and from these serene heights you appear to be part of another world. Dignified but relaxed, the stylishly understated rooms are done in naturally finished wood, fabric and marble.

SHIBUYA 渋谷

Granbell Hotel (Map p72; ☎ 5457-2681; fax 5457-2682; www.granbellhotel.jp; 15-17 Sakuragaokachō, Shibuya-ku; s/d/ste from ¥13,100/21,400/55,400; ✂ 🖳; 🚇 JR Yamanote line to Shibuya, south exit) Though the size of the Granbell's rooms are on par for Tokyo, the glass-walled bathrooms and bright tropical colour schemes give the illusion of spaciousness. In addition to amenities such as free LAN internet access, English-language TV and hairdryers, rooms in the main building feature curtains with fun Lichtenstein-esque designs and Simmons beds.

Shibuya Tōbu Hotel (Map p72; ☎ 3476-0111; fax 3476-0903; www.tobuhotel.co.jp/ shibuya; 3-1 Udagawachō, Shibuya-ku; s/d from ¥14,060/20,035; ✂ 🖳; 🚇 JR Yamanote line to Shibuya, Hachikō exit) One of Shibuya's nicest business hotels, the Tōbu has stylish, clean and relatively large rooms with LAN internet access.

Fish on skewers, restaurant at Park Hyatt Tokyo

ROPPONGI & AKASAKA
六本木・赤坂

Chisun Grand Akasaka (Map p72; ☎ 5572-7788; fax 5572-7789; www.solarehotels.com/english; 6-3-17 Akasaka, Minato-ku; s/d ¥14,600/17,900; ✗ 🖳 ; 🚇 Chiyoda line to Akasaka, exits 6 & 7) This business hotel has all of the comforts of its class (such as LAN internet) and then some: MP3-player-ready speakers, in-room clothes presses and full-sized beds even in single rooms.

b Akasaka (Map p72; ☎ 3586-0811; fax 3589-0575; theb-akasaka@ishinhotels.com; 7-6-13 Akasaka, Minato-ku; s/tw from ¥14,600/20,400; ✗ 🖳 ; 🚇 Chiyoda line to Akasaka, exit 3b) Curvy patterns, like circular windows and rounded shower stalls, characterise the modern rooms at b Akasaka. On a quiet street across from the TBS Broadcasting Center, this lovely business hotel offers free LAN internet, a light buffet breakfast and free coffee and tea 24 hours a day.

Grand Hyatt Tokyo (Map p72; ☎ 4333-1234; fax 4333-8123; www.tokyo.grand.hyatt .com; 6-10-3 Roppongi, Minato-ku; s/d from ¥50,400/55,650; 🅿 ✗ 🖳 🖳 ♿ ; 🚇 Hibiya & Toei Ōedo lines to Roppongi, exits 1c & 3) Set in uber-desirable Roppongi Hills, the Grand Hyatt gleams with polished refinement. Though the look is decidedly urban, the interior makes liberal use of natural materials, lending an earthy and comfortable feel to this modern hotel with details such as rain-shower fixtures and mahogany walls. Hi-tech luxuries include DVD players and flat-screen TVs in the bathrooms, while in-house facilities encompass a spa with wet and dry saunas, large indoor pool and gym, some of Tokyo's best dining and a number of bars.

EATING
KANDA & TOKYO STATION
神田・東京駅

Mimiu (Map p66; ☎ 3567-6571; www.mimiu .co.jp; 3-6-4 Kyōbashi, Chūō-ku; meals ¥1600; ⏱ 11.30am-9.30pm Mon-Sat, 11.30am-9pm Sun; 🚇 Ginza line to Kyōbashi, exits 1 & 2) Connoisseurs of udon say that Osaka-style broth is lighter in colour and more delicate in flavour than

Yakitori-ya (restaurant-bar serving skewers of grilled meats), Ginza

GREG ELMS

what Tokyoites favour. Try for yourself at Mimiu, an Osaka original that's said to have invented *udon-suki* (¥3500 per person; udon cooked sukiyaki-style in broth, with seafood, vegetables and meat). There's a picture menu. Look for the stately black corner building.

GINZA & SHIODOME
銀座・汐留

Sushi Zanmai (Map p66; ☎ 3541-1117; 4-11-9 Tsukiji, Chūō-ku; dinner from ¥1500; ⊙ 24hr; V ; 圓 Hibiya line to Tsukiji, exit 1) After the sunrise fish auctions of the Tsukiji Fish Market, it serves market-fresh sushi to weary fishermen; then tourists and townsfolk, office workers and retirees. In the evening, it remains open to bar and restaurant trade, and the ladies of the floating world. Zanmai has an English picture menu and English lettering on the sign; there's a proliferation of branches around the market.

Kyūbei (Map p66; ☎ 3571-6523; www.kyubey.jp; 8-7-6 Ginza, Chūō-ku; lunch/dinner from ¥4000/10,000; ⊙ lunch & dinner Mon-Sat; ✕ ; 圓 Ginza line to Shimbashi, exit 1) Established in 1936, this superb sushi restaurant continues to earn its reputation as one of Tokyo's best. If you treat yourself to one high-end, raw-fish experience, reserve a place at Kyūbei. An English menu is available online, not in-house, but English-speaking staff can help you order. Its minimalist facade has a discreet flagstone path on the left, one street west of Chūō-dōri.

UENO 上野

Ueno Yabu Soba (Map p68; ☎ 3831-4728; 6-9-16 Ueno, Taitō-ku; meals from ¥750; ⊙ 11.30am-9pm Thu-Tue; 齒 ; 圓 JR Yamanote line to Ueno, Hirokōji exit) Near the arcade, this famous *soba* (buckwheat noodles) shop has a peaceful, traditional atmosphere despite

its busyness. There's an English picture menu, but if you can't decide, try the filling *nabeyaki soba* (noodles topped with vegetables, egg and tempura shrimp). Look for the black granite sign on the corner shop that says 'Since 1892'.

ASAKUSA 浅草

Komagata Dojō (Map p68; ☎ 3842-4001; 1-7-12 Komagata, Taitō-ku; dishes ¥1500-3000; ⊙ 11am-9pm; 圓 Ginza & Toei Asakusa lines to Asakusa, exits 2 & A5) The sixth-generation chef running this marvellous restaurant continues the tradition of turning the simple *dojō* (a small, eel-like river fish) into rich deliciousness. It's all floor seating at the shared low, wooden-plank tables, and an English picture menu details your options. If you choose the *nabe* (¥1700; cast iron pot), the *dojō* will come on a charcoal-heated dish; heap it with chopped scallions and cook through before eating. Look for the restaurant's traditional facade between modern buildings.

Vin Chou (Map p68; ☎ 3845-4430; www .vinchou.jp/r-asakusa/asakusa.html, in Japanese; 2-2-13 Nishi-Asakusa, Taitō-ku; meals from ¥5000; ⊙ 5-11pm Mon, Tue & Thu-Sat, 4-10pm Sun) In a city enamoured of all things French, this is, *bien sûr*, a French-style *yakitori* (skewers of grilled chicken) joint, offering foie gras with your *tori negi* (chicken and leek). It's around the corner from Taitō Ryokan, with an English menu and small sign in French.

SHINJUKU 新宿

Nakajima (Map p70; ☎ 3356-7962; http://shin jyuku-nakajima.com, in Japanese; 3-32-5 Shinjuku, Shinjuku-ku; lunch/dinner from ¥800/12,500; ⊙ lunch & dinner Mon-Sat; 圓 Marunouchi line to Shinjuku-sanchōme, exit A1) The speciality of this warmly-lit, immaculate basement restaurant is the *iwashi* (sardine) – simmered in sweet broth with egg, served as sashimi, or delicately fried and laid on a bed of rice.

Though there's no English menu, the hostess will explain the options to you in flawless English. Dinners are *kaiseki* (Japanese haute cuisine), but lunches are fabulously inexpensive. Down the alley next to the Beams building, look for a black building with an outside stairwell leading down to this one-Michelin-star shop.

HARAJUKU & AOYAMA
原宿・青山

Maisen (Map p72; ☎ 3470-0071; 4-8-5 Jingūmae, Shibuya-ku; lunch sets ¥1500; ☺ 11am-10pm; ✗ ♿; ☒ Chiyoda, Ginza & Hanzōmon lines to Omote-sandō, exit A2) Maisen turns out righteous, crisp *tonkatsu* (deep-fried pork cutlets) that draws consistent queues. Thankfully, the place is housed in a converted bathhouse, so there's plenty of room for those craving Kagoshima *kurobuta* (black pork; ¥1260). If you're on the run, pick up a *bentō* (boxed meal) at the takeaway window.

SHIBUYA 渋谷

Sakana-tei (Map p72; ☎ 3780-1313; 4th fl, Koike Bldg, 2-23-15 Dōgenzaka, Shibuya-ku; meals from ¥3500; ☺ 5.30-11pm Mon-Sat; ☒ JR Yamanote line to Shibuya, Hachikō exit) This unpretentious, but slightly posh, *izakaya* is a sake specialist much sought after by connoisseurs, and it's great value to boot. There's no English menu; just point at the dishes on the counter to order. Call ahead for reservations, but turn off your mobile phone once you're in. From the Shibuya JR Station, take Bunkamura-dōri (to the right of the Shibuya 109 building), and take a left where the road splits. Take your first left, and the Koike Building will be the first on your right.

ROPPONGI 六本木

L'Atelier de Joël Robuchon (Map p72; ☎ 5772-7500; 2nd fl, Hillside, Roppongi Hills, 6-10-1 Roppongi, Minato-ku; lunch/dinner ¥5000/15,000; ☺ lunch & dinner; ☒ Hibiya & Toei Ōedo lines to Roppongi, exits 1c & 3) A two-star Michelin standout, L'Atelier is an upscale French diner whose main counter is fashioned after a sushi bar. Sip on wine or a cocktail from the well-rounded list as you watch the chefs, clad in black, working their magic in the open kitchen. The divine fusion cuisine combines Japanese, French and Spanish elements with refined style, and is best sampled in one of the tasting menus. The menu is in French and Japanese, but the servers speak English.

Inakaya (Map p72; ☎ 3408-5040; www .roppongi inakaya.jp; 5-3-4 Roppongi, Minato-ku; meals from ¥10,000; ☺ dinner; ☒ Hibiya & Toei Ōedo lines to Roppongi, exits 2 & 3) Once you're bombarded with greetings at the door, the action doesn't stop at this old-guard *robatayaki* (rustic bar-restaurant serving charcoal-grilled food that goes beautifully with booze; literally 'hearthside cooking'). Point at what you'd like to eat (there's no English menu, though prices are listed on the website) and it will be grilled for you.

AKASAKA 赤坂

Kikunoi (Map p72; ☎ 3568-6055; 6-13-8 Akasaka, Minato-ku; dinners from ¥20,000; ☺ dinner Mon-Sat; ☒ Chiyoda line to Akasaka, exit 6) This Kyoto-based *kaiseki* restaurant has built its reputation over three generations, and its fame has expanded to international recognition after being awarded with two Michelin stars in 2008. Exquisitely prepared seasonal dishes are as beautiful as they are delicious. The restaurant's Chef Murata has also written a book on *kaiseki*, and the staff helpfully use the book to explain the dishes you are served. There's no English menu, and reservations are essential.

DRINKING

GINZA & SHIODOME
銀座・汐留

Aux Amis des Vins (Map p66; ☎ 3567-4120; www.auxamis.com/desvins, in Japanese; 2-5-6 Ginza, Chūō-ku; ⏰ 5.30pm-2am Mon-Fri, noon-midnight Sat; ⓡ Yūrakuchō line to Ginza-itchōme, exits 5 & 8) Both the informal indoor and a small outdoor seating area at this wine bar feel welcoming in all seasons. A solid selection of mostly French wines comes by the glass (¥800) or by the bottle.

SHINJUKU 新宿

La Jetée (Map p70; ☎ 3208-9645; 1-1-8 Kabukichō, Shinjuku-ku; admission ¥700; ⏰ 7pm-late Mon-Sat; ⓡ Marunouchi & Toei Shinjuku lines to Shinjuku-sanchōme, exit B5) A favourite among cineastes (and run by one), this tidy little haven is the namesake for a film much admired by its French- speaking proprietor and a good introduction to these alleys.

Zoetrope (Map p70; ☎ 3363-0162; http://homepage2.nifty.com/zoetrope; 3rd fl, Gaia Bldg, 7-10-14 Nishi-Shinjuku, Shinjuku-ku; ⏰ 7pm-4am Mon-Sat; ⓡ Toei Ōedo line to Shinjuku-nishiguchi, exit D5) Spend a sociable, relaxed evening at this cosy bar, which features more than 300 kinds of Japanese whisky and screens silent films on the wall. An English menu will help you taste your way around.

ROPPONGI 六本木

Maduro (Map p72; ☎ 4333-8888; 4th fl, Grand Hyatt Tokyo, 6-10-3 Roppongi, Minato-ku; admission around ¥1500; ⏰ 6pm-2am Sun-Thu, to 3am Fri & Sat; ⓡ Hibiya & Toei Ōedo lines to Roppongi, exits 1c & 3) Inside the labyrinthine Grand Hyatt Tokyo, this sleek, swanky lounge is a chic spot to kick off your evening with a champagne or scotch. There's live music nightly, but arrive before 9pm to avoid the cover. charge

SuperDeluxe (Map p72; ☎ 5412 0515; www.super-deluxe.com; B1 fl, 3-1-25 Nishi-Azabu, Minato-ku; admission varies; ⏰ 6pm-late Mon-Sat; ⓡ Hibiya & Toei Ōedo lines to Roppongi, exits 1b & 3) Hard to categorise, easy to love, SuperDeluxe morphs from lounge to gallery to club to performance space from night to night.

ANTHONY PLUMMER

Shinjuku bar

ENTERTAINMENT

SUMŌ

Travellers who visit Tokyo in January, May or September should not miss their chance to attend a Grand Tournament at Tokyo's **Ryōgoku Kokugikan** (Ryōgoku Sumō Stadium; Map pp64-5; ☎ 3622-1100; www .sumo.or.jp; 1-3-28 Yokoami, Sumida-ku; ☺ 10am-4pm; 🚇 JR Sōbu line to Ryōgoku, west exit or Toei Ōedo line to Ryōgoku, exit A4). The best seats are all bought up by those with the right connections, but if you don't mind standing, you can get in for around ¥500. Tickets can be purchased up to a month prior to the tournament, or you can simply turn up on the day (you'll have to arrive very early, say 6am, to be assured of seats during the last days of a tournament).

SHOPPING

Akihabara (p63), Tokyo's discount electronics neighbourhood, carries a huge range of electrical appliances in a highly concentrated area – hence the nickname Denki-gai (Electric Town).

Photographers, take note: the area behind the Keiō department store (Map p70) on the west side of Shinjuku Station is home to Tokyo's largest camera stores, Yodobashi and Sakuraya.

GETTING THERE & AWAY

AIR

With the exception of a few Asian airlines, all international flights arrive at Narita International Airport rather than the more conveniently located Haneda airport.

TRAIN

All major JR lines radiate from Tokyo Station; northbound trains stop at Ueno Station, which, like Tokyo Station, is on the convenient JR Yamanote line. Private lines – often cheaper and quicker for making day trips out of Tokyo – start from various stations around Tokyo.

SHINKANSEN

Of these lines, the one most likely to be used by visitors to Japan is the Tōkaidō line, as it passes through Kyoto and Osaka. Nozomi (super express) trains between Tokyo and Kyoto (¥13,520, 2½ hours) are fastest, as they make only a few stops.

GETTING AROUND

Tokyo has an excellent public transport system, with everything of note conveniently close to a subway or JR station. Bus services are difficult to use if you don't read kanji, but the average visitor to Tokyo won't need the buses anyway.

TO/FROM NARITA AIRPORT

Narita airport is 66km from central Tokyo and is used by almost all the international airlines and a small number of domestic operators. Travel to or from Tokyo takes from 50 minutes to two hours, depending on your mode of transport and destination in town.

Depending on where you're headed, it's generally cheaper and faster to travel into Tokyo by train than by limousine bus. However, rail users will probably need to change trains somewhere, and this can be confusing on a jetlagged first visit. Limousine buses provide a hassle-free direct route to a number of Tokyo's top hotels, and you don't have to be a hotel guest to use the buses.

LIMOUSINE BUS

Airport Limousine Bus (www.limousinebus .co.jp/en) actually runs ordinary buses that take 1½ to two hours to travel between Narita airport and a number of major hotels. Check departure times before buying your ticket, as services are not all that frequent. The fare to or from hotels around Asakusa, to or from Ikebukuro, Akasaka, Ginza, Shiba, Shinagawa, Shinjuku or Haneda airport costs around ¥3000.

TRAIN

Two railway lines run between Tokyo and both terminals at Narita airport: the private **Keisei line** (☎ 3621-2232; www.keisei co.jp) and **JR East** (☎ 050-2016-1603; www jreast.co.jp/e/nex/index.html).

At the time of writing, the Keisei line has two services and will add a third in 2010. The Keisei Skyliner does the trip between Narita and Ueno (¥1920, 56 minutes) or Nippori (¥1920, 51 minutes). It's worth noting that it's much easier to transfer to the Yamanote line at Nippori Station. Keisei *tokkyū* (limited express; ¥1000) services are much more frequent than the Skyliner, and add another 15 or so minutes to the trip to Ueno, it's 71 minutes; to Nippori, 67 minutes). The third, highly anticipated service is the Skyliner Airport Express, which at 160km/h will whisk passengers from Narita to Tokyo Station in a mere 36 minutes (check www.keisei.co.jp for current fare information).

JR East runs the Narita Express (N'EX) to Tokyo Station (¥2940, 53 minutes), to Shinjuku Station (¥3110, 1½ hours), to or from Ikebukuro Station (¥3110, one hour and 40 minutes) and to or from Yokohama Station (¥4180, 1½ hours).

The Keikyū rail line runs between Narita and Haneda airports (¥1560, two hours), but you'll have to transfer to or from the Keisei line at Aoto Station.

TO/FROM HANEDA AIRPORT

Most domestic flights and Japan airlines (JAL), All Nippon Airlines (ANA), China Eastern Airlines, Shanghai Airlines and Air China use the convenient Haneda airport.

Transport to or from Haneda airport is a simple matter, as the **Tokyo Monorail** (www.tokyo -monorail.co.jp) runs from 5.15am to 11.15pm between the airport and Hamamatsuchō Station on the JR Yamanote line (¥470, 22 minutes, every 10 minutes).

Taxis from the airport to places around central Tokyo cost around ¥6000. Limousine buses connect Haneda with the Tokyo City Air Terminal (TCAT; ¥900), Tokyo Station (¥900), Ikebukuro and Shinjuku (¥1200), and several other destinations in Tokyo.

TAXI

Taxis are so expensive that you should only use them when there's no alternative. Flagfall is ¥710, which gives you 2km (1.5km after 11pm), after which the meter starts to clock an additional ¥100 for every

ANTHONY PLUMMER

Shopping in Harajuku (p70)

Ginza (p66)

350m; you also click up ¥100 for every two minutes you sit idly gazing at the scenery in a Tokyo traffic jam. If you don't speak Japanese, taxi drivers can plug a venue's telephone number into the GPS system to find its location.

TRAIN
JAPAN RAILWAYS (JR) LINES

Undoubtedly, the most useful line in Tokyo is the JR Yamanote line, which does a 35km-long loop around the city, taking in most of the important areas. Another useful aboveground JR route is the Chūō line, which cuts across the city centre between Shinjuku and Akihabara. Tickets are transferable on all JR lines.

Travellers planning to spend an extended period of time in Tokyo might consider get-

ting a Suica smart card – the Suica card can be swiped without being removed from a wallet, and they can be recharged at any JR vending machine. They can not only be used on most other metropolitan railway lines in addition to JR lines, but can even be used as debit cards at convenience stores and restaurants in the stations. Suica cards require a ¥500 deposit, refundable when you return it to a JR window.

SUBWAY LINES

Ticket prices on the Tokyo Metro start at ¥160 (¥170 on TOEI lines) for short hops, but if your trip involves a change of train it will probably cost upwards of ¥190. As with the JR system, if you're in doubt at all (there are still subway stations where the only pricing maps are in Japanese), buy the cheapest ticket and do a fare adjustment at your destination.

DISCOUNT TICKETS & TRAIN PASSES

There are no massively discounted tickets available for travel around Tokyo. The best deal is the Tokyo Combination Ticket (¥1580), which allows travel on any subway, tram, TOEI bus or JR train in the metropolitan area until the last train of the day. It's available from subway and JR stations and post offices.

NORTH OF TOKYO
NIKKŌ 日光

☎ 0288 / pop 93,000

Ancient moss clinging to a stone wall, rows of perfectly aligned stone lanterns, vermillion gates and towering cedars: this is only a pathway in Nikkō, a sanctuary that enshrines the glories of the Edo period (1600–1868). Scattered among hilly woodlands, Nikkō is one of Japan's major attractions. If there's any drawback, it's tha

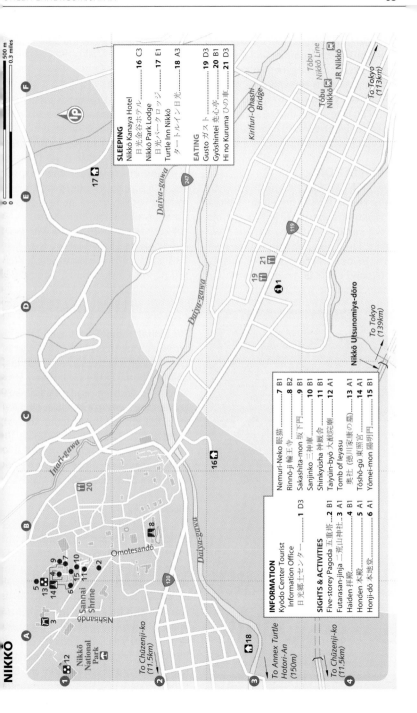

NIKKŌ

INFORMATION

Kyodo Center Tourist	
Information Office	
日光郷土センター	**1** D3

SIGHTS & ACTIVITIES

Five-storey Pagoda 五重塔	**2** B1
Futarasan-jinja 二荒山神社	**3** A1
Haiden 拝殿	**4** B1
Honden 本殿	**5** A1
Honji-dō 本地堂	**6** A1
Nemuri-Neko 眠猫	**7** B1
Rinnō-ji 輪王寺	**8** B2
Sakashita-mon 坂下門	**9** B1
Sanjinko 三神庫	**10** B1
Shinkyusha 神厩舎	**11** B1
Taiyūin-byō 大猷院廟	**12** A1
Tomb of Ieyasu	
奥社 (徳川家康の墓)	**13** A1
Tōshō-gū 東照宮	**14** A1
Yōmei-mon 陽明門	**15** B1

SLEEPING

Nikkō Kanaya Hotel	
日光金谷ホテル	**16** C3
Nikkō Park Lodge	**17** E1
Turtle Inn Nikkō	
タートルイン日光	**18** A3

EATING

Gusto ガスト	**19** D3
Gyōshintei 堯心亭	**20** B1
Hi no Kuruma ひの車	**21** D3

Sannai
Shrine

Omotesandō

Nishisandō

Inari-gawa

Daiya-gawa

Daiya-gawa

Daiya-gawa

Nikkō National Park

To Annex Turtle Hotori-An (150m)

To Chūzenji-ko (11.5km)

To Chūzenji-ko (11.5km)

Kirifuri-Ōhashi Bridge

Nikkō Utsunomiya-dōro

To Tokyo (139km)

To Tokyo (113km)

Tōbu Nikkō Line

Tōbu Nikkō

JR Nikkō

500 m
0.3 miles

plenty of other people have discovered it too; high season (summer and autumn) and weekends can be extremely crowded. Although Nikkō is certainly possible as a day trip from Tokyo, try to spend at least one night here so that the following morning you arrive at its World Heritage shrines and temples before the crowds do.

ORIENTATION

Both JR Nikkō Station and the nearby Tōbu Nikkō Station lie within a block of Nikkō's main road (Rte 119, the old Nikkō-kaidō), southeast of the town centre. From here, it's a 30-minute walk uphill to the shrine area, past restaurants, hotels and the main tourist information centre. From the stations to the shrines, you can take buses to the Shin-kyō bu stop for ¥190.

INFORMATION

The *Tourist Guide of Nikkō* has about every thing you need, and the bilingual *Centr Nikkō* shows the small streets.

Kyōdo Center tourist informatio office (☎ 54-2496; internet per 15min ¥5 ⏰ 9am-5pm) Has maps and English speak ers. You can also arrange for free guide tours in English. There are several com puters available for internet use.

Nikko Perfect Guide (www.nikko-jp.org english/index.html) This website to the cit also has a print version available fron the Kyōdo Center tourist informatio office for ¥1575.

SIGHTS

The World Heritage Sites around Tōshō-g are Nikkō's centrepiece. A ¥1000 'combi nation ticket', valid for two days and avail able at booths in the area, covers entr to Rinnō-ji, Tōshō-gū and Futarasan-jinja but not the Nemuri-Neko (Sleeping Cat in Tōshō-gū and Ieyasu's tomb. Separat admission tickets to these sights ar available.

Most sites are open from 8am to 5pn (until 4pm from November to March).

RINNŌ-JI 輪王寺

This Tendai-sect **temple** was founde 1200 years ago by Shōdō Shōnin, an today some 360m of zelkova trees mak up the pillars in the current building. Th three 8m gilded images in the Sambutsu dō (Three Buddha Hall) are the larges wooden Buddhas in Japan. The centra image is Amida Nyorai (one of the prima deities in the Mahayana Buddhist cannon flanked by Senjū (1000-armed Kannon deity of mercy and compassion) and Bat (a horse-headed Kannon), whose specia

ANTHONY PLUMMER

Ornamental footbath at Oedo Onsen Monogatari (p73)

domain is the animal kingdom. A room to the side contains a healing Buddha, holding his ring finger over a medicine bowl, and said to be the origin of the Japanese name for this finger (*kusuri-yubi* means 'medicine finger').

TŌSHŌ-GŪ 東照宮

A huge stone torii is a fittingly grand entrance to this storeyed **Shintō shrine**. To the left is a **five-storey pagoda** (34.3m) dating from 1650 and reconstructed in 1818. The pagoda has no foundations but contains a long suspended pole that swings like a pendulum, maintaining equilibrium in the event of an earthquake.

The entrance to the main shrine is through the torii at **Omote-mon**, a gate protected on either side by Deva kings. Just inside are the **Sanjinko** (Three Sacred Storehouses). On the upper storey of the last storehouse are imaginative relief carvings of elephants by an artist who famously had never seen the real thing. To the left of the entrance is **Shinkyūsha** (Sacred Stable), a plain building housing a carved white horse. The stable is adorned with allegorical relief carvings of monkeys, including the famous 'hear no evil, see no evil, speak no evil' monkeys, demonstrating three principles of Tendai Buddhism.

Pass through another torii, climb another flight of stairs, and on the left and right are a drum tower and a belfry. To the left of the drum tower is **Honji-dō** (Yakushido). This hall is best known for the painting on its ceiling of the Nakiryū (Crying Dragon). Monks demonstrate the acoustical properties of this hall by clapping two sticks together. The dragon 'roars' (a bit of a stretch) when the sticks are clapped beneath the dragon's mouth, but not elsewhere.

Next comes **Yōmei-mon** (Sunset Gate), dazzlingly decorated with glimmering gold leaf and intricate, coloured carvings and paintings of flowers, dancing girls, mythical beasts and Chinese sages. Worrying that its perfection might arouse envy in the gods, those responsible for its construction had the final supporting pillar placed upside down as a deliberate error. Although the style is more Chinese than Japanese and some critics deride it as gaudy, it's a grand spectacle.

Tōshō-gū's **Honden** (Main Hall) and **Haiden** (Hall of Worship) are across the enclosure. Inside (open only to *daimyō* – domain lords – during the Edo period) are paintings of the 36 immortal poets of Kyoto, and a ceiling-painting pattern from the Momoyama period; note the 100 dragons, each different. *Fusuma* (sliding door) paintings depict a *kirin* (a mythical beast that's part giraffe and part dragon). It's said that it will appear only when the world is at peace.

Through Yōmei-mon and to the right is **Nemuri-Neko**, a small wooden sculpture of a sleeping cat that's famous throughout Japan for its life-like appearance (though admittedly the attraction is lost on some visitors). From here, **Sakashita-mon** opens onto an uphill path through towering cedars to the appropriately solemn **Tomb of Ieyasu**. There's a separate entry fee (¥520) to see the cat and the tomb.

FUTARASAN-JINJA 二荒山神社

Shōdō Shōnin founded this **shrine**; the current building dates from 1619, making it Nikkō's oldest. It's the protector shrine of Nikkō itself, dedicated to the nearby mountain, Nantai-san (2484m), the mountain's consort, Nyotai-san, and their mountainous progeny, Tarō. There are other shrine branches on Nantai-san and by Chūzenji-ko.

Detail of a guardian statue at Tōshō-gū (p85)

BRENT WINEBRENN[...]

TAIYŪIN-BYŌ 大猷院廟

Enshrining Ieyasu's grandson Iemitsu (1604–51) is **Taiyūin-byō**. Though it houses many of the same elements as Tōshō-gū (storehouses, drum tower, Chinese-style gates etc), its smaller, more intimate scale and setting in a cryptomeria forest make it very appealing. It's unusual in that it's both a Buddhist temple and a mausoleum.

SLEEPING

Nikkō Park Lodge (☎ 53-1201; fax 53-4332; www.nikkoparklodge.com; 28285 Tokorono; dm from ¥3990; P) Friendly, cute, unpretentious and well kept, with pick-up available between 3pm and 5pm. It's mostly twin and double rooms, plus a couple of dorms, run by English-speaking Zen Buddhist monks; look for yoga classes. Breakfast/dinner is ¥395/1500.

Turtle Inn Nikkō (☎ 53-3168; fax 53-3883; www.turtle-nikko.com; 2-16 Takumi-chō; s/d without bathroom ¥4800/9000, s/d with bathroom ¥5600/10,600; P 🖳) Here you'll find large Japanese- and Western-style rooms, some

English-speaking staff and hearty meal[s] (breakfast/dinner ¥1050/2100). Take [a] bus to Sōgō-kaikan-mae, backtrack abou[t] 50m, turn right along the river and wal[k] for about five minutes; you'll see the turtle sign on the left.

Annex Turtle Hotori-An (☎ 53-3663; fax 53-3883; www.turtle-nikko.com; 8-28 Takumi chō; s/d ¥6500/12,400; P 🖳) The Turtle Inn's newer Annex is a more modern, pleasan[t] option. It has a windowed dining room (breakfast/dinner ¥1050/2100), well tended tatami and Western-style rooms and greenery surrounding the onsen (plus in-room baths).

Nikkō Kanaya Hotel (☎ 54-0001; fax 53-2487; www.kanayahotel.co.jp; 1300 Kami-Hatsuishi machi; tw from ¥17,325; P 🖳) One of the finest heritage Western hotels in Japan, this grand lady from 1893 wears her history like a fine dress. The best rooms have excellent vistas, spacious quarters and private bathrooms. The lobby bar is deliciously dark and amenable to drinking scotch. Rates do not include meals and rise steeply in high seasons.

EATING & DRINKING

Gusto (☎ 50-1232; mains ¥500-1000; ◷ 10am-2am Mon-Fri, 7am-2am Sat & Sun) Nikkō's only late-night restaurant makes up for what it lacks in individuality with value and variety. There's a detailed picture menu, and offerings include pizzas, pasta and *ribu rosu suteeki* (rib roast steak; ¥899). Look for the red circle sign.

Hi no Kuruma (☎ 54-2062; mains ¥500-1500; ◷ lunch & dinner Thu-Tue) A local favourite for *okonomiyaki* (savoury pancakes), which you cook yourself on a *teppan* (hot-steel table). Most choices are under ¥1000, or splurge on the works: pork, squid, beef, shrimp, corn etc (¥1500). There's an English menu. Look for the small cap park and red-black-and-white Japanese sign.

Gyōshintei (☎ 53-3751; set courses ¥3000-8000; ◷ lunch & dinner Fri-Wed) For *shōjin ryōri* (Buddhist vegetarian cuisine) in a setting to die for, Gyōshintei is worth the splurge. Set courses and prices change with the season, but a safe bet is the *omakase kaiseki* (chef's choice *kaiseki*; price varies). This elegant, traditional eatery overlooks a carefully tended garden, around 250m north of the Shin-kyō bridge. There's a three-peaked emblem on the door curtain.

GETTING THERE & AWAY

Nikkō is best reached from Tokyo via the Tōbu Nikkō line from Asakusa Station. You can usually get last-minute seats on reserved *tokkyū* (limited express) trains (¥2620, one hour 50 minutes) about every 30 minutes from 7.30am to 10am, hourly thereafter. *Kaisoku* (rapid) trains (¥1320, 2½ hours, hourly from 6.20am to 4.30pm) require no reservation. For either train, you may have to change at Shimo-imaichi. Be sure to ride in the first two cars to reach Nikkō (some cars may separate at an intermediate stop).

MINAKAMI & TAKARAGAWA ONSEN
水上温泉・宝川温泉

☎ 0278

In eastern Gunma-ken, Minakami is a thriving, sprawling onsen town with outdoor activities to match. The town of Minakami also encompasses Takaragawa Onsen (about 30 minutes away by road), a riverside hot springs oft-voted the nation's best.

The train station is in the village of Minakami Onsen, as are most of Minakami's lodgings. **Minakami Tourist Information Centre** (水上観光協会; ☎ 72-2611; www.minakami-onsen.com; ◷ 9am-5pm) is across from the station, has English pamphlets and can make accommodation reservations (in Japanese). Ask which inns in town have *higaeri nyuyoku* (day-use baths) open when you visit.

Hōshi Onsen Chōjūkan (法師温泉長寿館; ☎ 66-0005; fax 66-0003; www.houshi-onsen.jp, in Japanese; r per person incl 2 meals from ¥13,800), on the southwestern fringes of Minakami town, is one of Japan's finest onsen inns. To reach this perfectly rustic, supremely photogenic lodging, take a bus to Jōmō Kōgen Station (20 minutes), then another bus for Sarugakyō Onsen (35 minutes). At the last stop, take another bus for Hōshi Onsen (25 minutes). Be sure to check schedules at the tourist information centre.

Takaragawa Onsen (☎ 75-2611; adult/child ¥1500/1000; ◷ 9am-5pm) is idyllic and rangey. Most of its several pools on the river-banks (with slate, not natural, flooring) are mixed-bathing, and there's a women-only bath. Women are allowed to take modesty towels into the mixed baths. A fascinating antiques shop on the way down to the baths is full of junk and gems ranging from lacquered teapots to Buddha heads and abacuses.

The inn on the other side of the river, **Ōsenkaku** (汪泉閣; ☎ 75-2121; fax 75-2038; www.takaragawa.com; r per person incl 2 meals from ¥11,700) is spectacular, with gorgeous riverfront rooms over several buildings, a mighty old-style feel and 24-hour use of the outdoor onsen. Prices rise steeply for nicer rooms with better views, but aim for the 1930s-vintage No 1 annex. Note, the menu features bear-meat soup.

To reach Minakami Station, take the *shinkansen* from Ueno to Takasaki and transfer to the Jōetsu line (¥5140, two hours), or *tokkyū* Minakami trains run direct (¥4620, 2½ hours). You can also catch the *shinkansen* to Jōmō Kōgen (1¼ hours) from Tokyo/Ueno (¥5240/5040), from where buses run to Minakami (¥600) and Takaragawa Onsen (¥1450, April to early December). Buses to Takaragawa Onsen also run from Minakami Station (¥1100, year-round).

WEST OF TOKYO

MT FUJI AREA 富士山周辺

Always breathtaking, iconic Mt Fuji dominates the region west of Tokyo. Climbing this volcano is a tradition with sacred overtones, though many visitors are content to view it from its foothills.

MT FUJI 富士山

On clear days, particularly in winter, Mt Fuji (Fuji-san in Japanese) is visible from as far as Tokyo, 100km away. When Japan's highest mountain (3776m) is capped with snow, it's a picture-postcard perfect volcanic cone. For much of the year you need to be closer, and even then the notoriously shy mountain is often covered in haze or cloud. Spring is your next best bet for Fuji- spotting, yet even during this time the mountain may be visible only in the morning before it retreats behind its cloud curtain.

BOB CHARLTON

View to Mt Fuji

MT FUJI AREA

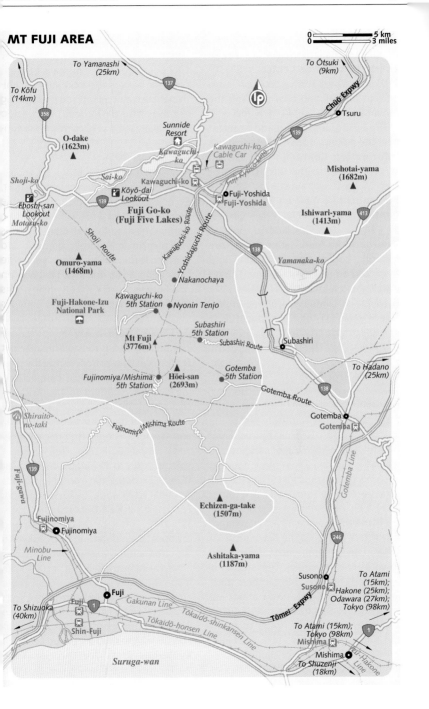

0 — 5 km
0 — 3 miles

To Yamanashi (25km)
To Ōtsuki (9km)
To Kōfu (14km)
358
137
139
Chūō Expwy
Tsuru
Sunnide Resort
O-dake (1623m)
Kawaguchi-ko Cable Car
Kawaguchi-ko
Mishotai-yama (1682m)
Sai-ko
Shoji-ko
139
Kōyō-dai Lookout
Kawaguchi-ko
Fuji-Yoshida
Fuji-Yoshida
Eboshi-san Lookout
Motosu-ko
Fuji Go-ko (Fuji Five Lakes)
Ishiwari-yama (1413m)
413
138
Yamanaka-ko
Shoji Route
Kawaguchi-ko Route
Yoshidaguchi Route
Omuro-yama (1468m)
Nakanochaya
Fuji-Hakone-Izu National Park
Kawaguchi-ko 5th Station
Nyonin Tenjo
Subashiri 5th Station
Subashiri Route
Subashiri
To Hadano (25km)
Mt Fuji (3776m)
Gotemba 5th Station
Fujinomiya/Mishima 5th Station
Hōei-san (2693m)
Gotemba Route
138
Shiraito-no-taki
Fujinomiya/Mishima Route
Gotemba
Gotemba
139
Fuji-gawa
Gotemba Line
Echizen-ga-take (1507m)
Fujinomiya
Fujinomiya
246
Minobu Line
Ashitaka-yama (1187m)
Susono
Susono
To Atami (15km); Hakone (25km); Odawara (27km); Tokyo (98km)
Fuji
Fuji
1
Gakunan Line
Tōkaidō-shinkansen Line
To Atami (15km); Tokyo (98km)
To Shizuoka (40km)
Shin-Fuji
Tōkaidō-honsen Line
Mishima
Mishima
Izu-Hakone Line
1
Suruga-wan
To Shuzenji (18km)
Tōmei Expwy

INFORMATION

Brochures available from the **Tokyo Tourist Information Center** (☎ 03-5321-3077) provide exhaustive detail on transport to Mt Fuji and how to climb the mountain.

The best tourist information centres near the mountain are the **Fuji-Yoshida Information Center** (☎ 0555-22-7000; ☯ 9am-5.30pm), to the left as you exit the Fuji-Yoshida train station, and the **Kawaguchi-ko Tourist Information Center** (☎ 0555-72-6700; ☯ 9am-5pm Sun-Fri, 8.30am-6.30pm Sat & holidays), next to Kawaguchi-ko train station. Both have friendly, English-speaking staff, and maps and brochures of the area. During the climbing season (1 July to 31 August), there is also climbing information provided by staff in English at a special office at **Fuji-Yoshida city hall** (☎ 0555-24-1236; ☯ 8.30am-5.15pm Mon-Fri).

CLIMBING MT FUJI

The mountain is divided into 10 'stations' from base (first station) to summit (10th), but most climbers start from one of the four fifth stations, reachable by road. From the fifth stations, allow about 4½ hours to reach the top and about three hours to descend, plus an hour for circling the crater at the top. The former Mt Fuji Weather Station, on the southwest edge of the crater, marks the mountain's actual summit.

North of Mt Fuji is the Kawaguchi-ko 5th Station (2305m), reachable from the town of Kawaguchi-ko. This station is particularly popular with climbers starting from Tokyo. Other fifth stations are at Subashiri (1980m), Gotemba (1440m; allow seven to eight hours to reach the summit) and Fujinomiya (Mishima; 2380m), which is best for climbers coming from the west (Nagoya, Kyoto and beyond).

To time your arrival for dawn you can either start up the slope in the afternoon, stay overnight in a mountain hut and continue early in the morning, or climb the whole way at night. You do not want to arrive on the top too long before dawn as it's likely to be very cold and windy.

MOUNTAIN HUTS

From the fifth to the eighth station, about a dozen lodges are scattered along the trails. Accommodation here is basic: most charge around ¥5000 for a blanket on the floor, sardined head-to-toe with other climbers. Staff prepare simple meals, and you're welcome to rest inside as long as you order something. If you don't feel like eating, a one-hour rest costs ¥500. Camping on the mountain is not permitted.

GETTING THERE & AWAY

The Mt Fuji area is most easily reached from Tokyo by bus; from Kansai the journey can require multiple connections via Mishima Station on the Kodama *shinkansen*. The two main towns on the north side of the mountain, Fuji-Yoshida and Kawaguchi-ko, are the principal gateways. See Fuji Go-ko (oposite).

From 1 July to 31 August, direct buses (¥2600, 2½ hours) run from Shinjuku bus terminal to Kawaguchi-ko 5th Station. For details call **Keiō Dentetsu Bus** (☎ 03-5376-2217). This is by far the fastest and cheapest way of getting from Tokyo to the fifth station. If you take two trains and a bus, the same trip can cost nearly ¥6000. If you're already in Kawaguchi-ko, there are bus services up to Kawaguchi-ko 5th Station (¥1500, 55 minutes) from 1 July to 31 August. The schedule varies considerably during the shoulder period – call **Fuji Kyūkō bus** (☎ 0555-72-6877) for details. At the height of the climbing season, there are buses until 9.15pm – ideal for climbers intending to make an overnight ascent. Taxis operate from Kawaguchi-ko train station to the Kawaguchi-ko 5th Station for around ¥10,000, plus tolls.

FUJI GO-KO 富士五湖

☎ 555

The Fuji Go-ko (Fuji Five Lakes) region is a postcardlike area around Fuji's northern foothills; its lakes provide perfect reflecting pools for the mountain's majesty. Yamanaka-ko is the largest and easternmost lake, followed by Kawaguchi-ko, Saiko, Shoji-ko (the smallest) and Motosu-ko. Particularly during the autumn *kōyō* (foliage) season, the lakes make a good overnight trip out of Tokyo, for a stroll or a drive, and the energetic can hike in nearby mountains.

On the lake of the same name, the sleepy town of Fuji-Kawaguchi-ko (河口湖) is closest to four of the five lakes and a popular departure point for climbing the mountain. Around 600m north of Kawaguchi-ko Station, on the lower eastern edge of the lake, is the **Kawaguchi-ko cable car** (☎ 72-0363; one-way/return ¥400/700) to the Fuji Viewing Platform (1104m). Ask at Kawaguchi-ko Tourist Information Center (opposite) for a map.

SLEEPING

If you're not overnighting in a mountain hut, Fuji-Yoshida and Kawaguchi-ko make good bases. Their respective tourist information offices (see opposite) can make reservations for you.

K's House Mt Fuji (☎ 83-5556; fax 83-5557; kshouse.jp; Kawaguchi-ko; dm from ¥2500, r from ¥3400; 💻) This clean, new hostel near the lake is in a renovated building with a cheery, welcoming atmosphere. There's a fully loaded kitchen, mountain bikes for hire and no curfew. Staff will pick you up for free.

Sunnide Resort (サニーデリゾート; ☎ 76-6004; fax 76-7706; www.sunnide.com, in Japanese; Kawaguchi-ko; r per person ¥6300, cottages from ¥16,000; 💻) A bit remote but with the best Fuji views in town, friendly Sunnide has hotel rooms and rental cottages with a delicious outdoor bath. Splash out in the stylish premium suites with private balcony baths or ask for the discounted 'backpacker' rates (¥4200) if same-day rooms are available. Breakfast/dinner is ¥1050/2100 (¥1575 for the backpacker dinner).

GETTING THERE & AWAY

Buses (¥1700, 1¾ hours) operate directly to Kawaguchi-ko from outside the western exit of Shinjuku Station in Tokyo. There are departures up to 16 times daily at the height of the Fuji climbing season. Some

DOMINIC BONUCCELLI

Donor plaques on a site in Fuji Go-ko

CHRIS MELLOR
Statues of the bodhisattva Jizō at Hase-dera, Kamakura

continue on to Yamanaka-ko and Motosu-ko. In Tokyo, call **Keiō Kōsoku Bus (Map p70; ☎ 03-5376-2217)** for reservations and schedule info. In Kawaguchi-ko, make reservations through **Tōmei Highway Bus (☎ 72-2922)**.

Trains take longer and cost more. JR Chūō line trains go from Shinjuku to Ōtsuki (*tokkyū*, ¥2980, one hour; *futsū*, ¥1280, 1½ hours), where you transfer to the Fuji Kyūkō line to Kawaguchi-ko (*futsū*, ¥1110, 50 minutes).

SOUTH OF TOKYO
KAMAKURA 鎌倉
☎ 0467 / pop 173,000

The capital of Japan from 1185 to 1333, Kamakura rivals Nikkō as the most cultur-ally rewarding day trip from Tokyo and is often considerably less crowded. Many Buddhist temples and the occasional Shintō shrine dot the surrounding coun-tryside here.

ORIENTATION

Kamakura's main attractions can be cov-ered on foot, with the occasional bus ride. Cycling is also practical (see p95 for details). Most sights are signposted in English and Japanese. You can start at Kamakura Station and travel around the area in a circle (Komachi-dōri 'shop-ping town' and broad Wakamiya-ōji are the main streets east of the station), or start one station north at Kita-Kamakura and visit the temples between there and Kamakura Station on foot.

INFORMATION

Tourist information center (☎ 22-3350; 9am-5.30pm Apr-Sep, to 5pm Oct-Mar) Just outside Kamakura Station's east exit, this helpful tourist office distrib-utes maps and brochures, such as the English guide *Oshiete Kamakura*, and can also make bookings for same-day accommodation.

SIGHTS & ACTIVITIES
TSURUGAOKA HACHIMAN-GŪ
鶴岡八幡宮

Further down the road, where it turns towards Kita-Kamakura Station, is **Tsurugaoka Hachiman-gū (☎ 22-0315; treasure hall admission adult/child ¥200/100; 6am-8.30pm)**, the main Shintō shrine of Kamakura. It was founded by Minamoto Yoriyoshi, of the same Minamoto clan that ruled Japan from Kamakura. This shrine's sprawl, with elongated paths, broad vistas and lotus ponds, presents the visitor with an atmosphere drastically different to the repose of the Zen temples

KAMAKURA

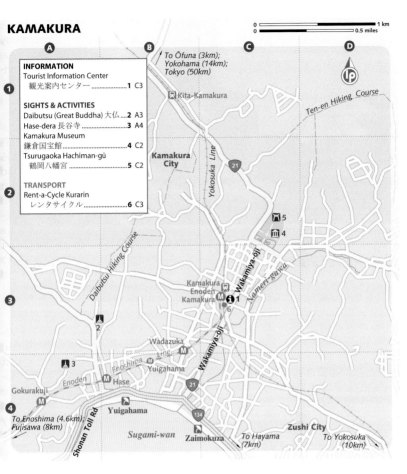

INFORMATION	
Tourist Information Center	
観光案内センター **1** C3	
SIGHTS & ACTIVITIES	
Daibutsu (Great Buddha) 大仏....**2** A3	
Hase-dera 長谷寺 **3** A4	
Kamakura Museum	
鎌倉国宝館.................................**4** C2	
Tsurugaoka Hachiman-gū	
鶴岡八幡宮 **5** C2	
TRANSPORT	
Rent-a-Cycle Kurarin	
レンタサイクル **6** C3	

clustered around Kita-Kamakura Station. The Gempei Pond (the name comes from the kanji for the Genji and Heike clans) is divided by bridges, said to symbolise the rift between the clans. Behind the Gempei Pond is the **Kamakura Museum** (☎ 22-0753; adult/child ¥300/100; ☯ 9am-4pm), housing some remarkable Zen Buddhist sculptures dating from the 12th to 16th centuries.

HASE-DERA 長谷寺
About 10 minutes' walk from the Daibutsu, **Hase-dera** (Hase Kannon; ☎ 22-6300; adult/ child ¥300/100; ☯ 8am-5pm Mar-Sep, to 4.30pm Oct-Feb) is one of the most popular temples in the Kantō region.

The walls of the staircases leading up to the main hall are lined with thousands of tiny statues of Jizō; ranked like a small army of urchins, many of them are clothed to keep them warm. It's quite charming until you realise that Jizō is the patron bodhisattva of travellers and departed children, and the statues were placed there by women who lost children through miscarriage or abortion.

BOB CHARLTON

Kamakura Daibutsu

↘ DAIBUTSU 大仏

The Kamakura **Daibutsu** (Great Buddha) is at Kōtoku-in temple. Completed in 1252, it is Japan's second-largest Buddha image and Kamakura's most famous sight. Once housed in a huge hall, today the statue sits in the open, the hall having been washed away by a tsunami in 1495. Cast in bronze and weighing close to 850 tonnes, the statue is 11.4m tall. Its construction is said to have been inspired by Yoritomo's visit to Nara (where Japan's biggest Daibutsu holds court) after the Minamoto clan's victory over the Taira clan. Even though Kamakura's Daibutsu doesn't quite match Nara's in stature, it is commonly agreed that it is artistically superior.

The Buddha itself is the Amida Buddha (*amitābha* in Sanskrit), worshipped by followers of the Jōdo school as a figure of salvation.

Buses from stops 1 to 6 in front of Kamakura Station run to the Daibutsu-mae stop. Alternatively, take the Enoden Enoshima line to Hase Station and walk north for about five minutes. Better yet, take the Daibutsu Hiking Course.

Things you need to know: ☎ 22-0703; adult/child ¥200/150; ☺ 7am-6pm Apr-Sep, to 5.30pm Oct-Mar

The focal point of the temple's main hall is the Kannon statue. Kannon (*avalokiteshvara* in Sanskrit), the goddess of mercy, is the bodhisattva of infinite compassion and, along with Jizō, is one of Japan's most popular Buddhist deities. This 9m-high carved wooden *jūichimen* (11-faced Kannon) is believed to date from the 8th century. The temple dates back to AD 736,

when it is said the statue washed up on the shore near Kamakura.

GETTING THERE & AWAY

JR Yokosuka line trains run to Kamakura from Tokyo (¥890, 56 minutes) and Shinagawa Stations, via Yokohama (¥330, 27 minutes). The Shōnan Shinjuku line runs from the west side of Tokyo (Shibuya,

Shinjuku and Ikebukuro, all ¥890) in about one hour; some trains require a transfer at Ōfuna, one stop before Kita-Kamakura.

GETTING AROUND

You can walk to most temples and shrines from Kamakura or Kita-Kamakura Station. Sites in the west, such as the Daibutsu, can be reached via the Enoden Enoshima line from Kamakura Station to Hase (¥190) or bus from Kamakura Station stops 1 to 6. Bus trips around the area cost either ¥170 or ¥190. Another good option is renting a bicycle; **Rent-a-Cycle Kurarin** (☎ 24-2319; per hr/day ¥600/1600; ⏱ 8.30am-5pm) is outside the east exit of Kamakura Station, and right up the incline. Local rickshaw rides start at ¥2000 per person for 10 minutes.

OGASAWARA-SHOTŌ 小笠原諸島

You won't believe you're still in Japan, much less Tokyo! About 1000km south of downtown in the middle of the Pacific Ocean, this far-flung outpost of Tokyo Prefecture has pristine beaches and star-studded night skies. Ogasawara is a nature-lover's paradise surrounded by tropical waters and coral reefs. Snorkelling, whale-watching, swimming with dolphins, and hiking are all on the bill.

The only way to get here is by a 25-hour ferry ride from Tokyo. The ferry docks at Chichi-jima (父島; Father Island), the main island of the group. A smaller ferry connects this island to Haha-jima (母島), the other inhabited island.

CHICHI-JIMA 父島

☎ 04998

Beautifully preserved, gorgeous Chichi-jima has plenty of accommodation, restaurants, even a bit of tame nightlife.

But the real attractions are the excellent beaches and outdoor activities.

SIGHTS & ACTIVITIES

The two best beaches for snorkelling are on the north side of the island, a short walk over the hill from the village. **Miya-no-ura** (宮之浦) has decent coral and is sheltered, making it suitable for beginners. About 500m along the coast (more easily accessed from town) is **Tsuri-hama** (釣浜), a rocky beach that has better coral but is more exposed.

Good swimming beaches line the west side of the island, getting better the further south you go. **Kominato-kaigan** (小港海岸) is the best, easily accessible on this side by bus from town, or by hitching.

SLEEPING & EATING

Ogasawara Youth Hostel (小笠原ユースホステル; ☎ 2-2692; fax 2-2692; www.oyh.jp, in Japanese; dm members/nonmembers incl 2 meals ¥5150/5750; 🅿 🖥) This is a clean, well-run, regimented hostel about 400m southwest of the pier, near the post office. Be sure to book early as it fills up quickly.

Chichi-jima View Hotel (父島ビューホテル; ☎ 2-7845; fax 2-7846; www16.ocn.ne.jp/~view1; r per person from ¥10,000; 🅿) Just a minute's walk west of the pier, this hotel has large, airy rooms with private bathroom and kitchen. It's one of the more upscale places on the island, with super views of the bay from guestroom balconies.

GETTING THERE & AWAY

The *Ogasawara-maru* sails about once a week between Tokyo's Takeshiba Pier (10 minutes from Hamamatsu-chō Station) and Chichi-jima (2nd class from ¥28,000 in July and August, from ¥22,000 September to June, 25 hours). Contact **Ogasawara Kaiun** (小笠原海運; ☎ 03-3451-5171; www.ogasawarakaiun.co.jp, in Japanese).

DAVID RYAN

Sake barrels at Tsurugaoka Hachiman-gū (p92), Kamakura

HAHA-JIMA 母島

☎ 04998

Haha-jima is a quieter, less developed version of Chichi-jima, with some fine beaches on its west side and good hiking along its spine. Certain bays along the east coast are particularly good for dolphin-watching. If you really want to get away from it all, this is the place.

INFORMATION

Haha-jima Tourist Association (母島観光協会; ☎ 3-2300; ⏰ 8am-5pm) is in the passenger waiting room at the pier.

SIGHTS & ACTIVITIES

A road runs south from the village to the start of **Minami-zaki Yūhodō** (南崎遊歩道), a hiking course that continues all the way to **Minami-zaki** (南崎; literally, 'southern point'). Along the way you'll find **Hōraine-kaigan** (蓬莱根海岸), a narrow beach with a decent offshore coral garden; Wai Beach, the best beach on the island, with a drop-off that attracts eagle rays; and Minami-zaki itself, which has a rocky, coral-strewn beach with ripping views of smaller

islands to the south. Above Minami-zaki you'll find **Kofuji** (小富士), an 86m-high mini Mt Fuji with great views in all directions. Scooter is the best way to get around the island (from ¥3000 per day).

SLEEPING & EATING

Anna Beach Haha-jima Youth Hostel (アンナビーチ母島ユースホステル; ☎ 3-2468; fax 3-2371; www.k4.dion.ne.jp/~annayh, in Japanese; dm members/nonmembers incl 2 meals ¥5320/5920) A young family runs this tidy, cheery youth hostel in a cosy Canadian-style house overlooking the fishing port.

Minshuku Nanpū (民宿ナンプー; ☎ 3-2462; fax 3-2458; r per person incl 2 meals ¥8400) This new guesthouse 500m northeast of the pier has friendly owners, good food, five rooms with large beds, and a jet bath.

GETTING THERE & AWAY

The *Hahajima-maru* sails about five times a week between Chichi-jima and Haha-jima (¥3780, two hours). Contact **Ogasawara Kaiun** (小笠原海運; ☎ 03-3451-5171; www.ogasawarakaiun.co.jp, in Japanese). Other operators run day cruises from Chichi-jima.

Kimono-clad woman in Kyoto

OLIVER STREW

KYOTO & KANSAI

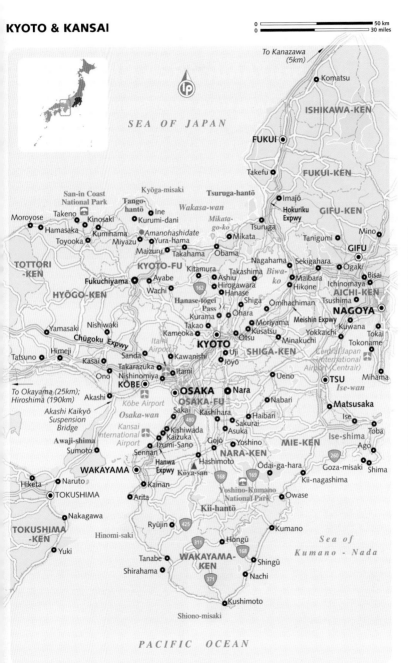

0 _____ 50 km
0 _____ 30 miles

To Kanazawa
(5km)

Komatsu

ISHIKAWA-KEN

SEA OF JAPAN

FUKUI

Takefu

FUKUI-KEN

Kyōga-misaki

Tsuruga-hantō

Imajō

Tango-
hantō

Ine

Wakasa-wan

Hokuriku
Expwy

GIFU-KEN

Moroyose

Takeno

Kinosaki

Kurumi-dani

Mikata-
go-ko

Tsuruga

Mino

Hamasaka

Kumihama

Amanohashidate

Mikata

Tanigumi

Toyooka

Miyazu

Yura-hama

GIFU

Maizuru

Takahama

Obama

Nagahama

Sekigahara

Ōgaki

TOTTORI
-KEN

KYOTO-FU

Kitamura

Takashima

Biwa-
ko

Bisai

Fukuchiyama

Ayabe

Ashiu

Hirogawara

Maibara

Ichinomaya

HYŌGO-KEN

Wachi

Hanase

Hikone

AICHI-KEN

Yamasaki

Nishiwaki

Hanase-tōge
Pass

Shiga

Omihachiman

Tsushima

NAGOYA

Chūgoku

Kurama

Ohara

Moriyama

Meishin Expwy

Kuwana

Himeji

Expwy

Itami
Airport

Takao

Kameoka

KYOTO

Kusatsu

Ōtsu

Yokkaichi

Tokai

Tokoname

Tatsuno

Kasai

Sanda

Kawanishi

Uji

SHIGA-KEN

Minakuchi

Central Japan
International
Airport (Centrair)

Mihama

Ono

Takarazuka

Itami

Jōyō

KŌBE

Nishinomiya

Ueno

TSU

Ise-wan

To Okayama (25km);
Hiroshima (190km)

Akashi

Kōbe Airport

OSAKA

Nara

Nabari

Matsusaka

Akashi Kaikyō
Suspension
Bridge

Osaka-wan

OSAKA-FU

Sakai

Kashihara

Haibari

Ise

Kansai
International
Airport

Kishiwada

Sakurai

Ise-shima

Toba

Awaji-shima

Kaizuka

Asuka

Ago

Sumoto

Izumi-Sano

Gojō

Yoshino

MIE-KEN

Shima

Sennan

NARA-KEN

Goza-misaki

WAKAYAMA

Hanwa
Expwy

Hashimoto

Kōya-san

Ōdai-ga-hara

Kii-nagashima

Hiketa

Naruto

Kainan

Yoshino-Kumano
National Park

Owase

TOKUSHIMA

Arita

Kii-hantō

Nakagawa

TOKUSHIMA
-KEN

Hinomi-saki

Ryūjin

Kumano

Sea of

Yuki

Kumano - Nada

Tanabe

WAKAYAMA-
KEN

Shingū

Shirahama

Nachi

Kushimoto

Shiono-misaki

PACIFIC OCEAN

HIGHLIGHTS

1 ARASHIYAMA AREA HIGHLIGHTS

BY IJUIN KOKO, PROFESSIONAL GUIDE & AUTHOR

Located 8km west of the city centre, Arashiyama is the romantic side of Kyoto. Here you can enjoy cool breezes by the river against a backdrop of mountains, with colours that change with the seasons. The area was originally developed as a detached villa for the imperial family so they could escape the heat of summer.

⬏ IJUIN KOKO'S DON'T MISS LIST

❶ TENRYŪ-JI

One of my favorite gardens in Kyoto is inside this temple (p128). When you stroll around the main hall to the far side, your breath will be taken away by the sight of the garden waiting for you. Stop to savour the view from many vantage points, as the pond garden is designed to have a perfect view from any point around the pond. This artificial landscape in the temple matches the natural landscape of mountains in the distance as if they are also part of the garden. This is *shakkei* o 'borrowed-landscape.'

❷ BAMBOO GROVE

Going out from the north garden exit o Tenryu-ji, suddenly you will find your self in a lane surrounded by towering bamboo trees (p127). You'll probably feel the temperature is several degrees cooler here. Early in the morning and on weekdays or in the low season, you may have the place all to yourself. This scene is often used to represent Kyoto.

Clockwise from top: Ōkōchi-sansō (p128); Autumn maple leaves; Detail of fountain at Ōkōchi-sansō (p128); Arashiyama bamboo grove (p127); Statue at Tenrū-ji (p128)

❸ ŌKŌCHI-SANSŌ

This magnificent villa and garden (p128) was the lifetime work of one of Ōkōchi Denjiro, who was a famous samurai movie actor. Ōkōchi's villa is now open for the public to enjoy strolling in different types of Japanese gardens, and to enjoy the views over Kyoto. The garden gives you ideas what you can do with your garden even if it is a small one, as each part is designed in a small scale.

❹ GIŌ-JI

Out of the 1600 temples in Kyoto, this is one of my all-time favourites. Giō-ji (p128) hardly looks like a temple at all, but more like a small three-room hut with an intimate garden. If you go expecting a grand temple, you'll be disappointed, but if you slow down and soak up the calm stillness of the garden, you will emerge refreshed and alive.

↘ THINGS YOU NEED TO KNOW

Ways to get there from downtown JR line from Kyoto or Nijō Stations; Hankyū line from downtown (with a change at Katsura); Keifuku line from Ōmiya; bus from downtown Be warned Arashiyama looks like a tourist trap until you get away from the main street See our author's review on p127

KYOTO & KANSAI

HIGHLIGHTS

2 | # CYCLING AROUND KYOTO

BY TAGA KAZUO, FOUNDER OF KYOTO CYCLING TOUR PROJECT & AUTHOR

A bicycle is the best and fastest way to get around Kyoto: it's economical and you don't have to worry about traffic jams. Most of Kyoto's sights are located in a compact area and there are no big hills. Kyoto is easy to navigate and a bicycle lets you get to the heart of the city.

HIGHLIGHTS

⬎ TAGA KAZUO'S DON'T MISS LIST

❶ NANZEN-JI TEMPLE

Zen is perhaps the most famous of all schools of Buddhism and this is a great example of a classic Zen temple. Nanzen-ji (p123) is surrounded by the rich nature of the Higashiyama area and the subtemples scattered around the temple precincts are spectacular.

❷ TETSUGAKU-NO-MICHI (PATH OF PHILOSOPHY)

The 20th-century philosopher Nishida Kitarō used this fine canal-side path (p126) for his daily walking meditation.

Almost every part of the 1.5km length is lined with some sort of blooming flower or tree.

❸ GINKAKU-JI

Ginkaku-ji (p126) was built as a villa for shōgun Ashikaga Yoshimasa in the late 15th century. It is said by some to be the birthplace of the Japanese *wabi-sabi* aesthetic. Here, beauty was found in simplicity and quietness rather than in splendour and luxury (although, the garden here is pretty splendid by almost any standard).

Clockwise from top: Hōnen-in (p126); Cherry blossom; Zen garden at Gingaku-ji (p126); San-mon at Nanzen-ji (p123)

❹ ŌTOYO-JINJA

This quaint mountainside shrine is commonly called the 'mouse shrine' because you will be welcomed by cute *koma nezumi* (stone guardian figures in the form of mice). These unusual figures come from a story of mice saving an important Shintō deity from a forest fire. Spread about the grounds are bird guardians and money carved out of stones, also to guard against evil.

❺ HŌNEN-IN

This quiet temple (p126) is a refuge among the greenery. Near the gate, you will see the sand mounds on either side of the path. These represent water and are said to purify the body and mind. Ever-changing patterns are drawn on them by the temple's gardeners.

❶ Nanzen-ji
❷ Tetsugaku-no-Michi (Path of Philosophy)
❸ Ginkaku-ji
❹ Ōtoyo-jinja
❺ Hōnen-in

0 ▭ 200 m
0 ▭ 0.1 miles

Imadegawa-dōri
Ginkaku-ji-Michi
Kyoto University
Kaguraoka-dōri
Shirakawa-dōri
Shinnyo-dō
Marutamachi-dōri
Okazaki-kōen
Kyoto Municipal Zoo
Nijō-dōri
Biwa-ko Sosui Canal

🔖 THINGS YOU NEED TO KNOW

Bicycle rental and bicycle tours Kyoto Cycling Tour Project (KCTP; p144)
Be warned The Higashiyama area can be very crowded during the cherry-blossom and autumn-foliage seasons See our author's review on p123

HIGHLIGHTS

3 NARA-KŌEN AREA

BY SHIBATA SUMIE, PROFESSIONAL NARA GUIDE

A fine park within easy strolling distance of Kintetsu Nara Station, Nara-kōen contains some of Japan's most important cultural and historical treasures. It also contains some virgin forest, said to be the world's only virgin forest inside a city. This park is lovely in any season.

↘ SHIBATA SUMIE'S DON'T MISS LIST

❶ KŌFUKU-JI

One of the first stops on any tour of Nara-kōen, the towering pagoda (p154) here is a masterpiece of Japanese architecture. The treasure hall contains some impressive Buddhist statues and the grounds make for pleasant strolling.

❷ ISUI-EN

A short walk from Kōfuku-ji brings you to Nara's finest garden: Isui-en (p154). This wonderful stroll garden is beautiful in any season and you'll

usually find something in bloom. The view over the pond takes in the roof of Tōdai-ji's Nandai-mon gate – it's a classic example of the technique of *shakkei*. To really enjoy the garden, buy a ticket for a hot cup of *matcha* (powdered green tea) and drink it while gazing over the scene.

❸ TŌDAI-JI

Dominating the east side of Nara-kōen, the Daibutsu-den (Great Buddha Hall) is an arresting sight. Prepare to be blown away by the sight of the Daibutsu

Clockwise from top: Tōdai-ji (p154); Kōfuku-ji (p154); Stone lanterns near Kasuga Taisha (p155); Daibutsu (p155) at Tōdai-ji; Architectural detail of Kasuga Taisha (p155)

(Great Buddha; p155) that it contains. This is truly one of the greatest sights in the entire Japanese archipelago.

❹ FEEDING THE DEER

Buy some *shika-senbei* (deer biscuits) from a vendor in the park and get ready: the hungry deer of Nara-kōen will mob you and try everything they can to get those crackers. The hundreds of sacred deer roam freely throughout the park and are said to be the divine messengers of Shintō deities at Kasuga Taisha. This is a must for those with kids in tow.

❺ WALKING TRAILS NEAR KASUGA TAISHA

After exploring Tōdai-ji, walk over to Kasuga Taisha (p155) and explore the many walking trails around this shrine. As you make your way through the tree-lined paths, you may find it hard to believe that you're still within Nara city limits. The thousands of stone lanterns to be found here add a mysterious feeling to the area.

↘ THINGS YOU NEED TO KNOW

Best way to get there from Kyoto Take a *tokkyū* (limited express) train on the Kintetsu line from Kintetsu Kyoto Station **Be warned** Nara-kōen can be packed with children on school excursions – to escape, hit the trails near Kasuga Taisha **See our author's review on p153**

HIGHLIGHTS

4

↘ KIYOMIZU-DERA

If you only see one temple in Kyoto, make it **Kiyomizu-dera** (p121). This flamboyant complex overlooking Kyoto is everything a temple shouldn't be: noisy, crowded and overtly mercantile. But, we're willing to forgive these failings because it's an awful lot of fun, it's gorgeous in the spring and autumn, and it has a holy spring that bestows longevity and health.

5

↘ KINKAKU-JI

Go early on a weekday to get a relatively uncrowded view of Kyoto's sublime Golden Pavilion, the temple of **Kinkaku-ji** (p126). Floating like an apparition over a serene pond, the main hall of this temple is one of Japan's loveliest sights. Under a dusting of new snow, it's breathtaking.

6

⬐ OSAKA AQUARIUM

The mother of all fish tanks can be found at the brilliant Osaka Aquarium (p148). The tank is home to a phenomenal collection of sharks, including two whale sharks, a tiger shark, a few leopard sharks and a hammerhead shark. A pair of mantas somehow cohabitates peacefully with this lot. If you've got kids in tow, this place is a must.

7

⬐ KINOSAKI ONSEN

On the Japan Sea coast in northern Kansai, the picturesque town of Kinosaki (p145) is *the* place for the classic Japanese onsen (hot spring) experience. Put on your *yukata* (light cotton kimono) and a pair of sandals and spend the evening hopping from one fine onsen to the next, then head back to your ryokan and feast on locally caught king crabs.

8

⬐ KŌYA-SAN

Deep in the mountains of Wakayama-ken, the monastic complex of Kōya-san (p157) provides a look into the heart of Japanese Buddhism. Stroll through the cedar-lined avenues of the magical Oku-no-in cemetery and then return to your *shukubō* (temple lodging) to sample exquisite *shōjin-ryōri* (Buddhist vegetarian fare).

4 & 5 SEAN CAFFREY; 6 IAIN MASTERTON/ALAMY; 7 JTB PHOTO/PHOTOLIBRARY; 8 RACHEL LEWIS

4 Kiyomizu-dera (p121); 5 Kinkaku-ji (p126); 6 Osaka Aquarium (p148); 7 Kinosaki (p145); 8 Oku-no-in (p158), Kōya-san

KYOTO & KANSAI

THE BEST...

THE BEST...

⬎ PLACES TO CONTEMPLATE

- Nanzen-ji (p123) A world of Zen temples and subtemples scattered amid the trees.
- Chion-in (p123) A vast Pure Land Buddhist temple – the Vatican of Japanese Buddhism.
- Ginkaku-ji (p126) The famed 'Silver Pavilion' boasts one of Kyoto's finest gardens.
- Hōnen-in (p126) A secluded retreat a short walk from the perpetually crowded Ginkaku-ji.

⬎ PLACES TO STAY

- Tawaraya (p134) Some say this sublime Kyoto ryokan is the finest accommodation in the world.
- Hyatt Regency Kyoto (p134) The slick, smooth and efficient Hyatt is Kyoto's best hotel.
- Hiiragiya (p133) The classic old wing and the pristine new wing are superb at this Kyoto ryokan.

⬎ BEST PLACES FOR A WALK

- Nara-kōen (p153) Spend a day with the deer at this temple-strewn park.
- Tetsugaku-no-Michi (Path of Philosophy; p126) Running along a canal in Kyoto's Higashiyama district, this path is picturesque in any season.
- Dōtombori (p147) Soak up the frenetic vibe along Osaka's hectic Dōtombori Canal.

⬎ FESTIVALS

- Daimon-ji Gozan Okuribi (p132) Five giant characters are set alight on mountains around Kyoto.
- Gion Matsuri (p131) The real fun is wandering downtown Kyoto in the nights before the main event.
- Tenjin Matsuri (p148) Join the down-to-earth Osakans for this raucous summer festival of fireworks and, um, drinking.

LEFT: FRANK CARTER; RIGHT: BRENT WINEBRENNER

Left: *Geta* (wooden sandals) at Daitoku-ji (p125); Right: Shopping arcade, Minami (p146), Osaka

THINGS YOU NEED TO KNOW

⬆ VITAL STATISTICS

- **Populations** Kyoto 1.47 million, Osaka 2.65 million, Nara 369,000
- **Area codes** Kyoto ☎ 075, Osaka ☎ 06, Nara ☎ 0742
- **Best times to visit** Cherry-blossom season (early April), autumn-foliage season (late October to early December)

⬆ PLACES IN A NUTSHELL

- **Kyoto** (p110) The cultural heart of Japan, this city belongs at the top of any Japan itinerary.
- **Kinosaki** (p145) A quaint onsen town on the Japan Sea coast, Kinosaki is a relaxing overnight trip out of Kyoto.
- **Osaka** (p146) The working heart of Kansai, Osaka is a good place to see Japan's modern side, particularly if you aren't going to Tokyo.
- **Himeji** (p149) This fine castle town makes a good stopover on the way to or from Western Honshū.
- **Nara** (p151) Japan's first capital, this history-rich city makes a brilliant day trip from Kyoto.
- **Kōya-san** (p157) A Buddhist retreat high in the mountains of southern Kansai.

⬆ RESOURCES

- **Kyoto Visitors Guide** Pick up a copy of this useful magazine at any major hotel in Kyoto. It's the best source of information on what's on while you're in town.

- **Kyoto Tourist Information Centre** (p114) Conveniently located in Kyoto Station, this should be your first stop in Kyoto.

⬆ EMERGENCY NUMBERS

- **Ambulance & Fire** ☎ 119
- **Police** ☎ 110

⬆ GETTING AROUND

- **Walk or cycle** around Kyoto and Nara.
- **Taxi** from Kyoto Station to your hotel or ryokan.
- **Subway** around Osaka.
- **Shinkansen** between Tokyo and Kyoto.

⬆ BE FOREWARNED

- **Cherry-blossom and autumn-foliage seasons** bring huge crowds to Kyoto (escape the crowds by going to lesser-known temples and shrines).
- **Summer** (July and August) is very hot and humid in Kansai, particularly in Kyoto.
- **Slip-on shoes** are useful for exploring the temples of Kyoto.

KYOTO & KANSAI

DISCOVER KYOTO & KANSAI

DISCOVER KYOTO & KANSAI

Kansai is the heart of Japan. It is here that a truly distinctive Japanese culture came into being, and with it, those things that so many of us associate with Japan: ancient temples, colourful shrines and peaceful Zen gardens. Indeed, nowhere else in the country can you find so much of historical interest in such a compact area.

Kansai's major drawcards are Kyoto and Nara. Kyoto was the imperial capital between 794 and 1868, and is still considered by many to be the cultural heart of Japan. Nara predates Kyoto as an imperial capital and also has an impressive array of temples, burial mounds and relics.

Other prefectures in Kansai include Mie-ken, which is home to Ise-jingū, Japan's most sacred Shintō shrine, and Wakayama-ken, which offers onsen (hot springs), a rugged coastline and the temple complex of Kōya-san, Japan's most important Buddhist centre.

KYOTO 京都

☎ 075 / pop 1.47 million

Kyoto is the storehouse of Japan's traditional culture and the stage on which much of Japanese history was played out. With 17 Unesco World Heritage Sites, more than 1600 Buddhist temples and over 400 Shintō shrines, Kyoto is also one of the world's most culturally rich cities. Indeed, it is fair to say that Kyoto ranks with Paris, London and Rome as one of those cities that everyone should see at least once in their lives. And, needless to say, it should rank at the top of any Japan itinerary.

Kyoto is where you will find the Japan of your imagination: raked pebble gardens, poets' huts hidden amid bamboo groves, arcades of vermilion shrine gates, geisha disappearing into the doorways of traditional restaurants, golden temples floating above tranquil waters. Indeed, most of the sites that make up the popular image of Japan probably originated in Kyoto.

That said, first impressions can be something of an anticlimax. Stepping out of Kyoto Station for the first time and gazing around at the neon and concrete

that awaits you, you are likely to feel that all you've heard and read about Kyoto is just so much tourist-literature hype. We can only advise you to be patient, for the beauty of Kyoto is largely hidden from casual view: it lies behind walls, doors, curtains and facades. But if you take a little time to explore, you will discover that there are hundreds, perhaps thousands of pockets of incredible beauty scattered across the city. And, the closer you look, the more there is to see.

HISTORY

The Kyoto basin was first settled in the 7th century, and by 794 it had become Heian-kyō, the capital of Japan. Like Nara, a previous capital, the city was laid out in a grid pattern modelled on the Chinese Tang-dynasty capital, Chang'an (contemporary Xi'an). Although the city was to serve as home to the Japanese imperial family from 794 to 1868 (when the Meiji Restoration took the imperial family to the new capital, Tokyo), the city was not always the focus of Japanese political power. During the Kamakura period

(1185–1333), Kamakura served as the national capital, and during the Edo period (1600–1867), the Tokugawa shōgunate ruled Japan from Edo (now Tokyo).

The problem was that from the 9th century, the imperial family was increasingly isolated from the mechanics of political power and the country was ruled primarily by military families, or shōgunates. While Kyoto still remained capital in name and was the cultural focus of the nation, imperial power was, for the most part, symbolic and the business of running state affairs was often carried out elsewhere.

Just as imperial fortunes have waxed and waned, the fortunes of the city itself have fluctuated dramatically. During the Ōnin War (1466–67), which marked the close of the Muromachi period, the Kyoto Gosho (Imperial Palace) and most of the city were destroyed. Much of what can be seen in Kyoto today dates from the Edo period. Although political power resided in Edo, Kyoto was rebuilt and flourished as a cultural, religious and economic centre. Fortunately Kyoto was spared the aerial bombing that razed other Japanese urban centres in the closing months of WWII.

ORIENTATION

Like Manhattan, Kyoto is laid out in a grid pattern and is extremely easy to navigate. Kyoto Station, the city's main station, is located at the southern end of the city, and the JR and Kintetsu lines operate from here. The real centre of Kyoto is located around Shijō-dōri, about 2km north of Kyoto Station via Karasuma-dōri. The commercial and nightlife centres are between Shijō-dōri to the south and Sanjō-dōri to the north, and between Kawaramachi-dōri to the east and Karasuma-dōri to the west.

Although some of Kyoto's major sights are in the city centre, Kyoto's best sight-

seeing is on the outskirts of the city, along the base of the eastern and western mountains (known as Higashiyama and Arashiyama, respectively). Sights on the east side are best reached by bus, bicycle or the Tōzai subway line. Sights on the west side are best reached by bus or train (or by bicycle if you're very keen).

MAPS

The Kyoto TIC (p114) stocks the following maps: the *Tourist Map of Kyoto,* a useful map with decent insets of the main tourist districts on the reverse; the colour *Welcome Inns Map of Kyoto/Nara,* which is fairly detailed; the *Bus Navi: Kyoto City Bus Travel map,* which is the most useful guide to city buses; and a leaflet called *Kyoto Walks,* which has detailed walking

FRANK CARTER

Kabuki actors (p141)

GREATER KYOTO

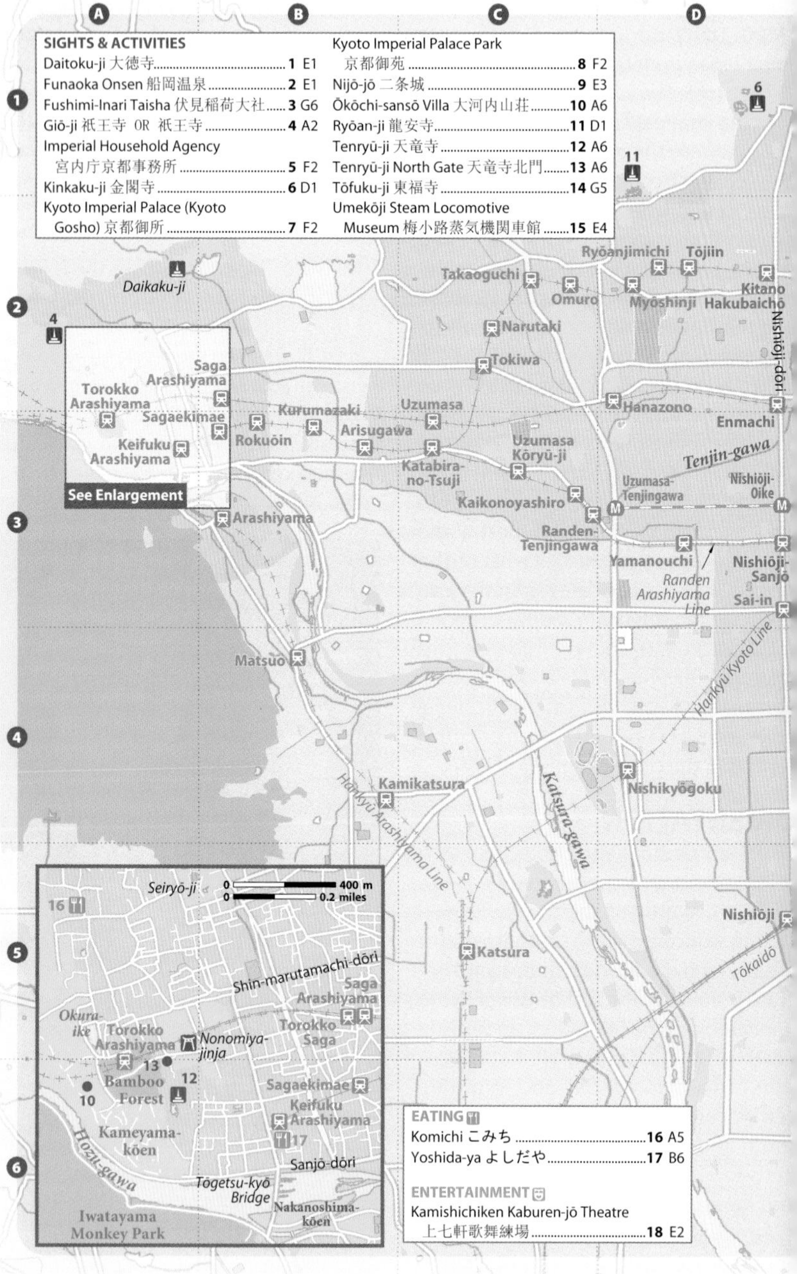
A
B
C
D
1
2
3
4
5
6
Daikaku-ji
Takaoguchi
Omuro
Ryōanjimichi
Tōjiin
Myōshinji
Kitano Hakubaichō
Nishiōji-dōri
Narutaki
Tokiwa
Hanazono
Enmachi
Kurumazaki
Uzumasa
Arisugawa
Rokuōin
Katabira-no-Tsuji
Uzumasa Kōryū-ji
Tenjin-gawa
Uzumasa-Tenjingawa
Nishiōji-Oike
Kaikonoyashiro
Randen-Tenjingawa
Yamanouchi
Randen Arashiyama Line
Nishiōji-Sanjō
Sai-in
Arashiyama
Matsuo
Hankyū Kyoto Line
Kamikatsura
Hankyū Arashiyama Line
Katsura-gawa
Nishikyōgoku
Nishiōji
Katsura
Tōkaidō
See Enlargement
Saga Arashiyama
Torokko Arashiyama
Sagaekimae
Keifuku Arashiyama
Seiryō-ji
400 m
0.2 miles
Shin-marutamachi-dōri
Saga Arashiyama
Okura-ike
Torokko Arashiyama
Nonomiya-jinja
Torokko Saga
Bamboo Forest
Sagaekimae
Keifuku Arashiyama
Kameyama-kōen
Hozu-gawa
Sanjō-dōri
Tōgetsu-kyō Bridge
Nakanoshima-kōen
Iwatayama Monkey Park

SIGHTS & ACTIVITIES

- Daitoku-ji 大徳寺 **1** E1
- Funaoka Onsen 船岡温泉 **2** E1
- Fushimi-Inari Taisha 伏見稲荷大社 **3** G6
- Giō-ji 祇王寺 OR 祇王寺 **4** A2
- Imperial Household Agency 宮内庁京都事務所 **5** F2
- Kinkaku-ji 金閣寺 **6** D1
- Kyoto Imperial Palace (Kyoto Gosho) 京都御所 **7** F2
- Kyoto Imperial Palace Park 京都御苑 **8** F2
- Nijō-jō 二条城 **9** E3
- Ōkōchi-sansō Villa 大河内山荘 **10** A6
- Ryōan-ji 龍安寺 **11** D1
- Tenryū-ji 天竜寺 **12** A6
- Tenryū-ji North Gate 天竜寺北門 **13** A6
- Tōfuku-ji 東福寺 **14** G5
- Umekōji Steam Locomotive Museum 梅小路蒸気機関車館 **15** E4

EATING

- Komichi こみち **16** A5
- Yoshida-ya よしだや **17** B6

ENTERTAINMENT

- Kamishichiken Kaburen-jō Theatre 上七軒歌舞練場 **18** E2

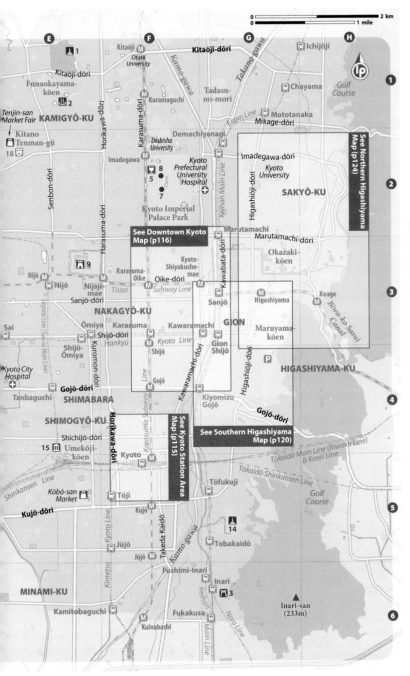

KYOTO & KANSAI

KYOTO

KYOTO & KANSAI

KYOTO

maps for major sightseeing areas in and around Kyoto (Higashiyama, Arashiyama, northwestern Kyoto and Ōhara).

INFORMATION
BOOKSHOPS

Junkudō (Map p116; ☎ 253-6460; Kyoto BAL Bldg, 2 Yamazaki-chō, Sanjō sagaru, Kawaramachi-dōri, Nakagyō-ku; ⏰ 11am-8pm) In the BAL Building, this shop has a great selection of English-language books on the 5th and 8th floors. This is Kyoto's best bookshop now that the old Maruzen and Random Walk bookshops have closed (you may remember these shops if you visited in the past).

TOURIST INFORMATION

Note that the following two information centres (along with the Welcome Inn

Kyoto Station

MARK HEMMINGS

Reservation counter, and the Prefectural International Centre) will move to the Suvaco shopping complex in spring 2010. Suvaco is on the 2nd floor of Kyoto Station, in the main concourse between the north side of the station and the *shinkansen* (bullet train) gates. It is just to the left (south) of the main entrance of Isetan department store.

Kyoto City Tourist Information Centre (Map p115; ☎ 343-6655; ⏰ 8.30am-7pm) Inside the new Kyoto Station building on the 2nd floor just across from Café du Monde. Though it's geared towards Japanese visitors, an English-speaking staff member is usually on hand and it's easier to find than the following.

Kyoto Tourist Information Centre (TIC; Map p115; ☎ 344-3300; ⏰ 10am-6pm, closed 2nd & 4th Tue of each month & new-year holidays) The best source of information on Kyoto, this is located on the 9th floor of the Kyoto Station building. To get there from the main concourse of the station, take the west escalator to the 2nd floor, enter Isetan department store and take an immediate left, then look for the elevator on your left and take it to the 9th floor. It's right outside the elevator, inside the Kyoto Prefectural International Centre. There is a Welcome Inn Reservation counter here that can help with accommodation bookings.

SIGHTS & ACTIVITIES
KYOTO STATION AREA
HIGASHI HONGAN-JI 東本願寺
A short walk north of Kyoto Station, this **temple** (Map p115; ☎ 371-9181; Shichijō agaru, Karasuma-dōri, Shimogyō-ku; admission free; ⏰ 5.50am-5.30pm Mar-Oct, 6.20am-4.30pm Nov-Feb) is the last word in all things grand and gaudy. Considering the proximity to the station, the free admission, the awesome

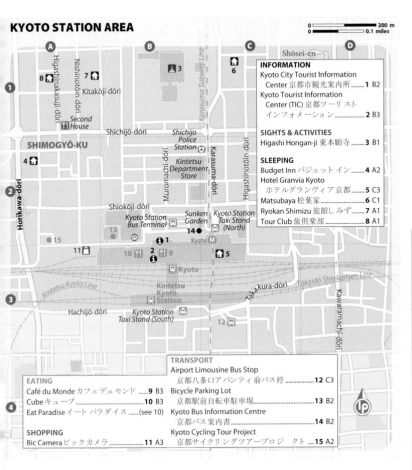

KYOTO STATION AREA

0 _____ 200 m
0 _____ 0.1 miles

KYOTO & KANSAI

KYOTO

Shōsei-en

INFORMATION
Kyoto City Tourist Information
　Center 京都市観光案内所 **1** B2
Kyoto Tourist Information
　Center (TIC) 京都ツーリスト
　インフォメーション **2** B3

SIGHTS & ACTIVITIES
Higashi Hongan-ji 東本願寺 **3** B1

SLEEPING
Budget Inn バジェット イン **4** A2
Hotel Granvia Kyoto
　ホテルグランヴィア京都 **5** C3
Matsubaya 松葉家 **6** C1
Ryokan Shimizu 旅館し みず....**7** A1
Tour Club 旅倶楽部 **8** A1

EATING
Café du Monde カフェデュモンド **9** B3
Cube キューブ **10** B3
Eat Paradise イート パラダイス ......(see 10)

SHOPPING
Bic Camera ビックカメラ **11** A3

TRANSPORT
Airport Limousine Bus Stop
　京都八条口アバンティ前バス停 **12** C3
Bicycle Parking Lot
　京都駅前自転車駐車場............................**13** B2
Kyoto Bus Information Centre
　京都バス案内書 **14** B2
Kyoto Cycling Tour Project
　京都サイクリングツアープロジ クト **15** A2

---

structures and the dazzling interiors, this temple is an obvious spot to visit if you find yourself near the station.

In 1602, when Tokugawa Ieyasu engineered the rift in the Jōdo Shin-shū school, he founded this temple as a competitor to Nishi Hongan-ji. Rebuilt in 1895 after a series of fires destroyed all of the original structures, the temple is now the headquarters of the Ōtani branch of Jōdo Shin-shū.

The enormous Goei-dō main hall is one of the world's largest wooden structures, standing 38m high, 76m long and 58m wide.

DOWNTOWN KYOTO
NISHIKI MARKET 錦市場

To see all the really weird and wonderful foods that go into Kyoto cuisine, wander through **Nishiki Market** (Map p116; ☎ 211-3882; Nishikikōji-dōri btwn Teramachi & Takakura; ⏰ 9am-5pm, varies for individual stalls, some shops closed on Wed) in the centre of town, one block north of (and parallel to) Shijō-dōri. It's a great place to visit on a rainy day or if you need a break from temple-hopping. The variety of foods on display is staggering, and the frequent cries of *Irasshaimase!* (Welcome!) are heart-warming.

DOWNTOWN KYOTO

KYOTO & KANSAI

KYOTO

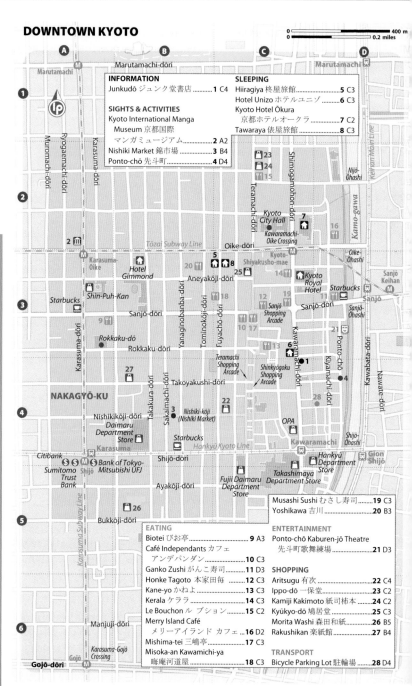

INFORMATION
Junkudō ジュンク堂書店 1 C4

SIGHTS & ACTIVITIES
Kyoto International Manga
  Museum 京都国際
  マンガミュージアム................2 A2
Nishiki Market 錦市場 3 B4
Ponto-chō 先斗町.........................4 D4

SLEEPING
Hiiragiya 柊屋旅館.......................5 C3
Hotel Unizo ホテルユニゾ 6 C3
Kyoto Hotel Ōkura
  京都ホテルオークラ 7 C2
Tawaraya 俵屋旅館 8 C3

Musashi Sushi むさし寿司........19 C3
Yoshikawa 吉川 20 B3

EATING
Biotei びお亭.................................. 9 A3
Café Independants カフェ
  アンデパンダン 10 C3
Ganko Zushi がんこ寿司........11 D3
Honke Tagoto 本家田毎 12 C3
Kane-yo かねよ 13 C3
Kerala ケララ 14 C2
Le Bouchon ル ブション 15 C2
Merry Island Café
  メリーアイランド カフェ ...16 D2
Mishima-tei 三嶋亭....................17 C3
Misoka-an Kawamichi-ya
  晦庵河道屋..............................18 C3

ENTERTAINMENT
Ponto-chō Kaburen-jō Theatre
  先斗町歌舞練場 21 D3

SHOPPING
Aritsugu 有次 22 C4
Ippo-dō 一保堂...........................23 C2
Kamiji Kakimoto 紙司柿本 24 C2
Kyūkyo-dō 鳩居堂......................25 C3
Morita Washi 森田和紙.............26 B5
Rakushikan 楽紙館.....................27 B4

TRANSPORT
Bicycle Parking Lot 駐輪場 28 D4

KYOTO INTERNATIONAL MANGA MUSEUM
京都国際マンガミュージアム

This fine museum (Map p116; ☎ 254-7414; www.kyotomm.com/english; Oike agaru, Karasuma-dōri, Nakagyō-ku; adult/child ¥500/100; ☽ 10am-6pm, closed Wed & the following Thu when Wed is a national holiday, & new-year holiday) has a collection of some 300,000 manga (Japanese comic books). Located in an old elementary school building, the museum is the perfect introduction to the art of manga. While most of the manga and displays are in Japanese, the collection of translated works is growing.

It's a short walk from the Karasuma-Oike Station on the Karuma line subway or the Tōzai line subway. Enter by 5.30pm.

PONTO-CHŌ 先斗町

A traditional nightlife district, Ponto-chō (Map p116) is a narrow alley running between Sanjō-dōri and Shijō-dōri just west of Kamo-gawa. It's best visited in the evening, when the traditional wooden buildings and hanging lanterns create a wonderful atmosphere of old Japan. It makes a nice stroll in the evening, perhaps combined with a walk in nearby Gion.

CENTRAL KYOTO

KYOTO IMPERIAL PALACE PARK
京都御所

The Kyoto Imperial Palace is surrounded by the spacious Kyoto Imperial Palace Park (Kamigyō-ku Kyoto gyoen; Map pp112-13; admission free; ☽ dawn-dusk), which is planted with a huge variety of flowering trees and open fields. It's perfect for picnics, strolls and just about any sport you can think of.

KYOTO IMPERIAL PALACE (KYOTO GOSHO) 京都御所

The original imperial palace (Map pp112-13) was built in 794 and was replaced several times after destruction by fire. The present building, on a different site and smaller than the original, was constructed in 1855. Enthronement of a new emperor and other state ceremonies are held there.

PRIVATE TOURS OF KYOTO

A private tour is a great way to see the sights and learn about the city without having to worry about transport and logistics. There's a variety of private tours on offer in Kyoto.

All Japan Private Tours & Speciality Services (www.kyotoguide.com/yjpt) This company offers private tours of Kyoto, Nara and Tokyo as well as business coordination and related services.

Chris Rowthorn's Walks & Tours of Kyoto & Japan (www.chrisrowthorn.com) Lonely Planet *Kyoto* and *Japan* author Chris Rowthorn offers private tours of Kyoto, Nara, Osaka and other parts of Japan.

Johnnie's Kyoto Walking (http://web.kyoto-inet.or.jp/people/h-s-love) Hirooka Hajime, aka Johnnie Hillwalker, offers an interesting guided walking tour of the area around Kyoto Station and the Higashiyama area.

Naoki Doi (☎ 090-9596-5546; www3.ocn.ne.jp/~doitaxi) This English-speaking taxi driver offers private taxi tours of Kyoto and Nara.

Windows to Japan (www.windowstojapan.com) Offers custom tours of Kyoto and Japan.

FRANK CARTER

Anime poster

The Gosho does not rate highly in comparison with other attractions in Kyoto and you must apply for permission to visit (see following). However, you shouldn't miss the park surrounding the Gosho (see p117).

To get there, take the Karasuma line subway to Imadegawa or a bus to the Karasuma-Imadegawa stop and walk 600m southeast.

RESERVATION & ADMISSION

Permission to visit the Gosho is granted by the Kunaichō, the Imperial Household Agency (Map pp112-13; ☎ 211-1215; ⏰ 8.30am-5.30pm Mon-Fri), which is inside the walled park surrounding the palace, a short walk from Imadegawa Station on the Karasuma line. You have to fill out an application form and show your passport. Children can visit if accompanied by adults over 20 years of age (but are forbidden entry to the other three imperial properties of Katsura Rikyū, Sentō Gosho and Shūgaku-in Rikyū). Permission to tour the palace is usually granted the

same day (try to arrive at the office at least 30 minutes before the start of the tour you'd like to join). Guided tours, sometimes in English, are given at 10am and 2pm from Monday to Friday. The tour lasts about 50 minutes.

The Gosho can be visited without reservation during two periods each year, once in the spring and once in the autumn. The dates vary each year, but as a general guide, the spring opening is around the last week of April and the autumn opening is in the middle of November. Check with the TIC for exact dates.

The Imperial Household Agency is also the place to make advance reservations to see the Sentō Gosho, Katsura Rikyū and Shūgaku-in Rikyū.

UMEKŌJI STEAM LOCOMOTIVE MUSEUM 梅小路蒸気機関車館

A hit with steam-train buffs and kids, this museum (Map pp112-13; ☎ 314-2996; Kannon-ji-chō, Shimogyō-ku; adult/child ¥400/100, train ride ¥200/100; ⏰ 9.30am-5pm, admission by 4.30pm, closed Mon) features 18 vintage steam locomotives (dating from 1914 to 1948) and related displays. It's in the former Nijō Station building, which was recently relocated here and carefully reconstructed. For an extra few yen, you can take a 10-minute ride on one of the fabulous old trains (departures at 11am, 1.30pm and 3.30pm).

From Kyoto Station, take bus 33, 205 or 208 to the Umekō-ji Kōen-mae stop (make sure you take a westbound bus).

SOUTHERN HIGASHIYAMA

The Higashiyama district, which runs along the base of the Higashiyama mountains (Eastern Mountains), is the main sightseeing district in Kyoto and it should be at the top of your Kyoto itinerary. It is thick with impressive sights: fine temples, shrines, gardens, museums, traditional neighbourhoods and parks. In this guide, we divide the Higashiyama district into two sections: southern Higashiyama and northern Higashiyama (p123).

This section starts at the southern end, around Shichijō-dōri, and works north, to Sanjō-dōri. You could cover these in the order presented in a fairly long day. The best way to see the highlights here is to take our walking tour (p130).

SANJŪSANGEN-DŌ 三十三間堂

The original Sanjūsangen-dō (Map p120; ☎ 525-0033; 657 Sanjūsangendōmawari-chō, Higashiyama-ku; admission ¥600; ☀ 8am-4.30pm, 9am-3.30pm 16 Nov-16 Mar) was built in 1164 at the request of the retired emperor Go-shirakawa. The temple burnt to the ground in 1249 but a faithful copy was constructed in 1266.

The temple's name refers to the *sanjūsan* (33) bays between the pillars of this long, narrow building that houses 1001 statues of the 1000-armed Kannon (the Buddhist goddess of mercy). The largest Kannon is flanked on either side by

500 smaller Kannon images, neatly lined up in rows.

The temple is a 1.5km walk east of Kyoto Station; alternatively, take bus 206 or 208 and get off at the Sanjūsangen-dō-mae stop. It's also very close to Keihan Shichijō Station.

KYOTO NATIONAL MUSEUM 京都国立博物館

The Kyoto National Museum (Map p120; ☎ 531-7509; www.kyohaku.go.jp/eng/index_top .html; 527 Chaya-machi, Higashiyama-ku; adult/student ¥500/250, extra for special exhibitions; ☀ 9.30am-5pm, closed Mon) is housed in two buildings opposite Sanjūsangen-dō temple. It was founded in 1895 as an imperial repository for art and treasures from local temples and shrines. There are 17 rooms

FRANK CARTER
Kiyomizu-dera (p121)

SOUTHERN HIGASHIYAMA

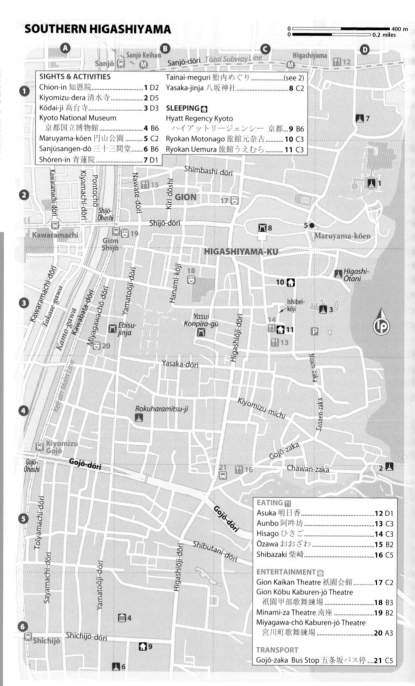

SIGHTS & ACTIVITIES

Chion-in 知恩院	**1** D2
Kiyomizu-dera 清水寺	**2** D5
Kōdai-ji 高台寺	**3** D3
Kyoto National Museum 京都国立博物館	**4** B6
Maruyama-kōen 円山公園	**5** C2
Sanjūsangen-dō 三十三間堂	**6** B6
Shōren-in 青蓮院	**7** D1
Tainai-meguri 胎内めぐり	(see 2)
Yasaka-jinja 八坂神社	**8** C2

SLEEPING

Hyatt Regency Kyoto ハイアットリージェンシー 京都	**9** B6
Ryokan Motonago 旅館元奈古	**10** C3
Ryokan Uemura 旅館うえむら	**11** C3

EATING

Asuka 明日香	**12** D1
Aunbo 阿吽坊	**13** C3
Hisago ひさご	**14** C3
Ōzawa おおざわ	**15** B2
Shibazaki 柴崎	**16** C5

ENTERTAINMENT

Gion Kaikan Theatre 祇園会館	**17** C2
Gion Kōbu Kaburen-jō Theatre 祇園甲部歌舞練場	**18** B3
Minami-za Theatre 南座	**19** B2
Miyagawa-chō Kaburen-jō Theatre 宮川町歌舞練場	**20** A3

TRANSPORT

Gojō-zaka Bus Stop 五条坂バス停	**21** C5

with displays of more than 1000 artworks, historical artefacts and handicrafts. The permanent collection is excellent but somewhat poorly displayed; unless you have a particular interest in Japanese traditional arts, we recommend visiting this museum only when a special exhibition is on.

KIYOMIZU-DERA 清水寺

This ancient **temple** (Map p120; ☎ 551-1234; 1-294 Kiyomizu, Higashiyama-ku; admission ¥300; ☻ 6am-6pm) was first built in 798, but the present buildings are reconstructions dating from 1633. As an affiliate of the Hossō school of Buddhism, which originated in Nara, it has successfully survived the many intrigues of local Kyoto schools of Buddhism through the centuries and is now one of the most famous landmarks of the city (for which reason it can get very crowded during spring and autumn).

The main hall has a huge verandah that is supported by hundreds of pillars and juts out over the hillside. Just below this hall is the waterfall **Otowa-no-taki**, where visitors drink sacred waters believed to have therapeutic properties. Dotted around the precincts are other halls and shrines. At **Jishu-jinja**, the shrine on the grounds, visitors try to ensure success in love by closing their eyes and walking about 18m between a pair of stones – if you miss the stone, your desire for love won't be fulfilled!

Before you enter the actual temple precincts, check out the **Tainai-meguri** (admission ¥100; ☻ 9am-4pm), the entrance to which is just to the left (north) of the pagoda that is located in front of the main entrance to the temple (you may have to ask a temple official as there is no English sign). We won't tell you too much about it as it will ruin the experience. Suffice to say that by entering the Tainai-meguri, you are symbolically entering the womb of a female bodhisattva. When you get to the rock in the darkness, spin it in either direction to make a wish.

To get there from Kyoto Station take bus 206 and get off at either the Kiyōmizu-michi or Gojō-zaka stop and plod up the hill for 10 minutes.

MARK HEMMINGS

Escalators at Kyoto Station

Monk exiting a hall at Chion-in

BRENT WINEBRENNER

MARUYAMA-KŌEN 円山公園

This **park** (Map p120; Maruyama-chō, Higashiyama-ku) is a great place to escape the bustle of the city centre and amble around gardens, ponds, souvenir shops and restaurants. Peaceful paths meander through the trees and carp glide through the waters of a small pond in the centre of the park.

For two weeks in late March/early April, when the park's many cherry trees come into bloom, the calm atmosphere of the park is shattered by hordes of revellers enjoying *hanami* (blossom-viewing). For those who don't mind crowds, this is a good place to observe the Japanese at their most uninhibited. It is best to arrive early and claim a good spot high on the eastern side of the park, from which point you can safely peer down on the mayhem below.

The park is a five-minute walk east of the Shijō-Higashiōji intersection. To get there from Kyoto Station, take bus 206 and get off at the Gion stop.

YASAKA-JINJA 八坂神社

This colourful **shrine** (Map p120; ☎ 561-6155; Gion-machi, Higashiyama-ku; admission free; ⏰ 24hr) is just down the hill from Maruyama-kōen. It's considered the guardian shrine of neighbouring Gion and is sometimes endearingly referred to as 'Gion-san'. This shrine is particularly popular as a spot for *hatsu-mōde* (the first shrine visit of the new year). If you don't mind a stampede, come here around midnight on New Year's Eve or over the next few days. Surviving the crush is proof that you're blessed by the gods! Yasaka-jinja also sponsors Kyoto's biggest festival, Gion Matsuri (p131).

GION 祇園周辺

Gion is Kyoto's famous entertainment and geisha district on the eastern bank of the Kamo-gawa. Modern architecture, congested traffic and contemporary nightlife establishments rob the area of some of its historical beauty, but there are still some lovely places left for a stroll. Gion falls roughly between Sanjō-dōri and

Gojō-dōri (north and south, respectively) and Higashiyama-dōri and Kawabata-dōri (east and west, respectively).

Hanami-kōji is the main north–south avenue of Gion. The section south of Shijō-dōri is lined with 17th-century restaurants and tea houses, many of which are exclusive establishments for geisha entertainment. If you wander around here in the late afternoon or early evening, you may glimpse geisha or *maiko* (apprentice geisha) on their way to or from appointments.

Another must-see spot in Gion is **Shimbashi** (sometimes called Shirakawa Minami-dōri), which is one of Kyoto's most beautiful streets, and, arguably, the most beautiful street in all of Asia, especially in the evening and during cherry-blossom season. To get there, start at the intersection of Shijō-dōri and Hanami-kōji and walk north, then take the third left.

Gion is very close to Gion Shijō Station on the Keihan line.

CHION-IN 知恩院

In 1234 **Chion-in** (**Map p120; ☎ 531-2111; 400 Rinka-chō, Higashiyama-ku; admission to grounds/inner buildings & garden free/¥400; 🕑 9am-4pm Mar-Nov, to 3.40pm Dec-Feb**) was built on the site where a famous priest by the name of Hōnen had taught and eventually fasted to death. Today it is still the headquarters of the Jōdo (Pure Land) school of Buddhism, which was founded by Hōnen, and a hive of activity. For visitors with a taste for the grand, this temple is sure to satisfy.

The oldest of the present buildings date back to the 17th century. The two-storey **San-mon**, a Buddhist temple gate at the main entrance, is the largest temple gate in Japan and prepares you for the massive scale of the temple. The immense main hall contains an image of Hōnen. It's connected to another hall, the Dai Hōjō, by a 'nightingale' floor (that sings and squeaks at every move, making it difficult for intruders to move about quietly).

Up a flight of steps southeast of the main hall is the temple's giant **bell**, which was cast in 1633 and weighs 74 tonnes. It is the largest bell in Japan. The combined muscle-power of 17 monks is needed to make the bell ring for the famous ceremony that heralds the new year.

The temple is close to the northeastern corner of Maruyama-kōen. From Kyoto Station take bus 206 and get off at the Chion-in-mae stop, or walk up (east) from Gion Shijō Station on the Keihan line.

NORTHERN HIGASHIYAMA

This area at the base of the Higashiyama mountains is one of the city's richest areas for sightseeing. It includes such first-rate attractions as Ginkaku-ji, Hōnen-in, Shūgaku-in Rikyū, Shisen-dō and Manshu-in. You can spend a wonderful day walking from Keage Station on the Tōzai subway line all the way north to Ginkaku-ji via the Tetsugaku-no-Michi (the Path of Philosophy), stopping in the countless temples and shrines en route. Sights further north should be tackled separately, as they are a little harder to reach.

NANZEN-JI 南禅寺

This is one of our favourite **temples** (**Map p124; ☎ 771-0365; http://nanzenji.com/english/index.html; Fukuchi-chō, Nanzen-ji, Sakyō-ku; admission to grounds/Hōjō garden/San-mon gate free/¥500/300; 🕑 8.40am-5pm Mar-Nov, to 4.30pm Dec-Feb**) in Kyoto, with its expansive grounds and numerous subtemples. It began as a retirement villa for Emperor Kameyama but was dedicated as a Zen temple on his death in 1291. Civil war in the 15th century destroyed most of the temple; the present buildings date from

NORTHERN HIGASHIYAMA

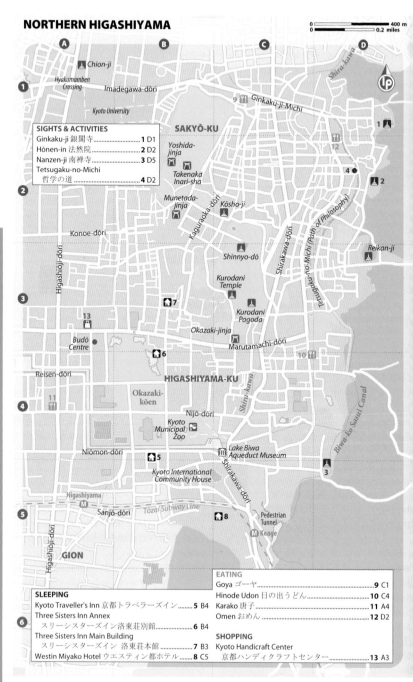

KYOTO & KANSAI

KYOTO

SIGHTS & ACTIVITIES
Ginkaku-ji 銀閣寺............................**1** D1
Hōnen-in 法然院............................**2** D2
Nanzen-ji 南禅寺............................**3** D5
Tetsugaku-no-Michi
哲学の道............................**4** D2

SLEEPING
Kyoto Traveller's Inn 京都トラベラーズイン........**5** B4
Three Sisters Inn Annex
スリーシスターズイン洛東荘別館....................**6** B4
Three Sisters Inn Main Building
スリーシスターズイン 洛東荘本館..................**7** B3
Westin Miyako Hotel ウエスティン都ホテル........**8** C5

EATING
Goya ゴーヤ............................**9** C1
Hinode Udon 日の出うどん............................**10** C4
Karako 唐子............................**11** A4
Omen おめん............................**12** D2

SHOPPING
Kyoto Handicraft Center
京都ハンディクラフトセンター............................**13** A3

BRENT WINEBRENNER

Stone tablet and maple leaves in the grounds of Nazen-ji

◥ IF YOU LIKE...

If you like Nanzen-ji, we think you'll like these other less-visited but wonderful Kyoto temples:

- **Daitoku-ji** (Map pp112-13; ☎ 491-0019; 53 Daitokuji-chō, Murasakino, Kita-ku; admission free; ☯ dawn-dusk) Like Nanzen-ji, this is an entire world of Zen temples. For garden lovers, this place is highly recommended.

- **Kōdai-ji** (Map p120; ☎ 561-9966; 526 Shimokawara-chō, Kōdai-ji, Higashiyama-ku; admission ¥600; ☯ 9am-5pm) Don't miss the night-time illuminations at this brilliant temple just down the hill from the more famous Kiyomizu-dera.

- **Sanjūsangen-dō** (Map p120; ☎ 525-0033; 657 Sanjūsangendōmawari-chō, Higashiyama-ku; admission ¥600; ☯ 8am-4:30pm, 9am-3:30pm 16 Nov-16 Mar) The 1001 statues of Kannon (Buddhist goddess of mercy) here are arresting sights.

- **Shōren-in** (Map p120; ☎ 561-2345; Sanjōbō-chō, Awataguchi, Higashiyama-ku; admission ¥500; ☯ 9am-5pm) Few tourists make it into this peaceful temple and that is definitely their loss.

the 17th century. It operates now as headquarters for the Rinzai school of Zen.

At its entrance stands the massive San-mon. Steps lead up to the 2nd storey, which has a fine view over the city. Beyond the gate is the main hall of the temple, above which you will find the Hōjō, where the Leaping Tiger Garden is a classic Zen garden well worth a look. (Try to ignore the annoying taped explanation of the garden.) While you're in the Hōjō, you can enjoy a cup of tea while gazing at a small waterfall (¥400, ask at the reception desk of the Hōjō).

To get to Nanzen-ji from JR Kyoto or Keihan Sanjō Station, take bus 5 and get off at the Nanzen-ji Eikan-dō-michi stop. You can also take the Tōzai subway line from the city centre to Keage and walk for five minutes downhill. Turn right (east, towards the mountains) opposite the police box and walk slightly uphill and you will arrive at the main gate of the temple.

TETSUGAKU-NO-MICHI (PATH OF PHILOSOPHY) 哲学の道

The Tetsugaku-no-Michi (Map p124; Sakyō-ku Ginkaku-ji) is a pedestrian path that runs along a canal near the base of the Higashiyama. It's lined with cherry trees and a host of other blooming trees and flowers. It takes its name from one of its most famous strollers: 20th-century philosopher Nishida Kitarō, who is said to have meandered along the path lost in thought. It only takes 30 minutes to complete the walk, which starts just north of Eikan-dō and ends at Ginkaku-ji (below).

HŌNEN-IN 法然院

This fine temple (Map p124; ☎ 771-2420; 30 Goshonodan-chō, Shishigatani, Sakyō-ku; admission free; ⏰ 6am-4pm) was established in 1680 to honour Hōnen, the charismatic founder of the Jōdo school. This is a lovely, secluded temple with carefully raked gardens set back in the woods. Be sure to visit in early April for the cherry blossoms and early November for the maple leaves, when the main hall is opened for a special viewing.

The temple is a 10-minute walk from Ginkaku-ji, on a side street that is accessible from the Tetsugaku-no-Michi; heading south on the path, look for the English sign on your left, then cross the bridge over the canal and follow the road uphill.

GINKAKU-JI 銀閣寺

Ginkaku-ji (Map p124; ☎ 771-5725; 2 Ginkaku-ji-chō, Sakyō-ku; admission ¥500; ⏰ 8.30am-5pm Mar-Nov, 9am-4.30pm Dec-Feb) is one of Kyoto's premier sights. In 1482 Shōgun Ashikaga Yoshimasa constructed a villa here as a genteel retreat from the turmoil of civil war. The villa's name translates as 'Silver Pavilion', but the shōgun's ambition to cover the building with silver was never realised. After Yoshimasa's death, the villa was converted into a temple.

From JR Kyoto or Keihan Sanjō Station take bus 5 and get off at the Ginkaku-ji-michi stop. From Demachiyanagi Station or Shijō Station, take bus 203 to the same stop.

NORTHWEST KYOTO

Northwest Kyoto has many excellent sights spread over a large swath of Kyoto. Highlights include Nijō-jō, a shōgun's castle; Kinkaku-ji, the famed Golden Pavilion; and Ryōan-ji, with its mysterious stone garden. Note that three of the area's main sites – Kinkaku-ji, Ryōan-ji and Ninna-ji – can easily be linked together to form a great half-day tour out of the city centre.

NIJŌ-JŌ 二条城

This castle (Map pp112-13; ☎ 841-0096; 541 Nijōjō-chō, Horikawa Nishi iru, Nijō-dōri, Nakagyō-ku; admission ¥600; ⏰ 8.45am-5pm, closed Tue in Dec, Jan, Jul & Aug, closed 26 Dec-4 Jan) was built in 1603 as the official Kyoto residence of the first Tokugawa shōgun, Ieyasu. The ostentatious style of construction was intended as a demonstration of Ieyasu's prestige and to signal the demise of the emperor's power. As a safeguard against treachery, Ieyasu had the interior fitted with 'nightingale' floors and concealed chambers where bodyguards could keep watch.

To reach the castle, take bus 9 from Kyoto Station to the Nijō-jō-mae stop. Alternatively, take the Tōzai subway line to the Nijō-jō-mae Station. Enter by 4pm.

KINKAKU-JI 金閣寺

Kyoto's famed 'Golden Pavilion', Kinkaku-ji (Map pp112-13; ☎ 461-0013; 1 Kinkaku-ji-chō, Kita-ku; admission ¥400; ⏰ 9am-5pm) is one of Japan's best-known sights. The original building was built in 1397 as a retirement villa for Shōgun Ashikaga Yoshimitsu. His son converted it into a temple.

Note that this temple can be packed almost any day of the year. We recommend going early in the day or just before closing.

To get to the temple from Kyoto Station, take bus 205 and get off at the Kinkaku-ji-michi stop. From Keihan Sanjō, take bus 59 and get off at the Kinkaku-ji-mae stop.

RYŌAN-JI 龍安寺

This **temple** (Map pp112-13; ☎ 463-2216; 13 Goryōnoshitamachi, Ryōan-ji, Ukyō-ku; admission ¥500; ☒ 8am-5pm Mar-Nov, 8.30am-4.30pm Dec-Feb) belongs to the Rinzai school of Zen and was founded in 1450. The main attraction is the garden arranged in the *kare-sansui* (dry landscape) style. An austere collection of 15 rocks, apparently adrift in a sea of sand, is enclosed by an earthen wall. The designer, who remains unknown, provided no explanation.

From Keihan Sanjō Station, take bus 59 to the Ryōan-ji-mae stop. Alternatively, you can walk to Ryōan-ji from Kinkaku-ji (see preceding) in about half an hour.

FUNAOKA ONSEN 船岡温泉

This old **bath** (Map pp112-13; ☎ 441-3735; 82-1 Minami-Funaoka-chō-Murasakino Kita-ku; admission ¥410; ☒ 3pm-1am Mon-Sat, 8am-1am Sun & holidays) on Kuramaguchi-dōri is Kyoto's best. It boasts an outdoor bath, a sauna, a cypress-wood tub, an electric bath, a herbal bath and a few more for good measure. Be sure to check out the *ranma* (carved wooden panels) in the changing room. Carved during Japan's invasion of Manchuria, the panels offer insight into the prevailing mindset of that era. (Note the panels do contain some violent imagery, which may disturb some visitors.)

To find the bath, head west about 400m on Kuramaguchi-dōri from the Kuramaguchi-Horiikawa intersection. It's

FRANK CARTER

Outdoor bath at Funaoka Onsen

on the left, not far past Lawson convenience store. Look for the large rocks out the front.

ARASHIYAMA & SAGANO AREA

Arashiyama and Sagano, at the base of Kyoto's western mountains (known as the Arashiyama), is Kyoto's second-most important sightseeing district after Higashiyama. On first sight, you may wonder what all the fuss is about: the main street and the area around the famous Tōgetsu-kyō bridge are a classic Japanese tourist circus. But once you head up the hills to the temples hidden in the greenery, you'll understand the appeal.

Arashiyama's most stunning sight is the famous **bamboo grove**, which begins just outside the north gate of Tenryū-ji (p128).

KYOTO & KANSAI

KYOTO

Garden path at Ōkōchi-sansō
BRENT WINEBRENNER

➘ ŌKŌCHI-SANSŌ
大河内山荘

This villa is the home of Ōkōchi Denjiro, an actor in samurai films. The superb gardens allow fine views over the city and are open to visitors. The gardens are particularly lovely during the autumn foliage season. The admission fee is hefty but includes tea and a cake (save the tea/cake ticket that comes with your admission). The villa is a 10-minute walk through the bamboo grove north of Tenryū-ji.

Things you need to know: Map pp112-13; ☎ 872-2233; 8 Tabuchiyama-chō, Ogurayama, Saga, Ukyō-ku; admission ¥1000; ☾ 9am-5pm

Walking through this expanse of swaying bamboo is like entering another world and it ranks high on the list of must-do experiences to be had in Japan.

Bus 28 links Kyoto Station with Arashiyama. Bus 11 connects Keihan Sanjō Station with Arashiyama. The most convenient rail connection is the ride from Shijō-Ōmiya Station on the Keifuku-Arashiyama line to Arashiyama Station (take the Hankyū train from downtown to get to Shijō-Ōmiya). You can also take the JR San-in line from Kyoto Station or Nijō Station and get off at Saga Arashiyama Station (be careful to take only the local train, as the express does not stop in Arashiyama).

TENRYŪ-JI 天龍寺
One of the major temples of the Rinzai school of Zen, Tenryū-ji (Map pp112-13; ☎ 881-1235; 68 Susukinobaba-chō, Saga Tenryū-ji, Ukyō-ku; admission ¥600; ☾ 8.30am-5.30pm, with slight seasonal variations) was built in 1339 on the former site of Emperor Go-Daigo' villa after a priest had dreamt of a dragon rising from the nearby river. The dream was interpreted as a sign that the emperor's spirit was uneasy and the temple was constructed as appeasement – hence the name tenryū (heavenly dragon). The present buildings date from 1900, but the main attraction is the 14th-century Zen garden.

Arashiyama's famous bamboo grove lies just outside the north gate of the temple.

GIŌ-JI 祇王寺
This quiet temple (Map pp112-13; ☎ 861-3574; 32 Kozaka, Toriimoto, Saga, Ukyō-ku; admission ¥300; ☾ 9am-4.30pm, with seasonal variations) was named for a Heian-era shirabyōshi (traditional dancer) named Giō. Aged 21, Giō committed herself here as a nun after her romance with Taira-no-Kiyomori, the commander of the Heike clan. She was usurped by a fellow entertainer, Hotoke Gozen (who later left Kiyomori to join Giō at the temple). Enshrined in the main hall are five statues: these are Giō, Hotoke Gozen, Kiyomori, and Giō's mother and sister (who were also nuns at the temple). It's next to Takiguchi-dera.

SOUTHEAST KYOTO
TŌFUKU-JI 東福寺
Founded in 1236 by the priest Enni, Tōfuku-ji (Map pp112-13; ☎ 561-0087; 15-778

onmahi, Higashiyama-ku; admission to grounds/ garden free/¥400; 9am-4pm Dec-Oct, 8.30am-.30pm Nov) belongs to the Rinzai sect of Zen Buddhism. As this temple was intended to compare with Tōdai-ji and Kōfuku-ji in Nara, it was given a name combining characters from the names of each of these temples. Enter by 30 minutes before closing.

The huge San-mon is the oldest Zen main gate in Japan. The *tōsu* (lavatory) and *yokushitsu* (bathroom) date from the 14th century. The present temple complex includes 24 subtemples; at one time there were 53.

The Hōjō was reconstructed in 1890. The gardens, laid out in 1938, are well worth a visit. The northern garden has stones and moss neatly arranged in a chequerboard pattern. From a viewing platform at the back of the gardens, you can observe the Tsūten-kyō (Bridge to Heaven), which spans a valley filled with maples.

Note that Tōfuku-ji is one of Kyoto's most famous autumn-foliage spots, and it is invariably packed during the peak of colours in November. Otherwise, it's often very quiet.

Tōfuku-ji is a 20-minute walk (2km) southeast of Kyoto Station. You can also take a local train on the JR Nara line and get off at JR Tōfukuji Station, from which it's a 10-minute walk southeast. Alternatively, you can take the Keihan line to Keihan Tōfukuji Station, from which it's also a 10-minute walk.

FUSHIMI-INARI TAISHA
伏見稲荷大社
This intriguing shrine (Map pp112-13; ☎ 641-7331; 68 Yabunouchi-chō, Fukakusa, Fushimi-ku; admission free; dawn-dusk) was dedicated to the gods of rice and sake by the Hata family in the 8th century. As the role of agriculture diminished, deities were enrolled to ensure prosperity in business. Nowadays the shrine is one of Japan's most popular, and is the head shrine for some 30,000 Inari shrines scattered the length and breadth of Japan.

KYOTO & KANSAI

KYOTO

MARK HEMMINGS

Garden at Ryōan-ji (p127)

The entire complex consisting of five shrines sprawls across the wooded slopes of Inari-yama. A pathway wanders 4km up the mountain and is lined with hundreds of red torii.

To get to the shrine from Kyoto Station, take a JR Nara line train to Inari Station. From Keihan Sanjō Station take the Keihan line to Fushimi-Inari Station. The shrine is just east of both of these stations.

SOUTHERN HIGASHIYAMA WALKING TOUR

If you had only one day in Kyoto, this 5km walk would be the best way to sample several of Kyoto's most important sights and neighbourhoods. It's pretty much a must-see route, heading right through the heart of Kyoto's premier sightseeing district. Be warned, though, that almost every visitor to Kyoto, both Japanese and foreign, eventually makes their way here so you'll have to hit it very early in the day to avoid the crush.

The walk begins at Gojō-zaka bus stop (Map p120) on Higashiōji-dōri. From here walk south for a few metres and turn up Gojō-zaka slope (there is an old noodle shop and pharmacy at the bottom of this street). Head uphill until you reach the first fork in the road; bear right and continue up Chawan-zaka (Teapot Lane). At the top of the hill you'll come to Kiyomizu-dera (p121), with its unmistakable pagoda rising against the skyline. Before you enter the main complex of Kiyomizu-dera, we recommend that you pay ¥100 to descend into the Tainai-meguri: the entrance is just to the left of the main temple entrance.

After touring Kiyomizu-dera, exit down Kiyomizu-michi, the busy approach to the temple. Walk down the hill for about 200m until you reach a four-way intersection; go right here down the stone-paved steps. This is Sannen-zaka, a charming street lined with old wooden houses, traditional shops and restaurants. There are many tea houses and cafes along this stretch.

Halfway down Sannen-zaka, the road curves to the left. Follow it a short distance, then go right down a flight of steps into Ninen-zaka, another quaint street lined with historic houses, shops and tea houses. At the end of Ninen-zaka, zigzag left (at the vending machines), then right (just past the car park), and continue north. Very soon, on your left, you'll come to the entrance to Ishibei-kōji – perhaps the most beautiful street in Kyoto, though it's actually a cobbled alley lined on both sides with elegant, traditional Japanese inns and restaurants. Take a detour to explore this, then retrace your steps and continue north, passing almost immediately the entrance to Kōdai-ji (p125) on the right up a long flight of stairs.

SOUTHERN HIGASHIYAMA WALKING TOUR

0 — 200 m
0 — 0.1 miles

Sanjō-dōri
Higashiyama
M END
Shōren-in
Chion-in
GION
Yasaka-jinja
Shijō-dōri
Maruyama-kōen
Ishibei-kōji
Kōdai-ji
Yasaka-dōri
Kiyomizu-michi
Gojō-zaka Bus Stop
START
Gojō-zaka
Chawan-zaka
Tainai-meguri
Kiyomizu-dera
Hanami-kōji
Higashiōji-dōri
Higashiōji-dōri
Ninen-zaka
Sannen-zaka

RACHEL LEWIS

Paper cranes at Fushimi-Inari Taisha (p129)

After Kōdai-ji continue north to the T-intersection; turn right at this junction and then take a quick left. You'll cross the wide pedestrian arcade and then descend into Maruyama-kōen (p122), a pleasant park in which to take a rest. In the centre of the park, you'll see the giant Gion *shidare-zakura,* Kyoto's most famous cherry tree. Opposite the tree there's a bridge that leads across a carp pond to the lovely upper reaches of the park – this is a good place for a picnic, but you'll have to have brought something with you to eat, since the offerings in the park are limited to junk food.

From the park, you can head west (downhill) into the grounds of Yasaka-jinja (p122) and descend from the shrine to Shijō-dōri and Gion and make your way home (it's about a 400m walk to Keihan Shijō Station from here). However, if you've got the energy, it's best to return back through the park and head north to tour the grounds of the impressive Chion-in (p123). From here

it's a quick walk to Shōren-in (p125), which is famous for its enormous camphor trees out the front. From Shōren-in descend to Sanjō-dōri (you'll see the giant shrine gate of Heian-jingū in the distance). By going left on Sanjō-dōri, you'll soon come to the Jingū-michi bus stop, where you can catch bus 5 or 100 to Kyoto Station, or continue west a little further on Sanjō-dōri and you'll soon come to the Higashiyama Station on the Tōzai line.

FESTIVALS & EVENTS

There are hundreds of festivals in Kyoto throughout the year. Listings can be found in the *Kyoto Visitor's Guide* or *Kansai Time Out.* The following are some of the major and most spectacular festivals. These attract hordes of spectators from out of town, so book accommodation well in advance.

Gion Matsuri Perhaps the most renowned of all Japanese festivals, this one reaches a climax on 17 July with a parade of more than 30 floats depicting ancient themes and decked out in incredible finery. On the three evenings preceding the main day, people gather on Shijō-dōri, many dressed in beautiful *yukata* (light summer kimonos), to look at the floats and carouse from one street stall to the next.

Daimon-ji Gozan Okuribi This festival, commonly known as Daimon-ji Yaki, is performed to bid farewell to the souls of ancestors on 16 August. Enormous fires are lit on five mountains in the form of Chinese characters or other shapes. The largest fire is burned on Daimonji-yama, just above Ginkaku-ji (p126), in northern Higashiyama. The fires start at 8pm and it is best to watch from the banks of the Kamo-gawa or pay for a rooftop view from a hotel.

Kurama-no-hi Matsuri (**Kurama Fire Festival**) In perhaps Kyoto's most dramatic festival, huge flaming torches are carried through the streets of Kurama by men in loincloths on 22 October (the same day as the Jidai Matsuri).

SLEEPING

The most convenient areas in which to be based, in terms of easy access to shopping, dining and sightseeing attractions, are downtown Kyoto and the Higashiyama area. The Kyoto Station area is also a good place to be based, with excellent access to transport and plenty of shops and restaurants about. Transport information in the following listings is from Kyoto Station unless otherwise noted.

KYOTO STATION AREA
BUDGET & MIDRANGE

Tour Club (Map p115; ☎ 353-6968; www .kyotojp.com; 362 Momiji-chō, Higashinakasuji Shōmen-sagaru, Shimogyō-ku; dm ¥2450, d ¥6980-7770, tr ¥8880-9720; ☒ ☐ ☞ ; ☒ Kyoto Station Karasuma central gate) Run by a charming and informative young couple, this clean, well-maintained guest house is a favourite of many foreign visitors. Facilities include bicycle rentals, laundry and free tea and coffee. Most private rooms have a bathroom, and there is a spacious quad room for families. It's a 10-minute walk from

Gion Matsuri (p131)

FRANK CARTE

Kyoto Station; turn north off Shichijō-dōri at the Second House coffee shop (looks like a bank) and keep an eye out for the English sign.

Budget Inn (Map p115; ☎ 344-1510; www budgetinnjp.com; 295 Aburanokōji-chō, Shichijō sagaru, Shimogyō-ku; dm/tr/q/5-person r ¥2500/ 10,980/12,980/14,980; ✗ 💻 🛜 ; 🚇 Kyoto Station, Karasuma central gate) This well-run guest house is an excellent choice. It's got two dorm rooms and six Japanese-style private rooms, all of which are clean and well maintained. All rooms have their own bathroom, and there is a spacious quad room which is good for families. The staff here is very helpful and friendly, and laundry and bicycle rental are available. It's a seven-minute walk from Kyoto Station; from the station, walk west on Shiokōji-dōri, turn north one street before Horikawa and look for the English-language sign out front.

Matsubaya (Map p115; ☎ 351-3727; www.matsubayainn.com; Nishi-iru Higashinotoin, Kamijizuyamachi-dōri, Shimogyō-ku; r per person from ¥4200; 💻 ; 🚇 Kyoto Station, Karasuma central gate) A short walk from Kyoto Station, this newly renovated ryokan has clean, well-kept rooms and a management that is used to foreign guests. Some rooms on the 1st floor look out on small gardens. There are internet terminals and local area network (LAN) cable-access points in rooms. Average room rates here run about ¥6500 per person.

Ryokan Shimizu (Map p115; ☎ 371-5538; www.kyoto-shimizu.net; 644 Kagiya-chō, Shichijō-dōri, Wakamiya agaru, Shimogyō-ku; r per person from ¥5250; ✗ 💻 ; 🚇 Kyoto Station, Karasuma central gate) A short walk north of Kyoto Station, this fine ryokan is quickly building a loyal following of foreign guests, and for good reason: it's clean, well run and friendly. Rooms are standard ryokan style with one difference: all have bathrooms.

TOP END

Hotel Granvia Kyoto (Map p115; ☎ 344-8888; www.granvia-kyoto.co.jp/e/index.html; Shiokōji sagaru, Karasuma-dōri, Shimogyō-ku; d/tw from ¥23,100/25,410; ✗ 💻 🚇 ; 🚇 Kyoto Station, Karasuma central gate) Imagine stepping straight out of bed and into the *shinkansen*. This is almost possible when you stay at the Granvia, an excellent hotel located directly above Kyoto Station. Rooms are clean, spacious and well appointed, with deep bathtubs. This is a very professional operation with some good on-site restaurants, some of which have good views over the city. There is LAN cable internet in rooms.

DOWNTOWN KYOTO
MIDRANGE & TOP END

Hotel Unizo (Map p116; ☎ 241-3351; www .sun-hotel.co.jp/ky_index.htm, in Japanese; Kawaramachi-dōri-Sanjō sagaru, Nakagyō-ku; s/d/tw from ¥7350/13,650/12,810; ✗ ; 🚌 bus 5 to Kawaramachi-Sanjō stop) They don't get more central than this downtown business hotel: it's smack-dab in the middle of Kyoto's nightlife, shopping and dining district and you can walk to hundreds of restaurants and shops within five minutes.

Kyoto Hotel Ōkura (Map p116; ☎ 211-5111; fax 254-2529; www.kyotohotel.co.jp/khokura/ english/index.html; Kawaramachi-dōri, Oike, Nakagyō-ku; s/d/tw from ¥21,945/31,185/31,185; ✗ 💻 ; 🚇 Tōzai subway line to Shiyakusho-mae Station, exit 3) This towering hotel in the centre of town has some of the best views in the city. Rooms here are clean, spacious and comfortable. There are several excellent on-site restaurants and bars, along with hundreds within easy walking distance of the hotel. There is LAN cable internet in rooms.

Hiiragiya (Map p116; ☎ 221-1136; fax 221-139; www.hiiragiya.co.jp/en; Anekōji-agaru,

GREG ELMS

Room at Tawaraya

▶ TAWARAYA

This ryokan has been operating for over three centuries and is classed as one of the finest places to stay in the world. Stepping inside is like entering another world and you just might not want to leave. The ryokan has an intimate, private feeling and all rooms have bathrooms. The gardens are sublime and the cosy study is the perfect place to linger with a book. A night here is sure to be memorable.

Things you need to know: Map p116; ☎ 211-5566; fax 221-2204; Fuyachō-Oike sagaru, Nakagyō-ku; r per person with 2 meals ¥42,263-84,525; ✕ ▣ ; ⌖ Tōzai & Karasuma subway lines to Karasuma-Oike Station, exit 3

Fuya-chō, Nakagyō-ku; r per person with 2 meals ¥30,000-60,000; ✕ ▣ ; ⌖ Tōzai & Karasuma subway lines to Karasuma-Oike Station, exit 3) This classic ryokan is favoured by celebrities from around the world. From the decorations to the service to the food, everything at the Hiiragiya is the best available. Rooms in the old wing have great old-Japan style, while those in the new wing are pristine and comfortable. It's centrally located downtown within easy walk of two subway stations and lots of good restaurants. There is LAN cable internet access in the new wing.

SOUTHERN HIGASHIYAMA
MIDRANGE & TOP END

Ryokan Uemura (Map p120; ☎ /fax 561-0377; Ishibe-kōji, Shimogawara, Higashiyama-ku; r with breakfast per person ¥9000; ✕ ; ⌖ bus 206 to Yasui stop) This beautiful little ryokan is at ease with foreign guests. It's on a quaint cobblestone alley, just down the hill from Kōdai-ji. Rates include breakfast and there is a 10pm curfew. Book well in advance, as there are only three rooms. Note that the manager prefers booking by fax and asks that cancellations also be made by fax (with so few rooms, it can be costly when bookings are broken without notice).

Ryokan Motonago (Map p120; ☎ 561-2087; fax 561-2655; www.motonago.com; 511 Washio-chō, Kōdaiji-michi, Higashiyama-ku; r per person with 2 meals from ¥17,850; ✕ ▣ ; ⌖ bus 206 to Gion stop) This ryokan may have the best location of any ryokan in the city, right on Nene-no-Michi in the heart of the Higashiyama sightseeing district. It's got traditional decor, friendly service, nice bathtubs and a few small Japanese gardens.

Hyatt Regency Kyoto (Map p120; ☎ 541-1234; fax 541-2203; www.kyoto.regency.hyatt.com; 644-2 Sanjūsangendō-mawari, Higashiyama-ku; r ¥22,000-46,000; ✕ ▣ ☎ ; ⌖ 5min walk from Keihan Shichijō Station) The new Hyatt Regency is an excellent, stylish, foreigner-friendly hotel at the southern end of Kyoto's southern Higashiyama sightseeing district. Many travellers consider this the best hotel in Kyoto, and almost all mention the great restaurants and bar and the highly professional staff. The stylish rooms and bathrooms have lots of neat touches.

NORTHERN HIGASHIYAMA

MIDRANGE & TOP END

Kyoto Traveller's Inn (Map p124; ☎ 771-0225; fax 771-0226; www.k-travelersinn.com/english/index.php; 91 Enshō-ji-chō, Okazaki, Sakyō-ku; s/tw from ¥5775/10,500; ✕ 💻 ; 🚌 bus 5 to Kyōto Kaikan Bijyutsukan-mae stop) This small business hotel is very close to Heian-jingū. It offers Western- and Japanese-style rooms. The restaurant on the 1st floor is open till 10pm. It's good value for the price and the location is dynamite for exploring the Higashiyama area.

Three Sisters Inn Main Building (Rakutō-sō Honkan; Map p124; ☎ 761-6336; fax 761-6338; 18 Higashifukunokawa-chō, Okazaki, Sakyō-ku; s/d/tr ¥10,280/15,014/22,521; ✕ ; 🚌 bus 5, Dōbutsuen-mae stop) This is a good foreigner-friendly ryokan with a loyal following of foreign guests. It's well situated in Okazaki for exploring the Higashiyama area.

Three Sisters Inn Annex (Rakutō-so Bekkan; Map p124; ☎ 761-6333; fax 761-6338; 89 Irie-chō, Okazaki, Sakyō-ku; s/d/tr ¥10,810/18,170/23,805, s/d without bathroom ¥5635/11,270; ✕ 💻 📶 ; 🚌 bus 5, Dōbutsuen-mae stop) In the same neighbourhood, this is run by another one of the three eponymous sisters, and is a good choice. The features are similar to the main building, but it's somewhat more intimate and the garden walkway adds to the atmosphere.

Westin Miyako Hotel (Map p124; ☎ 771-7111; fax 751-2490; www.westinmiyako-kyoto.com/english/index.html; Keage, Sanjō-dōri, Higashiyama-ku; s/d/tw from ¥26,600/33,500/33,500, Japanese-style r from ¥53,000; ✕ 💻 📶 🅿 ; 🚇 Tōzai subway line to Keage Station, exit 2) This sprawling complex is perched atop the Higashiyama area, making it one of the best locations for sightseeing in Kyoto. Rooms are clean, well maintained and tastefully decorated, and the staff is at home with foreign guests. Rooms on the north side have great views over the city to the Kitayama mountains. There is a fitness centre, as well as a private garden and walking trail. Rooms have LAN cable internet and wi-fi is in the lobby.

JOHN BANAGAN

Alleyway in Gion (p122)

Bowl of *rāmen* (egg noodles)   OLIVER STREW

EATING
KYOTO STATION AREA

The new Kyoto Station building is chock-a-block with restaurants, and if you find yourself anywhere near the station around mealtime, this is probably your best bet in terms of variety and price. For a quick cuppa while waiting for a train try Café du Monde (Map p115) on the 2nd floor overlooking the central atrium.

For more substantial meals there are several food courts scattered about. The best of these can be found on the 11th floor on the west side of the building: the Cube food court and Isetan department store's Eat Paradise food court. In Eat Paradise, we like Tonkatsu Wako for *tonkatsu* (deep-fried breaded pork cutlet), Tenichi for sublime tempura, and Wakuden for approachable *kaiseki* (Japanese haute cuisine). To get to these food courts, take the west escalators from the main concourse all the way up to the 11th floor and look for the Cube on your left and Eat Paradise straight in front of you.

Other options in the station include Kyoto Rāmen Koji, a collection of seven *rāmen* (egg noodle) restaurants on the 10th floor (underneath the Cube). Buy tickets for *rāmen* from the machines which don't have English but have pictures on the buttons.

DOWNTOWN KYOTO
BUDGET

Musashi Sushi (Map p116; ☎ 222-0634; Kawaramachi-dōri, Sanjō agaru, Nakagyō-ku; all plates ¥130; ⏰ 11am-10pm) This is the place to go to try *kaiten-sushi* (conveyor-belt sushi). Sure, it's not the best sushi in the world, but it's cheap, easy and fun. Look for the mini sushi conveyor belt in the window. It's just outside the entrance to the Sanjō covered arcade.

Café Independants (Map p116; ☎ 255-4312; B1F 1928 Bldg, Sanjō Gokomachi kado, Nakagyō-ku; salads/sandwiches from ¥400/800; ⏰ 11.30am-midnight) Located beneath a gallery, the cool subterranean cafe offers a range of light meals and good cafe drinks in a bohemian atmosphere. A lot of the food offerings are laid out on display for you to choose from – with the emphasis on healthy sandwiches and salads. Take the stairs on your left before the gallery.

Misoka-an Kawamichi-ya (Map p116; ☎ 221-2525; Sanjō agaru, Fuyachō-dōri, Nakagyō-ku; dishes ¥700-4000; ✪ 11am-8pm, closed Thu) This is the place to head for a taste of some of Kyoto's best *soba* (buckwheat noodles) in traditional surroundings. They've been handmaking noodles here for 300 years. Try a simple bowl of *nishin soba* (*soba* topped with fish), or the more elaborate *nabe* dishes (cooked in a special cast-iron pot). Look for the *noren* (Japanese curtains) and the traditional Japanese exterior. English menu.

Biotei (Map p116; ☎ 255-0086; 2F M&I Bldg, 28 Umetada-chō, Higashinotōin Nishi iru, Sanjō-dōri, Nakagyō-ku; lunch from ¥750; ✪ 11.30am-2pm & 5-8.30pm Tue-Fri, dinner Sat, closed Sun, Mon & holidays; **V**) Located diagonally across from the Nakagyō post office, this is a favourite of Kyoto vegetarians. Best for lunch, it serves a daily set of Japanese vegetarian food (the occasional bit of meat is offered as an option, but you'll be asked your preference). It's up the metal spiral steps. English menu.

Honke Tagoto (Map p116; ☎ 221-3030; 12 Ishibashi-chō, Kawaramachi Nishi iru, Sanjō-dōri, Nakagyō-ku; noodle dishes from ¥840; ✪ 11am-9pm) One of Kyoto's oldest and most revered *soba* restaurants makes a good break for those who have overdosed on *rāmen*. It's in the Sanjō covered arcade and you can see inside to the tables. English menu.

Kerala (Map p116; ☎ 251-0141; 2F KUS Bldg, Sanjō agaru, Kawaramachi, Nakagyō-ku; lunch/dinner from ¥850/2500; ✪ 11.30am-2pm & 5-9pm, closed irregularly) This is where we go for reliable Indian lunch sets – great thalis that include two curries, good naan bread,

some rice, a small salad etc. Dinners are à la carte and run closer to ¥2500 per person. It's on the 2nd floor; look for the display of food in the glass case on street level. English menu.

Kane-yo (Map p116; ☎ 221-0669; Rokkaku, Shinkyōgoku, Nakagyō-ku; unagi over rice from ¥950; ✪ 11.30am-9pm) This is a good place to try *unagi* (eel). You can sit downstairs with a nice view of the waterfall or upstairs on the tatami. The *kane-yo donburi* (eel over rice; ¥950) set is great value; it's served until 3pm. Look for the barrels of live eels outside and a wooden facade. English menu.

Le Bouchon (Map p116; ☎ 211-5220; 71-1 Enoki-chō, NIjō sagaru, Teramachi-dōri, Nakagyō-ku; lunch/dinner from ¥980/2500; ✪ 11.30am-2.30pm & 5.30-9.30pm, closed Thu) This reliable French place serves good lunch and dinner sets and has a pleasant, casual atmosphere. The kitchen does very good work with fish, salads and desserts. The owner speaks English and French as well as Japanese, and will make you feel right at home.

MIDRANGE & TOP END

Merry Island Café (Map p116; ☎ 213-0214; Oike agaru, Kiyamachi-dōri, Nakagyō-ku; weekend lunch from ¥1000; ✪ 2pm-midnight Tue-Fri, 11.30am-midnight Sat, Sun & holidays, closed Mon) This popular lunch/dinner restaurant strives to create the atmosphere of a tropical resort. The menu is *mukokuseki* (without nationality) and most of what is on offer is pretty tasty. It does a good risotto and occasionally has a nice piece of Japanese steak. English menu.

Ganko Zushi (Map p116; ☎ 255-1128; 101 Nakajima-chō, Kawaramachi Higashi iru, Sanjō-dōri, Nakagyō-ku; lunch/dinner ¥1000/3000; ✪ 11am-11pm) Near Sanjō-ōhashi bridge, this is a good place for sushi or just about anything else. There are plenty of sets to choose from, but we recommend ordering sushi à la carte. There's a full English menu, the kitchen is fast and the staff is used to foreigners. Look for the large display of plastic food models in the window.

Yoshikawa (Map p116; ☎ 221-5544; Oike sagaru, Tominokōji, Nakagyō-ku; lunch ¥3000-25,000, dinner ¥8000-25,000; ⊗ 11am-2pm & 5-8.30pm) This is the place to go for delectable tempura. It offers table seating, but it's much more interesting to sit and eat around the small counter and observe the chefs at work. It's near Oike-dōri in a fine traditional Japanese-style building. Reservation required for tatami room; counter and table seating unavailable on Sunday.

Mishima-tei (Map p116; ☎ 221-0003; 405 Sakurano-chō, Sanjō sagaru, Teramachi-dōri, Nakagyō-ku; sukiyaki lunch ¥8663-26,250, dinner ¥12,705-26,250, special until 3pm lunch ¥3350; ⊗ 11.30am-10pm, closed Wed) In the Sanjō covered arcade, this is an inexpensive place to sample sukiyaki: there is even a discount for foreign travellers! English menu; last orders 9pm.

SOUTHERN HIGASHIYAMA
BUDGET
Asuka (Map p120; ☎ 751-9809; 144 Nishi-machi, Jingū-michi Nishi iru, Sanjō-dōri, Higashiyama-ku; meals from ¥850; ⊗ 11am-10pm, closed Mon) With a staff of old Kyoto *mama-sans* (female managers) at home with foreign customers, this is a great place for a cheap lunch or dinner while sightseeing in the Higashiyama area. The tempura *moriawase* (assorted tempura set) is a big pile of tempura for only ¥1000. Look for the red lantern and the pictures of the set meals. English menu.

Hisago (Map p120; ☎ 561-2109; 484 Shimokawara-chō, Higashiyama-ku; ⊗ 11.30am-7.30pm, closed Mon) If you need a quick meal while in the main southern Higashiyama sightseeing district, this simple noodle and rice restaurant is a good bet. It's

within easy walking distance of Kiyomizu-dera and Maruyama-kōen. *Oyako-donbur* (chicken and egg over rice; ¥980) is the speciality of the house. There is no English sign; look for the traditional front and the small collection of food models on display. English menu.

MIDRANGE & TOP END
Shibazaki (Map p120; ☎ 525-3600; 4-190 3 Kiyomizu, Higashiyama-ku; soba from ¥1000 ⊗ 11am-9pm, closed Tue) For excellent *soba* noodles and well-presented tempura sets (among other things) in the area o Kiyomizu-dera, try this comfortable and spacious restaurant. After your meal, head upstairs to check out the sublime collection of Japanese lacquerware – it's the best we've seen anywhere. There's an English menu. Look for the low stone wall and the *noren* hanging in the entryway.

Aunbo (Map p120; ☎ 525-2900; Shimokawara chō, Yasaka Torii mae sagaru, Higashiyama-ku lunch from ¥2625, lunch course ¥6615, dinner course ¥6615-11,025; ⊗ noon-2pm & 5.30-10pm closed Wed) Aunbo serves elegant, creative Japanese cooking in traditional Japanese surroundings. Dishes include sashimi tempura-battered offerings and creative vegetable dishes. There's a small English sign and an English menu.

Ōzawa (Map p120; ☎ 561-2052; Minami gawa Gion Shirakawa Nawate Higashi iru, Higashiyama ku; meals from ¥3900; ⊗ 5-10pm, closed Thu, lunch available on advance request) On a beautifu street in Gion, this restaurant offers good tempura in traditional Japanese surroundings. English menu. Last orders 9pm.

NORTHERN HIGASHIYAMA
BUDGET
Hinode Udon (Map p124; ☎ 751-9251; 3 Kitanobō-chō, Nanzenji, Sakyō-ku; noodle dishe from ¥400; ⊗ 11am-6pm, closed Sun) Filling noodle and rice dishes are served at thi

OLIVER STREWE
Diners at a Kyoto *izakaya* (pub-eatery)

pleasant little shop with an English menu. Plain udon (thick white noodles) here is only ¥400, but we recommend you spring for the *nabeyaki udon* (pot-baked udon in broth) for ¥800. This is a good spot for lunch when temple-hopping near Ginkaku-ji or Nanzen-ji.

Karako (Map p124; ☎ 752-8234; 12-3 Tokusei-chō, Okazaki, Sakyō-ku; rāmen from ¥650; 🕑 11.30am-2pm & 6pm-2am, closed Tue) This is our favourite *rāmen* restaurant in Kyoto. While it's not much on atmosphere, Karako has excellent *rāmen* – the soup is thick and rich and the *chāshū* (pork slices) melt in your mouth. We recommend the *kotteri* (thick soup) *rāmen*. Look for the red lantern outside.

Goya (Map p124; ☎ 752-1158; 114-6 Nishida-chō, Jōdo-ji, Sakyō-ku; 🕑 noon-5pm & 6pm-midnight, closed Wed) We love this Okinawan-style restaurant for its tasty food, stylish interior and comfortable upstairs seating. It's the perfect place for lunch while exploring northern Higashiyama and it's just a short walk from Ginkaku-ji. There's an English sign and menu.

MIDRANGE

Omen (Map p124; ☎ 771-8994; 74 Jōdo-ji Ishibashi-cho, Sakyō-ku; noodles from ¥1050; 🕑 11am-10pm, closed Thu) This noodle shop is named after the thick, white noodles served in a hot broth with a selection of seven fresh vegetables. Just say *'omen'* and you'll be given your choice of hot or cold noodles, a bowl of soup to dip them in and a plate of vegetables (you put these into the soup along with some sesame seeds). It's about five minutes' walk from Ginkaku-ji in a traditional Japanese house with a lantern outside. English menu.

ARASHIYAMA & SAGANO AREA
BUDGET

Komichi (Map pp112-13; ☎ 872-5313; 23 Ōjōin-chō, Nison-in Monzen, Ukyō-ku, Saga; matcha ¥600; 🕑 10am-5pm, closed Wed) This friendly little tea house is perfectly located along the Arashiyama tourist trail. In addition to hot and cold tea/coffee drinks, it serves *uji kintoki* (sweet *matcha* over shaved ice, sweetened milk and sweet beans – sort of a Japanese Italian ice) in summer and a variety of light noodle dishes year-round. The picture menu helps with ordering. The sign is green and black on a white background.

Yoshida-ya (Map pp112-13; ☎ 861-0213; 20-24 Tsukurimichi-chō, Saga Tenryū-ji, Ukyō-ku; lunch from ¥800; 🕙 10am-6pm, closed Wed) This quaint and friendly little *teishoku-ya* (set-meal restaurant) is the perfect place to grab a simple lunch while in Arashiyama. All the standard *teishoku* favourites are on offer, including things like *oyako-donburi* for ¥850. You can also cool off here with a refreshing *uji kintoki* (¥650). It's the first place south of the station and it's got a rustic front.

ENTERTAINMENT
GEISHA DANCES

Annually in autumn and spring, *geiko* (geisha) and their *maiko* apprentices from Kyoto's five geisha districts dress elaborately to perform traditional dances in praise of the seasons. Cheap tickets cost about ¥1650 (unreserved on tatami mats), better seats cost ¥3000 to ¥3800, and spending an extra ¥500 includes participation in a quick tea ceremony. We highly recommend seeing one of these dances if you are in town when they are being held. Dates and times vary, so check with the TIC.

Gion Odori (祇園をどり; ☎ 561-0224; Higashiyama-ku-Gion; admission/with tea ¥3500/4000; 🕙 shows 1pm & 3.30pm) Held at Gion Kaikan Theatre (Map p120) near Yasaka-jinja; 1 to 10 November.

Kamogawa Odori (鴨川をどり; ☎ 221-2025; Ponto-chō-Sanjō sagaru; normal/special seat/special seat with tea ¥2000/3800/4300; 🕙 shows 12.30pm, 2.20pm & 4.10pm) Held at Ponto-chō Kaburen-jō Theatre (Map p116), Ponto-chō; 1 to 24 May.

Kitano Odori (北野をどり; ☎ 461-0148; Imadegawa-dōri-Nishihonmatsu nishi iru; admission/with tea ¥3800/4300; 🕙 shows 1pm & 3pm) At Kamishichiken Kaburen-jō Theatre (Map pp112-13), east of Kitano-Tenman-gū; 15 to 25 April.

Kyō Odori (京をどり; ☎ 561-1151; Kawabata-dōri-Shijō sagaru; admission/with tea ¥3800/4300; 🕙 shows 12.30pm, 2.30pm & 4.30pm) Held at Miyagawa-chō Kaburen-jō Theatre (Map p120), east of the

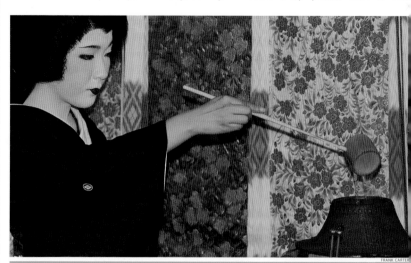

Geiko (geisha) performing the tea ceremony

FRANK CARTER

Kamo-gawa between Shijō-dōri and Gojō-dōri; from the first to the third Sunday in April.

Miyako Odori (都をどり; ☎ 561-1115; Higashiyama-ku-Gion-chō South; seat reserved/nonreserved/reserved with tea ¥3800/1900/4300; ☺ shows 12.30pm, 2pm, 3.30pm & 4.50pm) At Gion Kōbu Kaburen-jō Theatre (Map p120), Gion Corner; throughout April.

KABUKI
Minami-za Theatre (Map p120; ☎ 561-0160; Shijō-Ōhashi; performances ¥4200-12,600; ☺ irregular) In Gion, this is the oldest kabuki (stylised Japanese theatre) venue in Japan. The major event of the year is the Kao-mise Festival (1 to 26 December), which features Japan's finest kabuki actors. Other performances take place on an irregular basis. Those interested should check with the TIC. The most likely months for performances are May, June and September.

SHOPPING
The heart of Kyoto's shopping district is around the intersection of Shijō-dōri and Kawaramachi-dōri. The blocks to the north and west of here are packed with stores selling both traditional and modern goods. Kyoto's largest department stores (Hankyū, Takashimaya, Daimaru and Fujii Daimaru) are grouped together in this area.

Some of the best shopping and people-watching can be had along Kyoto's three downtown shopping arcades: Shinkyōgoku shopping arcade, Teramachi shopping arcade and Nishiki Market. Teramachi and Shinkyōgoku run parallel to each other in the heart of downtown. The former has a mix of tasteful and tacky shops; the latter specialises in tacky stuff for the hoards of schoolkids who visit Kyoto every year. Nishiki branches off Shinkyōgoku to the west, about 100m north of Shijō-dōri.

ELECTRONICS & CAMERAS
Bic Camera (Map p115; ☎ 353-1111; 927 Higashi Shiokōji-chō, Shimogyō-ku; ☺ 10am-9pm) This vast new electronics/camera shop is directly connected to Kyoto Station via the Nishinotōin gate; otherwise, it's accessed by leaving the north (Karasuma) gate and walking west. You will be amazed by the sheer amount of goods it has on display. Just be sure that an English operating manual is available. For computer parts, keep in mind that not all items on offer will work with English operating systems.

FOOD & KITCHEN UTENSILS
Nishiki Market (Map p116), in the centre of town, is Kyoto's most fascinating food market (see p115).

If you do choose to visit, be sure to stop into the knife shop **Aritsugu** (Map p116; ☎ 221-1091; 219 Kajiya-chō, Gokōmachi nishi iru, Nishikikōji-dōri, Nakagyō-ku; ☺ 9am-5.30pm) near the eastern end of the market. Here you can find some of the best kitchen knives available in the world, as well as a variety of other kitchenware.

For an even more impressive display of food, check the basements of any of the big department stores on Shijō-dōri (perhaps Daimaru has the largest selection). It's difficult to believe the variety of food on display, or some of the prices (check out the ¥10,000 melons or the Kōbe beef, for example).

JAPANESE ARTS & CRAFTS
North of the city hall, Teramachi-dōri (Map p116), between Oike-dōri and Marutamachi-dōri, has a number of classic old Kyoto shops, and this area is pleasant for strolling around and window-shopping.

Kamiji Kakimoto (Map p116; ☎ 211-3481; 54 Tokiwagi-chō, Nijō agaru, Teramachi, Nakagyō-ku; ☺ 9am-6pm Mon-Sat, 10am-5pm Sun &

holidays) This place sells a good selection of *washi* (Japanese paper). It's not as good as Morita Washi (below), but it's great for things such as *washi* computer paper.

Morita Washi (Map p116; ☎ 341-1419; 1F Kajioha Bldg, 298 Ōgisakaya-chō, Bukkō-ji agaru, Higashinotōin-dōri, Shimogyō-ku; ☒ 9.30am-5.30pm, to 4.30pm Sat, closed Sun & holidays) Not far from Shijo-Karasuma, it sells a fabulous variety of handmade *washi* for reasonable prices.

Rakushikan (Map p116; ☎ 221-1070; Takoyakushi-dōri Takakura nishi iru, Nakagyō-ku; ☒ 10.30am-6pm, closed Mon) This downtown Kyoto paper specialist carries an incredible variety of *washi* and other paper products in its spacious new store. You can also try your hand at making your own *washi* here (ask at the counter for details).

Ukiyo-e (wood-block prints)
FRANK CARTER

Kyūkyo-dō (Map p116; ☎ 231-0510; 52◼ Shimohonnōjimae-chō, Aneyakōji agaru, Teramachi◼ Nakagyō-ku; ☒ 10am-6pm Mon-Sat, closed Sun & 1-3 Jan) This old shop in the Teramachi cov◼ ered arcade sells a selection of incense◼ *shodō* (calligraphy) goods, tea-ceremon◼ supplies and *washi*. Prices are on the high◼ side but the quality is good.

Ippo-dō (Map p116; ☎ 211-3421; Teramachi◼ dōri, Nijō, Nakagyō-ku; ☒ 9am-7pm Mon-Sat, t◼ 6pm Sun & holidays, cafe 11am-5pm) This is an◼ old-fashioned tea shop selling all sorts o◼ Japanese tea. You can ask to sample the◼ tea before buying.

Kyoto Handicraft Center (Map p124◼ ☎ 761-5080; 21 Entomi-chō, Shōgoin, Sakyō-ku◼ ☒ 10am-6pm, closed 1-3 Jan) Just north o◼ the Heian-jingū, this is a huge coopera◼ tive that sells, demonstrates and exhibit◼ crafts (*ukiyo-e* – wood-block prints – and◼ *yukata* are a good buy here). It's the bes◼ spot in town for buying Japanese souve◼ nirs and is highly recommended.

GETTING THERE & AWAY
AIR
Kyoto is served by Osaka Itami aAirport◼ which principally handles domestic traffic◼ and the new Kansai International Airpor◼ (KIX), which principally handles interna◼ tional flights. There are frequent flight◼ between Tokyo and Itami (¥22,600, 6◼ minutes), but unless you're very lucky◼ with airport connections you'll probably◼ find it as quick and more convenient t◼ take the *shinkansen*.

TRAIN
SHINKANSEN (TOKYO, OSAKA, NAGOYA & HAKATA)
Kyoto is on the Tōkaidō-San-yō *shinkanse◼ line, which runs between Tokyo and◼ northern Kyūshū, with stops at place◼ such as Nagoya, Osaka, Kōbe, Hime◼ and Hiroshima en route. Fares and time◼

or Hikari (the second-fastest type of *hinkansen*) between Kyoto and the following cities are as follows: Tokyo (¥13,220, two hours 43 minutes); Nagoya (¥5440, 40 minutes); Osaka (¥2730, 15 minutes); Hiroshima (¥9540, 1½ hours); and Hakata (¥15,210, three hours 22 minutes). The *hinkansen* operates to/from Kyoto Station Kyoto's main train station).

NARA

The private Kintetsu line (sometimes written in English as the Kinki Nippon railway) links Kyoto (Kintetsu Kyoto Station, on the south side of the main Kyoto Station building) and Nara (Kintetsu Nara Station). There are fast direct *tokkyū* (limited express; ¥1110, 33 minutes) and ordinary express trains (¥610, 40 minutes), which may require a change at Saidai-ji.

The JR Nara line also connects Kyoto Station with JR Nara Station (express, ¥690, 41 minutes), and this is a great option for Japan Rail Pass holders.

OSAKA

The fastest train other than the *shinkansen* between Kyoto Station and Osaka is the JR *shinkaisoku* (special rapid train), which takes 29 minutes (¥540). In Osaka, the train stops at both Shin-Osaka and Osaka stations.

There is also the cheaper private Hankyū line, which runs between Hankyū Kawaramachi, Karasuma and Ōmiya Stations in Kyoto and Hankyū Umeda Station in Osaka (*tokkyū* or limited express Umeda–Kawaramachi, ¥390, 40 minutes).

Alternatively, you can take the Keihan main line between Demachiyanagi, Sanjō, Shijō or Shichijō Stations in Kyoto and Keihan Yodoyabashi Station in Osaka (*tokkyū* to/from Sanjō ¥400, 51 minutes).

TOKYO

The *shinkansen* line has the fastest and most frequent rail links. The journey can also be undertaken by a series of regular JR express trains, but keep in mind that it takes around eight hours and involves at least two (often three or four) changes along the way. The fare is ¥7980. Get the staff at the ticket counter to write down the exact details of each transfer for you when you buy your ticket.

GETTING AROUND
TO/FROM THE AIRPORT
OSAKA ITAMI AIRPORT
大阪伊丹空港

There are frequent limousine buses between Osaka Itami Airport (Map p99) and Kyoto Station (the Kyoto Station airport bus stop is opposite the south side of the station, in front of Avanti department store). Buses also run between the airport and various hotels around town, but on a less regular basis (check with your hotel). The journey should take around 55 minutes and the cost is ¥1280. Be sure to allow extra time in case of traffic.

At Itami, the stand for these buses is outside the arrivals hall; buy your tickets from the machines and ask one of the attendants which stand is for Kyoto (hint: you've got a better chance of getting a seat if you board at the South Terminal).

KANSAI INTERNATIONAL AIRPORT (KIX) 関西国際空港

The fastest, most convenient way to travel between KIX (Map p99) and Kyoto is on the special Haruka airport express, which makes the trip in about 78 minutes. Most seats are reserved (¥3290) but there are usually two cars on each train with unreserved seats (¥2980).

If you have time to spare, you can save some money by taking the *kankū kaisoku* (Kansai airport express) between the airport and Osaka Station and taking a regular *shinkaisoku* to/from Kyoto. The total journey by this method takes about 92 minutes with good connections and costs ¥1830, making it the cheapest option.

It's also possible to travel by limousine bus between Kyoto and KIX (¥2300, about 105 minutes). In Kyoto, the bus departs from the same place as the Itami-bound bus (see p143).

BICYCLE

Kyoto is a great city to explore on a bicycle; with the exception of outlying areas it's mostly flat and there is a bike path running the length of the Kamo-gawa.

Unfortunately, Kyoto must rank near the top in having the world's worst public facilities for bike parking and the city regularly impounds bikes parked outside of regulation bike-parking areas. If your bike does disappear, check for a poster in the vicinity (in both Japanese and English) indicating the time of seizure and the inconvenient place you'll have to go to pay a ¥2000 fine and retrieve your bike.

There are two bicycle-parking lots in town that are convenient for tourists: one in front of Kyoto Station (Map p115) and another on Kiyamachi-dōri, halfway between Sanjō-dōri and Shijō-dōri (Map p116).

BICYCLE RENTAL

A great place to rent a bike is Kyoto Cycling Tour Project (KCTP; Map p115; ☎ 354-3636; www.kctp.net/en/index.html; ⌚ 9am-7pm). These folk rent bikes (¥1000 per day) that are perfect for getting around the city. KCTP also conducts a variety of excellent bicycle tours of Kyoto with English-speaking guides.

BUS

Kyoto has an extensive network of bus routes providing an efficient way of getting around at moderate cost. Many of the routes used by visitors have announcements in English. The core timetable for buses is between 7am and 9pm, though a few run earlier or later.

The TIC (p114) stocks the *Bus Navi Kyoto City Bus Sightseeing Map,* which is a good map of the city's main bus lines. This map is not exhaustive. If you can read a little Japanese, pick up a copy of the regular (and more detailed) Japanese bus map available at major bus terminals throughout the city.

The Kyoto bus information centre (Map p115) is located in front of Kyoto Station. Here you can pick up bus maps, purchase bus tickets and passes (on all lines, including highway buses), and get additional information.

SUBWAY

Kyoto has two efficient subway lines, which operate from 5.30am to 11.30pm. The minimum fare is ¥210 (children ¥110).

TAXI

Kyoto taxi fares start at ¥640 for the first 2km. The exception is MK Taxis (☎ 778-4141), whose fares start at ¥580.

MK Taxis also provides tours of the city with English-speaking drivers. For a group of up to four, prices start at ¥21,800 for a three-hour tour. Another company offering a similar service is Kyōren Taxi Service (☎ 672-5111).

Most Kyoto taxis are equipped with satellite navigation systems. If you are going somewhere unusual, it will help the driver if you have the address or phone number of your destination, as both of these can be programmed into the system.

NORTHERN KANSAI 関西北部

KINOSAKI 城崎

☎ 0796 / pop 4140

Kinosaki is one of the best places in Japan to sample the classic Japanese onsen experience. A willow-lined canal runs through the centre of this town and many of the houses, shops and restaurants remain something of their traditional charm. Add to this the delights of crab fresh from the Sea of Japan in winter, and you'll understand why this is one of our favourite overnight trips from the cities of Kansai.

INFORMATION

Opposite the station is an **accommodation information office** (お宿案内所; ☎ 32-4141; ⏱ 9am-6pm) where the staff will gladly help you find a place to stay and make bookings, as well as provide maps to the town. The same office has rental bicycles available for ¥400/800 per two hours/day (return by 5pm).

SIGHTS & ACTIVITIES

Kinosaki's biggest attraction is its seven **onsen.** Guests staying in town stroll the canal from bath to bath wearing *yukata* and *geta* (wooden sandals). Most of the ryokan and hotels in town have their own *uchi-yu* (private baths), but also provide their guests with free tickets to the ones outside *(soto-yu)*.

SLEEPING

Mikuniya (三国屋; ☎ 32-2414; www.kinosaki3928.com, in Japanese; r per person with 2 meals from ¥18,900; 🖳) About 150m on the right on the street heading into town from the station, this ryokan is a good choice. The rooms are clean, with nice Japanese decorations, and the onsen is soothing. There is an English sign.

Nishimuraya Honkan (西村屋本館; ☎ 32-2211; honkan@nishimuraya.ne.jp; r per person with 2 meals from ¥37,950; 🖳) This is a classic and the ultimate of inns here. If you would like to try the high-class ryokan experience, this is a good place. The

KYOTO & KANSAI

NORTHERN KANSAI

Dōtombori (p147), Osaka

BRENT WINEBRENNER

two onsen are exquisite and most of the rooms look out over private gardens. The excellent food is the final touch. There is LAN cable internet access.

EATING
Crab from the Sea of Japan is a speciality in Kinosaki during the winter months. It's called *kani* and the way to enjoy it is in *kani-suki,* cooked in broth with vegetables right at your table.

Daikō Shōten (大幸商店; ☎ 32-3684; ☺ 10am-9pm, to 11pm in summer, closed irregularly) This seafood shop/*izakaya* (pub-eatery) is a great place to try freshly caught local seafood in a casual atmosphere. From November until mid-April (the busy tourist season for Kinosaki), the restaurant section is upstairs, while the downstairs is given over to selling vast quantities of crabs and other delights. For the rest of the year, the restaurant is on the ground floor. *Teishoku* (set meals) are available from ¥1380, but you'll never go wrong by just asking for the master's *osusume* (recommendations). It's diagonally across from Mikuniya (p145).

GETTING THERE & AWAY
Kinosaki is on the JR San-in line and there are a few daily *tokkyū* from Kyoto (¥4510, two hours 22 minutes) and Osaka (¥5250, two hours 42 minutes).

OSAKA 大阪
☎ 06 / pop 2.65 million

Osaka is the working heart of Kansai. Famous for the gruff manners of its citizens and the colourful *Kansai-ben* (Kansai dialect) they speak, it's a good counterpart to the refined atmosphere of Kyoto. First and foremost, Osaka is famous for good eating: the phrase *kuidaore* (eat 'til you drop) was coined to describe Osakans' love for good food. Osaka is also a good place to experience a modern Japanese city: it's only surpassed by Tokyo as a showcase of the Japanese urban phenomenon.

INFORMATION
TOURIST INFORMATION
All the offices listed here can help book accommodation if you visit in person. For information on upcoming events, pick up a copy of *Kansai Time Out* magazine from bookstores.

Umeda Visitors Information Office (☎ 6345-2189; Kita; ☺ 8am-8pm, closed 31 Dec-Jan) is the main tourist information office in Osaka. It's a little tricky to find: from JR Osaka Station, exit the Midō-suji ticket gate/exit, turn right, and walk about 50m. The office is just outside the station, beneath a pedestrian overpass. From the subway, go out exit 9, and look for it outside the station, beside the bus terminal. Note that the station is presently under construction and there is word that this office might move again.

Osaka Itami and Kansai International Airports also have information counters. **Kansai International Airport Information Center** (☎ 07-2455-2500; 2F/North 1F&4F/North, South & Central zones; ☺ 24hr) **Osaka Itami Airport Information Center** (☎ 6856-6781; 1F Terminal Arrival Lobby North & South zones; ☺ North zone 8am-9.15pm, South zone 6.30am-9.15pm)

SIGHTS & ACTIVITIES
MINAMI AREA ミナミ
A few stops south of Osaka Station on the Midō-suji subway line (get off at either Shinsaibashi or Namba Station), the Minami area is the place to spend the evening in Osaka. Its highlights include the Dōtombori Arcade, the National Bunraku Theatre, Dōguya-suji Arcade and Amerika-Mura.

DŌTOMBORI 道頓堀

Dōtombori is Osaka's liveliest nightlife area. It's centred on **Dōtombori-gawa** and **Dōtombori Arcade**, a strip of restaurants and theatres where a peculiar type of Darwinism is the rule for both people and shops: survival of the flashiest. In the evening, head to **Ebisu-bashi** bridge to sample the glittering nightscape, which brings to mind a scene from the science-fiction movie *Blade Runner*. Nearby, the banks of the Dōtombori-gawa have recently been turned into attractive pedestrian walkways and this is the best vantage point for the neon madness above.

Only a short walk south of Dōtombori Arcade you'll find **Hōzen-ji**, a tiny temple hidden down a narrow alley. The temple is built around a moss-covered **Fudō-myōō statue**. This statue is a favourite of people employed in *mizu shōbai* (water trade), who pause before work to throw some water on the statue. Nearby, you'll find **Hōzen-ji Yokochō**, a tiny alley filled with traditional restaurants and bars.

TEMPŌZAN AREA 天保山エリア

Trudging through the streets of Kita or Minami, you could easily be forgiven for forgetting that Osaka is actually a port city. A good remedy for this is a trip down to Tempōzan, the best of Osaka's burgeoning seaside developments. On an island amid the busy container ports of Osaka Bay, Tempōzan has several attractions to lure travellers, especially those with children in tow. To reach Tempōzan, take the Chūō subway line west from downtown Osaka and get off at Osakakō Station. Take exit 1 out of the station, go straight at the bottom of the stairs and walk for 300m to reach the following attractions.

Before hitting the main attractions, you might want to get some perspective on it all by taking a whirl on the **Giant Ferris Wheel** (大観覧車; Daikanransha; ☎ 6576-6222; 1-1-10 Kaigan-dōri, Minato-ku; admission ¥700; ☺ 10am-9.30pm). Said to be the largest Ferris wheel in the world, the 112m-high wheel offers unbeatable views of Osaka, Osaka Bay and Kōbe. Give it a whirl at night to enjoy

BRENT WINEBRENNER

Food stall in Dōtombori

the vast carpet of lights formed by the Osaka/Kōbe conurbation.

Next to the Ferris wheel, you'll find Tempōzan Marketplace (天保山マーケットプレース; ☎ 6576-5501; 1-1-10 Kaigan-dōri, Minato-ku; admission free; ☷ shops 11am-8pm, restaurants to 9pm), a shopping and dining arcade that includes the Naniwa Kuishinbō Yokochō (なにわ食いしんぼ横丁; ☎ 6576-5501; 1-1-10 Kaigan-dōri, Minato-ku; admission free; ☷ 11am-8pm Sep-Jun, 10am-9pm Jul & Aug), a faux-Edo-period food court where you can sample all of Osaka's culinary specialities.

OSAKA AQUARIUM 海遊館

Osaka Aquarium (Kaiyūkan; ☎ 6576-5501; 1-1-10 Kaigan-dōri, Minato-ku; adult/child ¥2000/900; ☷ 10am-8pm) is easily one of the best aquariums in the world and it's we worth a visit, particularly if you've go kids, or if you love sharks. The aquariur is built around a vast central tank, which houses the star attractions: two whal sharks and two mantas. But these ar only the beginning: you'll also find huge variety of other sharks, including leopard sharks, zebra sharks, hammer head sharks and even a tiger shark (th only one we've ever seen in an aquarium There are also countless other species c rays and other fish.

FESTIVALS & EVENTS

Tenjin Matsuri Held on 24 and 25 July this is one of Japan's three bigges festivals. Try to make the second day when processions of *mikoshi* (portabl shrines) and people in traditional attir start at Osaka Temman-gū and end u in O-kawa (in boats). As night falls, th festival is marked with a huge firework display.

Kishiwada Danjiri Matsuri Osaka' wildest festival, on 14 and 15 Septembe is a kind of running of the bulls excep with *danjiri* (festival floats), many weigh ing over 3000kg. The *danjiri* are haule through the streets of the city by hur dreds of people using ropes, and in a the excitement there have been a cou ple of deaths – take care and stand back Most of the action takes place on the sec ond day. The best place to see the pa rade and festivities is west of Kishiwad Station on the Nankai Honsen line (fror Nankai Station).

SLEEPING

There are plenty of places to stay i and around the two centres of Kita an Minami. You can also explore Osak from a base in Kyoto, and you'll fin more budget accommodation in the ol

RACHEL LEWIS

Kyoto schoolgirl

capital, which is only about 40 minutes away by train. Keep in mind, however, that the trains stop running a little before midnight (party-goers take note).

GETTING THERE & AWAY

AIR

Osaka is served by two airports: Osaka Itami Airport (ITM), which handles only domestic traffic, and the newer Kansai International Airport (KIX), which handles all international and some domestic flights. Itami is conveniently located right in Osaka itself; KIX is on an artificial island in Wakayama-ken.

TRAIN

SHINKANSEN

Osaka is on the Tōkaidō-San-yō *shinkansen* line that runs between Tokyo and Hakata (Kyūshū): Hikari *shinkansen* run to/from Tokyo (¥13,550, three hours) and to/from Hakata (¥14,390, three hours). Other cities on this line include Hiroshima, Kyoto, Kōbe and Okayama.

KYOTO

The *shinkansen* is the fastest way to travel between Kyoto and Osaka (¥2730, 15 minutes). The second-fastest way is a JR *shinkaisoku* train between JR Kyoto Station and JR Osaka Station (¥540, 28 minutes).

Another choice is the cheaper but more comfortable private Hankyū line that runs between Hankyū Umeda Station in Osaka and Hankyū Kawaramachi, Karasuma and Ōmiya Stations in Kyoto (*tokkyū* to Kawaramachi ¥390, 44 minutes).

Alternatively, you can take the private Keihan main line between Sanjō, Shijō or Shichijō Stations in Kyoto and Keihan Yodoyabashi Station in Osaka (*tokkyū* to Sanjō ¥400, 51 minutes). Yodoyabashi is on the Midō-suji subway line.

HIMEJI 姫路

☎ 079 / pop 536,500

Himeji-jō, the finest castle in all Japan, towers over the small city of Himeji, a quiet city on the *shinkansen* route between Osaka and Okayama. In addition to the castle, the city is home to the Hyōgo Prefectural Museum of History and Kōko-en, a small garden alongside the castle. If you're a fan of castles a visit to Himeji is a must, and you can visit it as a day trip from cities such as Kyoto, Nara or Osaka, or as a stopover between these cities and places like Hiroshima.

ORIENTATION & INFORMATION

In Himeji Station, you'll find a tourist information counter (☎ 285-3792; ⏲ 9am-5pm) on the ground floor to the left as you exit the central exit on the north side of the station. Between 10am and 3pm, an English-speaking staff is on duty. The castle is a 15-minute walk (1200m) straight up the main road from the north exit of the station. If you don't feel like walking, free rental cycles are available from an underground parking area halfway between the station and the castle; inquire at the information counter.

On the way to the castle you'll find Himeji Tourist Information (☎ 287-3658; ⏲ 9am-5pm), which has information on movies filmed in Himeji, public toilets, a fantastic model of the castle and free rental bicycles.

SIGHTS

HIMEJI-JŌ 姫路城

This castle (☎ 285-1146; 68 Honmachi; adult/child ¥600/200; ⏲ 9am-5pm Sep-May, to 6pm Jun-Aug) is the most magnificent castle in Japan. It's also one of only a handful of original castles in Japan (most others are modern concrete reconstructions). In

KYOTO & KANSAI

HIMEJI

HIMEJI

Japanese the castle is sometimes called *shirasagi*, or 'white heron', a title that derives from the castle's stately white form. Although there have been fortifications in Himeji since 1333, today's castle was built in 1580 by Toyotomi Hideyoshi and enlarged some 30 years later by Ikeda Terumasa. Ikeda was awarded the castle by Tokugawa Ieyasu when the latter's forces defeated the Toyotomi armies. In the following centuries the castle was home to 48 successive lords.

EATING

Me-n-me (☎ 225-0118; 68 Honmachi; noodles from ¥550; ✇ 11.30am-6pm, closed Wed) They make their own noodles at this homey little noodle joint a few minutes' walk from the castle. It's not fancy, but if you want an honest, tasty bowl of udon to power you through the day, this is the spot. There is usually an English sign on the street. English menu.

Fukutei (☎ 222-8150; 75 Kamei-chō; lunch/dinner from ¥1500/3000; ✇ 11.30am-2.30pm & 5-9pm Mon-Sat, 11.30am-2.30pm & 5-8pm Sun & holidays) This stylish, approachable restaurant is a great lunch choice if you want something a little civilised. The fare here is casual *kaiseki*: a little sashimi, some tempura and the usual nibbles on the side. At lunch try the excellent *omakese-zen* (tasting set; ¥1500). There's a small English sign that reads 'Omotenashi Dining Fukutei'. English menu.

JOHN BANAGAN

Himeji-jō (p149)

GETTING THERE & AWAY

A *shinkaisoku* on the JR Tōkaidō line is the best way to reach Himeji from Kyoto (¥2210, 91 minutes), Osaka (¥1450, 61 minutes) and Kōbe (¥950, 37 minutes). From Okayama, to the west, a *tokkyū* JR train on the San-yō line takes 82 minutes and costs ¥1450. You can also reach Himeji from these cities via the Tōkaidō/San-yō *shinkansen* line, and this is a good option for Japan Rail Pass holders or those in a hurry.

NARA 奈良

☎ 0742 / pop 369,000

The first permanent capital of Japan, Nara is one of the most rewarding destinations in the country. Indeed, with eight Unesco World Heritage Sites, Nara is second only to Kyoto as a repository of Japan's cultural legacy. The centrepiece is, of course, the Diabutsu, or Great Buddha, which rivals Mt Fuji and Kyoto's Golden Pavilion (Kinkaku-ji) as Japan's single most impressive sight. The Great

Buddha is housed in Tōdai-ji, a soaring temple that presides over Nara-kōen, a park filled with other fascinating sights that lends itself to relaxed strolling amid the greenery and tame deer.

HISTORY

Nara is at the northern end of the Yamato Plain, where members of the Yamato clan rose to power as the original emperors of Japan. The remains of these early emperors are contained in *kofun* (burial mounds), some of which date back to the 3rd century AD.

Until the 7th century, however, Japan had no permanent capital, as Shintō taboos concerning death stipulated that the capital be moved with the passing of each emperor. This practice died out under the influence of Buddhism and with the Taika reforms of 646, when the entire country came under imperial control.

At this time it was decreed that a permanent capital be built. Two locations were tried before a permanent

NARA

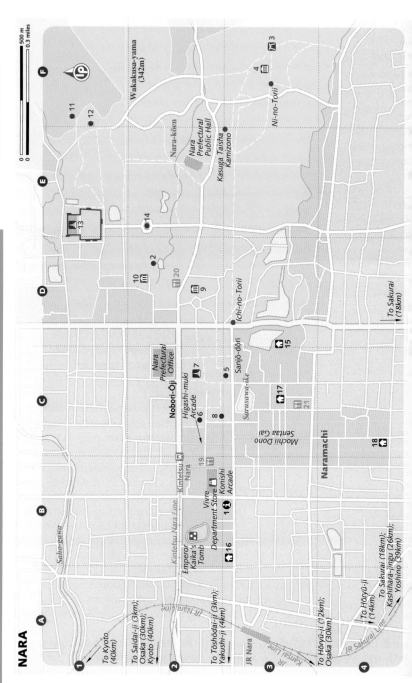

500 m
0.3 miles

Wakakusa-yama
(342m)

Ni-no-Torii

Nara-kōen

Nara
Prefectural
Public Hall

Kasuga Taisha
Kamizono

Ichi-no-Torii

To Sakurai
(18km)

Nara
Prefectural
Office

Nobori-Ōji

Higashi-muki
Arcade

Sanjō-dōri

Sarusawa-ike

Mochii Dono
Sentaa Gai

Naramachi

Kintetsu
Nara

Vivre
Department Store

Konishi
Arcade

Emperor
Kaika's
Tomb

Kintetsu Nara Line

JR Nara Line

JR Nara

Kansai Line

JR Sakurai Line

Saho-gawa

To Kyoto
(40km)

To Saidai-ji (3km);
Osaka (30km);
Kyoto (40km)

To Tōshōdai-ji (3km);
Yakushi-ji (4km)

To Hōryū-ji (12km);
Osaka (30km)

To Hōryū-ji
(14km)

To Sakurai (18km);
Kashihara-jingū (26km);
Yoshino (39km)

capital was finally established at Nara (which was then known as Heijōkyō) in 710. Permanent status, however, lasted a mere 75 years. When a priest by the name of Dōkyō managed to seduce an empress and nearly usurp the throne, it was decided to move the court to a new location, out of reach of Nara's increasingly powerful clergy. This led to the new capital being established at Kyoto, where it remained until 1868.

ORIENTATION

Nara retains the grid pattern of streets laid out in Chinese style during the 8th century. There are two main train stations: JR Nara Station and Kintetsu Nara Station. JR Nara Station is a little west of the city centre (but still within walking distance of the sights), while Kintetsu Nara is central. Nara-kōen, which contains most of the important sights, is on the eastern side, against the bare flank of

Wakakusa-yama. Most of the other sights are southwest of the city and are best reached by buses that leave from both train stations (or by train in the case of Hōryū-ji). It's easy to cover the city centre and the major attractions in nearby Nara-kōen on foot, though some may prefer to rent a bicycle.

MAPS
Nara tourist information offices stock the useful *Welcome to Nara Sight Seeing Map*.

INFORMATION
The main Nara City Tourist Center (☎ 22-3900; 23-4 Kamisanjō-chō; ☉ 9am-9pm, closed year-end/new-year holidays) is worth a stop if you start your sightseeing from JR Nara Station. If you start from Kintetsu Nara Station, try the helpful Kintetsu Nara Station information office (☎ 24-4858; ☉ 9am-5pm), which is near the top of the stairs above exit 3 from the station.

SIGHTS
NARA-KŌEN AREA 奈良公園
Many of Nara's most important sites are located in Nara-kōen, a fine park that occupies much of the east side of the city. The park is home to about 1200 deer, which in pre-Buddhist times were considered messengers of the gods and today enjoy the status of National Treasures. They roam the park and surrounding areas in search of handouts from tourists, often descending on petrified children who have the misfortune to be carrying food. You can buy *shika-sembei* (deer biscuits) from vendors for ¥150 to feed to the deer. Note: don't eat them yourself, as we saw one misguided foreign tourist doing.

Traditional parasol

BRENT WINEBRENNER

NARA NATIONAL MUSEUM
奈良国立博物館

The Nara National Museum (Nara Kokuritsu Hakubutsukan; ☎ 22-7771; 50 Noborioji-chō; admission ¥500; ⏱ 9.30am-5pm) is devoted to Buddhist art and is divided into two wings. The western gallery has a fine collection of *butsu-zō* (statues of Buddhas and bodhisattvas), while the new eastern gallery displays sculptures, paintings and calligraphy.

KŌFUKU-JI 興福寺

This temple was transferred here from Kyoto in 710 as the main temple for the Fujiwara family. Although the original temple complex had 175 buildings, fires and destruction as a result of power struggles have left only a dozen standing. There are two pagodas – three storeys and five

storeys – dating from 1143 and 1426 respectively. The taller of the two is the second-tallest in Japan, outclassed by the one at Kyoto's Tō-ji by a few centimetres.

ISUI-EN & NEIRAKU ART MUSEUM
依水園・寧楽美術館

This garden (☎ 25-0781; 74 Suimon-chō; admission museum & garden ¥650; ⏱ 9.30am-4pm, closed Tue & year-end/new-year holidays), dating from the Meiji era, is beautifully laid out and features abundant greenery and a pond with ornamental carp. It's without a doubt the best garden in the city and well worth a visit. For ¥450 you can enjoy a cup of tea on tatami mats overlooking the garden.

The adjoining art museum, Neiraku Bijutsukan, displays Chinese and Korean ceramics and bronzes (admission is included in garden entry).

There is no English sign outside the garden; look for the imposing wooden gate.

TŌDAI-JI 東大寺

Nara's famous Daibutsu (Great Buddha) is housed in the Daibutsu-den hall of this grand temple. It's Nara's star attraction and can often be packed with tour groups and schoolchildren from across the country, but it's big enough to absorb huge crowds and it belongs at the top of any Nara itinerary.

Before you enter the temple be sure to check out the Nandai-mon, an enormous gate containing two fierce-looking Niō guardians. These recently restored wooden images, carved in the 13th century by the sculptor Unkei, are some of the finest wooden statues in all of Japan, if not the world. They are truly dramatic works of art and seem ready to spring to life at any moment. The gate is about 200m south of the temple enclosure.

Note that most of Tōdai-ji's grounds can be visited free of charge, with the exception of the main hall: the Daibutsu-den.

DAIBUTSU-DEN 大仏殿

Tōdai-ji's **Daibutsu-den** (Hall of the Great Buddha; ☎ 22-5511; 406-1 Zōshi-chō; admission ¥500; ۞ 8am-4.30pm Nov-Feb, to 5pm Mar, 7.30am-5.30pm Apr-Sep, to 5pm Oct) is the largest wooden building in the world. Unbelievably, the present structure, rebuilt in 1709, is a mere two-thirds of the size of the original! The Daibutsu (Great Buddha) contained within is one of the largest bronze figures in the world and was originally cast in 746. The present statue, recast in the Edo period, stands just over 16m high and consists of 437 tonnes of bronze and 130kg of gold.

The Daibutsu is an image of Dainichi Buddha, the cosmic Buddha believed to give rise to all worlds and their respective Buddhas. Historians believe that Emperor Shōmu ordered the building of the Buddha as a charm against smallpox, which ravaged Japan in preceding years. Over the centuries the statue took quite a beating from earthquakes and fires, losing its head a couple of times (note the slight difference in colour between the head and the body).

NIGATSU-DŌ & SANGATSU-DŌ 二月堂・三月堂

Nigatsu-dō and Sangatsu-dō are halls (almost subtemples) of Tōdai-ji. They are an easy walk east (uphill from Daibutsu-den). You can walk straight east up the hill, but we recommend taking a hard left out of the Daibutsu-den exit, following the enclosure past the pond and turning up the hill. This pathway is among the most scenic walks in all of Nara. .

As you reach the plaza at the top of the hill, the **Nigatsu-dō** (☎ 22-5511; 406-1 Zōshi-chō; admission free) is the temple hall with the verandah overlooking the plaza. This is where Nara's Omizutori Matsuri (Water-Drawing Cenermony) is held each year on the evening of March 12. The verandah

affords a great view over Nara, especially at dusk. Opening hours here are the same as those of the Daibutsu-den.

A short walk south of Nigatsu-dō is **Sangatsu-dō** (admission ¥500), which is the oldest building in the Tōdai-ji complex. This hall contains a small collection of fine statues from the Nara period. It's open the same hours as the Daibutsu-den.

KASUGA TAISHA 春日大社

This **shrine** (☎ 22-7788; 160 Kasugano-chō; admission free; ۞ dawn-dusk) was founded in the 8th century by the Fujiwara family and was completely rebuilt every 20 years according to Shintō tradition until the end of the 19th century. It lies at the foot of the hill in a pleasant, wooded setting with herds of sacred deer awaiting handouts. As with similar shrines in Japan, you will find several subshrines around the main hall.

SLEEPING

Although Nara is often visited as a day trip from Kyoto, it is pleasant to spend the night here and this allows for a more relaxing pace.

BUDGET

Ryokan Seikan-sō (☎/fax 22-2670; 29 Higashikitsuji-chō; per person without bathroom from ¥4200; ▭) This traditional ryokan has reasonable rates and a good Naramachi location. The rooms are clean and spacious with shared bathrooms and a large communal bathtub. The management is used to foreign guests. The lovely Japanese garden is the icing on the cake here.

Ryokan Matsumae (☎ 22-3686; fax 26-3927; www.matsumae.co.jp/english/index_e.html; 28-1 Higashiterahayashi-chō; per person without bathroom from ¥5250; ▭) This friendly little ryokan boasts a great location in Naramachi, a short walk from all the sights. The rooms are typical of a ryokan: tatami mats, low tables, TVs and futons. Some rooms are a little dark, but the feeling here is warm and relaxing. English is spoken here.

MIDRANGE & TOP END

Nara Washington Hotel Plaza (☎ 27-0410; http://nara.wh-at.com; 31-1 Shimosanjō-chō; s/d/tw from ¥6900/12,000/12,000; 🖳) Located right downtown, this reliable hotel is another excellent choice in this price range. Rooms are clean and comfortable and there is LAN internet access. Right outside are endless restaurants to choose from.

Nara Hotel (☎ 26-3300; fax 23-5252; www .narahotel.co.jp/english/index.html; 1096 Takabatake-chō; s/tw from ¥18,480/33,495; 🖳) This grande dame of Nara hotels is a classic, with high ceilings and the smell of polished wood all around. All the rooms are spacious and comfortable with big beds. Unfortunately,

some of the bathrooms have cramped unit baths. The rooms in the Shinkan (new wing) are nice, but we recommend the Honkan (main building) for its great retro atmosphere. LAN internet access.

EATING

Shizuka (☎ 27-8030; 59-11 Noboriōji-chō; rice dishes from ¥892; 🕙 11am-8pm, closed Tue) Shizuka is a cosy little traditional restaurant that serves a Nara speciality known as *kamameshi* (rice cooked in a small iron pot with various vegetables, meat or fish thrown in). It's in a two-storey building that looks like a private home, with a white-and-black paper lantern-sign. English menu.

Mellow Café (☎ 27-9099; 1-8 Konishi-chō; lunch from ¥980; 🕙 11am-11.30pm) Located down a narrow alley (look for the palm tree), this open-plan cafe tries to create the ambience of a South Seas resort in downtown Nara. Offerings include international and pan-Asian cuisine. Lunch specials are displayed in front to help you choose and order. There's an English sign and menu.

Tempura Asuka (☎ 26-4308; 11 Shōnami-chō; meals ¥1500-5000; 🕙 11.30am-2.30pm & 5-9.30pm, closed Mon) This reliable restaurant serves attractive tempura and sashimi sets in a relatively casual atmosphere. At lunchtime try its *yumei-dono bentō* (a box filled with a variety of tasty Japanese foods) for ¥1600. There is an English sign and menu.

GETTING THERE & AWAY

TRAIN

The Kintetsu line, which runs between Kintetsu Kyoto Station (in Kyoto Station) and Kintetsu Nara Station, is the fastest and most convenient way to travel between Nara and Kyoto. There are *tokkyū* (¥1110, 33 minutes) and *kyūkō* (¥610, 40 minutes). The *tokkyū* trains run directly

FRANK CARTER

Timber lantern in Oku-no-in (p158), Koya-san

and are very comfortable; the *kyūkō* usually require a change at Saidai-ji.

The JR Nara line also connects JR Kyoto Station with JR Nara Station (*JR miyakoji kaisoku*, ¥690, 41 minutes) and there are several departures an hour during the day.

KII-HANTŌ
紀伊半島

KŌYA-SAN 高野山
☎ 0736 / pop 4090

Kōya-san is a raised tableland in northern Wakayama-ken covered with thick forests and surrounded by eight peaks. The major attraction here is the Kōya-san monastic complex, which is the headquarters of the Shingon school of Esoteric Buddhism. Though not quite the

Shangri-la it's occasionally described as, Kōya-san is one of the most rewarding places to visit in Kansai, not just for the natural setting of the area but also as an opportunity to stay in temples and get a glimpse of long-held traditions of Japanese religious life.

INFORMATION		
Kōya-san Tourist Association 高野山観光協会	**1**	B3
SIGHTS & ACTIVITIES		
Dai-tō 大塔	**2**	A3
Ichi-no-hashi 一の橋	**3**	C3
Kondō (Main Hall) 金堂	**4**	A3
Kongōbu-ji 金剛峯寺	**5**	B3
Mimyo-no-hashi 御廟橋	**6**	D2
Oku-no-in 奥の院	**7**	D1
Sai-tō 西塔	**8**	A3
Tōrō-dō 灯ろう堂	(see 7)	
SLEEPING		
Ekō-in 永光院	**9**	C3
Henjōson-in 遍照尊院	**10**	A3
Rengejō-in 蓮華定院	**11**	A2

KŌYA-SAN

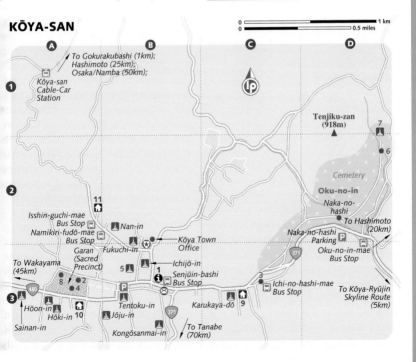

Keep in mind that Kōya-san tends to be around 5°C colder than down on the plains, so bring warm clothes if you're visiting in winter, spring or autumn.

ORIENTATION & INFORMATION

The precincts of Kōya-san are divided into two main areas: the Garan (Sacred Precinct) in the west, where you will find interesting temples and pagodas, and the Oku-no-in, with its vast cemetery, in the east.

Kōya-san Tourist Association (☎ 56-2616; fax 56-2889; ☼ 8.30am-5.30pm Jul & Aug, to 4.30pm Sep-Jun) In the centre of town in front of the Senjūin-bashi bus stop, this tourist information centre stocks maps and brochures, and English speakers are usually on hand.

SIGHTS

OKU-NO-IN 奥の院

Any Buddhist worth their salt in Japan has had their remains, or just a lock or two of hair, interred in this cemetery-temple to ensure pole position when Miroku Buddha comes to earth.

The best way to approach Oku-no-in is to walk or take the bus east to Ichi-no-hashi-mae bus stop. From here you cross the bridge, Ichi-no-hashi, and enter the cemetery grounds along a winding, cobbled path lined by tall cedar trees and thousands of tombs. As the trees close in and the mist swirls the atmosphere can be enchanting, especially as night falls.

At the northern end of the graveyard, you will find the Tōrō-dō (Lantern Hall), which is the main building of the complex. It houses hundreds of lamps, including two believed to have been burning for more than 900 years. Behind the hall you can see the closed doors of the Kūkai mausoleum.

On the way to the Lantern Hall is the bridge Mimyo-no-hashi. Worshippers ladle water from the river and pour it over the nearby Jizō statues as an offering for the dead. The inscribed wooden plaques in the river are in memory of aborted babies and those who died by drowning.

KONGŌBU-JI 金剛峯寺

This is the headquarters of the Shingon school and the residence of Kōya-san's abbot. The present structure (☎ 56-2011; admission ¥500; ☼ 8.30am-5pm) dates from the 19th century and is definitely worth a visit.

The main hall's Ohiro-ma room has ornate screens painted by Kanō Tanyu in the 16th century. The Yanagi-no-ma (Willow Room) has equally pretty screen paintings of willows but the rather grisly distinction of being the place where Toyotomi Hidetsugu committed *seppuku* (ritual suicide by disembowelment).

Admission includes tea and rice cakes served beside the stone garden. Last entry 4.30pm.

GARAN 伽藍

This is a temple complex (☎ 56-2011; admission to each bldg ¥200; ☼ 8.30am-5pm) of several halls and pagodas. The most important buildings are the Dai-tō (Great Pagoda) and Kondō (Main Hall). The Dai-tō, rebuilt in 1934 after a fire, is said to be the centre of the lotus-flower mandala formed by the eight mountains around Kōya-san. It's well worth entering the Dai-tō to see the Dainichi-nyōrai (Cosmic Buddha) and his four attendant Buddhas. It's been repainted recently and is an awesome sight. The nearby Sai-tō (Western Pagoda) was most recently rebuilt in 1834 and is more subdued. Last entry 4.30pm.

SLEEPING

There are more than 50 temples in Kōya-san offering *shukubō*. It's worth staying the night at a temple here, especially to try *shōjin-ryōri* (Buddhist vegetarian food – no meat, fish, onions or garlic).

Most lodgings *start* at ¥9500 per person including two meals.

Make advance reservations by fax through the Kōya-san Tourist Association (opposite) or directly with the temples (getting a Japanese speaker to help will make this easier). Even if you contact the temples directly, you will usually be asked to go to the Tourist Association to pick up a reservation slip-voucher.

Rengejō-in (☎ 56-2233; fax 56-4743; r per person with 2 meals from ¥9500, single travellers ¥11,550) This lovely temple has superb rooms, many with garden views, fine painted *fusuma* (sliding doors) and interesting art on display. English is spoken here and sometimes explanation of Buddhist practices and meditation is available. It is highly recommended.

Ekō-in (☎ 56-2514; fax 56-2891; ekoin@mbox.co.jp; r per person with 2 meals from ¥10,000; 🖳) One of the nicer temples in town, Ekō-in is run by a friendly bunch of young monks and the rooms look onto beautiful gardens. This is also one of the two temples in town (the other is Kongōbu-ji) where you can study *zazen* (seated meditation). Call ahead to make arrangements.

Henjōson-in (☎ 56-2434; fax 56-3641; r per person with 2 meals from ¥15,750) This is another good choice. The rooms here also have good garden views and are quite spacious. High-quality meals are served in the dining hall. The communal bathtubs here are huge and have nice views. And the flowers in the entryway are usually stunning.

GETTING THERE & AWAY

Unless you have a rental car, the best way to Kōya-san is the Nankai-Dentetsu line from Osaka's Namba Station to Kōya-san. The trains terminate at Gokurakubashi, at the base of the mountain, where you board a funicular railway (five minutes, price included in train tickets) up to Kōya-san itself. From the cable-car station, you take a bus into the centre of town (walking is prohibited on the connecting road).

From Osaka (Namba Station) you can travel directly on a Nankai-Dentetsu line *kyūkō* to Kōya-san (¥1230, 100 minutes). For the slightly faster *tokkyū* service with reserved seats you pay a supplement (¥760).

From Kyoto go via Namba in Osaka. From Nara you can take the JR line to

STAEVEN VALLÁK
Dai-tō, Garan temple complex

Hashimoto, changing at Sakurai and Takadate en route.

GETTING AROUND

Buses run on three routes from the top cable-car station via the centre of town to Ichi-no-hashi and Oku-no-in. An all-day bus pass (*ichi-nichi furee kippu;* ¥800) is available from the bus office outside the top cable-car station, but once you get into the centre of town you can reach most destinations quite easily on foot (including Oku-no-in, which takes about 30 minutes).

ISE-SHIMA
伊勢志摩
ISE 伊勢

☎ 0596 / pop 135,250

Although the city of Ise-shi is rather drab, it's worth making the trip here to visit the spectacular Ise-jingū. This is arguably Japan's most impressive shrine; its only rival to this claim is Nikkō's Tōshō-gū, which is as gaudy as Ise-jingū is austere.

SIGHTS & ACTIVITIES
ISE-JINGŪ 伊勢神宮

Dating back to the 3rd century, Ise-jingū is the most venerated Shintō **shrine (admission free; ☀ sunrise-sunset)** in Japan. Shintō tradition has dictated for centuries that the shrine buildings be replaced every 20 years with exact imitations built on adjacent sites according to ancient techniques – no nails, only wooden dowels and interlocking joints.

Upon completion of the new buildings, the god of the shrine is ritually transferred to its new home in the Sengū No Gi ceremony, first witnessed by Western eyes in 1953. The wood from the old shrine is then used to reconstruct the torii at the shrine's entrance or is sent to shrines around Japan for use in rebuilding their structures. The

present buildings were rebuilt in 1993 (fo the 61st time) at a cost exceeding ¥5 bil lion. They'll next be rebuilt in 2013.

You may be surprised to discove that the main shrine buildings are al most completely hidden from view be hind wooden fences. Only members o the imperial family and certain shrine priests are allowed to enter the sacrec inner sanctum. This is unfortunate, as the buildings are stunning examples of pre Buddhist Japanese architecture. Don' despair, though, as determined neck craning over fences allows glimpses o the upper parts of buildings (at least i you're tall).

There are two parts to the shrine, Gekū (Outer Shrine) and Naikū (Inner Shrine) The former is an easy 10-minute walk from Ise-shi Station; the latter is accessible by bus from the station or from the stop out side Gekū (see below). If you only have time to visit one of the shrines, Naikū is the more impressive of the two.

GEKŪ 外宮

The Outer Shrine dates from the 5th century and enshrines the god o food, clothing and housing, Toyouke-no-Ōkami. Daily offerings of rice are made by shrine priests to the goddess who is charged with providing food to Amaterasu-Ōmikami, the goddess en shrined in the Naikū. A stall at the en trance to the shrine provides a leaflet in English with a map.

The main shrine building here is the Goshōden, which is about 10 minutes walk from the entrance to the shrine Across the river from the Goshōden, you'll find three smaller shrines that are worth a look (and are usually less crowded).

From Ise-shi Station or Uji-Yamada Station it's a 10-minute walk down the main street to the shrine entrance.

NAIKŪ 内宮

The Inner Shrine is thought to date from the 3rd century and enshrines the sun goddess, Amaterasu-Ōmikami, who is considered the ancestral goddess of the imperial family and the guardian deity of the Japanese nation. Naikū is held in even higher reverence than Gekū because it houses the sacred mirror of the emperor, one of the three imperial regalia (the other two are the sacred beads and the sacred sword).

A stall just before the entrance to the shrine provides the same English leaflet given out at Gekū. Next to this stall is the Uji-bashi, which leads over the crystal-clear Isuzu-gawa into the shrine. Just off the main gravel path is a Mitarashi, the place for pilgrims to purify themselves in the river before entering the shrine.

The path continues along an avenue lined with towering cryptomeria trees to the Goshōden, the main shrine building. As at Gekū, you can only catch a glimpse of the top of the structure here, as four rows of wooden fences obstruct the view.

To get to Naikū, take bus 51 or 55 from bus stop 11 outside Ise-shi Station or the stop on the main road in front of Gekū (¥410, 12 minutes). Note that bus stop 11 is about 100m past the main bus stop outside Ise-shi Station (walk south on the main street). Get off at the Naikū-mae stop. From Naikū there are buses back to Ise-shi Station via Gekū (¥410, 18 minutes from bus stop 2). Alternatively, a taxi between Ise-shi Station or Gekū and Naikū costs about ¥2000.

SLEEPING

Ise City Hotel (伊勢シティホテル; ☎ 28-2111; 1-11-31 Fukiage; s/tw ¥6510/13,650; ⊚) This is a good business hotel with small, clean rooms and a convenient location less than 10 minutes' walk from the station. Some staff members speak a bit of English. To get there from Ise-shi Station, take a left (east) outside the station, walk past a JTB travel agency, take a left at the first traffic light, and cross the tracks. You'll see it on the left.

JAPAN TRAVEL BUREAU/PHOTOLIBRARY

Ise-jingū

KYOTO & KANSAI

ISE-SHIMA

Preparing *tako-yaki* (octopus balls)
BRENT WINEBRENNER

Hoshide-kan (星出館; ☎ 28-2377; fax 27-2830; 2-15-2 Kawasaki; r per person with/without 2 meals ¥7500/5000; 💻) This is a quaint wooden ryokan with some nice traditional touches. Go straight past Ise City Hotel, and it's on the right (there is a small English sign). It's at the second light (400m) past the train tracks. Look for the large traditional building with cedars poking out of tiny gardens. Free internet.

EATING & DRINKING
Daiki (大善; ☎ 28-0281; meals from ¥1500; 🕙 11am-9pm) Our favourite place to eat in Ise-shi bills itself as 'Japan's most famous restaurant'. It's a great place to sample seafood, including *ise-ebi* (Japanese lobsters), served as set meals for ¥5000; ask for the *ise-ebi teishoku* and specify *yaki* (grilled), *niita* (boiled) or *sashimi* (raw). Simpler meals include tempura *teishoku* (¥1500). It's outside and to the right of Uji-Yamada Station; there's a small English sign reading 'Kappo Daiki' and 'Royal Family Endorsed'. English menu.

At Naikū you'll find plenty of good restaurants in the Okage-yokochō Arcade just outside the shrine (when walking from the bus stop towards the shrine look to the left and you will see the covered arcade).

The arcade **Nikōdōshiten** (二光堂支店; ☎ 24-4409; 19 Ujiimazaike-chō; 🕙 11am-4pm, closed Thu) is a good place to try some of the local specialities in a rough, roadhouse atmosphere. *Ise-udon* (thick noodles in a dark broth; small/large bowl ¥420/570) is the speciality. For a bigger meal, try the *ise-udon teishoku* (*ise-udon* with rice and side dishes; ¥1000). The restaurant is 100m up from the southern (shrine) end of the arcade.

GETTING THERE & AWAY
There are rail connections between Ise-shi and Nagoya, Osaka and Kyoto on both the JR and the Kintetsu lines. For those without a Japan Rail Pass, the Kintetsu line is by far the most convenient way to go and the *tokkyū* are comfortable and fast.

Kintetsu fares and travel times to/from Ise-shi include Nagoya (*tokkyū*, ¥2690, 85 minutes), Osaka (Uehonmachi or Namba Stations, *tokkyū*, ¥3030, 106 minutes) and Kyoto (*tokkyū*, ¥3520, 123 minutes).

There are two stations in Ise: Ise-shi Station and Uji-Yamada Station, which are only a few hundred metres apart (most trains stop at both). Get off at Ise-shi Station for destinations and accommodation described in this section.

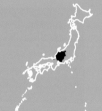

DENNIS WALT

Portrait of girl at a festival near Takayama

CENTRAL HONSHŪ

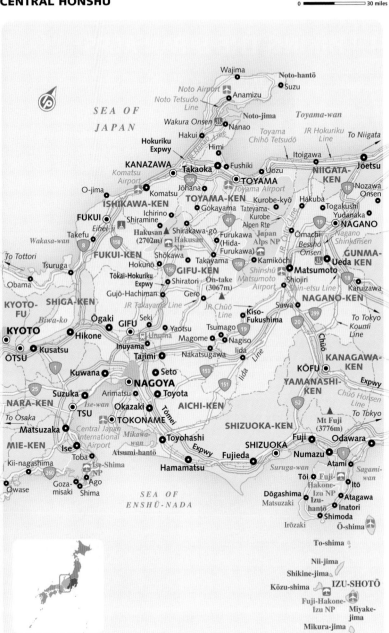

CENTRAL HONSHŪ

HIGHLIGHTS

HIGHLIGHTS

1 HIKING THE JAPAN ALPS

BY NAKANISHI NORIO, PROFESSIONAL MOUNTAIN GUIDE

The northern Japan Alps offer world-class hiking and an extensive system of mountain huts. This region of the Alps is unique because you can reach Murodō-daira Plateau, right in the middle of the highest peaks, by a series of buses and lifts. Once there, you can stay in a variety of comfortable accommodations.

➢ NAKANISHI NORIO'S DON'T MISS LIST

❶ TSURUGI-DAKE CLIMB

The 2999m peak of Tsurugi-dake is one of Japan's most impressive sights: the jagged ridges leading to the summit will tempt any serious hiker or mountain climber. The standard route is from Murodō via Tsurugi-sawa-goya hut and back to Murodō. You can also start at Murodō, cross the summit and descend right into the Tsurugi-sawa valley or do this in reverse. Keep in mind that this climb is fairly serious and is only for expe-

rienced climbers comfortable with heights and exposed routes.

❷ MURODŌ TO TARŌBEI-DAIRA TRAVERSE

This is the classic North Alps traverse. Start by taking the Tateyama–Kurobe Alpen Route from Toyama up to the Murodō-daira Plateau and spend the night there (don't miss the onsens). Climb off the plateau and traverse the long mountain ridge to the south, stopping for the night en route at the huts at Goshiki-ga-hara and Tarōbei-

Clockwise from top: Yuki-no-Ōtani; Hikers; Camping at Murodō (p194); Kurobe Dam (p194)

daira, before exiting at Oritate or continuing south in the direction of Shin-Hotaka Onsen or even Kamikōchi.

❸ ABOVE KAMIKŌCHI: YARIGA-TAKE & THE HOTAKAS

Kamikōchi is an alpine sanctuary surrounded by high mountains on all sides. Unlike Murodō, Kamikōchi sits at the base of the mountains. You can enjoy gentle hikes along the Azusa-gawa in the valley or climb the peaks that loom over the valley. The route over the Hotaka Range to the Matterhorn-like spire of 3180m Yariga-take is a classic.

❹ YUKI-NO-ŌTANI

Just west of the 2450m Murodō Terminal on the Tateyama–Kurobe Alpen Route (p193), you'll find one of Japan's most incredible sights: Yuki-no-Ōtani (Great Snow Valley). Snowdrifts of up to 19m pile up here during the winter and spring. From the opening of the route in April until the end of June, the drifts tower high over either side of the road – it's like travelling through the heart of a glacier.

⬊ THINGS YOU NEED TO KNOW

Hiking Season Trails are usually free from snow between June and October **Hiking Maps** Shōbunsha's Japanese-language *Yama-to-Kōgen-no-Chizu* maps (¥900; available at major Japanese bookshops) are the best hiking maps for this area **See our author's reviews on p183 and p193**

CENTRAL HONSHŪ

HIGHLIGHTS

HIGHLIGHTS

2   TAKAYAMA

BY OHNO JIRO, DIRECTOR OF THE SANMACHI PRESERVATION ORGANIZATION

Takayama's Sanmachi-suji district contains an incredible collection of well-preserved Edo-era and Taishō-era *machiya* (town houses). People in this area try very hard to preserve these old houses by actually living in them. All the residents are like one big family and this makes all the local events, such as the Takayama Matsuri, all the more enjoyable.

⤵ OHNO JIRO'S DON'T MISS LIST

❶ OLD HOUSES IN SANMACHI-SUJI

While the area around Takayama Station looks like any other modern Japanese city, as soon as you cross the Miya-gawa and enter Sanmachi-suji you'll feel like you've entered another world. Here, the streets and alleys are lined with atmospheric old wooden houses. You can enter some of them, including Yoshijima-ke and Kusakabe Mingeikan. They built these houses to last – check out their incredible exposed-beam structures.

❷ TEMPLES & SHRINES IN HIGASHIYAMA

An almost unbroken line of Buddhist temples and Shintō shrines stretches along the base of Higashiyama (literally 'Eastern Mountains') area. A walking path, the Higashiyama Yuhodō, connects all of them. Walking the path is a great way to spend half a day in Takayama. The highlight of the walk is Sakurayama Hachiman-gū (p178), a shrine backed by magnificent cedar trees.

Clockwise from top: Takayama Matsuri (p179); Stack of roof shingles at Hida-no-Sato (p179); Detail of a carving on a *yatai* (float) at Sannō Matsuri (p179); *Gasshō-zukuri* (thatched-roof houses) at Hida-no-Sato (p179)

❸ TAKAYAMA MATSURI

The Takayama Matsuri (Takayama Festival; p179) is one of Japan's most impressive festivals – a mountain counterpart to Kyoto's famous Gion Matsuri. The festival is held twice a year. The spring festival, known as the Sannō Matsuri, is held on 14 and 15 April, while the autumn festival, known as the Hachiman Matsuri, is held on 9 and 10 October. In both festivals, wonderfully decorated *yatai* (floats) are displayed and puppet shows are performed. On the evening of the first day of the festival, the *yatai* are covered with lanterns and are pulled through the town by chanting float teams.

❹ HIDA-NO-SATO

Few buildings fit into their landscape as perfectly as *gasshō-zukuri* (thatched-roof houses). Some of the finest examples were built in the mountain villages surrounding Takayama. Hida-no-Sato (p179) a collection of these houses moved from the surrounding area, contains more than 30 traditional buildings and six fine *gasshō-zukuri*.

⬆ THINGS YOU NEED TO KNOW

Transport An express train from Nagoya is the best way to reach Takayama; a rental car is useful for exploring the surrounding area Reservations If you plan to attend the Takayama Matsuri, make accommodation and transport reservations well in advance See our author's review on p176

HIGHLIGHTS

⬂ KANAZAWA

Sometimes called 'Little Kyoto', Kanazawa (p194) is packed with worthwhile attractions. It has one of Japan's best gardens, attractive traditional streetscapes, some fine temples and a handful of museums. With regular express train services to Kyoto, Kanazawa is a nice addition to the usual Kyoto–Tokyo itinerary. It can easily be paired with excursions to Noto-hantō, the Japan Alps and Takayama.

⬃ KAMIKŌCHI

A pristine sanctuary surrounded by the high mountains walls, Kamikōchi (p183) is arguably the most scenic spot in the entire Japan Alps. With several lodges and hotels scattered along the banks of the crystal-clear Azusa-gawa, it makes a great base for hiking. You can choose from gentle day hikes along the mostly flat river valley, or set off for multiday treks among the high peaks.

CENTRAL HONSHŪ

HIGHLIGHTS

⬇ **TATEYAMA–KUROBE ALPEN ROUTE**

A testament to Japanese engineering skills, the Tateyama–Kurobe Alpen Route (p193) is a series of lifts, buses and trolleys that works its way up and over (and sometimes through) the northern Japan Alps. For those who want to get high up among the peaks without breaking a sweat, this is the way to go.

⬇ **NOTO-HANTŌ**

Noto-hantō (p200) is one of the best reasons to bring an international driving licence to Japan. Jutting 90km into the Sea of Japan, this peninsula offers some incredibly scenic vistas: rocky coastal scenery, stepped rice paddies and traditional villages. Along the way, you can stay in fine onsen (hot springs) ryokan and sample the region's famous seafood.

⬇ **SKIING**

While foreign skiers make a beeline for Hokkaidō's Niseko, savvy local skiers head to the Japan Alps for their winter fun. The mountain town of Hakuba (p189) is surrounded by world-class ski resorts. Nozawa Onsen (p188) combines great skiing, a European atmosphere and 13 free onsen. Finally, sprawling Shiga Kōgen (p188) offers 80 runs spread over 21 areas.

3 JOHN ASHBURNE; 4 MUNEO ABE/SEBUN PHOTO/GETTY IMAGES; 5 JTB PHOTO/PHOTOLIBRARY; 6 ANTHONY GIBLIN; 7 JOHN BORTHWICK

3 Kenroku-en (p197); 4 Asuza-gawa (p183); 5 Tateyama–Kurobe Alpen Route (p193); 6 Bundles of drying rice; 7 Snowbaorder at Shiga Kōgen (p188)

THE BEST...

⤵ HIKING AREAS

- **Kamikōchi** (p183) An alpine sanctuary with comfortable lodges and fantastic hiking.
- **Shin-hotaka Onsen** (p185) Take the ropeway (tramway) to the ridge and keep on climbing.
- **Tateyama-Murodō Plateau** (p193) Take the Alpen Route to this plateau high in the Alps and set out on an adventure.
- **Hakuba** (p189) This ski resort town has brilliant hiking in the summer, some of it lift served.

⤵ ONSEN

- **Shin-hotaka Onsen** (p185) This riverside onsen is one of Japan's most scenic. Ryokan nearby have great private baths.
- **Lamp no Yado** (p203) This seaside onsen on the far-flung Noto-hantō boasts private outdoor baths.
- **Nozawa Onsen** (p188) Spend an evening soaking in the 13 free

(scalding hot) onsen in this mountain town.

⤵ OVERNIGHT GETAWAYS

- **Takayama** (p176) Take an express from Nagoya to this fine old town on the doorstep of the Japan Alps.
- **Kanazawa** (p194) Take an express from Kyoto to this culture-rich city on the Sea of Japan.
- **Matsumoto** (p190) Take an express from Tokyo or Nagoya to this castle town at the foot of the Japan Alps.

⤵ DRIVES

- **Noto-hantō** (p200) Cruise quiet seaside roads, stopping at onsen and ryokan en route.
- **Shirakawa-go & Gokayama** (p180) Hire a car in Takayama and explore the thatch-roof villages of Shirakawa-go and Gokayama.
- **Nagano** (p186) A car is best way to explore Nagano's mountains.

LEFT: CHRISTOPHER GROENHOUT; RIGHT: MARTIN MOO

Left: Craftsperson at Hida-no-Sato (p179); Right: Matsumoto-jō (p190)

THINGS YOU NEED TO KNOW

VITAL STATISTICS

- Populations Nagano 377,000, Matsumoto 227,000, Kanazawa 456,000, Takayama 95,300
- Area codes Nagano ☎ 026, Matsumoto ☎ 0263, Kanazawa ☎ 076, Takayama ☎ 0577
- Best time to visit Cherry-blossom season (early April), autumn foliage season (September and October in the mountains), ski season (December to March)

PLACES IN A NUTSHELL

- Takayama (p176) This town of traditional riverside houses is a gateway to the Japan Alps.
- Kamikōchi (p183) An alpine sanctuary boasting wondrous views and world-class hiking.
- Nagano (p186) The former host city of the Winter Olympics makes an ideal base for exploring the surrounding mountains.
- Hakuba (p189) A ski resort town with numerous onsen and hiking opportunities.
- Matsumoto (p190) This popular destination at the foot of the Japan Alps is home to Japan's oldest wooden castle.
- Kanazawa (p194) A small city packed with cultural delights and attractive streetscapes.
- Noto-hantō (p200) See traditional lifestyles and enjoy fresh seafood along this peninsula on the Sea of Japan coast.

RESOURCES

- Japan National Tourism Organization (JNTO; www.jnto.go.jp, www.japantravelinfo.com)

EMERGENCY NUMBERS

- Ambulance & Fire ☎ 119
- Police ☎ 110

GETTING AROUND

- Walk around Takayama, Kanazawa and the Japan Alps.
- Drive the Tateyama–Kurobe Alpen Route across the Japan Alps, and explore the quiet roads of Noto-hantō.
- Train or bus between cities and towns.

BE FOREWARNED

- Winter (December to March) can be very cold in Central Honshū, particularly in the mountains.
- An International Driving Licence is necessary to rent a car and drive in Japan.
- The Japan Alps are steep and fairly high (peaks around 3000m). Training is helpful if you intend to climb.

CENTRAL HONSHŪ ITINERARIES

TAKAYAMA & THE JAPAN ALPS Three Days

If you've only got limited time in Japan but would like to see a little bit more than just Tokyo and Kyoto, this Central Honshū jaunt is the perfect add-on. A bit over two hours north of Nagoya, which is on the Tōkaidō *shinkansen* (bullet train) line that runs between Tokyo and Kyoto, Takayama is the perfect place to base yourself for this itinerary.

Take a *shinkansen* from Kyoto or Tokyo to **(1) Nagoya** and switch to an express train north to **(2) Takayama** (p176). Spend your first day exploring Takayama itself. Check out the traditional wooden houses in Sanmachi-suji (p177); walk over to the Takayama Yatai Kaikan (p178), which houses the festival floats used in the Takayama Matsuri (p179); and take a bus, taxi or bicycle over to Hida-no-Sato (p179), a collection of thatched-roof houses from the region. Then take the bus (actually two buses) to **(3) Kamikōchi** (p183), do some hiking, spend the night and then make your way back to Kyoto or Tokyo via Takayama (or Matsumoto).

KANAZAWA & THE ALPEN ROUTE Five Days

A brilliant way to diversify a Kyoto–Tokyo itinerary is this loop that takes you from Kyoto to Kanazawa and up and over the Japan Alps via the Tateyama–Kurobe Alpen Route. If you start in Tokyo and travel to Kyoto by *shinkansen,* this allows you to return to Tokyo without retracing your steps.

Catch a direct express train from Kyoto to **(1) Kanazawa** (p194). Spend a day in Kanazawa enjoying Kenroku-en (p197) and the city's temples. Then, take an express train to Toyama and switch to local trains for the journey to the western terminus of the **(2) Tateyama-Kurobe Alpen Route** (p193), which will bring you by a funicular and bus to the Murodō-daira Plateau. Consider spending a night here in one of the hiking lodges, which will allow you to do some hiking – maybe you can bag the 3015m peak of Tateyama. Then, continue east along the Alpen Route to the JR Oito line, which will bring you to the city of **(3) Matsumoto** (p190), where you can catch an express train to Tokyo.

BEST OF CENTRAL HONSHŪ One Week

A full week gives you time to make a more thorough exploration of Central Honshū. The best way to do this itinerary is by rental car, although you can do the entire route by public transport if you don't mind some long waits for buses and trains.

SEA OF JAPAN

Noto-hantō

KANAZAWA

Gokayama

Shirakawa-gō

Tateyama-Kurobe
Alpen Route

Takayama

Kamikōchi   Matsumoto

ROUTES
— Takayama & the Japan Alps
— Kanazawa & the Alpen Route
— Best of Central Honshū

NAGOYA

Travel by express train from (1) Nagoya to (2) Takayama (p176). Spend a day exploring Takayama and the following day, pick up your rental car and drive west to check out the old thatch-roof villages of (3) Shirakawa-gō (p181) and (4) Gokayama (p182). Then, continue north to the city of (5) Kanazawa (p194) where you should spend a day exploring the city. Then, spend a day or two driving around the penisula of (6) Noto-hantō (p200) enjoying the coastal scenery. Return to Takayama via the city of Toyama. Return your car and, if you have time, consider an overnight trip via bus to (7) Kamikōchi (p183) before continuing on to Tokyo or Kyoto.

DISCOVER CENTRAL HONSHŪ

Japan's heartland in both geography and attitude, Central Honshū (本州中部) stretches between the two great megalopolises of Kantō (Greater Tokyo) and Kansai (Osaka, Kyoto and Kōbe), between the Pacific Ocean and the Sea of Japan. This region is filled with modern commercial centres and traditional towns, the majestic Japan Alps and the rugged northern coastline.

In Central Honshū's southern prefectures, called 'Chūbu' in Japanese, hiking takes you through the Japan Alps National Park, and onsen (hot-spring) villages offer welcome recovery for skiers drawn to the Olympic slopes of Nagano-ken. The Sea of Japan side of this region ('Hokuriku' in Japanese) boasts clifftop vistas, remarkable temples and incredibly fresh seafood.

Hokuriku's hub is Kanazawa, a historic yet thriving city where handsomely preserved streets once housed samurai and geisha. Lovely Takayama is admired for its traditional riverside houses, wood crafts, delicious cuisine and verdant countryside. Matsumoto is another favourite with visitors for its striking 16th-century black-and-white castle and many galleries.

HIDA DISTRICT
飛驒地域

TAKAYAMA 高山
☎ 0577 / pop 95,300

With its old inns, shops and sake breweries, Takayama is a rarity: a 21st-century city (admittedly a small one) that's also retained its traditional charm. Vibrant morning markets, hillside shrines and a laid-back populace add to the town's allure, mean that Takayama should be a high priority on any visit to Central Honshū. Give yourself at least two days to enjoy the place; it's easily tackled on foot or bicycle.

Takayama was established in the late 16th century as the castle town of the Kanamori clan, but in 1692 it was placed under direct control of the *bakufu* (field headquarters) in Edo. The present layout dates from the Kanamori period, and its sights include more than a dozen mu-seums, galleries and exhibitions that cover lacquer and lion masks, folk craft and architecture.

Takayama remains the region's administrative and transport hub, and it makes a good base for trips around Hida and Japan Alps National Park (p183).

ORIENTATION
All of the main sights except Hida-no-Sato (Hida Folk Village) are in the centre of town, within walking distance of the station. Northeast of the station Kokubun-ji-dōri, the main street, heads east, across the Miya-gawa (about 10 minutes' walk), where it becomes Yasugawa-dōri. South of Yasugawa-dōri is the historic, picturesque Sanmachi-suji (Sanmachi district) of immaculately preserved old homes.

Hida-no-Sato is a 10-minute bus ride west of the station.

INFORMATION

Takayama's main tourist information office (☎ 32-5328; ⏱ 8.30am-5pm Nov-Mar, to 6.30pm Apr-Oct), directly in front of JR Takayama Station, has knowledgeable English-speaking staff, as well as English-language maps and information on sights (the *Hida Takayama* pamphlet is a good start), accommodation, special local events and regional transit. A tourist information office branch (☎ 32-2177; Kami-san-no-machi; ⏱ 10am-4pm) is in the centre of Sanmachi-suji and is useful for quick enquiries.

SIGHTS & ACTIVITIES

SANMACHI-SUJI 三町筋

The centre of the old town, this district of three main streets (Ichi-no-Machi, Ni-no-Machi and San-no-Machi) is lined with traditional shops, restaurants and museums. Sake breweries are easily recognised by the spheres of cedar fronds: some open to the public in January and early February (schedule available at tourist offices); most of the year they just sell their wares. For beautiful night-time shots, bring a tripod and set your camera's exposure to long.

TAKAYAMA-JINYA 高山陣屋

These sprawling grounds south of the Sanmachi district house the only remaining prefectural office building of the Tokugawa shōgunate. Takayama-jinya (Historical Government House; ☎ 32-0643; 1-5 Hachiken-machi; adult/child ¥420/free; ⏱ 8.45am-5pm Mar-Oct, to 4.30pm Nov-Feb) was originally built in 1615 as the administrative centre for the Kanamori clan but was later taken over by the *bakufu*. The main gate was once reserved for high officials. The present main building dates back to 1816 and it was used as the local government office until 1969.

As well as government offices, a rice granary and a garden, there's a torture chamber with explanatory detail. Free guided tours in English are available (reservations advised). Takayama-jinya is a 15-minute walk east of the train station.

MERCHANT HOUSES

吉島家・日下部民芸館

North of Sanmachi are two excellent examples of Edo-period merchants' homes, with the living quarters in one section and the commercial/warehouse areas in another. Design buffs shouldn't miss Yoshijima-ke (Yoshijima house; ☎ 32-0038; 1-51 Ōshinmachi; adult/child ¥500/300; ⏱ 9am-5pm Mar-Nov, to 4.30pm Wed-Sun Dec-Feb), which is well covered in architectural publications. Its lack of ornamentation allows you to focus on the spare lines, soaring roof and skylight. Admission includes a cup of delicious shiitake tea, which you can also purchase for ¥600 per can.

PETER PTSCHELINZEW

Higashi Chaya-gai (p197), Kanazawa

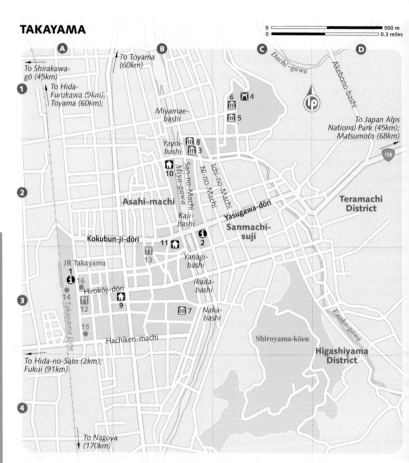

TAKAYAMA

Down the block, **Kusakabe Mingeikan** (Kusakabe Folk Art Museum; ☎ 32-0072; 1-52 Ōshinmachi; adult/child ¥500/300; ☃ 9am-4.30pm Mar-Nov, to 4pm Wed-Mon Dec-Feb), built during the 1890s, showcases the striking craftsmanship of traditional Takayama carpenters. Inside is a collection of folk art.

TAKAYAMA YATAI KAIKAN
高山屋台会館

A rotating selection of four of the 23 multi-tiered *yatai* (floats) used in the Takayama Matsuri can be seen at **Takayama Yatai Kaikan** (Festival Floats Exhibition Hall; ☎ 32-5100; 178 Sakura-machi; adult/child/high-school student ¥820/410/510; ☃ 8.30am-5pm Mar-Nov, 9am-4.30pm Dec-Feb). These spectacular creations, some dating from the 17th century, are prized for their flamboyant carvings, metalwork and lacquerwork. A famous feature of some floats is *karakuri*, mechanical puppets that perform amazing tricks and acrobatics courtesy of eight accomplished puppeteers using 36 strings. A video gives a sense of the festival.

The Yatai Kaikan is on the grounds of the stately hillside shrine Sakurayama

Hachiman-gū; the shrine's main buildings are behind the Yatai Kaikan. Dedicated to the protection of Takayama, the shrine also oversees the festival.

Your ticket also admits you to the Sakurayama Nikkō-kan diagonally across from the shrine, with intricate models of the famous shrines at Nikkō (p82). Lighting takes you from dawn to dusk and back again, allowing you to witness these sites in different kinds of light.

HIDA-NO-SATO 飛騨の里

The large, open-air Hida-no-Sato (Hida Folk Village; ☎ 34-4711; 1-590 Okamoto-chō; adult/child ¥700/200; ⏰ 8.30am-5pm) is highly recommended for its dozens of traditional houses, dismantled at their original sites throughout the region and rebuilt here. Allow at least three hours. During clear weather, there are good views across the town to the peaks of the Japan Alps.

Hida-no-Sato is a 30-minute walk west from Takayama Station, but the route is

Zen garden in Takayama
BRENT WINEBRENNER

↘ IF YOU LIKE...

If you like Takayama we think you'll like these other less visited but wonderful Central Honshū destinations:

- **Inuyama** This castle town has some quaint streets and nearby rivers. It's about 30 minutes north of Nagoya by train.
- **Hida-Furukawa** This town has some a fine carp-filled canal lined by old *kura* (storehouses). It's about 15 minutes north of Takayama by train.
- **Bessho Onsen** With some fine temples, this mountain onsen resort makes a relaxing getaway. It's about one hour northeast of Nagoya; change trains at Ueda.

not enjoyable. Either hire a bicycle, or catch a bus from Takayama bus station (¥200, 10 minutes). The 'Hida-no-Sato setto ken' ticket combines return fare and admission to the park for ¥900. Be sure to check return times for the bus.

FESTIVALS & EVENTS

One of Japan's greatest festivals, the Takayama Matsuri, is in two parts. On 14 and 15 April is the Sannō Matsuri; a dozen *yatai*, decorated with carvings, dolls, colourful curtains and blinds, are paraded through the town. In the evening the floats are decked out with lanterns and the procession is accompanied by sacred music. Hachiman Matsuri, on 9 and 10 October, is a slightly smaller version.

SLEEPING

Spa Hotel Alpina (☎ 33-0033; www.spa-hotel -alpina.com, in Japanese; 5-41 Nada-cho; s/tw from ¥6300/11,000; ✗ 🖳) This business hotel, which opened in 2008, is minimalist without being cold – crisp bedding, modular bathrooms and a variety of room types. The best part, though, is the onsen baths on the top floor, including *rotemburo* (outdoor baths) with views across the city. LAN cable is available.

Sumiyoshi Ryokan (☎ 32-0228; www .sumiyoshi-ryokan.com; 4-21 Hon-machi; r per person with 2 meals from ¥11,550; 🖳) This delightfully traditional inn is set in an old merchant's house from the late Meiji period and is filled with antiques. Some rooms have river views through windows of antique glass, and the common baths are made of wood and slate tiles. One room has a private bath (¥13,650).

Tanabe Ryokan (☎ 32-0529; fax 35-1955; www.tanabe-ryokan.jp; 58 Aioi-chō; r per person with 2 meals from ¥15,000; ✗ 🖳) Central, family-run inn with sweet, welcoming staff. There's art throughout, stone paths line the carpeted hallways, the 21 rooms are spacious, and dinner is Hida *kaiseki* (Japanese haute cuisine). Rooms have en-suite bath, but the common baths with their beamed ceilings are worth a try. Some English is spoken.

EATING

Origin (☎ 36-4655; 4-108 Hanasato-chō; most dishes ¥315-819; ☼ dinner) This wonderful local *izakaya* (pub-eatery) located a minute from the station has the usual *kushiyaki* (grilled skewers) and tofu steak, plus original dishes like sardines rolled

in *yuba* (tofu skin), or big-as-a-beer-can grilled daikon in miso sauce. Or go for broke with Hida beef (¥1575). Look for the bamboo poles out the front. There's an English menu.

Suzuya (☎ 32-2484; 24 Hanakawa-chō; sets ¥1155-3100; ☼ 11am-3pm & 5-8pm Wed-Mon) In the centre of town, Suzuya is one of Takayama's longstanding favourites, and it's highly recommended for local specialities such as Hida beef, *hoba-miso* and various stews. The menu is available in English.

GETTING THERE & AWAY

From Tokyo or Kansai, Takayama is most efficiently reached by *tokkyū* (limited express) via Nagoya on the JR Takayama line (Hida *tokkyū*, ¥5670, 2¼ hours); the mountainous train ride along the Hida-gawa is *gorge*-ous. The same train continues to Toyama (¥3480, 90 minutes), with connections to Kanazawa (additional ¥2050, 40 minutes).

You'll find Eki Rent-a-Car System (☎ 33-3522), Toyota Rent-a-Car (☎ 36-6110) and Mazda Rent-a-Car (☎ 36-1515) all near the station.

SHIRAKAWA-GŌ & GOKAYAMA
白川郷・五箇山

These remote, dramatically mountainous districts between Takayama and Kanazawa are best known for farmhouses in the thatched, A-frame style called *gasshō-zukuri*. They're rustic and lovely particularly in clear weather or in the region's copious snows, and they hold a special place in the Japanese heart.

In the 12th century the region's remoteness is said to have attracted stragglers from the Taira (Heike) clan, virtually wiped out by the Minamoto (Genji) clan in a brutal battle in 1185. During feudal times Shirakawa-gō, like the rest of Hida, was under direct control of the Kanamori

MICHAEL GEBICKI

Farm building and rice fields near Gokayama

clan, connected to the Tokugawa shōgun, while Gokayama was a centre for the production of gunpowder for the Kaga region, under the ruling Maeda clan.

Fast-forward to the 1960s: when construction of the gigantic Miboro Dam over the river Shōkawa was about to submerge some local villages, many *gasshō* houses were moved to their current sites for safekeeping. Although much of what you'll find has been specially preserved for, and supported by, tourism, it still presents a view of rural life found in few other parts of Japan.

Most of Shirakawa-gō's sights are in the heavily visited community of Ogimachi; a new expressway from Takayama has made it even more crowded. In less-crowded Gokayama (technically not in Hida but in Toyama-ken), the community of Ainokura has the greatest concentration of attractions; other sights are spread throughout hamlets over many kilometres along Rte 156. Ogimachi and Ainokura are Unesco World Heritage Sites (as is the Gokayama settlement of Suganuma).

SHIRAKAWA-GŌ 白川郷

☎ 05769

The region's central settlement, **Ogimachi**, has some 600 residents and more than 110 *gasshō-zukuri* buildings, and is the most convenient place to orient yourself for tourist information and transport.

Ogimachi's **main tourist office** (Deai no Yakata; ☎ 6-1013; www.shirakawa-go.org; 9am-5pm) is near the Shirakawa-gō bus stop. There's a free English map of Ogimachi. Limited English is spoken. There's a smaller tourist information office near the Ogimachi car park.

SIGHTS & ACTIVITIES

On the site of the former castle, **Shiroyama Tenbōdai** (observation point) provides a lovely overview of the valley. It's a 15-minute walk via the road behind the east side of town. You can climb the path (five minutes) from near the intersection of Rtes 156 and 360, or there's a shuttle bus (¥200 one-way) from the Shirakawa-gō bus stop.

Gasshō-zukuri Minka-en (☎ 6-1231; adult/child ¥500/300; ☼ 8.40am-5pm Apr-Jul & Sep-Nov, 8am-5.30pm Aug, 9am-4pm Fri-Wed Dec-Mar) features more than two dozen relocated *gasshō-zukuri* buildings, reconstructed in this open-air museum amid seasonal flowers. Several houses are used for demonstrating regional crafts such as woodwork, straw handicrafts and ceramics; many items are for sale.

Shirakawa-gō's largest *gasshō* house, **Wada-ke** (☎ 6-1058; adult/child ¥300/150; ☼ 9am-5pm) is a designated National Treasure. It once belonged to a wealthy silk-trading family and dates back to the mid-Edo period. Upstairs are silk-harvesting equipment and a valuable lacquerware collection.

Of the other *gasshō* houses, **Kanda-ke** (☎ 6-1072; adult/child ¥300/150; ☼ 9am-5pm) is the least cluttered with exhibits, which leaves you to appreciate the architectural details – enjoy a cup of herb tea in the 36-mat living room on the ground floor. **Nagase-ke** (☎ 6-1047; adult/child ¥300/150; ☼ 9am-5pm) was the home of the doctors to the Maeda clan; look for displays of herbal medicine equipment. The *butsudan* (Buddhist altar) dates from the Muromachi period. In the attic, you can get an up-close look at the construction of the roof, which took 530 people to re-thatch.

GOKAYAMA DISTRICT 五箇山
☎ 0763

Along the Shōkawa, Gokayama is so isolated that road links and electricity didn't arrive until 1925.

Villages with varying numbers of *gasshō-zukuri* buildings are scattered over many kilometres along Rte 156. The following briefly describes some of the communities you'll come across as you travel north from Shirakawa-gō or the Gokayama exit from the Tōkai-Hokuriku

Expressway; if your time is limited, head straight for Ainokura.

SUGANUMA 菅沼
This riverside **World Heritage Site** (www.gokayama.jp/english/index.html), 15km north of Ogimachi and down a steep hill, features an attractive group of nine *gasshō-zukuri* houses. The **Minzoku-kan** (民族館 Folklore Museum; ☎ 67-3652; adult/child ¥300/150; ☼ 9am-4pm) consists of two houses, with items from traditional life, and displays illustrating traditional gunpowder production.

AINOKURA 相倉
This World Heritage Site is the most impressive of Gokayama's villages, with more than 20 *gasshō* buildings in an agricultural valley amid splendid mountain views. It's less equipped for visitors than Ogimachi, which can be either a drawback or a selling point. Pick up an English pamphlet at the booth by the central car park.

Stroll through the village to the **Ainokura Museum of Life** (相倉民族館 ☎ 66-2732; admission ¥200; ☼ 8.30am-5pm) with displays of local crafts and paper.

GETTING THERE & AWAY
Nōhi Bus Company (☎ 0577-32-1688 Japanese only; www.nouhibus.co.jp/english) operates seven buses daily linking Shirakawa-gō with Takayama (one-way/ return ¥2400/4300, 50 minutes). Some buses require a reservation. Two buses a day connect Kanazawa and Takayama (¥3300/5900, 2¼ hours), from Shirakawa-gō (¥1800/3200, 1¼ hours). Weather delays and cancellations are possible between December and March.

Just before Ainokura, buses divert from Rte 156 for Rte 304 towards Kanazawa. From the Ainokura-guchi bus stop it's about 400m uphill to Ainokura.

Kaetsuno Bus (☎ 0766-22-4888) operates at least four buses a day between Takaoka on the JR Hokuriku line, Ainokura (¥1450, 90 minutes) and Ogimachi (¥2350, 2½ hours), stopping at all major sights.

By car, this region is about 50 minutes from Takayama, with interchanges at Gokayama and Shōkawa. From Hakusan, the scenic toll road Hakusan Super-Rindō ends near Ogimachi (cars ¥3150). In colder months, check conditions in advance with regional tourist offices.

JAPAN ALPS NATIONAL PARK
中部山岳国立公園

Boasting some of Japan's most dramatic scenery, this mountain-studded park – also called Chūbu-Sangaku National Park – is a favourite of alp-lovers. Highlights include hiking the valleys and peaks of Kamikōchi and Shin-Hotaka Onsen, and soaking up the splendour of Shirahone Onsen or Hirayu Onsen. The northern part of the park extends to the Tateyama–Kurobe Alpen Route (p193).

GETTING THERE & AROUND
The main gateway cities are Takayama to the west and Matsumoto to the east. Service from Takayama is by bus, while most travellers from Matsumoto catch the private Matsumoto Dentetsu train to Shin-Shimashima Station (¥680, 30 minutes) and transfer to buses – the ride in from either side is breathtaking. In the park, the main transit hubs are Hirayu Onsen (Gifu-ken side) and Kamikōchi (Nagano-ken side).

Hiring a car may save money, time and nerves. However, some popular routes, particularly the road between Naka-no-yu and Kamikōchi, are open only to buses and taxis.

KAMIKŌCHI 上高地
☎ 0263
The park's biggest drawcard, Kamikōchi offers some of Japan's most spectacular scenery along the rushing Azusa-gawa, and a variety of hiking trails from which to see it.

In the late 19th century, foreigners 'discovered' this mountainous region and coined the term 'Japan Alps'. A British missionary, Reverend Walter Weston, toiled from peak to peak and sparked Japanese interest in mountaineering as a sport. He is now honoured with a festival (on the first Sunday in June, the official opening of the hiking season), and Kamikōchi has become a base for strollers, hikers and climbers. It's a pleasure just to meander

FRANK CARTER
Gasshō-zukuri (thatched-roof houses) in Gokayama (p180)

Kamikōchi's riverside paths lined with *sasa* (bamboo grass).

Kamikōchi is closed from mid-November to late April, and in high season (late July to late August, and during the foliage season in October) can seem busier than Shinjuku Station. Arrive early in the day, especially during the foliage season. June to mid-July is the rainy season, making outdoor pursuits depressingly soggy. It's perfectly feasible to visit Kamikōchi as a day trip, but you'll miss out on the pleasures of staying in the mountains and taking uncrowded early-morning or late-afternoon walks.

KAMIKŌCHI

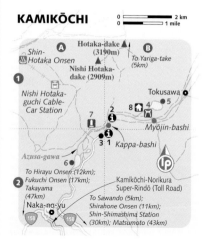

INFORMATION
Kamikōchi Information Centre
上高地インフォメーションセンター 1 B2
Kamikōchi Visitor Centre
上高地ビジターセンター 2 B1
Kankō Ryokan Kumiai 3 A2

SIGHTS & ACTIVITIES
Hotaka-jinja 穂高神社 4 B1
Myōjin-ike 明神池 5 B1
Taishō-ike 6 A2
Weston Relief ウェストン像 7 A1

SLEEPING
Kamikōchi Gosenjaku Lodge
上高地五千尺ロッヂ 8 B1

ORIENTATION

Visitors arrive at Kamikōchi at the bus station, which is surrounded by visitor facilities. A 10-minute walk from the bus station along the Azusa-gawa takes you to the bridge Kappa-bashi, named for a water sprite of Japanese legend, where most of the hiking trails start.

INFORMATION

The **Kankō Ryokan Kumiai** (Ryokan Association; ☎ 95-2405; ☷ 9am-5pm late Apr–mid-Nov) at the Kamikōchi bus station is geared to booking accommodation, though non-Japanese speakers may want to book through the tourist information office in Matsumoto (p190) for Kamikōchi and Shirahone Onsen as it has English-speaking staff.

A little bit further along and to the left, the **Kamikōchi Information Centre** (☎ 95-2433; ☷ 8am-5pm late Apr–mid-Nov) provides hiking instructions and info on weather conditions, and also distributes the useful English *Kamikōchi Pocket Guide* with a map of the main walking tracks.

A 10-minute walk from the bus station along the main trail, the spiffy **Kamikōchi Visitor Centre** (☎ 95-2606; ☷ 8am-5pm late Apr–mid-Nov) has displays on Kamikōchi's flora and fauna, and explanations of its geological history.

SIGHTS & ACTIVITIES
HIKING & CLIMBING

The river valley offers mostly level, short-distance walks. A four-hour round trip starts east of Kappa-bashi along the right-hand side of the river past Myōjin-bashi (one hour) to Tokusawa (another hour) before returning. By Myōjin-bashi is the idyllic **Myōjin-ike** (admission ¥300), a pond whose clear waters mark the innermost shrine of **Hotaka-jinja**.

West of Kappa-bashi, you can amble along the right-hand side of the river to **Weston Relief** (a monument to Kamikōchi's most famous hiker, Walter Weston; 15 minutes) or keep to the left-hand side of the river and walk to the pond **Taishō-ike** (40 minutes).

Dozens of long-distance options vary in duration from a couple of days to a week. Japanese-language maps of the area show routes and average hiking times between huts, major peaks and landmarks. Favourite hikes and climbs (which can mean human traffic jams during high seasons) include Yariga-take (3180m) and Hotaka-dake (3190m) – also known as Oku-Hotaka-dake.

SLEEPING & EATING
Kamikōchi Gosenjaku Lodge (☎ 95-2221; fax 95-2511; www.gosenjaku.co.jp; 'skier's bed' per person ¥10,500, d/tr/q ¥17,850/16,800/15,750) This is a polished little place. Its 34 rooms are mostly Japanese-style plus some 'skier's beds', which are basically curtained-off bunk beds. Rooms all have sink

and toilet, but baths are shared. Buffet-style meals are Japanese, Chinese and Western.

GETTING AROUND
Private vehicles are prohibited between Naka-no-yu and Kamikōchi; access is only by bus or taxi, and then only as far as the Kamikōchi bus station. Those with private cars can use car parks en route to Naka-no-yu in the hamlet of Sawando for ¥500 per day; shuttle buses (¥1800 return) run a few times per hour.

Buses run via Naka-no-yu and Taishō-ike to the bus station. Hiking trails commence at Kappa-bashi, which is a short walk from the bus station.

SHIN-HOTAKA ONSEN
新穂高温泉
☎ 0578
The reason to visit Shin-Hotaka Onsen, north of Fukuchi Onsen, is the **Shin-Hotaka Ropeway** (新穂高ロープウェイ; ☎ 89-2252; www.okuhi.jp/rop/frtop.html; one-way/return ¥1500/2800; ⏰ 6am-5.15pm

MARCO BETTI/ALAMY
Kamikōchi

1 Aug–last Sun in Aug, 8.30am–4.45pm late Aug–Jul, additional hours in high seasons). At 1308m, this two-stage cable car is Japan's – some say Asia's – longest, whisking you 2156m up Nishi Hotaka-dake (2909m). The entrance is a few minutes' walk uphill from Shin-Hotaka Onsen bus station.

Assuming clear weather, views from the top are spectacular, from observation decks and walking trails – in winter, snows can easily be shoulder deep. In season (only, please!), fit, properly equipped hikers with ample time can choose longer hiking options from the top cable-car station, Nishi Hotaka-guchi, including over to Kamikōchi (p183, three hours), which is *much* easier than going the other way.

Adjacent to the bus terminal is a spartan **public onsen** (新穂高温泉アルペン浴場; admission free; 9.30am–4pm). During summer it's crowded with tourists, but in the low season your only company is likely to be a few weary shift workers from the nearby hydroelectric plant.

NAGANO-KEN
長野県
NAGANO 長野
☎ 026 / pop 377,000

The mountain-ringed prefectural capital, Nagano has been a place of pilgrimage since the Kamakura period. Back then it was a temple town centred on the magnificent Zenkō-ji. The temple still draws more than four million visitors every year.

Following Nagano's flirtation with international fame, hosting the Winter Olympic Games in 1998, the city has reverted to its friendly small-town self, if just a bit more worldly. While Zenkō-ji is the only real attraction in the city centre, Nagano is a great regional base for day trips.

ORIENTATION
Nagano is laid out on a grid, with Zenkō-ji occupying a prominent position overlooking the city centre from the north. Chūō-dōri leads south from the temple, doing a quick dogleg before hitting JR Nagano Station, 1.8km away; it is said that street-planners considered Zenkō-ji so auspicious that it should not be approached directly from the train. The private Nagano Dentetsu ('Nagaden') train line and most bus stops are just outside JR Nagano Station's Zenkō-ji exit.

INFORMATION
Nagano Tourist Information Centre (☎ 226-5626; 9am–6pm) Inside JR Nagano Station, this friendly outfit has good English-language colour maps and guides to Nagano and the surrounding areas. Staff can book accommodation in the city centre.

SIGHTS
ZENKŌ-JI 善光寺
This **temple** (☎ 234-3591; 491 Motoyoshi-chō; admission free; 4.30am–4.30pm summer, 6am–4pm winter, varied hours rest of year) is believed to have been founded in the 7th century and is the home of the revered statue Ikkō-Sanzon, who was allegedly the first Buddhist image to arrive in Japan (in AD 552).

The original site was south of the current temple, off what's now the busy shopping street Nakamise-dōri; however, in that location it was destroyed 11 times by fires originating in neighbouring homes and businesses – and rebuilt each time with donations from believers throughout Japan. Finally, the Tokugawa shōgunate decreed that the temple be moved to its present, safer location. The current building dates from 1707 and is a National Treasure.

NOBORU KOMINE

Hondō (main hall) at Zenkō-ji

Visitors ascend to the temple via Nakamise-dōri and the impressive gates **Niō-mon** and **Sanmon**. In the *hondō* (main hall), the Ikkō-Sanzon image is in an ark left of the central altar, behind a dragon-embroidered curtain. To the right of the altar, visitors may descend a staircase to **Okaidan** (admission ¥500), a pitch-black tunnel that symbolises death and rebirth and provides the closest access to the hidden image (taller visitors: watch your head!). As you navigate the twisting tunnel, dangle your arm along the right-hand wall until you feel something heavy, moveable and metallic – said to be the key to salvation, a bargain for the admission price.

Any bus from bus stop 1 in front of JR Nagano Station's Zenkō-ji exit will get you to the temple (¥100, about 10 minutes; alight at the Daimon bus stop).

SLEEPING

Hotel Metropolitan Nagano (☎ 291-7000; www.metro-n.co.jp; 1346 Minami-Ishido-chō; s/d/tw from ¥9240/18,480/19,635) An excellent choice by the station. The modern, elegant Metropolitan features airy, comfortable rooms, and there's a cafe, restaurant and top-floor lounge with broad views. Japan Rail Pass holders get a 20% discount. It's just outside the station's Zenkō-ji exit; sensitive sleepers should reserve a room facing away from the tracks.

EATING

Yayoi-za (☎ 232-2311; 503 Daimon-chō; mains ¥945-2650; ☺ lunch & dinner, closed Tue & 2nd Wed each month) A homey 150-year-old shop specialising in *seiro-mushi* (ingredients steamed in a wood and bamboo box). The standard is *monzen seiro-mushi* (local beef and vegetables; ¥1680), while vegetarians can enjoy *onyasai salada* (steamed vegetables in sesame sauce). For dessert, try *kurian cream* (chestnut-paste mousse; ¥525).

Sukitei (すき亭; ☎ 234-1123; 112-1 Tsumashina; lunch sets ¥1150-2950, sukiyaki from ¥2500; ☺ lunch & dinner Tue-Sun) Tops in town for succulent sukiyaki. Set menus include udon, *gyusashi* (beef sashimi) and more. The price of the top-grade beef is sky-high, but if you try it you may never go back to the cheaper stuff.

GETTING THERE & AWAY

Nagano *shinkansen* run twice hourly from Tokyo Station (Asama, ¥7970, 1¾ hours). The JR Shinonoi line connects Nagano with Matsumoto (Shinano *tokkyū*, ¥2970, 50 minutes) and Nagoya (Shinano *tokkyū*, ¥7330, 2¾ hours).

SHIGA KŌGEN 志賀高原
☎ 0269

The site of several events in the 1998 Nagano Olympics, Shiga Kōgen (☎ 34-2404; www.shigakogen.gr.jp/english; 1-day lift ticket ¥4800; ⏱ 8.30am-4.30pm Dec-Apr) is Japan's largest ski resort and one of the largest in the world: 21 linked areas covering 80 runs. One lift ticket gives access to all areas as well as the shuttle bus between the various base lodges. There is a huge variety of terrain for all skill levels, as well as ski-only areas.

Direct buses run between Nagano Station and Shiga Kōgen, with frequent departures in ski season (¥1600, 70 minutes). You can also take a train from Nagano to Yudanaka and continue to Shiga Kōgen by bus – take a Hase-ike-bound bus and get off at the last stop (¥760, approximately 40 minutes).

NOZAWA ONSEN
野沢温泉
☎ 0269 / pop 4050

A compact town that is tucked into a corner of the eastern Japan Alps, Nozawa Onsen is the quintessential Japanese onsen–ski resort. Nozawa feels like a Swiss ski resort, and you may wonder where you are – until you see a sign written entirely in kanji. Although Nozawa is worth visiting any time of year, skiing is the main attraction for foreign visitors.

SIGHTS & ACTIVITIES
NOZAWA ONSEN SKI RESORT
野沢温泉スキー場

The town is dominated by the Nozawa Onsen Ski Resort (☎ 85-3166; www .nozawaski.com/winter/en/; 1-day lift ticket ¥4600; ⏱ Dec-Apr), which is one of Honshū's best. The ski area here is more compact than, say, nearby Shiga Kōgen, and it's relatively easy to navigate and enjoy. The main base

Shiga Kōgen
JOHN BORTHWICK

rea is right around the Higake gondola tation. There is a good variety of terrain t all levels, and snowboarders should try he Karasawa terrain park or the half-pipe t Uenotaira. Advanced skiers will enjoy he steep and often mogulled Schneider Course, while beginners and families will njoy the Higake Course.

ONSEN
After skiing or hiking, check out the 13 ree onsen (6am-11pm) dotted about the own. Our favourite is Ō-yu, with its fine vooden building, followed by the scald-ng-hot Shin-yu, and the atmospheric old Kuma-no-tearai (Bear's Bathroom). The lo-cals like to say about some of these that hey're so hot 'humans can't even enter'. f you have silver jewellery, leave it in your oom unless you don't mind it turning olack for a day or so.

GETTING THERE & AWAY
There are direct buses between Nagano Station's east exit and Nozawa Onsen ¥1400, 90 minutes, six buses per day in winter, three buses per day in summer). Alternatively, take a JR Iiyama-line train be-ween Nagano and Togari Nozawa Onsen Station (¥740, 55 minutes). Regular buses connect Togari Nozawa Onsen Station and Nozawa Onsen (¥300, 15 minutes, nine per day). The bus station/ticket office is about 200m from the main bus stop, which is di-ectly in the middle of town. This can be a ittle confusing, but there are staff around to nelp get people where they need to be.

HAKUBA 白馬
☎ 0261
At the base of one of the highest sections of the northern Japan Alps, Hakuba is one of Japan's main ski and hiking centres. In winter, skiers from all over Japan and in-creasingly from overseas flock to Hakuba's

seven ski resorts. In summer, the region is crowded with hikers drawn by easy access to the high peaks. There are many onsen in and around Hakuba-mura, the main vil-lage, and a long soak after a day of action is the perfect way to ease your muscles.

For information, maps and lodging as-sistance, visit the Hakuba Shukuhaku Jōhō Centre (白馬宿泊情報センター; ☎ 72-6900; www.hakuba1.com, in Japanese; 7am-6pm), to the right of the Hakuba train/bus station, or Hakuba-mura Kankō Kyōkai Annai-jo (白馬村観光協会案内所; ☎ 72-2279; 8.30am-5.15pm), just out-side the station to the right (look for the 'i' symbol). Online, visit www.vill.hakuba .nagano.jp/e/index.htm.

SIGHTS & ACTIVITIES
HAPPŌ-ONE SKI RESORT 八方尾根
Host of the men's and women's down-hill races at the 1998 Winter Olympics, Happō-One (☎ 72-3066; www.hakuba-happo .or.jp, in Japanese; 1-day lift ticket ¥4800; Dec-Apr) is one of Japan's best ski areas. The mountain views here are superb – the entire Hakuba massif looks close enough to touch with your ski poles. Beginner, intermediate and advanced runs cater to skiers and snowboarders.

From Hakuba Station, a five-minute bus ride (¥260) takes you into the middle of Hakuba-mura; from there it's a 10-minute walk to the base of Happō-One and the main 'Adam' gondola base station. In win-ter, a shuttle bus makes the rounds of the village, lodges and ski base.

GETTING THERE & AWAY
Hakuba is connected with Matsumoto by the JR Ōito line (tokkyū, ¥2770, 56 min-utes; futsū, ¥1110, 99 minutes). Continuing north, change trains at Minami Otari to meet the JR Hokuriku line at Itoigawa, with connections to Niigata, Toyama

CENTRAL HONSHŪ

NAGANO-KEN

and Kanazawa. From Nagano, buses leave from Nagano Station (¥1500, approximately 70 minutes). There are also buses between Shinjuku Nishi-guchi, in Tokyo, and Hakuba (¥4700, 4½ hours).

MATSUMOTO 松本

☎ 0263 / pop 227,000

A traveller's favourite, Matsumoto has a superb castle, some pretty streets and an atmosphere that's both laid-back and surprisingly cosmopolitan.

Nagano-ken's second-largest city has been around since at least the 8th century. Formerly known as Fukashi, it was the castle town of the Ogasawara clan during the 14th and 15th centuries, and it continued to prosper through the Edo period. Today, Matsumoto's street aesthetic combines the black and white of its castle with *namako-kabe* (lattice-pattern-walled) *kura* (stone houses) and Edo-period streetscapes in the Nakamachi district, and some smart 21st-century Japanese architecture. Plus, views of the Japan Alps are never much further than around the corner. The area by the Metoba-gawa and Nakamachi boast galleries, comfortable cafes and reasonably priced, high-quality accommodation.

INFORMATION

Matsumoto's **tourist information office** (☎ 32-2814; 1-1-1 Fukashi; ⏰ 9.30am-5.45pm) inside Matsumoto Station, has English-language pamphlets and maps, and can book accommodation. For train and bus reservations, try **JTB** (☎ 35-3311; 1-2-11 Fukashi).

SIGHTS & ACTIVITIES

MATSUMOTO-JŌ 松本城

Even if you spend only a couple of hours in Matsumoto, be sure to visit **Matsumoto-jō** (☎ 32-2902; 4-1 Marunōchi; adult/child ¥600/300; ⏰ 8.30am-5pm early-Sep–mid-Jul, to 6pm mid-Jul & Aug), Japan's oldest wooden castle and one of four castles designated National Treasures – the others are Hikone, Himeji (p149) and Inuyama.

The magnificent three-turreted *donjon* (main keep) was built c 1595, in contrast

Feeding pigeons on the causeway at Matsumoto-jō

DOMINIC BONUCCEL

ng black and white, leading to the nickname Karasu-jō (Crow Castle). Steep steps
lead up six storeys, with impressive views
from each level. Lower floors display guns,
bombs and gadgets with which to storm
castles, and a delightful *tsukimi yagura*
(moon-viewing pavilion). It has a tranquil moat full of carp, with the occasional
swan gliding beneath the red bridges. The
basics are explained over loudspeakers in
English and Japanese.

SLEEPING

Nunoya (☎ /fax 32-0545; 3-5-7 Chūō; r per
person from ¥4500) Few inns have more
heart than this pleasantly traditional
charmer, with shiny wood floors and
quality tatami rooms with shared bathrooms. No meals are served, but the cafes
(and shops and galleries) of Nakamachi
are just outside.

Marumo (☎ 32-0115; fax 35-2251; 3-3-10
Chūō; r per person without bathroom ¥5250, with
breakfast ¥6300) Between Nakamachi and
the rushing Metoba-gawa, this beautiful
wooden ryokan dates from 1868 and has
lots of traditional charm, including a bamboo garden and coffee shop. Although
rooms aren't huge and don't have private facilities, it's quite popular, so book
ahead.

EATING & DRINKING

Shizuka (☎ 32-0547; 4-10-8 Ōte; dishes ¥525-
1365; ⊗ lunch & dinner Mon-Sat) Friendly, traditional *izakaya* serving favourites such
as *oden* (stew) and *yakitori* (skewers of
grilled chicken) as well as some more
challenging local specialties.

GETTING THERE & AWAY

AIR

Shinshū Matsumoto airport has flights to
Fukuoka, Osaka and Sapporo.

BUS

Alpico (☎ 35-7400) runs buses between
Matsumoto and Shinjuku in Tokyo (¥3400,
3¼ hours, 18 daily), Osaka (¥5710, 5¼
hours, two daily), Nagoya (¥3460, 3½
hours, six daily) and Takayama (¥3100,
2½ hours, four daily). Reservations are
advised. Matsumoto's bus station is in
the basement of the Espa building across
from the train station.

TRAIN

Matsumoto is connected with Tokyo's
Shinjuku Station (*tokkyū*, ¥6510, 2¾
hours, hourly), Nagoya (*tokkyū*, ¥5670,
two hours) and Nagano (Shinano *tokkyū*,
¥2970, 50 minutes; *futsū*, ¥1110, 70
minutes).

GETTING AROUND

The castle and the city centre are easily covered on foot, or free bicycles are
available for loan; inquire at the tourist
information office. Three 'town sneaker'
bus routes loop through the centre of
the city between 9am and 6pm from
April to November (to 5.30pm December
to March) for ¥100/300 per ride/day;
the blue and orange routes cover the
castle.

KISO VALLEY REGION
木曽
☎ 0264

Thickly forested and alpine, southwest
Nagano-ken is traversed by the twisting,
craggy former post road, the Nakasendō..
Like the more famous Tōkaidō, the
Nakasendō connected Edo (present-day
Tokyo) with Kyoto, enriching the towns
along the way. Today, several small towns
feature carefully preserved architecture of
those days, making this a highly recommended visit.

TSUMAGO & MAGOME
妻籠・馬篭

These are two of the most attractive Nakasendō towns. Both close their main streets to vehicular traffic and they're connected by an agreeable hike.

Tsumago feels like an open-air museum, about 15 minutes' walk from end to end. It was designated by the government as a protected area for the preservation of traditional buildings, so no modern developments such as telephone poles are allowed to mar the scene. The dark-wood glory of its lattice-fronted houses and gently sloping tile roofs is particularly beautiful in early morning mist. Many films and TV shows have been shot on its main street.

Tsumago's tourist information office (観光案内館; ☎ 57-3123; fax 57-4036; ✆ 8.30am-5pm) is in the centre of town, by the antique phone booth. Some English is spoken and there's English-language literature.

Down the street and across, Waki-honjin (脇本陣; ☎ 57-3322; adult/child ¥600/300; ✆ 9am-5pm) is a former rest stop for retainers of *daimyō* (domain lords) on the Nakasendō. Reconstructed in 1877 under special dispensation from the emperor Meiji, it contains a lovely moss garden and a special toilet built in case Meiji happened to show up (apparently he never did). If some elements remind you of Japanese castles, that's because Waki-honjin was built by a former castle builder, out of work due to Meiji's antifeudal policies. The Shiryōkan (資料館; local history museum) here houses elegant exhibitions about Kiso and the Nakasendō, with some English signage.

Across from Shiryōkan, Tsumago Honjin (妻籠本陣; ☎ 57-3322; adult/child ¥300/150; ✆ 9am-5pm) is where the *daimyō* themselves spent the night, though this building is more noteworthy for its architecture than its exhibits. A combined ticket (¥700/350) gives you admission to Waki-honjin and Shiryōkan as well.

The 7.8km hike connecting Tsumago and Magome peaks at the top of the steep pass, Magome-tōge (elevation 801m). From here, the trail to/from Tsumago passes waterfalls, forest and farmland, while the Magome approach is largely on paved road. It takes around 2½ hours to hike between these towns. It's easier from Magome (elevation 600m) to Tsumago (elevation 420m) than the other way. English signage marks the way. The Magome–Tsumago bus (¥600, 30 minutes, at least three daily in each direction, except Monday to Friday from December to February) also stops at the pass.

If you're hiking between Magome and Tsumago, the towns offer a handy baggage-forwarding service (per bag ¥500; ✆ daily late Jul-Aug, Sat, Sun & holidays late Mar-late Nov) from either tourist office to the other. Deposit your bags between 8.30am and 11.30am for delivery by 1pm.

SLEEPING & EATING

It's worth a stay in these towns, particularly Tsumago, to have them to yourself once the day-trippers clear out. Both tourist information offices can help book accommodation at numerous ryokan (from around ¥9000 per person) and *minshuku* (guesthouses, from around ¥7000); prices include two meals. Don't expect en-suite bath or toilet, but you will get heaps of atmosphere.

Fujioto (藤乙; ☎ 57-3009; www.takenet .or.jp/~fujioto; r per person ¥11,550) Another much-photographed, excellent ryokan, this place has impressive old-style rooms and a graceful garden, which you can enjoy over lunch such as Kiso Valley *teishoku* (trout; ¥1500). It's a few doors down from the Waki-honjin in Tsumago.

GETTING THERE & AWAY

Nakatsugawa and Nagiso Stations on the JR Chūō line serve Magome and Tsumago, respectively, though both are still at some distance. Nakatsugawa is connected with Nagoya (*tokkyū*, ¥2740, 47 minutes) and Matsumoto (*tokkyū*, ¥3980, 1¼ hours). A few *tokkyū* daily stop in Nagiso (from Nagoya ¥3080, one hour); otherwise change at Nakatsugawa (*futsū* ¥320, 20 minutes).

Buses leave hourly from Nakatsugawa station for Magome (¥540, 30 minutes). There's also an infrequent bus service between Magome and Tsumago (¥600, 45 minutes), via Magome-tōge.

Buses run between Tsumago and Nagiso Station (¥270, 10 minutes, eight per day), or it's an hour's walk.

Highway buses operate between Magome and Nagoya's Meitetsu Bus Centre (¥1810, 1½ hours), as well as Tokyo's Shinjuku Station (¥4500, 4½ hours). These stop at the nearby interchange (Magome Intah, 馬籠インター), from where it's about 1.3km on foot uphill, unless it's timed with the bus from Nakatsugawa.

TOYAMA-KEN
富山県

TATEYAMA–KUROBE ALPEN ROUTE 立山黒部 アルペンルート

This seasonal, 90km route, popular with tourists, connects Toyama with Shinano-omachi in Nagano-ken via a sacred mountain, a deep gorge, a boiling-hot spring and glory-hallelujah mountain scenery. It is divided into nine sections with different modes of transport: train, ropeway, cable car, bus, trolley bus and your own two feet. Travel is possible in either direction; instructions here are from Toyama.

BRENT WINEBRENNER

Wooden votive plaques

The website www.alpen-route.com/english/index.html has details.

The fare for the entire route is ¥10,560/17,730 one-way/return; individual tickets are available. The route can be completed in under six hours one-way, although you'll probably want to stop en route; some visitors find that a trip as far as Murodō, the route's highest point, is sufficient (¥6530 return). The route is open from mid-April to mid-November. Precise dates vary, so check with a tourist office. During high season (August to October), transport and accommodation reservations are strongly advised.

From Toyama Station take the chug-a-lug regional Chitetsu line (¥1170, one hour) through rural scenery to Tateyama (立山; 475m). There are plenty of ryokan in Tateyama if you make an early start or late finish.

From Tateyama, take the cable car (¥700, seven minutes) to **Bijodaira** (美女平) and then the bus (¥1660, 50 minutes) via the spectacular alpine plateau of Midagahara Kōgen to **Murodō** (室堂; 2450m). You can break the trip at Midagahara and do the 15-minute walk to see **Tateyama caldera** (立山カルデラ), the largest nonactive crater in Japan. The upper part of the plateau is often covered with deep snow until late into the summer; the road is kept clear by piling up the snow to form a virtual tunnel (great fun to drive through).

Murodō's beauty has been somewhat spoilt by a monstrous bus station, but short hikes take you back to nature. Just 10 minutes' walk north is the pond **Mikuri-ga-ike** (みくりが池). Twenty minutes further on is **Jigokudani Onsen** (Hell Valley Hot Springs): no bathing here, the waters are boiling!

To the east, you can hike for about two hours – including a very steep final section – to the peak of **O-yama** (雄山; 3003m) for an astounding panorama. Keen long-distance hikers with several days or a week to spare can continue south to Kamikōchi (p183).

Continuing on the route from Murodō, there's a bus ride (¥2100, 10 minutes) via a tunnel dug through Tateyama to **Daikanbō** (大観峰), where you can pause to admire the view before taking the cable car (¥1260, seven minutes) to Kurobe-daira, where another cable car whisks you down (¥840, five minutes) to Kurobeko beside the vast **Kurobe Dam** (黒部ダム).

There's a 15-minute walk from Kurobeko to the dam, where you can descend to the water for a cruise, or climb up to a lookout point, before taking the trolley bus to **Ogizawa** (扇沢; ¥1260, 16 minutes). From here, a bus ride (¥1330, 40 minutes) takes you down to Shinano-ōmachi Station (712m). From here there are frequent trains to Matsumoto (one hour), from where you can connect with trains for Tokyo, Nagoya and Nagano.

ISHIKAWA-KEN 石川県

KANAZAWA 金沢

☎ 076 / pop 456,000

Kanazawa's wealth of cultural attractions makes it a highlight for visitors to Hokuriku. It is most famed for Kenroku-en, the fine former castle garden that dates from the 17th century. The experience is rounded out by handsome streetscapes of the former geisha and samurai districts, attractive temples and a great number of museums for a city of its size.

ORIENTATION

Kanazawa's labyrinthine layout befits its castle-town past, but bus service makes it easy to get from the train station to the main sightseeing districts, which can then be covered on foot.

The site of the former Kanazawa-jō (Kanazawa Castle) and its gardens, including Kenroku-en, occupy the centre of town. The Katamachi district, just south, is Kanazawa's commercial and business hub, around the Kōrinbō 109 department store; its busiest intersection is known as the Scramble. The Nagamachi samurai district is a short walk west from Kōrinbō 109. Northeast of the castle, across the Asano-gawa, is the picturesque Higashi Chaya-gai (east geisha district); the hills of Higashiyama to its east offer walks and city views. Just south of Katamachi, across the Sai-gawa, is the Teramachi temple district.

INFORMATION

Kanazawa tourist information office (☎ 232-6200; 1 Hiro-oka-machi; ⏰ 9am-7pm) Friendly office inside Kanazawa Station. Pick up the bilingual map *Kanazawa Japan* (with details of sights,

CENTRAL HONSHŪ

ISHIKAWA-KEN

KANAZAWA

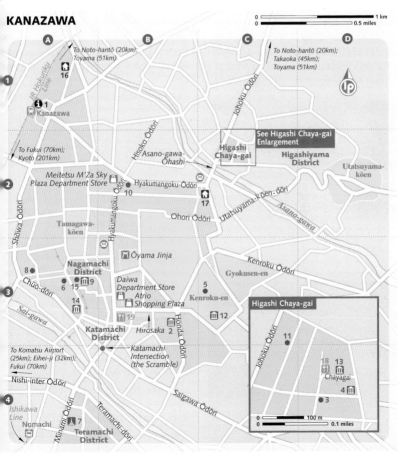

crafts and local specialities) and the English-language *Eye On Kanazawa,* which focuses on restaurants.

SIGHTS & ACTIVITIES

NAGAMACHI DISTRICT 長町

Once inhabited by samurai, this attractive, well-preserved district (Nagamachi Buke Yashiki) framed by two canals features winding streets lined with tile-roofed mud walls. Nomura Samurai House (☎ 221-3553; 1-3-32 Nagamachi; adult/child/student ¥500/250/400; ☺ 8.30am-5.30pm Apr-Sep, to 4.30pm Oct-Mar), though partly transplanted from outside Kanazawa, is worth a visit for its decorative garden.

Towards Sai-gawa, Shinise Kinenkan (☎ 220-2524; 2-2-45 Nagamachi; adult/child ¥100/free; ☺ 9.30am-5pm) offers a peek at a former pharmacy and, upstairs, a moder-

ate assortment of local traditional products. If the flowering tree made entirel of candy gives you a sweet tooth, slake i at *wagashi* (Japanese sweet) shops. Tarc (☎ 223-2838; ☺ 8.30am-5.30pm), next to the Nomura Samurai House, makes unusua flavours of *yōkan* (bean-paste gelatin – our favourite is choco. Murakam (☎ 264-4223; ☺ 8.30am-5pm), across the canal, makes *fukusamochi* (red-bea paste and pounded rice in a crêpe) and *kakiho* (*kinako* – soybean flour – rolled in *kurogoma,* which are black sesame seeds).

In a nonhistoric building just out side Nagamachi (about 250m from the Nomura Samurai House), Nagamachi Yūzen-kan (☎ 264-2811; admission ¥350 ☺ 9am-noon & 1-4.30pm Fri-Wed) display some splendid examples of *Kaga yūzen* kimono-dyeing and demonstrates the process. Inquire ahead about trying the silk-dyeing process yourself (¥4000).

21ST CENTURY MUSEUM OF CONTEMPORARY ART
金沢21世紀美術館

Designed by the acclaimed Tokyo archi tecture firm SANAA, this ultramoder museum (☎ 220-2800; www.kanazawa21.jp 1-2-1 Hirosaka; permanent collection adult/high school student & child/university student & senio ¥350/free/280; ☺ 10am-6pm Tue-Thu & Sun to 8pm Fri & Sat) opened in late 2004 and instantly became an 'it' building. A low slung glass cylinder, 113m in diameter forms the perimeter, and inside gallerie and auditoria are arranged like boxes o a tray. Nongallery portions of the building are open daily from 9am to 10pm.

Oh yes, there's art too: temporary ex hibits by leading contemporary artist from Japan and abroad, plus occasiona music and dance performances. Check the website for events; admission charge

NOBORU KOMINE
21st Century Museum of Contemporary Art

MICHAEL GEBICKI

Tree trussed with ropes to protect it from snow in Kenroku-en

⇘ KENROKU-EN 兼六園

Kanazawa's star attraction, Kenroku-en is ranked as one of the great gardens of the Edo period and one of the top three gardens in Japan (the other two are Kairaku-en in Mito and Kōraku-en in Okayama).

The name (*kenroku* means 'combined six') refers to a renowned garden from Sung-dynasty China that required six attributes for perfection: seclusion, spaciousness, artificiality, antiquity, abundant water and broad views (on clear days you can see to the Sea of Japan). In 1676 Kenroku-en started as the garden of an outer villa of Kanazawa-jō, but later it was enlarged to serve the castle itself, reaching completion in the early 19th century; the garden opened to the public in 1871. In winter the branches of Kenroku-en's trees are famously suspended with ropes via a post at each tree's centre, forming elegant conical shapes that protect the trees from breaking under Kanazawa's heavy snows. In spring, irises turn Kenroku-en's waterways into rivers of purple.

Inside the park, Seison-kaku is a retirement villa built by a Maeda lord for his mother in 1863. Elegant chambers named for trees and animals are filled with furniture and clothings. A detailed English-language pamphlet is available.

Things you need to know: Kenroku-en (☎ 234-3800; 1-1 Marunouchi; adult/senior/child ¥300/free/100; ⏰ 7am-6pm Mar-15 Oct, 8am-4.30pm 16 Oct-Feb); Seison-kaku (☎ 221-0580; 2-1 Dewa-machi; adult/elementary-school student/student ¥700/250/300; ⏰ 9am-5pm Thu-Tue)

may increase up to ¥1000 during special exhibitions.

HIGASHI CHAYA-GAI 東茶屋街

North of the Ōhi Pottery Museum and across Asano-gawa, Higashi Chaya-gai (Higashi Geisha District) is an enclave of narrow streets that was established early in the 19th century as a centre for geisha to entertain wealthy patrons. The slatted wooden facades of the geisha houses are romantically preserved.

One famous, traditional former geisha house is **Shima** (☎ 252-5675; 1-13-21 Higashiyama; adult/child ¥400/300; ❂ 9am-6pm), dating from 1820. Note the case of elaborate combs and *shamisen* (three-stringed traditional instrument) picks. Across the street, **Kaikarō** (☎ 253-0591; 1-14-8 Higashiyama; admission ¥700; ❂ 9am-5pm) is an early-19th-century geisha house refinished with contemporary fittings and art, including a red lacquered staircase.

The **Sakuda Gold Leaf Company** (☎ 251-6777; 1-3-27 Higashiyama; admission free; ❂ 9am-6pm) is a good place to observe the *kinpaku* (gold leaf) process and pick up gilded souvenirs (including pottery, lacquerware and, er, golf balls). The tea served here contains flecks of gold leaf, meant to be good for rheumatism. Even the walls of the loos are lined with gold and platinum.

On most nights you can visit the local *sentō* (public bath), **Higashi-yu** (☎ 252-5410; 1-13-2 Higashiyama; admission ¥370; ❂ 2pm-12.30am Mon & Wed-Sat, 1pm-12.30am Sun).

TERAMACHI DISTRICT 寺町

This hilly neighbourhood across Sai-gawa southwest of the centre, was established as a first line of defence and contains dozens of temples. **Myōryū-ji** (Ninja-dera; ☎ 241-0888; 1-2-12 Nomachi; admission ¥800; ❂ 9am-4.30pm Mar-Nov, to 4pm Dec-Feb, reservations required) is a five-minute walk from the river. Completed in 1643, it was designed as a hideout in case of attack, and contains hidden stairways, escape routes, secret chambers, concealed tunnels and trick doors. The popular name refers to the temple's connection with ninja. Admission is by tour only – it's in Japanese but visual enough. Take Minami Ō-dōri across the river, take a left at the first major intersection, then the first right.

ŌMICHŌ MARKET 近江町市場

A warren of several hundred shops and restaurants, many of which specialise in seafood, this **market** (35 Ōmichō; ❂ 9am-5pm) bustles all day and is a great place for a break from sightseeing and to watch everyday people in action. Ōmichō func

Takayama (p176)

...ions like the outer market of Tokyo's Tsukiji Fish Market, but thanks to a recent makeover it's a lot more orderly and polished. It's between Katamachi district and Kanazawa Station. The nearest bus stop is Musashi-ga-tsuji.

SLEEPING

Hotel Dormy Inn Kanazawa (☎ 263-9888; fax 263-9312; www.hotespa.net, in Japanese; 2-25 Horikawa-shinmachi; s/d/tw ¥8500/12,000/15,000; ✗ ☐) This brand-new hotel steps from the station is filled with futuristic art. Most of its 304 rooms are singles and have an inner door to keep out extraneous noise. There's a naturium- and calcium-rich onsen *rotemburo* on the top floor, and a coin laundry.

Matsumoto (☎ 221-0302; fax 221-0303; 1-7-2 Owari-chō; r per person with 2 meals ¥25,000) This upscale inn bills itself as a *ryōri* (cuisine) ryokan; expect a culinary treat of local specialities. Huge rooms have private bathrooms. It's near the intersection of Hyakumangoku-ōdōri and Jūhoku-dōri, down a narrow street across from the post office. No English is spoken.

EATING

Janome-sushi Honten (☎ 231-0093; 1-1-12 Kōrinbō; mains ¥1200-3400, Kaga ryōri sets from ¥4000; ❀ lunch & dinner Thu-Tue) Highly regarded for sashimi and Kaga cuisine. One of our Japanese friends says that when he eats here, he knows he's really in Kanazawa. It's across a little stream from Siena clothing store.

Hotaruya (☎ 251-8585; 1-13-24 Higashi-yama; lunch/dinner courses from ¥3675/6300; ❀ lunch & dinner) To splurge on *Kaga ryōri* and step back in time, visit this shop in Higashi Chaya-gai. You'll be rewarded with wood-beam and tatami-room surroundings, and understated, standard-setting course dinners.

House facade in Higashi Chaya-gai (p197)

GETTING THERE & AWAY
BUS
JR Highway Bus (☎ 234-0111; ❀ reservations 9am-7pm) operates express buses from in front of Kanazawa Station's east exit, to Tokyo (¥7840, Ikebukuro seven hours, Shinjuku 7½ hours) and Kyoto (¥4060, 4¼ hours). **Hokutetsu Bus** (☎ 234-0123; ❀ reservations 8am-7pm) serves Nagoya (¥4060, four hours).

TRAIN
The JR Hokuriku line links Kanazawa with Fukui (*tokkyū*, ¥2940, 50 minutes; *futsū*, ¥1280, 1½ hours), Kyoto (*tokkyū*, ¥6710, 2¼ hours), Osaka (*tokkyū*, ¥7440, 2¾ hours) and Toyama (*tokkyū*, ¥2810, 35 minutes), with connections to Takayama (total ¥5840, additional 90 minutes).

From Tokyo take the Jōetsu *shinkansen* and change at Echigo-Yuzawa in Northern Honshū (¥12,710, four hours).

GETTING AROUND

Any bus from station stop 7, 8 or 9 will take you to the city centre (¥200, day pass ¥900). The Kanazawa Loop Bus (single ride/day pass ¥200/500, every 15 minutes from 8.30am to 6pm) circles the major tourist attractions in 45 minutes. On Saturday, Sunday and holidays, the Machi-bus goes to Kōrinbō for ¥100.

NOTO-HANTŌ 能登半島

With rugged seascapes, traditional rural life, fresh seafood and a light diet of cultural sights, this peninsula atop Ishikawa-ken is highly recommended. Noto juts out from Honshū like a boomerang, with sights dotting its flat west coast. The lacquer-making town of Wajima is the hub of the rugged north, known as Oku-Noto, and the best place to stay overnight. Famous products include *Wajima-nuri* lacquerware, renowned for its durability and rich colours, Suzu-style pottery and locally harvested sea salt and *iwanori* seaweed.

Day trips from Kanazawa, while possible, don't do the peninsula justice – buzzing through the sights leaves little time to savour the day-to-day pace. Unless you're under your own power, a speedy trip may not be an option anyway: public transport is infrequent. If staying overnight, be sure to reserve; accommodation fills up in summer, and many lodgings close in winter.

Kanazawa's **tourist information office** (☎ 076-232-6200) stocks the *Unforgettable Ishikawa* map and guide, which includes the peninsula. On the peninsula, the most user-friendly tourist office is in Wajima.

GETTING THERE & AROUND

In the centre of Oku-Noto, **Noto airport** (NTQ; ☎ 0768-26-2100) connects the peninsula with Tokyo's Haneda airport. **ANA** (☎ 0120-029-222) offers two return flights daily (one-way ¥19,800, 65 minutes). **Furusato Taxi** (☎ 0768-22-7411) is a van service to locations around the peninsula

Garden at Nomura Samurai House (p196), Kanazawa

MICHAEL GEBICKI

Fares start at ¥700 to nearby communities including Wajima (about 30 minutes).

Although there are trains, most sights can be reached by road only. For the west Noto coast, get off the JR Nanao Line at Hakui (*tokkyū*, ¥1370; *futsū*, ¥740), and connect to buses. For Oku-Noto, trains continue to Wakura Onsen, connecting to less frequent buses. Check departure and arrival times with the bus company **Hokutetsu** (☎ in Kanazawa 076-234-0123) to avoid long waits. Hokutetsu also runs express buses between Kanazawa and Wajima (¥2200, two hours, 10 daily), with a couple continuing to Sosogi (¥2510, 2¾ hours). Buses leave from outside Kanazawa Station.

Daily tour buses from Kanazawa (¥7200, 8.10am to 3.30pm) include Wajima's morning market (p202), Ganmon and more, plus lunch, a Japanese-speaking guide and admission fees, with a very quick turnaround.

Driving has become a popular option. The 83km Noto Yūryo (能登有料; Noto Toll Rd) speeds you as far as Anamizu (toll ¥1180); allow two hours to complete the journey to Wajima via Rte 1. The toll road does not serve most of Noto's west-coast sights, so allow a day to see those sights en route to Wajima.

Noto's mostly flat west coast appeals to cyclists. However, cycling is not recommended on the Noto-kongō coast and east because of steep, blind curves.

WEST NOTO COAST
☎ 0767

KITA-KE 喜多家
During the Edo period, the Kita family administered more than 200 villages from this **house** (☎ 28-2546; adult/child ¥500/200; ☺ 8.30am-5pm Apr-Oct, to 4pm Nov-Mar), at the pivotal crossroads of the Kaga, Etchū and Noto fiefs. Inside this splendid, sprawl-

Terraced rice paddies by the sea in Noto-hantō
FRANK CARTER

ing home and adjacent museum, still in the hands of the same family (about 400 years), are displays of weapons, ceramics, farming tools, fine and folk art, and documents. The garden has been called the Moss Temple of Noto.

Kita-ke is about 1km from the Komedashi exit on the Noto Toll Rd. By train, take the JR Nanao line to Menden Station; it's about 20 minutes' walk.

MYŌJŌ-JI 妙成寺
Founded in 1294 by Nichizō, a disciple of Nichiren, the imposing **Myōjō-ji** (☎ 27-1226; admission ¥500; ☺ 8am-5pm Apr-Oct, to 4.30pm Nov-Mar) remains an important temple for the sect. The grounds comprise many buildings, including 10 Important Cultural Properties, notably the strikingly elegant **Gojū-no-tō** (Five-Storeyed

Pagoda). Pick up an English-language pamphlet.

The Togi-bound bus from Hakui Station can drop you at Myōjō-ji-guchi bus stop (¥420, 18 minutes); from here, it's under 10 minutes' walk.

NOTO-KONGŌ COAST 能登金剛
☎ 0768

This rocky, cliff-lined shoreline extends for about 16km between Fukuura and Sekinohana, and is set with dramatic rock formations like the gate-shaped **Ganmon** (best reached under your own power, or by tour bus with the usual caveats).

The manicured little town of **Monzen**, about 25km northeast of Ganmon, is home to majestic **Sōji-ji** (☎ 42-0005, dial 186 for caller ID; fax 42-1002; adult/child/high-school student ¥400/150/300; ⏰ 8am-5pm), the temple established in 1321 as the head of the Sōtō school of Zen. After a fire severely damaged the buildings in 1898 the temple was restored, but it now functions as a branch temple; the main temple is now in Yokohama. Sōji-ji welcomes visitors to experience one hour of *zazen* (seated meditation; ¥300; 9am to 3pm) and serves *shōjin-ryōri* (Buddhist vegetarian cuisine; ¥2500 to ¥3500); reserve at least two days in advance.

Monzen is a bus hub with service to Kanazawa (¥2200, 2½ hours), Hakui (¥1510, 1½ hours) and Wajima (¥740, 35 minutes). For the temple, tell the driver 'Sōji-ji-mae'.

WAJIMA 輪島
☎ 0768 / pop 31,500

About 20km from Monzen, this fishing port on the north coast is the largest town in Oku-Noto and a historic centre for the production of *Wajima-nuri* (Wajima lacquerware) and, now, tourism. There's a prettily refurbished town centre and a lively morning market.

The **tourist information office** (☎ 22 1503; ⏰ 8am-7pm) at the former Wajima train station (now called Michi-no-eki, 道の駅 still the bus station) provides English leaflets and maps, and staff can book accommodation. Limited English is spoken.

SIGHTS & ACTIVITIES
ISHIKAWA WAJIMA URUSHI ART MUSEUM 石川輪島漆芸美術館

In the southwest corner of the town centre this stately, contemporary **museum** (☎ 22 9788; adult/junior-high & elementary-school student, student ¥600/150/300; ⏰ 9am-5pm) has a large rotating collection of lacquerware in galleries on two floors; works are both Japanese and foreign, ancient and contemporary. It's about a 15-minute walk west of the train station. Phone ahead, as this museum closes between exhibitions.

SLEEPING & EATING
Wajima (わじま; ☎ 22-4243; sakaguti@quartz ocn.ne.jp; s/d per person with 2 meals ¥7875/7350) This 10-room *minshuku* has subdued woodwork, a mineral onsen and *Wajima-nuri* bowls and chopsticks for eating your home-grown rice and catch of the day. It's across Futatsuya-bashi, south of the city centre.

Madara-yakata (まだら館; ☎ 22-3453; mains ¥800-2100; ⏰ lunch & dinner, closed irregularly) This restaurant serves local specialities, including *zosui* (rice hotpot), *yaki-zakana* (grilled fish) and seasonal seafood, surrounded by folk crafts. It's near the morning market street.

SHOPPING
The **asa-ichi** (morning market; ⏰ 8am-noon, closed 10th & 25th of month) is highly entertaining, though undeniably touristy. Some 200 fishwives ply their wares – seafood, crafts etc – with sass and humour that cuts across the language barrier. To

Festival decorations in Noto-hantō

FRANK CARTER

find the market, walk north along the river from the Wajima Shikki Shiryōkan and turn right just before Iroha-bashi.

GETTING THERE & AWAY

See p201 for information on Hokutetsu buses to Wajima (☎ 22-2314). Buses to Monzen (¥740, 35 minutes) leave every one to two hours.

SUZU & NOTO-CHŌ
珠洲・能登町

☎ 0768

Heading east from central Wajima towards the end of the peninsula, you'll pass the famous slivered *dandan-batake* (rice terraces) at Senmaida (千枚田) before arriving in the coastal village of Sosogi (曽々木). After the Taira were defeated in 1185, one of the few survivors, Taira Tokitada, was exiled to this region. The Tokikuni family, which claims descent from Tokitada, eventually divided into two clans and established separate family residences here, both now Important Cultural Properties. From Wajima, buses bound for Ushitsu stop in Sosogi (¥740, 40 minutes).

The first residence, Tokikuni-ke (Tokikuni Residence; ☎ 32-0075; adult/junior high-school student/high-school student ¥600/300/400; ☯ 8.30am-5pm daily Apr-Dec, Sat & Sun Jan-Mar), was built in 1590 in the style of the Kamakura period and has a *meishō tei-en* (famous garden). A few minutes' walk away, Kami Tokikuni-ke (Upper Tokikuni Residence; ☎ 32-0171; adult/child ¥500/400; ☯ 8.30am-5.30pm Jul-Sep, to 5pm Oct-Jun), with its impressive thatched roof and elegant interior, was constructed early in the 19th century. Entry to either home includes a leaflet in English.

Lamp no Yado (☎ 86-8000; www.lampno yado.co.jp; r per person with 2 meals from ¥19,000; ☯), in remote Suzu, is a place that sparkles. This 14-room wood-built waterside village, far from the main drag, has been an inn since the 1970s, but the building goes back four centuries, to when people would escape to its curative waters for weeks at a time. Rooms (some two-storey) have private bathrooms and their own *rotemburo*. The pool is almost superfluous. A very worthy splurge; reservations are required.

CENTRAL HONSHŪ

FUKUI-KEN

FRANK CARTER

Young girls at a festival in Kanazawa (p194)

FUKUI-KEN
福井県

EIHEI-JI 永平寺

☎ 0776

In 1244 the great Zen master Dōgen (1200–53), founder of the Sōtō sect of Zen Buddhism, established Eihei-ji in a forest near Fukui. Today it's one of Sōtō's two head temples, one of the world's most influential Zen centres and a palpably spiritual place amid mountains, mosses and ancient cedars. Serious students of Zen should consider a retreat here – there are commonly some 150 priests and disciples in residence – but all are welcome to visit.

The **temple** (☎ 63-3102; adult/child ¥500/200; ⏱ 9am-5pm) receives huge numbers of visitors as sightseers or for rigorous Zen training. Among the approximately 70 buildings, the standard circuit concentrates on seven major ones: San-mon (main gate), Butsuden (Buddha Hall), Hattō (Dharma Hall), Sō-dō (Priests' Hall), plus the *daikuin* (kitchen), *yokushitsu* (bath) and, yes, *tōsu* (lavatory). You walk among the buildings on wooden walkways in your stockinged feet (pretty chilly in cold weather). The Shōbōkaku exhibits many Eihei-ji treasures.

The temple is often closed for periods varying from a week to 10 days for religious observance. Before setting out, be sure to check www.sotozen-net.or.jp/kokusai/list/eiheiji.htm or with tourist offices.

You can attend the temple's four-day, three-night **sanzen program** (religious trainee program; ☎ 63-3640; fax 63-3631; www.sotozen-net.or.jp/kokusai/list/eiheiji.htm; fee ¥12,000), which follows the monks' training schedule, complete with 3.50am prayers, cleaning, *zazen* and ritual meals in which not a grain of rice may be left behind. Japanese-language ability is not necessary, but it helps to be able to sit in the half-lotus position. Everyone we've spoken to who has completed this course agreed it is a remarkable experience. Book at least one month in advance. A single night's stay, *sanrō*, is also possible for ¥8000 (with two meals). Day visitors can eat a lunch of *shōjin-ryōri* (¥3000) by reservation.

To get to Eihei-ji from Fukui (which has JR links to Kanazawa, Osaka and Kyoto) take the Keifuku bus (¥720, 35 minutes, at least three daily) from stop 5, a couple of blocks from Fukui; buses (¥720, 35 minutes) depart from the east exit of Fukui Station.

NORTHERN HONSHŪ & HOKKAIDŌ

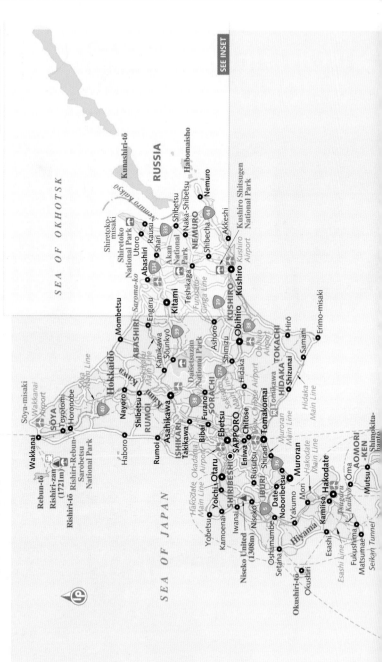

SEE INSET

RUSSIA

SEA OF OKHOTSK

SEA OF JAPAN

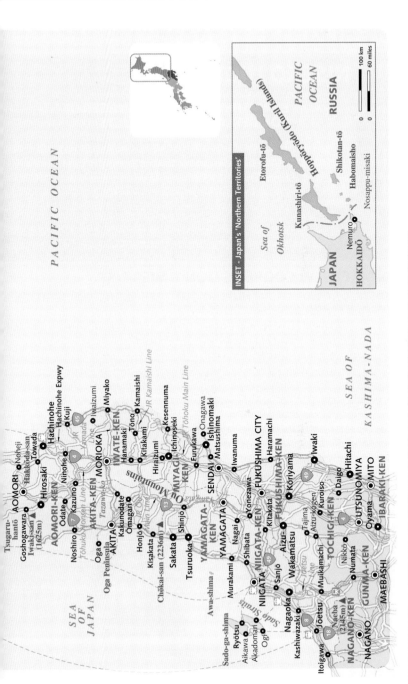

PACIFIC OCEAN

INSET - Japan's 'Northern Territories'

RUSSIA

PACIFIC OCEAN

Happōryōdo (Kuril Islands)

Etorofu-tō

Kunashiri-tō

Shikotan-tō

Habomaisho

Nosappu-misaki

Sea of Okhotsk

Nemuro

JAPAN

HOKKAIDŌ

0   100 km
0   60 miles

SEA OF JAPAN

PACIFIC OCEAN

Hachinohe Expwy

Hachinohe

Iwaizumi

Miyako

Kuji

Kamaishi

JR Kamaishi Line

Tōhoku Shinkansen Line

Tsugaru-hantō

Noheji

Goshogawara

Iwaki-san (1625m)

Hakkōda-san

Towada

Hirosaki

AOMORI

AOMORI-KEN

Odate

Ninohe

Kazuno

Tazawako

Tōhoku Shinkansen Line

MORIOKA

IWATE-KEN

Hanamaki

Tōno

Kitakami

Kesennuma

Noshiro

AKITA-KEN

Ōmagari

Ou Mountains

Ichinoseki

Onagawa

Ishinomaki

Matsushima

Oga

Oga Peninsula

AKITA

Kakunodate

Honjō

Hiraizumi

Furukawa

Ou Main Line

Tōhoku Main Line

Chōkai-san (2236m)

Kisakata

Sakata

Shinjō

YAMAGATA-KEN

Nagai

Iwanuma

SENDAI

MIYAGI-KEN

Haramachi

FUKUSHIMA CITY

Iwaki

Hitachi

Tsuruoka

YAMAGATA

Yonezawa

Kōriyama

FUKUSHIMA-KEN

Awa-shima

Murakami

Shibata

Kitakata

Tajima

Aizu-Kōgen

Daigo

UTSUNOMIYA

MITO

IBARAKI-KEN

SEA OF JAPAN

Sado-ga-shima

Ryōtsu

Aikawa

Akadomari

Ogi

Sado Straits

NIIGATA

Sanjō

Wakamatsu

Aizu

NIIGATA-KEN

Muikamachi

Kuroiso

Nikkō

Numata

TOCHIGI-KEN

Ōyama

KASHIMA-NADA

Nagaoka

Kashiwazaki

Jōetsu

Naeba (2145m)

GUNMA-KEN

MAEBASHI

Itoigawa

NAGANO-KEN

NAGANO

Chōkai-san

Ōu Mountains

HIGHLIGHTS

1 NISEKO HIGHLIGHTS

BY MATHEW COOPER, MANAGER OF POWDERLAND SKI PRODUCTS

The attraction of Niseko is the extremely light dry fluffy powder snow that is brought over steadily from the cold Siberian lands to the west. Off-course skiing is allowed, and there are all types of terrain available. This is some of the most reliable lift-served powder skiing around and you can ever ski it at night, under the lights.

⤵ MATTHEW COOPER'S DON'T MISS LIST

❶ BACK BOWLS OF AN'NUPURI

After one of Niseko's regular dumps of powder, experienced skiers make their way to the top of Mt An'nupuri, accessible via a 20-minute hike from the top of the lifts. Here, there's a great variety of open and partially treed terrain, and you can usually find untracked powder long after the snow stops falling. You can make your way back to the base of the An'nupuri Gondola after a run if you cut out early, or you can head all the way to the bottom and get a friend to drive you back to the base of the area.

❷ TREE SKIING ON HIRAFU

The easternmost of the three main sk areas at Niseko, Niseko Grand Hirafu offers some spectacular lift-served tree skiing. A favourite is the Miharashi run which is 880m of pure powder pleas ure served by the Hirafu Gondola.

❸ NIGHT POWDER SKIING

Niseko offers something you won' find anywhere else in the world: night powder skiing. With a view of the vol cano Yōtei-zan under the moon in the

Clockwise from top: Downhill skiing at Niseko (p236); Sunset at Niseko (p236); Powder skiing

CLOCKWISE FROM TOP: TONY HARRINGTON/STOCKSHOT/ALAMY; FELIX RIOUX; FELIX RIOL

istance, the shadows of the birch rees as you glide by, and the spray of loodlit snow, it's a truly spellbinding xperience.

GOSHIKI ONSEN

About 25 minutes from the base of the ki area, Goshiki Onsen is a must for the obligatory après-ski soak. With a fine otemburo (outdoor bath), this is the place to enjoy the classic experience of snow falling on your head while oaking in hot spring water.

❺ FOREIGNER-FRIENDLY BARS & RESTAURANTS

In winter, you might get the impression that Niseko is part of Australia, given the number of Aussie skiers who make the journey from down under to enjoy the famous powder. The popularity of the area with foreign skiers ensures that Niseko is a very foreigner-friendly area.

⊾ THINGS YOU NEED TO KNOW

Out of bounds skiing The back bowls and nongroomed areas are only open when the ski patrol judges them to be safe from avalanche danger; don't ski closed areas **Be warned** Niseko can be brutally cold, particularly near the summit of Mt An'nupuri; dress accordingly **See our author's review on p236**

HIGHLIGHTS

2

⬎ DAISETSUZAN NATIONAL PARK

The roof of Hokkaidō, this national park (p239) is the premier outdoor destination in Hokkaidō and one of the best in all of Japan. Many visitors base themselves in onsen towns around the periphery of the park and make day trips into the mountains, using gondolas and chairlifts to make the initial ascent. Serious hikers set out on the multiday Daisetsuzan Grand Traverse right across the park.

3

⬎ SAPPORO

Sapporo (p227) is one of Japan's most attractive cities and a great place to make a thorough exploration of Hokkaidō's brilliant seafood and produce – find yourself an *izakaya* (dining pub) and feast on salmon, crab and local vegetables. Then, explore the botanical garden, the Ainu Museum and the fish market. If you're here in February, don't miss the famous Sapporo Yuki Matsuri (Sapporo Snow Festival).

⤳ DEWA SANZAN

An ancient pilgrimage track runs across the three peaks of Dewa Sanzan (p222) in Northern Honshū. *Yamabushi* (mountain mystics who practise the Shūgendō sect of Buddhism) come from all across Japan to hike the three mountains, which represent birth, death and rebirth. Join them on the pilgrimage route and stay in mountain huts along the way.

⤳ SADO-GA-SHIMA

About 35km off the coast of Niigata-ken in Northern Honshū, Japan's sixth-largest island of Sado-ga-shima (p225) is the home of Japan's famous Kodo Drummers. Traditional Japanese taiko drumming is performed each August in the Earth Celebration. Rugged coastal scenery and rolling hills make the island a great place to explore by rental car.

⤳ HIRAIZUMI

Located in Northern Honshū, Hiraizumi (p218) once rivalled Kyoto for grandeur. Wealth from the region's gold mines was used to build a series of Buddhist temples which remain to this day, including the impressive Chūson-ji. While many of the original buildings were destroyed by fire, those that survived give some hint of the complex's original splendour.

2 MARTIN MOOS; 3 OLIVER STREWE; 4 MASON FLORENCE; 5 BRENT WINEBRENNER; 6 JTB PHOTO/PHOTOLIBRARY
2 Asahi-dake (p241), Daisetsuzan National Park; 3 Carving ice sculptures at Sapporo Yuki Matsuri (p230); 4 Collecting butterflies on Gas-san (p222); 5 Taiko drumer; 6 Chūson-ji (p219), Hiraizumi

THE BEST...

⚐ EXPERIENCES

- **Powder Skiing at Niseko** (p236) Some of the world's most reliable lift-served powder.
- **Gorging on Seafood in Sapporo** (p227) Japan's northern island of Hokkaidō has some seriously tasty seafood.
- **Riding the Cassiopeia from Tokyo to Sapporo** (p234) Go to sleep on the outskirts of Tokyo and wake up in another world.

⚐ FESTIVALS

- **Sapporo Yuki Matsuri** (p231) An icy wonderland.
- **Earth Celebration** (p226) The Kodo Drummers here play music you can really feel.
- **Matsushima Tōrō Nagashi Hanabi Taikai** (p217) This fireworks and lantern festival is a feast for the eyes.

⚐ DRIVES

- **Hokkaidō** (p227) The roads of Hokkaidō will bring out the driver in you.
- **Sado-ga-shima** (p225) The roads around this island were made for driving.
- **Tazawa-ko Area** (p220) Northern Honshū is good driving country, with great scenery and fewer cars than down south.

⚐ ONSEN

- **Nyūtō Onsen** (p221) This onsen in Northern Honshū is one of Japan's best.
- **Sukayu Onsen Ryokan** (p219) An old-school classic near the Hakkōda-san ropeway in Northern Honshū.
- **Sōunkyō Onsen** (p243) Great for a soak after a hike in nearby Daisetsuzan National Park.

Left: *Bento* (boxed meal); Right: Sculpture at Sapporo Yuki Matsuri (p231)

THINGS YOU NEED TO KNOW

⫸ VITAL STATISTICS

- **Populations** Sapporo 1.89 million, Matsushima 20,000, Niseko 6000
- **Area codes** Sapporo ☎011, Matsushima ☎022, Niseko ☎0136
- **Best time to visit** Autumn foliage season (September to November); ski season (December to March)

⫸ PLACES IN A NUTSHELL

- **Sapporo** (p227) Hokkaidō's main city famous for great seafood and Western-style streets.
- **Niseko** (p236) A world-class ski resort and a town that feels like 'Little Australia' during the winter months.
- **Daisetsuzan National Park** (p239) Hokkaidō's 'Big Snow Mountain' park offers great hiking and excellent onsen.
- **Matsushima** (p216) The island-strewn bay of this northern Honshū town is one of Japan's 'three famous views'.
- **Hiraizumi** (p218) A collection of splendid Buddhist temples in Northern Honshū.
- **Kakunodate** (p222) One of Japan's many 'little Kyotos', this Northern Honshū town has a great preserved samurai district.

⫸ ADVANCE PLANNING

- **Get in shape** if you plan to do any hiking in places such as Daisetsuzan National Park (these hikes are strenuous).

Book accommodation far in advance if you intend to visit Niseko over the Christmas/New Year period.

Visit a large bookstore in Tokyo or Sapporo to pick up hiking maps of the main hiking areas in Northern Honshū and Hokkaidō.

⫸ RESOURCES

- **Japan National Tourism Organization** (JNTO; www.jnto.go.jp, www.japantravelinfo.com)

⫸ EMERGENCY NUMBERS

- **Ambulance & Fire** ☎119
- **Police** ☎110

⫸ GETTING AROUND

- **Walk** around Sapporo, Hiraizumi and Kakunodate.
- **Hike** across Daisetsuzan National Park and the Dewa Sanzan.
- **Drive** around Hokkaidō and Sado-ga-shima.
- **Train** between cities in northern Honshū.

⫸ BE FOREWARNED

- **Winter** (November to April) can be very cold with a lot of snow in Northern Honshū and Hokkaidō.
- **Book in advance** for overnight express trains between Tokyo and Hokkaidō.

NORTHERN HONSHŪ & HOKKAIDŌ ITINERARIES

NIGHT TRAIN NORTH TO SAPPORO Three Days

For those who love the romance of rail, the overnight trip in a sleepe car on the *Cassiopeia* express from Tokyo to Sapporo is an interesting addition to a standard Japan itinerary (but book well in advance).

After exploring **(1) Tokyo** for a few days, show up at the appointed time to claim your berth on the *Cassiopeia* (p234) and settle in for the relaxing ride north through Honshū, through the Seikan Tunnel and or to **(2) Sapporo** (p227), the main city on the northern island of Hokkaidō Spend a day or two exploring the city of Sapporo, checking out such sights as the Hokudai Shokubutsuen botanical gardens (p228) and gorg ing on the city's famous seafood before flying back to Tokyo.

SAPPORO & DAISETSUZAN Five Days

The island of Hokkaidō positively begs to be explored by car. If you plan to be in Japan during the warm months of May to September and have an international licence, a driving trip around Hokkaidō is a great way to enjoy Japan. This is especially good during June and July, when the main island of Honshū is likely to be in the grip of the rainy season.

Start by flying from Tokyo to **(1) Sapporo** (p227). Explore the city for a day or two before picking up your rental car. There are plenty o good places to explore by car in Hokkaidō, but the real highlight is **(2) Daisetsuzan National Park** (p239). Base yourself at Sōunkyō Onsen (p243) or Asahidake Onsen (p240) and use the lifts to get you up onto the Daisetsuzan Massif, which offers incredible hiking and scenic vistas.

JULIAN BENTLE

Japanese tree frog

NORTHERN HONSHŪ HIGLIGHTS One Week

For those who want to explore a side of Japan rarely seen by foreign tourists, a trip from Tokyo to the northern tip of Honshū is a good choice, particularly during the warm months from April to September. This route can be done by public transport, though a car will make everything easier and allow you to work more efficiently. One possibility is taking trains for most of the route and renting cars when you want to explore a bit.

Head north from (1) Tokyo on the *shinkansen* (bullet train) to Sendai, where you can catch a local train to (2) Matsushima (p216). Check out one of Japan's 'three famous views' at Matsushima-wan bay and then return to Sendai and continue north to the town of (3) Hiraizumi (p218), which is famous for Chūson-ji temple (p219). From here, head north to Morioka, where renting a car will allow you relatively easy access to the sights at the very north end of Honshū. First, drive west to the onsen, lake and hiking resort area of (4) Tazawa-ko (p220), where you can spend the night at one of the ryokan at Nyūto Onsen (p221). Enjoy the hot springs here and take a drive to (5) Kakunodate (p222) to visit the samurai district (p222), then head north to Aomori and the mountains of (6) Hakkōda-san (p219), where you can take a dip in the wonderful Sukayu Onsen (p219). Head back to Morioka and then on to Tokyo.

DISCOVER NORTHERN HONSHŪ & HOKKAIDŌ

Northern Honshū (Tōhoku in Japanese) is a place of rugged mountains and remote valleys, terminating at the very tip of Japan's main island. The time-honoured travellers' route through this region takes you along ancient watercourses that feed fertile rice paddies, and around hulking volcanic massifs that fuel natural onsen (hot springs).

Across the Tsugaru-kaikyō Straits, the island of Hokkaidō is where all of your preconceived notions of Japan will be shattered. For the thrill-seeking traveller in search of sweeping vistas, amazing wildlife, wide open roads and overwhelming emptiness, Hokkaidō is a refreshing contrast to the often claustrophobic density of Honshū. In winter, the ski resort of Niseko offers some of the world's best lift-served powder skiing, while summer turns the island into a hiker's paradise.

Hokkaidō is best travelled by car – or better yet motorcycle – which is fortunate as public transport here leaves a lot to be desired.

NORTHERN HONSHŪ
本州の北部

MATSUSHIMA & OKU-MATSUSHIMA
松島・奥松島

☎ 022 / pop 20,000

Centuries ago, the haiku poet Bashō had initial misgivings about journeying through Tōhoku. Although he famously lamented: 'I may as well be travelling to the ends of the earth', the north's special charms eventually rendered him lost for words. Upon his encounter with Matsushima Bay, Bashō wrote: 'Matsushima, ah! Matsushima! Matsushima!'

It's easy to see why Bashō was so taken by Matsushima. The bay features around 250 islands covered in pines that have been shaped by the wind, and rock formations that have been shaped by the ceaseless slapping of waves, resulting in spectacular monuments to natural forces. This conglomeration is one of Japan's *Nihon Sankei*

(Three Great Sights) – the other two are the floating torii of Miyajima Island and the sand-spit at Amanohashidate.

ORIENTATION & INFORMATION

There's a Matsushima Station, but Matsushima-kaigan is the one you want – it's closer to the main sights. Outside, the **tourist information office** (☎ 354-2618 ⊙ 8.30am-5pm Apr-Nov, to 4.30pm Dec-Mar) provides maps.

Inside Oku-Matsushima's Nobiru Station, the **tourist information office** (☎ 588-2611; ⊙ 9am-6pm) has a few bicycles for rent.

SIGHTS & ACTIVITIES
MATSUSHIMA

Zuigan-ji (admission ¥1000; ⊙ 8am-3.30pm Jan & Dec, to 4pm Feb & Nov, to 4.30pm Mar & Oct to 5pm Apr-Sep), one of Tōhoku's finest Zen temples, was founded in AD 828. The present buildings were constructed in 1606 by Date Masamune to serve as a family temple. Look out for **Seiryū-den** (青龍殿; Treasure Hall), displaying works of art associated with the Date family. The temple is accessed via an avenue lined with tall cedars, with weathered Buddhas and altars to the sides – a frequently spooky, deeply contemplative approach.

The **Kanran-tei** (admission ¥200; 8.30am-5pm Apr-Oct, to 4.30pm Nov-Mar) pavilion was presented to the Date family by Toyotomi Hideyoshi in the late 16th century. It served as a genteel venue for tea ceremonies and moon viewing – the name means 'a place to view ripples on the water'. Today *matcha* (powdered green tea) is served here, and the garden includes the **Matsushima Hakubutsukan**, a small museum housing a collection of relics from the Date family.

OKU-MATSUSHIMA

Natural beauty is the order of the day here. **Sagakei** (嵯峨渓) is a 40m-high scenic canyon overhanging the Pacific Ocean, notable for its crashing waves; **Ōtakamori** (大高森) is a small hill in the middle of Miyato Island offering a ter-

rific panorama, including Mt Zaō and Kinkasan; and **Nobiru Beach** (野蒜海岸) is a swimming beach popular with day trippers from Sendai.

FESTIVALS & EVENTS

On 17 August, **Matsushima Tōrō Nagashi Hanabi Taikai** honours the souls of the departed with the O-Bon (Festival of the Dead) ritual, when lighted lanterns are floated out to sea accompanied by an extensive fireworks display.

SLEEPING

Matsushima Century Hotel (354-4111; www.centuryhotel.co.jp, in Japanese; 8 Aza-Senzui; d from ¥12,700; P □ 🛜) The pick of the resorts, the Century enjoys a stunning location, resting elegantly on one of the islands in Matsushima Bay. Western- and Japanese-style rooms vary in price depending on their furnishings and location (upmarket rooms have sea-view balconies), though everyone can enjoy the panoramic vistas from the on-site communal bath. LAN cable internet available.

NORTHERN HONSHŪ & HOKKAIDŌ

NORTHERN HONSHŪ

Detail of rock sculpture at Zuigan-ji
P NARAYAN/AGE FOTOSTOCK/PHOTOLIBRARY

Shintō shrine on a hiking path in Hakkōda-san

MASON FLORENC

GETTING THERE & AWAY

There are frequent *kaisoku* (rapid) on the JR Senseki line between Sendai and Matsushima-kaigan (¥400, 35 minutes). To reach Oku-Matsushima from Matsushima-kaigan Station, take the JR Senseki line six stations east (two stops by *kaisoku*) to Nobiru (¥230, 10 minutes).

HIRAIZUMI 平泉

☎ 0191 / pop 9000

Hiraizumi's grandeur once rivalled Kyoto's, and the tale of its ruin is one of the most bittersweet sagas in Tōhoku's history. From 1089 to 1189, three generations of the Fujiwara family, headed by Fujiwara Kiyohira, created a political and cultural centre in Hiraizumi. Kiyohira had made his fortune from local gold mines and, at the behest of Kyoto priests, he used his wealth and power to commence work on the creation of a 'paradise on earth', devoted to the principles of Buddhist thought as a reaction against the feudal wars that were plaguing the land.

Although his son and grandson continued along this path, Kiyohira's great grandson, Yoshihira, yielding to both internal and external pressures, brough this short century of fame and prosperity to an abrupt end. Today only a few sights scattered around this rural town bear testament to Hiraizumi's faded glory, though they do represent a singular experience, and remain a regional highlight.

INFORMATION

Turning right outside Hiraizumi Station the **tourist information office** (☎ 46 2110; 8.30am-5pm) has English-language pamphlets. The post office, with an international ATM, is 400m northwest of the station heading towards Mōtsū-ji. Free internet access is available at the public library (open 9am to 5pm Tuesday to Sunday), 1500m southwest of the station.

SIGHTS & ACTIVITIES

CHŪSON-JI 中尊寺

This **temple complex** (☎ 46-2211; admission incl Konjiki-dō, Sankōzō & Kyōzō ¥800; ☼ 8am-5pm Apr-Oct, 8.30am-4.30pm Nov-Mar) was established in AD 850 by the priest Ennin, though it was Fujiwara Kiyohira who decided in the early 12th century to expand the complex into a site with around 300 buildings, including 40 temples. Ironically, in the face of the grand scheme to build a Buddhist utopia, Hiraizumi was never far from tragedy: a massive fire here in 1337 destroyed most of the buildings, although two of the original constructions remain alongside the newer temples. The site is accessed via a steep approach along an avenue lined with trees and Jizō statues.

The approach snakes past the **Hon-dō** (Main Hall) to an enclosure featuring the splendid **Konjiki-dō** (金色堂; Golden Hall; ☼ 8am-4.30pm Apr-Oct, 8.30am-4pm Nov-Mar). Built in 1124, Konjiki-dō is quite a sight, with gold detailing, black lacquerwork and inlaid mother-of-pearl (the region was known for its gold and lacquer resources). The centrepiece of the hall is the fabulously ornate statue of the Amida Buddha, along with attendants. Beneath the three side altars are the mummified remains of three generations of the Fujiwara family.

SLEEPING & EATING

Hotel Musashibō (☎ 46-2241; fax 46-2250; www.musasibou.co.jp, in Japanese; r per person incl 2 meals from ¥8550; 💻) If you're looking for a bit of privacy, the Musashibō is something of a cross between a business hotel and a ryokan, offering Japanese-style rooms, an onsen bath, formal sit-down dinners and an informal snack bar. From the station, walk straight for 500m and turn right, pass the temple, then look on the corner after the second road on the left. LAN cable internet available.

GETTING THERE & AWAY

Hourly trains run along the JR Tōhoku *shinkansen* between Sendai and Ichinoseki (¥3320, 30 minutes). Local trains run about every hour or two on the JR Tōhoku Main line between Ichinoseki and Hiraizumi (¥190, 10 minutes). There are also frequent local buses running between Ichinoseki and Chūson-ji (¥350, 20 minutes) via JR Hiraizumi Station.

Ichinoseki is connected to Morioka by the JR Tōhoku *shinkansen* (¥3920, 40 minutes) and the JR Tōhoku Main line by *futsū* (local train; ¥1620, 1½ hours).

HAKKŌDA-SAN 八甲田山

☎ 017

Just south of Aomori, Hakkōda-san is a scenic region of soaring peaks that serves as a popular day trip for both hikers and skiers. There is reason enough to spend the night here, especially since the mountains are also home to one of Tōhoku's best onsen, Sukayu.

The Hakkōda-san **ropeway** (八甲田山ロープウエイ; one-way/return ¥1150/1800, 5-trip pass ¥4900; ☼ 9am-4.20pm) whisks you up Tamoyachi-dake to the 1324m summit. From there you can follow an elaborate network of hiking trails. One particularly pleasant route scales the three peaks of Akakura-dake (1548m), Ido-dake (1550m) and Ōdake (1584m), and then winds its way down to Sukayu Onsen. This 8km hike can be done in a leisurely four hours.

Sukayu Onsen Ryokan (酸ヶ湯温泉; ☎ 738-6400; www.sukayu.jp, in Japanese; r per person with/without 2 meals from ¥9600/5925, onsen-only admission ¥600; ☼ 7am-5.30pm; 🅿) is a place plucked right out of an *ukiyo-e* (wood-block print) – a delight for all five senses. On a cold day, relaxing here is hard to beat. One of the baths is rumoured to hold up to 1000 people (though you'll rarely see more than 25 at any one time).

Two daily buses leave from stop 8 outside Aomori Station, pass by the Hakkōda Ropeway-eki stop (¥1070, 50 minutes), and terminate at the next stop, Sukayu Onsen (¥1300, one hour).

TAZAWA-KO 田沢湖
☎ 0187 / pop 13,000

At 423m, Tazawa-ko is Japan's deepest lake, complete with sandy beaches, wooded shores and vacationing families either paddling rowboats across still waters or skiing down snow-covered slopes. The area is also home to the atmospheric Nyūtō Onsen, which is tucked up at the top of a winding mountain road, and is famous for its mineral-enriched milky white water. As if all of this isn't enough of a hard sell, consider the fact that Tazawa-ko also has its own *shinkansen* station, which makes it an easy-to-access rural getaway.

ORIENTATION & INFORMATION
JR Tazawa-ko Station is located a few kilometres southeast of the lake, and serves as the area's access point. Buses connect the station to Tazawa Kohan, a small transport hub on the eastern shores of the lake. From here, it takes about 40 minutes travelling northwesterly by bus or car to reach Nyūtō Onsen and the ski slopes. Tazawa Kohan is also the jumping-off point for hikes up Akita Komaga-take.

Inside the train station, **Folake** (☎ 43 2111; 🕙 8.30am-6.30pm) is a tourist information office that has excellent bilingual maps and free internet.

A 20km perimeter road surrounds the lake, and you can rent bicycles (¥400 per hour) or scooters (¥1200 per hour) in Tazawa Kohan. A car makes getting around easier, though there is a decent public transport network here.

SIGHTS & ACTIVITIES
TAZAWA-KO
Public beaches surround the lake itself, though swimming is a frigid proposition outside the balmy summer months. If you're not a member of the polar-bear club, you can rent all manner of boats in Tazawa Kohan during the spring, summer and autumn months. A stroll by the lake at sunset is a treat at any time of year.

GETTING THERE & AROUND
BUS
Frequent local buses run between the JR Tazawa-ko Station to Tazawa Kohan (¥350, 10 minutes), and between Tazawa Kohan and Nyūtō Onsen (¥650, 40 minutes). Note that these services terminate after sunset.

MASON FLORENCE
Tsuru-no-yu Onsen

MASON FLORENCE

Rotemburo (outdoor baths) at Nyūtō Onsen

🔺 NYŪTŌ ONSEN 乳頭温泉

One of Japan's choicest hot springs, Nyūtō Onsen is must-visit for any aspiring onsen aficionado. The area is home to seven rustic ryokan, each with a different character and different baths, though all offer healing waters that are great for soaking away from it all. All of the ryokan offer overnight lodging, and many feature *konyoku* (mixed-sex baths) – when it comes to bathing, the Japanese certainly aren't shy! The two most famous bathhouses are Tsuru-no-Yu and Kuroyu:

Tsuru-no-yu Onsen is the most storied onsen in Nyūtō. It was the official bathhouse of the Akita clan's ruling elite, and you can still relax under a thatched villa that was used during samurai times. A mineral-rich spring containing sulphur, sodium, calcium chloride and carbonic acid, Tsuru-no-yu is famous for its unique milky colour.

Kuroyu Onsen is at streamside Kuroyu, where you'll easily feel like you've stepped back into a Japanese wood-block print. With a bathing tradition dating back more than 300 years, Kuroyu is famous for its hydrogen sulphide spring that is said to ease high blood pressure, diabetes and arteriosclerosis.

Things you need to know: Tsuru-no-yu Onsen (鶴の湯温泉; ☎ 46-2139; fax 46-2100; 50 Kokuyurin, Sendatsuzawa; www.tsurunoyu.com; r per person ¥8400, bath ¥500; Ⓟ); Kuroyu Onsen (黒湯温泉; ☎ 46-2214; fax 46-2280, www.kuroyu.com, in Japanese; 2-1 Aza-kuroyuzawa, Obonai; r per person incl 2 meals from ¥11,700, bath ¥500; Ⓟ)

From April to October buses run three times daily (both directions) between JR Tazawa-ko Station and Hachimantai Chōjō (¥1990, 2¼ hours); six times daily (both directions) between the station and Komagatake Hachigōme (¥1000, one hour).

TRAIN

Several hourly trains on the Akita *shinkansen* line run between Tazawa-ko and Tokyo (¥14,900, three hours) via Morioka (¥13,640, 2½ hours), and between Tazawa-ko and Akita (¥3080, one hour) via Kakunodate (¥1360, 15 minutes). Infrequent local trains also run on the JR Tazawako line between Tazawa-ko and Kakunodate (¥320, 25 minutes).

KAKUNODATE 角館
☎ 0187 / pop 30,000

Established in 1620 by Ashina Yoshikatsu, the lord of the Satake clan, Kakunodate is known as 'Little Kyoto', and presents a thoughtful, immersive experience for anyone interested in catching a glimpse of old Japan. While the original castle that once guarded over the feudal town is no more, the *buke yashiki* – or samurai district – is splendidly preserved. A veritable living museum of Japanese culture and history, the *buke yashiki* consists of original samurai mansions surrounded by cherry trees and lush garden expanses. It takes an hour or so to stroll through the district, which makes Kakunodate a pleasant stopover en route between Tazawa-ko and Akita.

INFORMATION

Tourist information office (☎ 54-2700; ☯ 9am-6pm mid-Apr–Sep, to 5.30pm Oct–mid-Apr) Outside the station in a small building shaped like a *kura* (earth-walled storehouse). There are English maps, and some staff speak English.

SIGHTS

Each of the samurai mansions is impressive in its own right, though the highlight of the district is the **Kakunodate Rekishimura Aoyagi-ke** (☎ 54-3257; www.samuraiworld.com/english/index.html; 3 Omotemachi, Shimochō; admission ¥500; ☯ 9am-5pm Apr-Oct, to 4pm Nov-Mar). This agglomeration of minimuseums exhibits everything from Aoyagi family heirlooms and folk art to valuable antiques including old-time cameras, gramophones and classic jazz records.

SLEEPING & EATING

Tamachi Bukeyashiki Hotel (☎ 52-2030; fax 52-1701; www.bukeyashiki.jp, in Japanese; 52 Tamachi; r with/without 2 meals from ¥17,850/13,125) A Western-style hotel of mind-blowing opulence that preserves the original character and structure of the samurai mansion.

Several of the old houses in the *buke yashiki* serve noodles, though the town's most historically significant lunch spot is **Kosendō** (☎ 53-2902; noodles from ¥750; ☯ lunch & dinner), an old wooden schoolhouse – try the *inaniwa udon* (udon noodles in a clear mushroom soup; ¥850).

GETTING THERE & AWAY

Several hourly trains on the Akita *shinkansen* line run between Kakunodate and Tazawa-ko (¥1360, 15 minutes), and between Kakunodate and Akita (¥2740, 45 minutes). Infrequent local trains also run on the JR Tazawako line between Kakunodate and Tazawa-ko (¥320, 25 minutes), and between Kakunodate and Akita (¥1280, 1¾ hours), with a change at Ōmagari to the JR Ōu line.

Buses run from Kakunodate to Tazawa Kohan (¥840, 52 minutes) and Tazawa-ko Station (¥490, 35 minutes), as well as to Akita (¥1330, 1½ hours). From December to March, these buses do not stop at Tazawa Kohan. Kakunodate bus station is 10 minutes north of the train station.

DEWA SANZAN 出羽三山
☎ 0235

Dewa Sanzan is the collective title for three sacred peaks – Haguro-san, Gas-san and Yudono-san – which are believed to represent birth, death and rebirth, respectively. Together, they have been worshipped for centuries by *yamabushi* and followers of the Shugendō sect. During the annual pilgrimage seasons, you can

Gardeners at the base of Haguro-san

MASON FLORENCE

...ee white-clad pilgrims equipped with ...vooden staff, sandals and straw hat, and ...eece-clad hikers equipped with poles, ...rekking boots and bandana.

ORIENTATION & INFORMATION
Theoretically, if you hiked at a military ...pace and timed the buses perfectly, you ...night be able to cover all three peaks in ...one day. However, this would leave you ...no time to enjoy the scenery, and the ...chances of missing a key bus connection ...are very high. If you want to tackle all ...three mountains, it's best to devote two ...or three days, especially if you eschew ...ouses in favour of foot leather.

Before setting out, it's recommended ...hat you book accommodation, and stock ...up on maps, at the tourist information of-...ice in Tsuruoka. Also note that transport ...can grind to a halt once the snow starts ...to pile up – it's best to time your visit be-...ween July and September when all three ...nountains are open to hikers.

SIGHTS & ACTIVITIES
Tradition dictates that you start at Haguro-san and finish at Yudono-san, which is why we're presenting the pilgrimage in this order. However, feel free to follow the circuit in the opposite direction, which is certainly one way of going against the crowd.

HAGURO-SAN 羽黒山
Because it has the easiest access, Haguro-san (419m) attracts a steady flow of tourists. At the base of the mountain is Haguro village, consisting of *shukubō* (temple lodgings) and the **Ideha Bunka Kinenkan** (☎ 62-4727; admission ¥400; ⏰ 9am-4.30pm Wed-Mon Apr-Nov, 9.30am-4pm Wed-Mon Dec-Mar), a small history museum featuring films of *yamabushi* rites and festivals.

The orthodox approach to the shrine on the summit requires pilgrims to climb 2446 steps, but buses run straight to the top. The climb can be done in a leisurely hour, though you might be lapped by gaggles of sprightly senior citizens.

Hikers on Gas-san

MASON FLORE

From the Haguro Centre bus stop, walk straight ahead through the torii, and continue across the bridge. En route you'll pass **Gojū-no-tō**, a weather-beaten, five-storey pagoda dating from the 14th century. Then comes a very long slog up the hundreds of stone steps arranged in steep sections. Pause halfway at the **tea house** (8.30am-5pm Apr-Nov) for refreshment and breathtaking views. If you detour to the right, just past the tea house, you'll come upon the temple ruins of **Betsu-in**, visited by Bashō during his pilgrimage here.

At the top of Haguro-san, you have a number of options to consider. In summer, there are a couple of morning buses that travel directly from the summit to the eighth station of Gas-san. If you miss these buses, you can walk back down to the village, or spend the night at Saikan (see opposite). Alternatively, purists can follow the 20km ridge hike to the peak of Gas-san.

GAS-SAN 月山
Accessible from July to September, Gas-san (1984m) is the highest of the three

sacred mountains. Coming from Haguro-san, the peak is usually accessed from the trailhead at **Hachigōme** (eighth station). This route then passes through an alpine plateau to **Kyūgōme** (ninth station) in 1¾ hours, and then grinds uphill for another 1¼ hours. At the summit, pilgrims flock to **Gassan-jinja** (admission with ritual purification ¥500; 6am-5pm), though not without first being purified: bow your head to receive priest's benediction before rubbing you head and shoulders with sacred paper which is then placed in the fountain.

From the summit, you could retrace your steps to eighth station, though almost everybody will be pressing on with the steep descent to Yudono-san-jinja This takes another three hours or so, and you'll have to carefully descend rusty ladders chained to the cliff sides, and pic your way down through a slippery stre ambed at the end of the trail.

YUDONO-SAN 湯殿山
Accessible from May to October, Yudono-san (1504m) is the spiritual culmination o

he Dewa Sanzan trek. Coming from Gas-an, it's just a short walk from the stream ped at the end of the down climb to **'udono-san-jinja** (admission ¥500; 6am-pm, closed Nov-Apr). This sacred shrine is not building, but rather a large orange rock ontinuously lapped by water from a hot pring. It has the strictest rituals of the hree, with pilgrims required to perform barefoot circuit of the rock, paddling hrough the cascading water.

To finish the pilgrimage, it's a mere 10-ninute hike further down the mountain p the trailhead at **Yudono-san-sanrōsho**, vhich is marked by a torii, or you can give our feet a break by taking a shuttle bus.

From here, you have a number of op-ions: spend the night at Yudono-san anrōjo (see below), catch a direct bus pack to Tsuruoka, catch the bus or walk long the 3km toll road to the Yudono-an Hotel, or take a detour to Dainichibō nd Chūren-ji.

SLEEPING & EATING

Saikan (62-2357; r per person incl 2 meals 7350) The most famous *shukubō*, located t the top of Haguro-san, this atmospheric odging has sweeping views over the val-y below, and is a good spot to spend the light and break up the hike.

Yudono-san Sanrōjo (54-6131; r per erson incl 2 meals from ¥7350; closed Nov-Apr) t the end of your second day, consider taying here. It's conveniently located lext to Sennin-zawa bus terminal and is fun spot to unwind with other success-ul pilgrims.

GETTING THERE & AROUND

Hourly buses run from Tsuruoka to the Haguro Centre bus stop (¥680, 45 min-ites), several of which then continue on o Haguro-sanchō (Haguro summit; ¥990, ne hour).

From early July to late August, and then on weekends and holidays until late September, there are up to four daily buses from Haguro-sanchō to Gas-san as far as Hachigōme (¥1240, one hour).

Between June and early November, there are up to four daily buses from the Yudono-san Sanrōjo trailhead at Yudono-san to Tsuruoka (¥1480, 1½ hours), which also passes by the Yudono-san Hotel (¥100, five minutes) and Ōami (¥910, 45 minutes). Regular buses between Tsuruoka and Yamagata also run via the Yudono-san Hotel.

SADO-GA-SHIMA 佐渡島

0259 / pop 69,500

Japan's sixth-largest island, Sado-ga-shima has always been something of a far-flung destination, albeit not always a voluntary one. During the feudal era, Sado-ga-shima was a notorious penal colony where out-of-favour intellectu-als were forever banished. The illustrious list of former prisoners includes Emperor Juntoku, *nō* (stylised dance-drama) mas-ter Ze-Ami, and Nichiren, the founder of one of Japan's most influential Buddhist sects. When gold was discovered near the village of Aikawa in 1601, there was a sudden influx of gold-diggers, who were often vagrants press-ganged from the mainland and made to work like slaves.

Despite this history of ill repute, Sado is now one of Tōhoku's top tourist des-tinations. Compared with Honshū, the island is relatively undeveloped, and is characterised by rugged natural beauty and eccentric reminders of its rich and evocative past. While a good number of hikers descend on the island in the warmer months, crowds peak during the third week in August for the three-day Earth Celebration, which is headlined by the world-famous Kodo Drummers.

Rāmen Yokochō (p233), Sapporo

PAUL DYMO·

While there is a comprehensive and fairly regular bus network between major towns on Sado-ga-shima, you really need a private vehicle to access the island's most scenic parts, and a good number of accommodation options are situated far from bus stops. Fortunately, car rental is readily available in the town of Ryōtsu, which also serves as the island's primary access point and transport hub.

RYŌTSU & AROUND 両津

Considering that Ryōtsu is essentially a port town, Sado's main hub is surprisingly beautiful, and serves as an excellent introduction to the rustic splendour of the island. While there isn't too much here in the way of sights, Ryōtsu is where you can get your bearings, make onward arrangements and get a good night's rest.

The island's main **tourist information centre** (☎ 23-3300; ☷ 8.30am-5pm, to 6.50pm Jun-Aug) is in Ryōtsu, in the street behind the coffee and souvenir shops across from the ferry terminal. Be sure to stock up on

comprehensive maps, bus timetables an· tourist pamphlets for the entire island.

Kunimisō (☎ 22-2316; Niibo-Shomyōji; pe· person incl 2 meals from ¥7000; ℙ) is one o· Sado's most popular *minshuku* (Japanes· guesthouse), due to its collection o· *bunya* puppets, which the owner like· to demonstrate to guests. It's 15 minute· by bus from Ryōtsu to the Uryūya bu· stop, then a long walk along a countr· road to this small house (follow th· signs). Alternatively, phone ahead for · pick-up from the ferry terminal, or ge· directions from tourist information i· you're driving.

Located about 2km from Ryōtsu a· Sumiyoshi Onsen (look for the large whit· building), **Sado Seaside Hotel** (☎ 27-721· fax 27-2713; http://sadoseasidehotel.yuyado.ne· in Japanese; 80 Sumiyoshi; s/d from ¥5925/10,80· breakfast/dinner ¥840/1575; ℙ ▯) is a Western· style drive-up motel with sea-view room· an attractive onsen, free internet and a· obliging free shuttle service to and fro· the port.

FESTIVALS & EVENTS

One of Sado's biggest draws is the Earth Celebration (アースセレブレーション; www.kodo.or.jp), a three-day music, dance and arts festival usually held during the third week in August. The event features *kesa* (folk dances), *onidaiko* (demon drum dances) and *tsuburosashi* (a phallic dance with two goddesses). However, the focal point of the Earth Celebration is the performance of the Kodo Drummers, who live in a small village north of Ogi, but spend much of the year on tour across the world.

GETTING THERE & AWAY

Sado Kisen (☎ 03-5390-0550) passenger ferries and hydrofoils run between Niigata and Ryōtsu. There are up to six regular ferries daily (one-way from ¥3170, 2½ hours). As many as 10 jetfoils zip across daily in merely an hour (one-way/return ¥6340/11,490), but service is greatly reduced between December and February. Before embarking, you need to buy a ticket from the vending machines and to fill in a white passenger ID form.

GETTING AROUND

Local buses are fine on the main routes, though services to other parts of the island are often restricted to two or three a day, and sharply restricted in the winter.

To explore less-touristed areas, car rental is desirable. There are numerous car-rental firms close to the Ryōtsu terminal; rates start from ¥7000/9000 per day/24 hours. Tell the proprietor your plan, as construction, unpassable bridges or snow may mean the map's routes are unavailable.

If you plan to make extended use of local buses, there's an English-language timetable available from the ferry terminals and tourist information offices. The ¥2000 unlimited-ride bus pass, also in English, is a good-value option valid for two consecutive days on weekends only.

Cycling is an enjoyable way to get off the beaten track. Bicycle rental is available at various locations in all major towns (per day ¥400 to ¥1500).

HOKKAIDŌ
北海道
SAPPORO 札幌

☎ 011 / pop 1.89 million

Japan's fifth-largest city, and the prefectural capital of Hokkaidō, Sapporo is a surprisingly dynamic and cosmopolitan urban centre that pulses with energy despite its extreme northerly latitude. Designed by European and American architects in the late 19th century, Sapporo is defined by its wide grid of tree-lined streets and ample public-park space, which contribute to the city's surprising level of liveability. Even if you get cold easily, you can always get your energy back over a hot meal, a great proposition given Sapporo's wholly deserved gastronomic reputation.

As the island's main access point and transport hub, Sapporo serves as an excellent base for striking out into the wilds that lie just beyond the city limits. But, while it might be hard to resist the pull of Hokkaidō's world-class national parks, especially after travelling this far north, don't give Sapporo a quick pass – on the contrary, you'll most definitely be surprised by how good life can be in the capital of the north country. Sapporo is a major tourist destination itself, especially for those partial to the delicious liquid gold that is Sapporo beer. And, if you're planning long periods of time hiking in isolation, you might want to first indulge in a bit of the raucous nightlife of the Susukino district.

In February, the city also hosts the world-famous Snow Festival, which is highlighted by huge ice sculptures of everything from brown bears and *tanuki* (Japanese raccoon dog) to Hello Kitty and Doraemon.

ORIENTATION

Sapporo, laid out in a Western-style grid pattern, is relatively easy to navigate. Blocks are labelled East, West, North and South in relation to a central point near the TV Tower in the city centre. For example, the famous landmark Tokei-dai (Clock Tower) is in the block of North 1, West 2 (Kita Ichi-jo, Nishi Ni-chōme) – N1W1. Ōdōri-kōen, a narrow grass-covered section ending at the TV Tower, is a major city feature, dividing the city east–west, into north–south halves. South of Ōdōri is the downtown shopping district with shops and arcades. Susukino, the club and entertainment district, is located mainly between the South 2 and South 6 blocks.

INFORMATION

Hokkaidō-Sapporo Food & Tourism Information Centre (北海道さっぽろ食と観光情報館; ☎ 213-5088; fax 213-5089; www.welcome.city.sapporo.jp/english/index.html; N5W3 Chūō-ku, JR Sapporo Station Nishi-dōri Kita-guchi; ⏰ 8.30am-8pm) Located on the 1st floor of Sapporo Stellar Place inside JR Sapporo Station. This is the island's mother load of tourist information, so stock up on maps, timetables, brochures and pamphlets, and be sure to make use of the friendly and helpful bilingual staff.

SIGHTS

HOKUDAI SHOKUBUTSUEN
北大植物園

One of Sapporo's must-see attractions, this beautiful **botanical garden** (☎ 221-0066; N3W8 Chūō-ku; adult ¥400; ⏰ 9am-4.30pm Apr-Sep, 9am-3.30pm Oct-Nov) boasts more than 4000 varieties of plants, all attractively set on a meandering 14-hectare plot just 10 minutes on foot southwest

Fish displayed at market

PHIL WEYMOUTH

SAPPORO

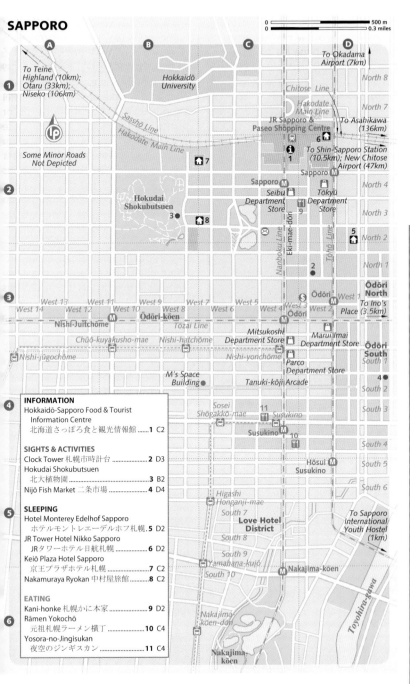

0 — 500 m
0 — 0.3 miles

To Teine
Highland (10km);
Otaru (33km);
Niseko (106km)

Hokkaidō
University

To Okadama
Airport (7km)

North 8

Chitose Line

Hakodate
Main Line

JR Sapporo &
Paseo Shopping Centre

To Asahikawa
(136km)

North 7

Sasshō Line

Hakodate Main Line

Some Minor Roads
Not Depicted

To Shin-Sapporo Station
(10.5km); New Chitose
Airport (47km)

Sapporo

North 4

Hokudai
Shokubutsuen

Sapporo
Seibu
Department
Store

Tōkyū
Department
Store

North 3

Eki-mae-dōri

North 2

Nanboku Line

Tōhō Line

North 1

West 13   West 11   West 9   West 7   West 5
West 14   West 12   West 10   West 8   West 6   West 4   West 3

Ōdōri
North

Ōdōri   West 1   To Ino's
West 2   Place (3.5km)

Ōdōri

Nishi-Juitchōme

Ōdōri-kōen

Tōzai Line

Chūō-kuyakusho-mae   Nishi-hatchōme

Nishi-jūgochōme   Nishi-yonchōme

Mitsukoshi
Department Store

Marui Imai
Department Store

Ōdōri
South

South 1

Parco
Department Store

South 2

M's Space
Building

Tanuki-kōji Arcade

INFORMATION
Hokkaidō-Sapporo Food & Tourist
Information Centre
北海道さっぽろ食と観光情報館 **1** C2

SIGHTS & ACTIVITIES
Clock Tower 札幌市時計台 **2** D3
Hokudai Shokubutsuen
北大植物園 **3** B2
Nijō Fish Market 二条市場 **4** D4

SLEEPING
Hotel Monterey Edelhof Sapporo
ホテルモントレーエーデルホフ札幌.**5** D2
JR Tower Hotel Nikko Sapporo
JRタワーホテル日航札幌 **6** D2
Keiō Plaza Hotel Sapporo
京王プラザホテル札幌 **7** C2
Nakamuraya Ryokan 中村屋旅館 **8** C2

EATING
Kani-honke 札幌かに本家 **9** D2
Rāmen Yokochō
元祖札幌ラーメン横丁 **10** C4
Yosora-no-Jingisukan
夜空のジンギスカン **11** C4

Sosei
Shōgakkō-mae

Susukino

Susukino

South 3

South 4

Hōsui
Susukino

South 5

South 6

Higashi
Honganji-mae

South 7

Love Hotel
District

South 8

To Sapporo
International
Youth Hostel
(1km)

South 9

Yamahana-kujō

South 10

Nakajima-kōen

Nakajima-
kōen-dōri

Toyohira-gawa

Nakajima-
kōen

PAUL DYMOND

Ainu woman playing a *mukkur* (stringed mouth harp)

of the station. The botannical gardens suffered from serious typhoon damage in 2004, but has since made a near total recovery.

In addition to the obvious outdoor sights, the Hokudai is also home to two museums: the **Natural History Museum**, a grand, old building dating from 1882 that has a comprehensive taxidermy collection of the island's wildlife, and the smaller **Ainu Museum**, which displays an extensive collection of anthropological artefacts from Hokkaidō's indigenous inhabitants.

During the winter months, the botanical gardens are frozen over and the museums are closed, though you can still head to the **greenhouse** (admission ¥110; ☺ 10am-

3pm Mon-Fri, 10am-noon Sat, closed Sun) for some hothouse flowers.

CLOCK TOWER 札幌市時計台

While it may not be at the top of your own list, no Japanese tourist can leave Sapporo without snapping a photo of the city's signature landmark, the **Clock Tower** (Tokei-dai; ☎ 231-0838; www .15.ocn.ne.jp/~tokeidai/english.html; N1W2 Chūō-ku; admission ¥200; ☺ 8.45am-5pm Tue-Sun). Built in 1878, the clock has never missed tolling the hour for more than 130 years. Impressive – though the clock tower is also known as one of Japan's top three *gakkari* (disappointing) spots, mainly because the brochure photos often remove the urban metropolis that dwarfs the small building. The clock tower is just two minutes on foot from exit 7 of Ōdōri Station – careful as you might walk by before realising it's right in front of you.

NIJŌ FISH MARKET 二条市場

Buy a bowl of rice and select your own sashimi toppings, gawk at the fresh delicacies or sit down at a shop in **Nijō Fish Market** (S3E1&2 Chūō-ku; ☺ 7am-6pm), one of Hokkaidō's best. Sea urchin and salmon roe are favourites; as is Hokkaidō's version of Mother and Child (*oyakodon*), a bowl of rice topped with salmon and roe. Get there early for the freshest selection and the most variety; things close up by 6pm and individual restaurants have their own hours.

FESTIVALS & EVENTS

Drawing more than two million visitors, the annual **Sapporo Yuki Matsuri** (さっ ぽろ雪まつり; Snow Festival; www.snowfe .com/english) takes place in February, and is arguably one of Japan's top festivals. The humble origins of the festival date back o 1950 when local high school students built six snow statues in Ōdōri-kōen. Five years later, the Japan Self-Defence Force from the nearby Makomanai base upped the ante by building the city's first gigantic snow sculptures. By 1974, the event had grown into an international contest and was attracting teams from more than a dozen countries. Taking weeks and weeks to carve, past snow sculptures have included life-sized statues of Hideki Matsui, entire frozen stages for visiting musical acts, ice slides and mazes for the kiddies and – of course – the obligatory Hello Kitty statue or two. You can view these icy behemoths in Ōdōri-kōen as well as in various other locations around the city.

The Snow Festival also highlights the best in regional food and drink from across the island, and you can expect all kinds of wild and drunken revelry, particularly once the sun sets (at these latitudes, it's quite early!). Finding reasonably priced accommodation can be extremely difficult during the festival, so it's a good idea to book as far in advance as possible.

SLEEPING
BUDGET

Sapporo International Youth Hostel (札幌国際ユースホステル; ☎ 825-3120; www .youth hostel.or.jp/kokusai; 6-5-35 Toyohira-ku; dm/s/tw from ¥3200/3800/6600; 🖳 🛜) Housed in a surprisingly modern and stylish building that could give most business hotels a run for their money, this well-conceived youth hostel has perfected the basics by offering simple but sparkling rooms to budget travellers. Both Western- and Japanese-style private rooms are available, as well as so-called 'dorm-rooms' featuring four full-sized beds. The closest subway stop is Gakuen-mae (Exit 2) on the Toho line; the hostel is just two minutes from the station behind the Sapporo International Student Center. Note that twin rooms are only for married couples.

PAUL DYMOND

Festival street parade in Sapporo

Ino's Place (イノーズプレイス; ☎ 832-1828; http://inos-place.com/e/; dm/s/d from ¥3400/4800/8600; 🖳 📶) While youth hostels in Japan are often stale and sterilised affairs with strict rules and little to no English on hand, Ino's Place is a true backpackers' spot with all the fixings. Friendly and bilingual staff are on hand to make your stay warm and welcoming, while clean rooms, private lockers, free internet, no curfew, a steamy Japanese bath, laundry facilities, a kitchen and communal lounge space sweeten the deal. To reach Ino's, take the Tōzai line to the Shiroishi stop (four past Ōdōri); take Exit 1 and walk straight for a few minutes along the main street in the direction of the Eneos petrol station. Turn right at the Marue supermarket and you'll see a detached two-storey white building – you've arrived!

MIDRANGE

Keiō Plaza Hotel Sapporo (☎ 271-0111; www.keioplaza-sapporo.co.jp/english/index2.html; N5W7 Chūō-ku; s/d from ¥7000/11,000; ❌ 🖳 🈁) One of the more stylish options in this price bracket, the Keiō Plaza lie at the northeast corner of the botanica gardens, and boasts some impressive amenities including a full-sized swimming pool, sauna complex and athletic training room. Rooms increase in price as you ascend the tower, though you can easily stick to your budget by choosing a standard room on the 12th floor or below. LAN cable internet available.

Nakamuraya Ryokan (☎ 241-2111 241-2118; www.nakamura-ya.com/english.html N3W7-1 Chūō-ku; r per person high season from ¥7875, low season ¥7350; 🖳 📶) Located directly across from the botanical gardens, this charming little Japanese-style inn is a wonderful introduction to the pleasures of the island. A variety o different plans are available, featuring tatami rooms of varying shapes and sizes, as well as lavish feasts incorporating the unique flavours of Hokkaidō. All guests can also relax in the large on-site bath, and the owner-managers are well equipped to deal with the needs o foreigner travellers.

PAUL DYMON

Neon signs in Susukino

TOP END

Hotel Monterey Edelhof Sapporo (☎ 242-7111; fax 232-1212; www.hotelmonterey.co.jp/eng/index.htm; N2W1 Chūō-ku; s/d from ¥17,000/32,340; 🖳 🛜) A few minutes south of the station, opposite the JR Sapporo Railway Hospital, this seemingly modern hotel lords over the street like a concrete monolith, though the interior is fully decked out in a bizarre but surprisingly amenable Austrian-theme. While the opulent lobby and lavish rooms are Continental-inspired, the various dining rooms and onsen are Japanese through and through. LAN cable internet available.

JR Tower Hotel Nikko Sapporo (JRタワーホテル日航札幌; ☎ 251-2222; fax 251-6370; www.jrhotelgroup.com/eng/hotel/eng101.htm; N5W2 Chūō-ku; s/d from ¥18,000/26,000; 🖳 🛜) You can't beat the location at this soaring tower, which is firmly attached to the JR Sapporo Station. Taking advantage of such great heights, the Hotel Nikko Sapporo offers plush rooms priced by floor, a spa with a view on the 22nd floor, and both Western and Japanese restaurants perched at the top on the 35th floor. LAN cable internet available.

EATING

Rāmen Yokochō (🕙 11am-3am) This famous alleyway in the Susukino entertainment district is crammed with dozens of *rāmen* (egg noodle) shops, and you'll most likely wind up here in a noble attempt to vanquish your hang-over. Anyone with a yen for *rāmen* shouldn't miss it, but it can be difficult to find. Take the Nanboku line to Susukino and walk south to the first crossroad. Turn left (east); Rāmen Yokochō is halfway down on the right. If you can't find it just ask – it's one place people *will* know. Hours and holidays vary for different shops.

Yosora-no-Jingisukan (☎ 219-1529; 10th fl, S4W4 Chūō-ku; plates from ¥850; 🕙 5pm-2.30am) Genghis Khan is on the menu everywhere, though at this speciality restaurant, located on the 10th floor of the My Plaza building, across from a 7-Eleven, you can grill up tender slices of locally raised lamb, as well as more exotic cuts from far-flung destinations including Australia and Iceland. There is no English, though the handy picture-menu makes ordering a breeze.

Kani-honke (☎ 222-0018; N3W2 Chūō-ku; set course from ¥3625; 🕙 11.30am-10pm) The frigid seas surrounding Hokkaidō are extremely bountiful and yield some of the tastiest crustaceans on the planet. There is no better place to dine on all manner of exotic crab than at the famous Kani-honke, which serves up elaborate *kaiseki-ryōri* (Japanese cuisine following strict rules of etiquette) centred on these juicy little critters. Seasonal set courses are priced according to the size and rarity of the crab, so simply choose depending on how much you want to spend.

GETTING THERE & AWAY
AIR

Sapporo's main airport is **New Chitose Airport** (新千歳空港; **Shin-Chitose Kūkō**), about 40km south of the city. Domestic destinations include Tokyo, Osaka, Nagoya, Hiroshima, Sapporo and many others.

There's a smaller airport at **Okadama** (丘珠空港; **Okadama Kūkō**), about 10km north of the city, which has limited service to cities in Hokkaidō.

BUS

Highway buses connect Sapporo with the rest of Hokkaidō, and are generally cheaper than trains and even time-competitive on some routes. Sapporo Eki-mae is the main bus station, just southeast of JR Sapporo Station, beneath Esta. The Chūō bus station (southeast of JR Sapporo Station) and Ōdōri bus centre are also departure spots. At all three departure points, you will find ticket booths from where you can purchase tickets to major cities throughout Hokkaidō.

Some popular destinations, which have frequent daily departures from Sapporo Eki-mae bus terminal, include Wakkanai (¥6000, six hours), Asahikawa (¥2000, two hours), Muroran (¥2250, 2¼ hours), Noboribetsu Onsen (¥1900, two hours), Tōya-ko Onsen (¥2700, 2¾ hours), Niseko (¥2300, three hours), Furano (¥2100, three hours) and Otaru (¥590, one hour).

From the Chūō bus station there are a few departures a day to Obihiro (¥3670, 4¼ hours) and Abashiri (¥6210, 6¼ hours). Buses to Hakodate depart from both the Chūō and Ōdōri bus stations (¥4680, 5¼ hours).

Discounted round-trip tickets are available for most routes.

CAR

The best place in Hokkaidō to pick up a rental car is at the New Chitose Airport. While you might have to backtrack a bit if you're heading north, some people find this preferable to picking up a vehicle in Sapporo, and subsequently navigating through the busy city centre. There are just under a dozen different companies located in the arrivals area on the first floor, which makes it easy to shop around the various booths and quickly compare prices.

If you'd prefer to pick up your vehicle in Sapporo, it's recommended that you deal with **Toyota Rent a Car** (☎ 281-0100; N5E2-1 Chūō-ku; ☼ 8am-10pm). In addition to being conveniently located near JR Sapporo

Station, the company is a bit better at dealing with foreigners than most rental car dealers. There's no guarantee the staff will speak English – if you have problems, you can always try to make arrangements in advance through the tourist information centre.

TRAIN

The *Hokutosei* (北斗星) is a *tokkyū* (limited express) sleeper train that runs between Tokyo's JR Ueno Station and JR Sapporo Station. There are two departures in both directions every evening, and the total journey time is around 16½ hours, which puts you in your destination the following morning.

The base fare for a journey between Tokyo and Sapporo is ¥16,080, plus an additional ¥2890 limited-express train charge. On top of this, you need to pay an additional fee for accommodation – prices range from ¥6300 for a private sleeping berth to ¥17,180 for the 'royal room'. Note that this flat fee is charged regardless of starting or ending location. If you're travelling on a JR Pass, you do not have to pay the base fare and limited express charge, but you will have to pay the accommodation fare. Full-on French and formal Japanese meals are available on board with advanced reservation, though meal service is not included in the ticket price.

A much more luxurious option is the *Cassiopeia* (カシオペア), a *tokkyū* sleeper train that runs three times a week between Tokyo and Sapporo. There are three evening departures in both directions every week, and the total journey time is also around 16½ hours. Base fares and limited-express train charges are equivalent to the *Hokutosei*, and are again waived if you have a JR Pass, though accommodation is more expensive, ranging

OLIVER STREWE
Crab for sale at a Sapporo street stall

from ¥13,350 for a twin room to ¥25,490 for a full-on suite. These prices are on par with an upmarket hotel, and sleeper cars on the *Cassiopeia* are something akin to a four-star resort on wheels. The night train also has sophisticated dining cars offering Michelin-star quality meals, which are not included in the ticket price, and must be booked in advance. Note that single travellers must pay for the full price of a room, so it's advised that you have a travel companion.

Reservations for both the *Hokutosei* and the *Cassiopeia* can be made at any JR ticket counter or travel agency. These trains are very popular and often booked solid, particularly in the summer months, so make a reservation as far in advance as possible.

Additionally there are hourly trains on the JR Tōhoku *shinkansen* between Tokyo and Hachinohe (¥15,150, three hours). Hachinohe is connected to Sapporo by the JR Tsugaru Kaikyō line and Hakodate lines – hourly *tokkyū* trains run through

the Seikan Tunnel between Hachinohe and Hakodate (¥7030, three hours), and between Hakodate and Sapporo (¥8390, 3½ hours).

There are hourly *kaisoku* trains on the JR Hakodate line between Sapporo and Otaru (¥620, 40 minutes). Finally, Super Kamui *tokkyū* trains run twice an hour between Sapporo and Asahikawa (¥4480, 1½ hours).

GETTING AROUND
TO/FROM THE AIRPORTS
New Chitose Airport is accessible from Sapporo by *kaisoku* train (¥1340, 35 minutes) or bus (¥1000, 1¼ hours). There are convenient bus services connecting the airport to various destinations in Hokkaidō, including Shikotsu-ko, Tōya-ko Onsen, Noboribetsu Onsen and Niseko.

For Okadama airport, buses leave every 20 minutes or so from in front of the All Nippon Airways (ANA) ticket offices, opposite JR Sapporo Station (¥400, 30 minutes).

BUS & TRAM

JR Sapporo Station is the main terminus for local buses. From late April to early November, tourist buses loop through major sights and attractions between 9am and 5.30pm; a one-day pass costs ¥750, single trips are ¥200 (basic fee).

There is a single tram line that heads west from Ōdōri, turns south, then loops back to Susukino. The fare is a flat ¥170.

SUBWAY

Sapporo's three subways are efficient. Fares start at ¥200 and one-day passes cost ¥800 (per day ¥500 weekend only). There are also ¥1000 day passes that include the tram and buses as well. Or get a pay-in-advance With You card (various denominations available), which can be used on subways, buses, trams, Jōtetsu and Chūō buses; unlike the one-day passes, the With You card does not expire at midnight.

NISEKO ニセコ

☎ 0136 / pop 6000

Hokkaidō is dotted with world-class ski resorts, but the reigning prince of powder is unquestionably Niseko. Despite its village status, Niseko boasts four interconnected resorts, namely Hirafu, Higashiyama, An'nupuri and Hanazono, which together contain more than 800 skiable hectares. Because of its blessed location, Niseko experiences northwest to southeast Siberian weather fronts, which produce a soft and light powdery snow that skiers and snowboarders love to carve. In fact, Niseko was recently named the world's second snowiest ski resort, with an annual average snowfall of more than 15m! (Pipped at the post by Mt Baker Ski Area in Washington State, USA, according to *Forbes* magazine.)

Of course, the secret is out, and Niseko is currently experiencing an unprecedented boom, primarily fuelled by Australians and Singaporeans. Property values are soaring, new resorts and condos are springing up left and right, and the tiny village of Hirafu is rapidly becoming an international hotspot. Depending on whom you ask, Niseko is either losing its traditional Japanese character and in danger of rapid overdevelopment, or becoming floridly cosmopolitan in light of increased foreign investment. Regardless of your opinion, however, skiing at Niseko with its jaw-dropping views of mountains is unequalled.

ORIENTATION

The ski resorts of Hirafu, Higashiyama, An'nupuri and Hanazono are run together as a single administrative unit, appropriately dubbed Niseko United. At the base of the ski slopes lie several towns and villages that comprise Niseko's population centre. Most of the hotels, restaurants, bars and tourists are clustered together in **Hirafu** (ひらふ), while Higashiyama, An'nupuri and Hanazono are much quieter and less developed.

Further east are **Kutchan** (倶知安) and **Niseko** (ニセコ) proper, which are more permanent population centres that remain decidedly Japanese. While there is a JR Hirafu Station, it is far from the town and poorly serviced by infrequent buses. As a result, incoming passengers on the train disembark at either JR Kutchan or JR Niseko Stations, and then switch to local buses. During the ski season, there are also direct buses connecting the Welcome Centre in Hirafu village to Sapporo's New Chitose Airport.

To the east of the valley lies **Yōtei-zan** (羊蹄山), a perfectly conical volcano reminiscent of Mt Fuji. Yōtei-zan draws its fair hare of hikers in the summer months, though there is something almost holy about the snow-covered crater on a chilly winter day.

INFORMATION

There are very small **tourist information offices** (☎ Niseko 44-2468, Kutchan 22-2151; www.niseko.gr.jp/eigo.html; ⏰ 10am-7pm) in both JR Niseko and Kutchan Stations that can provide pamphlets, maps, bus timetables and help with bookings.

To meet the winter crush, the **Hirafu Welcome Centre** (ひらふウエルカムセンター; ☎ 22-0109; www.grand-hirafu.jp/winter/en/index.html; ⏰ 8.30am-9pm), which is where direct buses to/from New Chitose Airport originate and terminate, also provides English-language information.

The Niseko area is packed throughout the ski season. If you're coming from Sapporo, it is recommended that you first visit one of the larger regional tourist information centres, and try to arrange accommodation in advance. Most of the accommodation places in Niseko are very internet savvy, which means that it's also fairly easy to make all of your reservations online well ahead of your trip.

SIGHTS & ACTIVITIES
SKIING & SNOWBOARDING

Niseko United (www.niseko.ne.jp/en; ⏰ day 8.30am-4.30pm, night 4.30-9pm, Nov-Apr) is the umbrella name for four resorts: Niseko An'nupuri, Niseko Higashiyama, Niseko Grand Hirafu and the Hanazono area.

What makes Niseko United stand out from the competition is that you can access all four ski slopes by purchasing a single **All-Mountain Pass** (day/night ¥4300/1900). This electronic tag gives you access to 20 different lifts and gondolas, as well as free rides on the intermountain shuttle bus. If you're planning on skiing for several days, a week or even the season, you can also buy discounted multi-day passes.

Rental equipment is of very high quality, and can be picked up virtually everywhere

Wine produced in Sapporo (p227)

OLIVER STREWE

at fairly standard but affordable prices. In fact, a good number of rental shops will deliver and pick up equipment straight to your accommodation. As with the All-Mountain Pass, you can save a bit of money by renting equipment over a longer period of time.

Niseko caters for skiers and snowboarders of all skill levels, and it's possible to spend several days here without repeating the same course. In total there are around 60 different beginner, intermediate and advanced runs with a 2m to 3m snow base that wind through varied terrain. While it's difficult to generalise such a massive area, Niseko United is arguably some of the finest skiing in Japan and Asia, and the whole world for that matter.

SLEEPING & EATING

Niseko Tourist Home (ニセコツーリスト ホーム; ☎ 44-2517; http://niseko-th.com, in Japanese; dm Nov-Apr/Mar-Oct ¥3500/2500, incl 2 meals ¥5500/4500; ℗ ⌨) A clean and inexpensive wooden A-frame about 4km

from Niseko Station, the always-popula Tourist Home is a great budget base Attracting a more Japanese crowd than the internationally minded youth hostels the delightful owners have a lot of pride in their small ski town.

Hilton Niseko Village (ニセコヒル トンヴィレジ; ☎ 44-1111; fax 44-3224 www.hiltonworldresorts.com/Resorts/Niseko Higashiyama Onsen; r from ¥19,000; ℗ ⌨ ⌥ There is no shortage of resort hotels ir Niseko, though the Hilton enjoys the bes location of all – it is quite literally attachec to the Niseko Gondola in Higashiyama As you might expect from the luxury moniker, Western-style rooms at the Hilton are complemented by a whole slew of amenities spread out across a veritable village. Check the website before arriving as special deals are usually available. LAN cable internet available.

Annupuri Village (アンヌプリ・ ヴィレジ; ☎ 59-2111; fax 59-2112; www .annupurivillage.com; 432-21 Niseko; 4-8 person sk chalet from ¥74,000-98,000; ℗ ⌨ ⌥) If you're

Enjoying *rāmen* (egg noodle) soup, Sapporo (p227)

PAUL DYMON

ravelling with a large group of friends, onsider giving the resort hotels a pass, nd renting an immaculately designed ski halet in Annupuri Village, located at the ase of the An'nupuri ski slopes. Natural ardwoods and picture windows are featured prominently from floor to ceiling, vhile rich stone fireplaces, spa-quality athroom fixtures, professional kitchens nd plasma TVs add a touch of modern lass. Summer discounts available.

GETTING THERE & AWAY

BUS
During the ski season, a couple of companies run regular highway buses from JR apporo Station and New Chitose Airport o Niseko, a few of which stop in Rusutsu. he trip takes 3¼ hours, costs ¥2300 (return ¥3850) and provides the most direct ccess to the various slopes.

Reservations are necessary, and it's recommended that you book well ahead of our departure date. If you don't speak apanese, ask the staff at the tourist information centres or your accommodation o make a reservation for you.

Chūō Bus (☎ 011-231-0500; www.chuo-bus co.jp, in Japanese)

Donan Bus (☎ 0123-46-5701; www.donan us.co.jp, in Japanese)

Hokkaidō Resort Liner (☎ 011-219-4411)

Trans Orbit Hokkaidō (☎ 011-242-2040)

CAR
Scenic Rte 5 winds from Sapporo to Otaru around the coast, and then cuts nland through the mountains down to Niseko. Having a car will certainly make t easier to move between the various ki slopes. In the summer (low season), ublic transport drops off, which provides more incentive to pick up a car in apporo.

TRAIN
Frequent *futsū* run on the JR Hakodate line between Sapporo and Otaru (¥620, 40 minutes), and between Otaru and Niseko (¥1410, 1½ hours) via Kutchan (¥1040, 1¼ hours). In the peak of the ski season, there are also a few daily *tokkyū* between Niseko and Sapporo (¥4560, two hours).

While there is a JR Hirafu Station, it is far from the town itself, and is not well serviced by local buses. From JR Niseko and JR Kutchan Stations, you will need to switch to local buses to access the villages at the base of the ski slopes.

GETTING AROUND
There are twice-hourly local buses linking JR Kutchan and JR Niseko Stations to Hirafu, Higashiyama and An'nupuri villages. Pick up a schedule from the tourist information centres so that you don't miss your connection.

If you've purchased an All-Mountain Pass, you can ride the free hourly shuttle bus between Hirafu, Higashiyama and An'nupuri.

DAISETSUZAN NATIONAL PARK 大雪山国立公園
Known as Nutakukamushupe in Ainu, Daisetsuzan or Big Snow Mountain is Japan's largest national park, covering more than 2300 sq km. A vast wilderness area of soaring mountains, active volcanoes, remote onsen, clear lakes and dense forests, Daisetsuzan is the kind of place that stressed-out workers in Tokyo and Osaka dream about on their daily commute.

Daisetsuzan National Park is virtually untouched by human hands. Tourism in the park is minimal, with most visitors basing themselves in the hot-spring villages on the periphery. From the comfort

DAISETSUZAN NATIONAL PARK

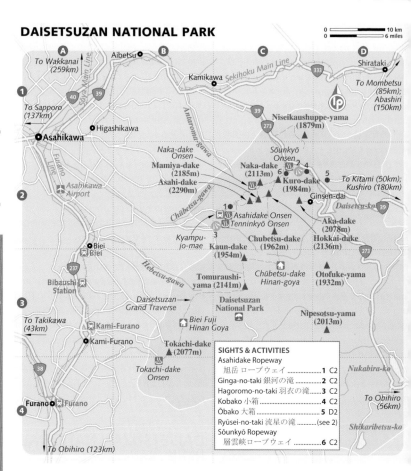

SIGHTS & ACTIVITIES

Asahidake Ropeway
旭岳 ロープウェイ 1 C2
Ginga-no-taki 銀河の滝 2 C2
Hagoromo-no-taki 羽衣の滝 3 C2
Kobako 小箱 4 C2
Ōbako 大箱 5 D2
Ryūsei-no-taki 流星の滝 ....(see 2)
Sōunkyō Ropeway
層雲峡ロープウェイ 6 C2

of your onsen hotel, you can make small forays into the park's interior, summiting peaks and trekking through valleys on challenging day hikes.

However, if you're properly equipped with the right gear, and you've done a bit of advanced planning, you can tackle Japan's most hardcore multiday trek, the Daisetsuzan Grand Traverse. No matter how far you venture into the park, though, any notions you have of Japan being small and densely packed will be shattered.

ASAHIDAKE ONSEN 旭岳温泉
☎ 0166

This forested hot-springs resort consist of around a dozen or so small inns lying at the base of Asahi-dake. Serious hikers head here for the start of the Daisetsuzan Grand Traverse, though there are plenty of other hiking options, many of which wind through unique terrain offering mix of volcanic activity, fields and foliage Whether you're here for full-on trek or just a few day hikes, be good to your body by spending ample time luxuriating in the area's healing onsen.

MARTIN MOOS

Shiretoko National Park

⚓ IF YOU LIKE...

If you like Daisetsuzan National Park we think you'll like these other national parks in Hokkaidō:

- **Shiretoko National Park** This peninsula on the east coast of Hokkaidō is considered one of the last true wilderness areas in the country. The park is famous for its bears, which is perhaps why many people are content to check out the view from boats.
- **Rishiri-Reibun-Sarobetsu National Park** These islands off the northern tip of Hokkaidō offer great hikes through fields of wildflowers in July and August (much of the rest of the year is downright arctic).
- **Akan National Park** Lakes and volcanoes are the main attractions at this fine park in eastern Hokkaidō.
- **Kushiro Shitsugen National Park** This swampland in eastern Hokkaidō is popular with birdwatchers who come in hopes of catching a glimpse of a *tanchō-zuru* (red-crested white crane).

INFORMATION

Hikers should pay a visit to the Asahidake Visitors Centre (☎ 97-2153; www.town.higashi kawa.hokkaido.jp/vc, in Japanese; ⏱ 9am-5pm daily Jun-Oct, 9am-4pm Tue-Sun Nov-May), which has excellent maps that the staff will mark with daily track conditions. An onsen map is also available here, which lists the locations, prices and hours of the various baths.

SIGHTS & ACTIVITIES

HIKING

At the base of Asahi-dake, the Asahidake ropeway (☎ 68-9111; one-way/return Jul–mid-Oct ¥1500/2800, mid-Oct–Jun ¥1000/1800; ⏱ 6am-4.30pm Jul–mid-Oct, 9am-4pm mid-Oct–Jun) runs to within easy hiking distance of the peak.

Once you've climbed Asahi-dake, you can either return to the ropeway, embark on the Daisetsuzan Grand Traverse or descend to Sōunkyō Onsen. There is also a 1.7km loop track that leads for about 50 minutes around the area before returning to the ropeway's upper terminal.

There are *rotemburo* off the northern route at Nakadake Onsen; branch left at Nakadake-bunki just before ascending Nakadake. Beware: the water in Yudoku Onsen is poisonous – don't touch it.

From Asahidake Onsen there's also a 5.5km track leading through the forest in about two hours to Tenninkyō Onsen, a small hot-springs resort with a scenic gorge and the beautiful **Hagoromo-no-taki** (Angel's Robe Waterfall).

SLEEPING & EATING

Hotel Beamonte (ホテルベアモンテ; ☎ 97-2321; www.bearmonte.jp, in Japanese; r per person incl 2 meals from ¥10,650; **P**) Across from the visitors centre, Asahi-dake's most sophisticated accommodation is this European-style resort hotel, which combines elegant rooms (some with polished wooden floors) with a stunne of an onsen, offering a variety of indoo and outdoor rock tubs. Prices vary sub stantially depending on the season, an it can be quite full at times; calling ahea is a good plan. Visiting the bath only possible for ¥1500.

GETTING THERE & AWAY

From 15 June to October, there are fiv buses in both directions between bu stop 4 at the in front of the JR station i Asahikawa and Asahidake Onsen (¥132(1½ hours). The first bus, which leave Asahikawa and Asah-idake at 9.10ar and 9.15am, respectively, is direct, whil all others require a quick transfer i Higashikawa. All other times of the yea there are only one or two daily buses i both directions.

If you're driving, follow Rtes 237, 21 and 160 from Asahikawa to Asahidak Onsen. Note that these roads are ver

View from Kuro-dake

dangerous in the snowy winter months, so drive with extreme caution.

SŌUNKYŌ ONSEN 層雲峡温泉
☎ 01658

The second major gateway to Daisetsuzan National Park is this onsen town on the park's northeastern edge, which provides secondary access to the multiday hike, the Grand Traverse. Once again, even if you're not hiking through the length of the park, Sōunkyō Onsen is still a nice base for shorter forays into the park's interior, and there are some impressive natural attractions in the area that are worth seeking out between dips in the hot springs.

INFORMATION

The **tourist information office** (☎ 5-3350; www.sounkyo.net/english/index.html; ☷ 8.30am-5pm), on the 1st floor of the public bath Kurodake-no-yu, has several maps and English-language pamphlets. Its booking service may be useful if you arrive in high season. Next to the ropeway terminus, the park **visitor centre** (☎ 9-4400; http://sounkyovc.town.kamikawa.hokkaido.jp, in Japanese; ☷ 8am-5.30pm daily Jun-Oct, 9am-5pm Tue-Sun Nov-May) can provide information on park conditions.

SIGHTS & ACTIVITIES

SŌUNKYŌ 層雲峡
This **gorge** stretches for about 8km beyond Sōunkyō Onsen, and is renowned for its waterfalls – **Ryūsei-no-taki** (流星の滝; Shooting Stars Falls) and **Ginga-no-taki** (Milky Way Falls) are the main ones – and for two sections of perpendicular rock columns that give an enclosed feeling; hence their names, **Ōbako** (Big Box) and **Kobako** (小箱; Little Box). If you don't have a rental car, a number of shops along the main street rent **mountain bikes** (¥2000 per day).

HIKING
The combination of the **Sōunkyō Ropeway and chairlift** (☎ 5-3031) provides fast access to **Kuro-dake** (黒岳; 1984m) for hikers and sightseers. One-way/return tickets on the ropeway cost ¥900/1750 and on the chairlift ¥400/600. Hours of operation vary seasonally (8am to 7pm in July and August, closed intermittently in winter).

From July to the end of September, one bus a day goes to Ginsen-dai, where the trailhead **Aka-dake** (赤岳; 2078m) is located. The bus leaves Sōunkyō Onsen at 6am and returns from Ginsen-dai at 2.15pm (¥800, one hour), leaving you plenty of time for your ascent and descent.

A short, steep and very pretty track runs up to Soūbakudai, a scenic overlook of the two waterfalls, Ryūsei-no-taki and Ginga-no-taki. Look for the steps leading up the hill directly behind where the bus stops. It takes about 20 minutes to reach the top.

After a hard day of cycling or hiking, **Kurodake-no-yu** (黒岳の湯; ☎ 5-3333; admission ¥600; ☷ 10am-9pm Thu-Tue) offers handsome onsen (including *rotemburo*). It's on the town's main pedestrian street. You can also soothe your aching feet in the free **ashi-no-yu** (foot bath), next to the Ginsenkaku Hotel.

SLEEPING
Ginsenkaku (銀泉閣; ☎ 5-3003; www.ginsenkaku.com, in Japanese; r per person incl 2 meals high/low season from ¥15,900/10,500; ℗) A Japanese-style inn with the appearance of an alpine chalet, Ginsenkaku is a very professional operation located in the centre of the village. Traditionally minded tatami rooms are the scene of

Ōbako rock formation (p243), Sōunkyō, Daisetsuzan National Park

PAUL DYMON

lavish nightly feasts, though not before you give yourself a good scrub down in the steamy common baths, including a *rotemburo* with a view.

GETTING THERE & AWAY

There are up to seven buses a day in both directions between Sōunkyō Onsen and Asahikawa (¥1950, 1¾ hours) via Kamikawa. JR Rail Pass holders can travel for free between Asahikawa and Kamikawa, and then catch the bus between Kamikawa and Sōunkyō Onsen (¥800, 35 minutes). These buses also run between Sōunkyō Onsen and Akan Kohan (¥3260, 3½ hours) in Akan National Park.

There are also a couple of buses a day to Kushiro (¥4790, 5¼ hours) via Akan Kohan (¥3260, 3½ hours). Finally, there are two buses a day to Obihiro (¥2200, 80 minutes), which follow a scenic route via Nukabira-ko.

If you're driving, Rte 39 connects Sōunkyō Onsen to Asahikawa in the west and Abashiri in the east.

WESTERN HONSHŪ, SHIKOKU & KYŪSHŪ

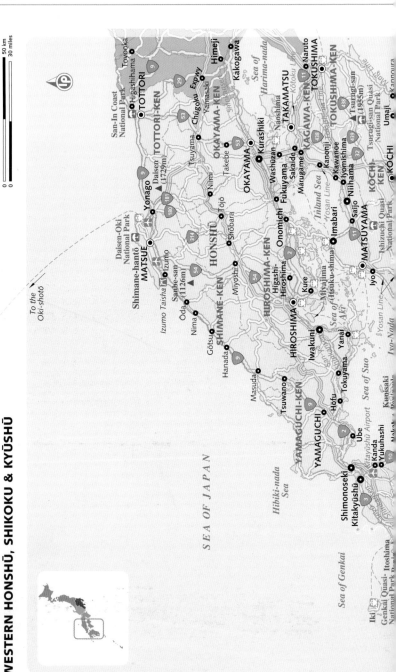

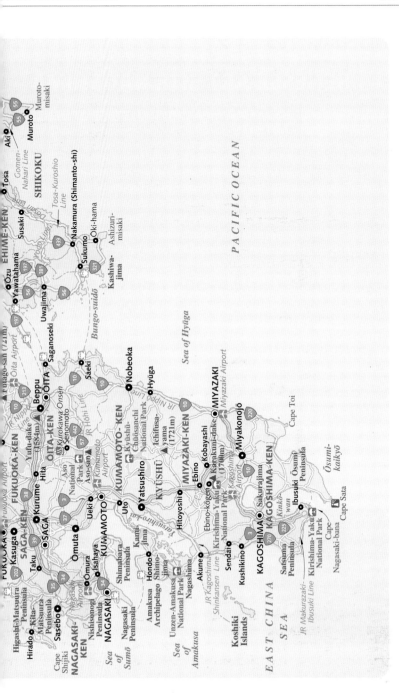

HIGHLIGHTS

1 BENESSE ART SITE NAOSHIMA

BY MARUYAMA CHIYUKI, STAFF AT BENESSE ART SITE

Benesse Art Site represents the perfect interplay of art, architecture and nature. The island showcases the architecture of Andō Tadao, who created a museum where art is illuminated only by natural light. People who live on Naoshima have a deep appreciation of art and they welcome people from around the world who come to visit the island.

◥ MARUYAMA CHIYUKI'S DON'T MISS LIST

❶ BENESSE HOUSE

Surely one of the world's most unusual art museums, Benesse House (p265) is a *residential* art museum – a hotel-cum-museum where the guests can peruse the galleries even after the museum has closed its doors to day visitors. This Andō-designed museum contains a variety of guest rooms, a spa, a cafe, two restaurants and artworks by Andy Warhol, David Hockney and Jasper Johns, among others.

❷ ART HOUSE PROJECT

Taking the idea of residential art ever further, the Benesse Art Site directors invited artists from several nations to transform several island structures into free-standing installations. The Art House Project (p265) includes a mesmerising local shrine with a glass staircase, a house with watery pools in place of tatami mats, and Minami-dera, where the artwork coalesces out of the darkness as your eyes adjust to the gloom.

Clockwise from top: Pumpkin sculpture (p265); Interior of Chichū Art Museum (p265); Courtyard of Chichū Art Museum (p265); Views from Benesse Art Site (p264); Courtyard of Benesse House (p265)

❸ CHICHŪ ART MUSEUM

Built into the earth (the name means 'in the middle of the earth'), this museum (p265) houses works by Monet, Walter de Maria and James Turrell. Andō Tadao's clever design allows natural light to enter and illuminate each work to its best advantage.

❹ NIGHT VIEWS OF THE SETO-NAIKAI

As night falls on the island, an array of twinkling lights appear on all quarters of the horizon around the island: cities, villages, boats and buoys. The views from Miyanoura port are great, but for the best view, head to the terrace of the Benesse House Museum Café – it's worth eating late to enjoy the night view.

❺ I ♥ YU

One of Naoshima's newest attractions, this whimsical *sentō* (public bath) near the island's Miyanoura port, may be the most unusual *sentō* in the country. Designed by artist Ohtake Shinro, the outside of the building is a riot of coloured tiles and posters, while inside, the bathtubs are lined with a wild assortment of collages.

❱ THINGS YOU NEED TO KNOW

Stopover Naoshima makes a good stop on the journey between Kansai (Kyoto etc) and Hiroshima. **Be warned** Naoshima can be cold and windy from November to March See our author's review on p264

WESTERN HONSHŪ, SHIKOKU & KYŪSHŪ

HIGHLIGHTS

HIGHLIGHTS

2

⬊ HIROSHIMA

Reborn from the ashes of the 1945 atomic blast, **Hiroshima** (p256) is not a highlight in the traditional sense of the word. Rather, it is a chance to learn about the horrors of nuclear war and the power of the human spirit to overcome adversity. While the displays relating to the blast are sobering in the extreme, they are also enlightening, and the vibrant modern city of Hiroshima inspires hope for the future.

3

⬊ MIYAJIMA

An hour from Hiroshima, the island of **Miyajima** (p262) is home to one of Japan's most iconic sights: the floating torii (Shintō shrine gate) of Itsukushima-jinja. After snapping the obligatory shot of the gate, head up nearby Misen, a 530m peak that offers sweeping views of the area. Miyajima is a great place to stay after visiting Hiroshima and these two destinations make a great overnight trip from Kansai.

4

↘ ASO-SAN

For those who like their hiking with a faint whiff of danger, Kyūshu's semiactive volcanic massif of Aso-san (p279) is sure to please. Hikers can explore the five main peaks within the vast 128km caldera, and a cable car allows easy access to the heights. Needless to say, with all the geothermal activity, there are onsen (hot springs) nearby for your posthike soak.

5

↘ KUROKAWA ONSEN

Within striking distance of Aso-san in central Kyūshū, Kurokawa Onsen (p282) is one of the best places in Japan for an onsen-ryokan experience. If you have a rental car, this place makes a great base for hiking in the surrounding hills, and nothing beats slipping into a private onsen after a day on the trails.

6

↘ DŌGO ONSEN

One of the best reasons to head off the beaten track to Matsuyama on the island of Shikoku is this fine old onsen (p270), which calls to mind the bathhouse from the Miyazaki animated film *Spirited Away*. An overnight stay in Matsuyama can be paired with a trip to Hiroshima and Miyajima.

2 Peace Memorial Park (p257), Hiroshima; 3 Itsukushima-jinja (p263), Miyajima; 4 Caldera of Aso-san (p279); 5 Eggs cooking in onsen, Kurokawa Onsen (p282); 6 Dōgo Onsen Honkan (p270)

THE BEST...

⬎ EXPERIENCES

- **Eating okonomiyaki in Hiroshima** (p260) Hiroshima's signature dish is this pancakelike savoury delight.
- **Staying in a yurt on Naoshima** (p265) Go Mongolian in the Inland Sea.
- **Seeing the 'floating torii' at Miyajima** (p263) This is the mother of all Shintō shrine gates.

⬎ PLACES FOR A HIKE

- **Aso-san** (p279) Hike around the craters of these semiactive volcanoes in central Kyūshū.
- **Miyajima** (p262) Head down from Misen to the famous floating torii on this scenic island.
- **Kirishima-Yaku National Park** (p283) The volcanic peaks of this superb park in southern Kyūshū rival those of Aso-san and are usually less crowded.

⬎ ONSEN

- **Kurokawa Onsen** (p282) A collection of fine onsen and ryokan beside a river in central Kyūshū.
- **Dōgo Onsen** (p270) One of Japan's most picturesque bathhouses is in Matsuyama, Shikoku.
- **Ebino-kōgen** (p284) A fine onsen hotel that's perfect for a soak after a hike in Kyūshū's Kirishima-Yaku National Park.

⬎ PLACES TO STAY

- **Iwasō Ryokan** (p264) An ideal place for spending a night on the island of Miyajima, a World Heritage site.
- **Sanga Ryokan** (p283) A classic onsen ryokan at Kurokawa Onsen near Aso-san in central Kyūshū.
- **Funaya** (p272) Old-school elegance and a fine garden in Matsuyana, Shikoku.

LEFT: FRANK CARTER RIGHT: MASON FLORENCE

Left: Floating torii (p263), Miyajima; Right: Walking the Shikoku Pilgrimage (p269)

THINGS YOU NEED TO KNOW

⤲ VITAL STATISTICS

- **Populations** Hiroshima 1.15 million, Matsuyama 513,000, Nagasaki 451,000
- **Area codes** Hiroshima ☎ 082, Matsuyama ☎ 089, Nagasaki ☎ 095
- **Best time to visit** Summer (July and August) can be too hot, but the rest of the year is comfortable.

⤲ PLACES IN A NUTSHELL

- **Hiroshima** (p256) A thriving port city with a tragic past.
- **Miyajima** (p262) A scenic island near Hiroshima with a famous shrine.
- **Naoshima** (p264) An 'art island' in the Inland Sea.
- **Matsuyama** (p269) The largest city on the island of Shikoku; home to a great onsen.
- **Kurokawa Onsen** (p282) A small onsen village in the heart of Kyūshū.
- **Aso-san** (p279) A region of volcanic peaks in central Kyūshū that offers incredible hiking.

⤲ ADVANCE PLANNING

- **Book in at Benesse House** If you plan to stay at Benesse House on Naoshima, make reservations as far in advance as possible.

- **Get an International Driving Licence** You'll appreciate one of these if you plan to explore places such as Kyūshū.

⤲ RESOURCES

- **Japan National Tourism Organization** (JNTO; www.jnto.go.jp, www.japantravelinfo.com)
- **Kōchi University Weather Home Page** (weather.is.kochi-u.ac.jp/index-e.html) This site posts satellite images of Japan updated several times a day, which can be useful when the typhoons blow in between July and October.

⤲ EMERGENCY NUMBERS

- **Ambulance & Fire** ☎ 119
- **Police** ☎ 110

⤲ GETTING AROUND

- **Walk or cycle** around Hiroshima, Naoshima and Nagasaki.
- **Hike** among the volcanic peaks of Kyūshū.
- **Ferry** around the islands of the Inland Sea.
- **Train** between cities and between Western Honshū and Kyūshū.
- **Shinkansen** (bullet train) between Tokyo and Kyoto and Hiroshima and points west.

⤲ BE FOREWARNED

- **Summer** (July and August) is very hot and humid in Western Honshū and Kyūshū.

WESTERN HONSHŪ, SHIKOKU & KYŪSHŪ ITINERARIES

HIROSHIMA & MIYAJIMA Three Days

If you find yourself in Kyoto with a Japan Rail Pass and a few extra days on your hands before you have to head home, consider this excellent addition to the normal Kyoto–Tokyo itinerary.

Grab a *shinkansen* heading west out of **(1) Kyoto**. If you're not in a rush, make a stop in **(2) Himeji** to check out Himeji-jō castle and then continue on to **(3) Hiroshima** (p256). Visit the Peace Memorial Park (p257) to learn about the city's tragic history, then spend the evening sampling the delights of Hiroshima's famous oysters and *okonomiyak* (p260). The next day, make the short journey to **(4) Miyajima** (p262) where you can see one of Japan's most famous sights, the 'floating torii' (Shintō shrine gate) at Itsukushima-jinja (p263). If you have time, climb up Misen (p263) to savour the views over then Inland Sea. Finally, return to Hiroshima and catch a *shinkansen* east to Kyoto or Tokyo.

ALONG THE INLAND SEA Five Days

Five days is enough to see the major highlights of Western Honshū, most of which are located along the Inland Sea (Seto-nai-kai), the island-studded waterway that runs between the main Japanese island of Honshū and Shikoku.

Start in **(1) Kyoto**, where you can catch a *shinkansen* west to Okayama, where you can switch to a local train and then ferry to the wonderful 'art island' of **(2) Naoshima** (p264). Explore the incredible installations on the island, then return to the mainland, and, time permitting, make a quick stop in **(3) Kurashiki** (p274) before continuing west to **(4) Hiroshima** (p256). Allot at least half a day for the Peace Memorial Park (p257) to learn about the city's tragic history, and don't forget to try Hiroshima's famous oysters and *okonomiyaki* (p260). The following day, head to nearby **(5) Miyajima** (p262) to check out the famous 'floating torii' at Itsukushima-jinja (p263) and climb up Misen (p263). If you've got another day to spare, consider taking a ferry from Hiroshima to **(6) Matsuyama** (p269), where you can try one of Japan's most famous hot springs, Dōgo Onsen (p270).

SOUTHWESTERN ADVENTURE One Week

A full week allows you to add the main island of Kyūshū to the standard Western Honshū itinerary. This is a good itinerary for those who visit Japan during the cool/cold months (late September to late March). It allows you to see a lot of varied terrain and makes the perfect addition to the standard Kyoto–Tokyo route.

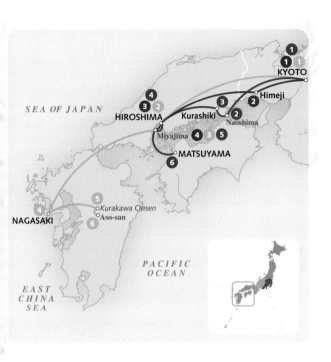

Start in (1) Kyoto and head west to (2) Hiroshima (p256) on the *shinkansen*. Check out the Peace Memorial Park (p257) to learn about the atomic bombing. Then, try some of the city's famous speciality cuisines (p260). Make a quick side trip to (3) Miyajima (p262) to see the 'floating torii' at Itsukushima-jinja (p263). Then, hop on another *shinkansen* and head down to Kyūshū. If you are interested in wartime history, visit (4) Nagasaki (p273). Otherwise, rent a car either in Fukuoka or Kumamoto and continue to wonderful (5) Kurokawa Onsen (p282). Use this as a base for a day or two of hiking in the (6) Aso-san (p279) area before heading back to Honshū and home.

DISCOVER WESTERN HONSHŪ, SHIKOKU & KYŪSHŪ

Overlooking the island-strewn Inland Sea, Western Honshū has plenty to lure the traveller, starting with Hiroshima, a city whose tragic history is brightened by its present-day vitality. Not far away, the island of Miyajima is home to Japan's most iconic sights, the floating torii (shrine gate) of Itsukushima-jinja. A few islands away, Naoshima has been turned into one of Japan's most compelling art museums.

Relatively few foreigners visit nearby Shikoku, but those who do can expect a friendly welcome. In addition to all the temples, hiking and some excellent seafood, Shikoku offers the chance to discover glimpses of an older, quieter Japan.

Kyūshū's rolling hills give way to rugged volcanic peaks. Hikers flock to Aso-san and Kirishima-Yaku National Park for excellent trekking amid the occasionally smoking craters. Needless to say with all this geothermal activity, there are plenty of excellent onsen scattered about. Finally, there is cosmopolitan Nagasaki, a vibrant city whose rebirth is a message of hope.

WESTERN HONSHŪ
本州西部

HIROSHIMA 広島

☎ 082 / pop 1,154,000

Although it's a prosperous and attractive city with excellent nightlife and a cosmopolitan population, to most people, Hiroshima means just one thing. The city will forever be remembered for the terrible instant on 6 August 1945 when it became the target of the world's first atomic-bomb attack. Hiroshima's Peace Memorial Park is a constant reminder of that day, and it attracts visitors from all over the world. But Hiroshima is a far from depressing place; its citizens have recovered from nuclear holocaust to build a thriving and internationally minded community. It's worth spending a night or two here and seeing the city at its vibrant best.

The city dates to 1589, when Mōri Terumoto established his castle here.

ORIENTATION

Hiroshima is built on a series of sandy islands in the Ōta-gawa delta. JR Hiroshima Station is east of the city centre. The city's main island is traversed east–west by the busy Aioi-dōri (with the main tram line from the station). South of this is another east–west boulevard, Heiwa-Ōdōri. Between these two major roads is the Hon-dōri covered arcade, along with most of the shops, bars and restaurants.

The A-Bomb Dome and Peace Memorial Park are at the western end of Aioi-dōri.

INFORMATION

Hiroshima Rest House (☎ 247-6738; 1 1 Nakajima-machi, Naka-ku; ☉ 9.30am-6pm Apr-Sep, 8.30am-5pm Oct-Mar) In the Peace Memorial Park, next to Motoyasu-bashi. Comprehensive information about the city and the island of Miyajima.

Spring flowers in the Aso-san area (p279)

MASON FLORENCE

Tourist information office JR Hiro-shima Station South (☎ 261-1877; ⌚ 9am-5.30pm); JR Hiroshima Station North (☎ 263-6822; ⌚ 9am-5.30pm) There's also another branch in the Shareo underground shopping mall at Kamiya-cho Station.

SIGHTS

A-BOMB DOME 原爆ドーム

Perhaps the starkest reminder of the destruction visited upon Hiroshima is the **A-Bomb Dome** (Gembaku Dōmu), across the river from Peace Memorial Park. Built by a Czech architect in 1915, the building served as the Industrial Promotion Hall until the bomb exploded almost directly above it. Everyone inside was killed, but the building itself was one of very few left standing anywhere near the epicentre. Despite local misgivings, a decision was taken after the war to preserve the shell of the building as a memorial. Declared a Unesco World Heritage Site in December 1996, the propped-up ruins are floodlit at night, and have become a grim symbol of the city's tragic past.

PEACE MEMORIAL PARK
平和記念公園

From the A-Bomb Dome, cross over into **Peace Memorial Park** (Heiwa-kōen), which is dotted with memorials, including the **cenotaph** that contains the names of all the known victims of the bomb. The cenotaph frames the **Flame of Peace**, which will only be extinguished once the last nuclear weapon on earth has been destroyed, and the A-Bomb Dome across the river.

Just north of the road crossing through the park is the **Children's Peace Monument**, inspired by leukaemia victim Sadako Sasaki. When Sadako developed leukaemia at 11 years of age in 1955 she decided to fold 1000 paper cranes. In Japan, the crane is the symbol of longevity and happiness, and she was convinced that if she could achieve that target she would recover. She died before reaching her goal,

HIROSHIMA

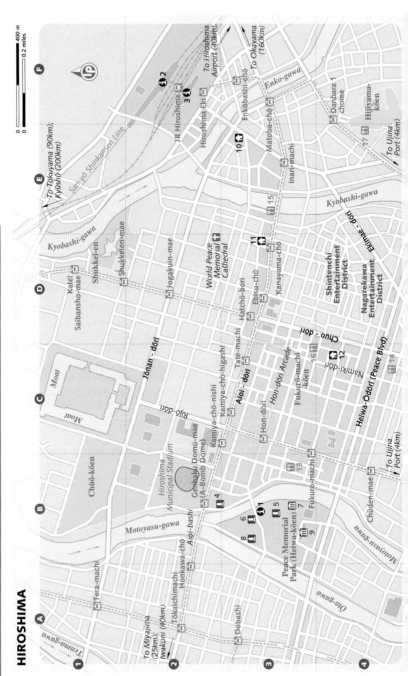

0   400 m
0   0.2 miles

To Tokuyama (90km);
Kyūshū (200km)

To Hiroshima
Airport (40km)

To Okayama
(160km)

San-yō Shinkansen Line

JR Hiroshima

Hiroshima Eki

2

3

K

Enkōbashi-chō

Enko-gawa

Danbara 1
chome

Hijiyama-
kōen

To Ujina
Port (4km)

Matoba-chō

10

Inari-machi

Kyōbashi-gawa

Kyōbashi-gawa

Shukkei-en

Shukkeien-mae

Jōgakuin-mae

Ehime - dōri

15

World Peace
Memorial
Cathedral

11

Ebisu-chō

Kanayama-chō

Shintenchi
Entertainment
District

Nagarekawa
Entertainment
District

Hatchō-bori

Katei

Saibansho-mae

Jōnan - dōri

Rijō-dōri

Kamiya-chō-nishi

Tate-machi

Kamiya-chō-higashi

Aioi - dōri

Hon-dōri Arcade

Hon-dōri

Chūō - dōri

Namiki-dōri

16

12

Heiwa-Ōdōri (Peace Blvd)

14

Chūō-kōen

Moat

Moat

Hiroshima
Municipal Stadium

Genbaku Dōmu-mae
(A-Bomb Dome)

4

Fukurō-machi
kōen

Fukuro-machi

13

Chūden-mae

To Ujina
Port (4km)

Motoyasu-gawa

Aioi-bashi

Honkawa-chō

6
1

8

5

Peace Memorial
Park (Heiwa-kōen)

7

9

Tera-machi

Tenma-gawa

To Miyajima
(25km);
Iwakuni (40km)

Tōkaichimachi

Dobashi

Dōbashi

Ōta-gawa

Motoyasu-gawa

A   B   C   D   E   F

1   2   3   4

MASON FLORENCE

Waterfall in Kirishima-Yaku National Park (p283)

ut her classmates folded the rest. The story
nspired a nationwide bout of paper-crane
olding that continues to this day.

Nearby is the recently relocated Korean
-Bomb Memorial. Many Koreans were
hipped over to work as slave labourers
luring WWII, and Koreans accounted for
nore than one in 10 of those killed by the
tomic bomb.

PEACE MEMORIAL MUSEUM
平和記念資料館

Hiroshima's Peace Memorial Museum
(☎ 241-4004; 1-2 Nakajima-chō, Naka-ku; admission ¥50; ☉ 8.30am-5pm, to 6pm Mar-Jul &
ep-Nov, to 7pm Aug) presents a balanced
arrative of events leading up to the war
nd the bombing. There are some harrow-
ng exhibits documenting the horror of
vhat happened on 6 August 1945, and a
lepressing display showing the develop-
nent of even more destructive weapons
n the years since. A visit to the museum
an be an overwhelming experience.

HIROSHIMA NATIONAL PEACE MEMORIAL HALL FOR THE ATOMIC BOMB VICTIMS
国立広島原爆死没者追悼平和祈念館

Opened in August 2002, Peace Memorial
Hall (☎ 543-6271; 1-6 Nakajima-chō, Naka-ku; admission free; ☉ 8.30am-6pm Mar-Jul & Sep-Nov, to
7pm Aug, 8.30am-5pm Dec-Feb) contains a contemplative underground hall of remem-
brance and a room where the names and
photographs of atomic-bomb victims are
kept, along with survivors' testimonies in
several languages. It was built by architect
Tange Kenzō, who also designed the museum, cenotaph and eternal flame. These
testimonies, which can be viewed on
video, vividly evoke the chaos of the time.
It's worth taking time here to get first-hand
accounts of the after-effects of the bomb.

SLEEPING

Hotel Active! (☎ 212-0001; fax 211-3121; www
.hotel-active.com, in Japanese; 15-3 Nobori-chō
Naka-ku; s/d with breakfast ¥6279/7875; P ✕ 🖳)
This very chic hotel has designer couches,
satiny coverlets and onsen. It's right in the
heart of things, within stumbling distance
of the entertainment district. Free internet
in the lobby.

Hiroshima Grand Intelligent Hotel
(☎ 263-5111; fax 262-2403; www.intellig
enthotel.co.jp, in Japanese; 1-4 Kyōbashi-chō; s/
tw ¥6300/7300; P ✕ 🖳) A recently renovated business-hotel-style place a short
walk from the station, with a suit of ar-
mour standing to attention as you enter.
Comfortable rooms have all the mod cons,
including LAN internet. There are computers in the lobby, and there's a pleasant
coffee shop.

Sera Bekkan (☎ 248-2251; fax 248-2768;
www.yado.to, in Japanese; 4-20 Mikawa-chō Naka-
ku; per person with/without meals ¥12,600/8400;
P) A very friendly traditional ryokan near
Fukurō-machi-kōen. There are large baths
and a peaceful garden on the 2nd floor.

EATING

Hassei (☎ 242-8123; 4-17 Fujimi-chō Naka-k
dishes ¥450-1200; ☯ lunch & dinner, dinner onl
Sun, closed Mon) The walls of this popula
okonomiyaki joint are covered in th
signatures of celebrity visitors. There'
an English menu. Unless you're a sum
wrestler who hasn't eaten for a week
you'll probably find a half-order mor
than enough to be getting on with a
lunchtime. The *shīfūdo supeshiaru* (sea
food special; ¥1300) is stuffed with squic
shrimp and octopus. Look for the rising
sun pattern on the sign over the door.

Okonomi-mura (☎ 241-2210; 5-1
Shintenchi Naka-ku; dishes ¥700-1000; ☯ 11am
2am) Twenty-five stalls spread over thre
floors, all of them serving the same thing
this Hiroshima institution is an atmos
pheric place to get acquainted with th
local speciality of *okonomiyaki*. It's close t

Worshippers praying at Itsukushima-jinja (p263)

STAEVEN VALL

he Parco department store; the entrance
s decorated with dozens of red-and-white
anterns, and the name is written in red
luminated characters.

Kaki-tei (☎ 090-8062-0378; 11 Hashimoto-chō
Naka-ku; ☺ lunch & dinner, closed Tue) This intimate bistro on the riverbank specialises in
oysters prepared in a variety of mouthwa-
ering ways. Grilled options include *champagne cream yaki* (¥850 for two). The daily
oyster lunch is ¥1200. There's no English
menu, but the friendly staff will help you
figure things out. Look for the green *noren*
(Japanese curtains) decorated with oysters
and the words 'Oyster Conclave'.

Tōshō (☎ 506-1028; 6-24 Hijiyama-chō
Minami-ku; lunch/dinner menus from ¥1575/3000;
☺ lunch & dinner)** In a traditional wooden
building overlooking a delightful pond
and garden, Tōshō specialises in delicious
homemade tofu (the menu has some
pictures). It's a short walk from Danbara
chōme tram stop, left uphill after the
Hijiyama shrine.

Cha Cha Ni Moon (☎ 241-7444; 2-6-26
Otemachi Naka-ku; dishes from ¥3000; ☺ 5-11.30pm)**
sophisticated minimalist chic prevails in
this softly lit old house. There's a cosy bar
downstairs and two floors of intimate semi-
private dining rooms upstairs. The beautifully presented dishes here are based on
traditional Kyoto cuisine. Look for the tiny
'Moon' sign across from the small park.

GETTING THERE & AWAY

Hiroshima's main **airport** (☎ 0848-86-
8151; www.hij.airport.jp; 64-31 Zennyūji, Hongō-
chō, Mihara-shi) is 40km east of the city,
with bus connections to/from Hiroshima
station (¥1300, 48 minutes). There are
flights to/from Tokyo (¥30,800, one hour
and 15 minutes), Sapporo (¥45,700, one
hour and 50 minutes), Sendai (¥39,000,
one hour and 20 minutes) and Naha
¥32,000, two hours), as well as flights to

Bridge over the Nakajima-gawa, Nagasaki (p273)

Seoul, Dalian, Beijing, Shanghai, Taipei (all
daily), Bangkok (Monday and Friday) and
Guam (Monday and Thursday).

Hiroshima is an important stop on
the Tokyo–Osaka–Hakata *shinkansen*
route. The trip from Hiroshima to Hakata
(Fukuoka) takes roughly 1¼ hours (¥8190);
to Osaka, it's 1½ hours (¥9470), and to
Tokyo it's four hours (¥17,540).

GETTING AROUND

Hiroshima has an extensive tram service
that will get you almost anywhere you want
to go for a flat fare of ¥150. There's even
a tram that runs all the way to Miyajima
port (¥270). If you have to change trams
to get to your destination, you should ask
for a *norikae-ken* (transfer ticket). Pay when
you get off. A day pass covering unlimited
travel on the tram network is ¥600.

MIYAJIMA 宮島

☎ 0829 / pop 1970

The small island of Miyajima is a Unesco World Heritage Site and one of Japan's biggest tourist attractions. The vermilion torii of the Itsukushima-jinja is one of the most photographed sites in the country, and has traditionally been ranked as one of the three best views in Japan. The shrine itself seems to float on the waves at high tide. Besides the main shrine, there are some good hikes on Misen, and large numbers of cheeky deer that wander the streets hitting up tourists for something (anything!) to eat.

INFORMATION

There's a **tourist information counter** (☎ 44-2011; 1162-18 Miyajima-chō; ⏰ 9am-5pm) in the ferry terminal. Turn right as you emerge and follow the waterfront for 10 minutes to get to the shrine. The shopping street, packed with souvenir outlets and restaurants, as well as the world's largest *shakushi* (rice scoop), is a block back from the waterfront.

MIYAJIMA (ITSUKU-SHIMA)

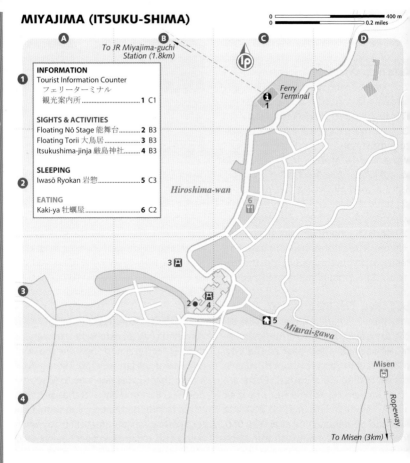

0	400 m
0	0.2 miles

INFORMATION
Tourist Information Counter
フェリーターミナル
観光案内所 **1** C1

SIGHTS & ACTIVITIES
Floating Nō Stage 能舞台 **2** B3
Floating Torii 大鳥居 **3** B3
Itsukushima-jinja 厳島神社 **4** B3

SLEEPING
Iwasō Ryokan 岩惣 **5** C3

EATING
Kaki-ya 牡蠣屋 **6** C2

To JR Miyajima-guchi
Station (1.8km)

Ferry Terminal

Hiroshima-wan

Miarai-gawa

Misen

Ropeway

To Misen (3km)

RACHEL LEWIS
Deer in Miyajima

SIGHTS

ITSUKUSHIMA-JINJA 厳島神社

Going back as far as the late 6th century, **Itsukushima-jinja** (☎ 44-2020; 1-1 Miyajima-chō; admission ¥300; ☉ 6.30am-6pm Mar-mid-Oct, to 5.30pm mid-Oct-Nov, Jan & Feb, to 5pm Dec) gives the island its real name. The shrine's present form dates from 1168, when it was rebuilt under the patronage of Taira no Kiyomori, head of the doomed Heike clan. Its pierlike construction is a result of the island's holy status: commoners were not allowed to set foot on the island and had to approach the shrine by boat through the **floating torii** out in the bay. Much of the time, however, the shrine and torii are surrounded by mud: to get the classic view of the torii that adorns the brochures, you'll need to come at high tide.

On one side of the floating shrine is a **floating nō stage** built by local lord Asano Tsunanaga in 1680 and still used for performances every year from 16 to 18 April. The famous torii, dating in its present form from 1875, is floodlit at night.

MISEN 弥山

The ascent of Misen (530m) is the island's finest walk. You can avoid most of the uphill part of the climb by taking the two-stage **ropeway** (one-way/return ¥1000/1800), which leaves you with a 20-minute walk to the top. There are monkeys and deer around the cable-car station, and some fantastic views – on clear days you can see across to the mountain ranges of Shikoku. Close to the summit is a temple where Kōbō Daishi meditated for 100 days following his return from China in the 9th century. Next to the main temple hall close to the summit is a flame that's been burning continually since Kōbō Daishi lit it 1200 years ago. From the temple, a path leads down the hillside to Daishō-in and Itsukushima-jinja. The descent takes a little over an hour. A four-hour hike of Misen is detailed in Lonely Planet's *Hiking in Japan*.

A parasol maker speaks to a class of Shikoku schoolchilden

MASON FLORENCE

SLEEPING & EATING

Iwasō Ryokan (☎ 44-2233; www.iwaso.com; Momijidani Miyajima-chō; per person with 2 meals from ¥19,950; **P**) The Iwasō, open since 1854, offers the grand ryokan experience in exquisite gardens, a few minutes' walk from the throng. It's worth the splurge, especially in autumn when Momiji-dani (Maple Valley) explodes with colour. There's a relaxing onsen in the main building.

Kaki-ya (☎ 44-2747; 539 Miyajima-chō; plate of 4 oysters ¥1000; ⏱ 11am-6pm) A sophisti-cated oyster bar in a converted building on the main street. It serves delicious local oysters freshly grilled on the barbecue by the entrance, along with beers and wines by the glass. There is an English menu.

GETTING THERE & AWAY

The mainland ferry terminal for Miyajima is a short walk from Miyajima-guchi Station on the JR San-yō line, halfway between Hiroshima and Iwakuni. Miyajima trams from Hiroshima terminate at the Hiroden-Miyajima-guchi stop by the ferry terminal. Trams from Hiroshima (¥270, 70 minutes) take longer than *futsū* (slowest trains that stop at all stations; ¥400, 25 minutes), but can be boarded in central Hiroshima.

Regular ferries shuttle across from Miyajima-guchi (¥170, 10 minutes). JR passholders should use the one oper-ated by JR. High-speed ferries (¥1800, 30 minutes, six to eight daily) operate direct to Miyajima from Hiroshima's Ujina port. Another ferry (¥1900, 45 minutes, 12 daily) runs between Miyajima and Peace Memorial Park in Hiroshima.

NAOSHIMA 直島

☎ 087 / pop 3500

Naoshima is a special place. Until not too long ago, this small island was no different from many others in the Inland Sea: home to a dwindling population subsisting on the joint proceeds of a dying fishing in-dustry and their old-age pensions. Today, as the location of the **Benesse Art Site Naoshima** (www.naoshima-is.co.jp), Naoshima s one of the area's biggest tourist attractions, offering a unique opportunity to see some of Japan's best contemporary art in stunning natural settings.

The project started in the early '90s, when the Benesse Corporation chose Naoshima as the setting for its growing collection of modern art. Award-winning architect Andō Tadao was hired to design the company's **Benesse House** (ベネッセハウス; ☎ 892-2030; Gotanji Nao-shima-chō; admission ¥1000; 8am-9pm), a stunning museum and hotel on the south coast of the island. There are works here by Andy Warhol, David Hockney and Jasper Johns, among many others.

A short walk away is the **Chichū Art Museum** (地中美術館; ☎ 892-3755; www.chichu.jp; 3449-1 Naoshima; admission ¥2000; 10am-6pm Mar-Sep, to 5pm Oct-Feb, closed Mon), another Andō creation completed in 2004. Largely underground, yet lit entirely by natural light, the museum provides a remarkable setting for several Monet 'Water Lilies', some monumental sculptures by Walter de Maria and three unforgettable installations by James Turrell.

At the **Art House Project** (家プロジェクト; ☎ 892-2030; combined ticket ¥1000; 10am-4.30pm, closed Mon), in the old fishing village of Honmura (本村), half-a-dozen traditional buildings have been restored and turned over to contemporary artists to use as the setting for some impressive installations. In a converted fisherman's house called **Kadoya**, Miyajima Tatsuo's red, yellow and green LEDs float serenely on a pond where you would expect to find tatami mats. Another of James Turrell's experiments with light occupies **Minami-dera**, where the viewer sits in total darkness for up to 10 minutes before the eyes grow used to the dim light and the art slowly starts

to reveal itself. Elsewhere, Sugimoto Hiroshi's glass staircase and underground 'Stone Chamber' make striking use of the traditional **Go'o Shrine**.

In addition to the main sites, numerous works of outdoor art are situated around the coast, including the **pumpkin sculpture** by Kusama Yayoi that has become a symbol of the island.

With an early ferry from Takamatsu or Uno it's possible to cover the sights as a day trip, but there is a growing range of accommodation options available for those who want to soak up the special atmosphere of the island overnight. **Tsutsuji-sō** (つつじ荘; ☎ 892-2838; fax 892-3871; per person from ¥3675; P) is an encampment of Mongolian-style yurt tents by the beach, not far from the two museums. Meals are available.

OLIVER STREWE

Daikon for sale at a market in Kōchi (p267)

For upmarket accommodation, there's **Benesse House** (☎ 892-2030; www.naoshima -is.co.jp/english/benessehouse/index.html; r from ¥30,000; P ✕) itself, where guests can view the artworks at leisure, 24 hours a day.

In Honmura, close to the Art House Project buildings, **Café Maruya** (まるや; ☎ 892-2714; lunch special ¥800; ⏱ 11am-6pm, closed Mon) is a civilised spot for coffee or *higawari ranchi* (daily lunch special).

The **tourist information desk** (☎ 892-2299; www.naoshima.net/en/accommodations/index.html; ⏱ 9am-7pm) in the Marine Station by the ferry port has a full list of accommodation options (also outlined on the website) and a useful bilingual map of the island.

Minibuses link the sights (¥100), and **bike hire** (per day ¥500; ⏱ 9am- 7pm) is available at the ferry port. The main areas of interest are easily covered on foot.

There are six to seven ferries a day to the main port of Miyaura from Takamatsu (高松; ¥510, one hour, 8.10am to 8.05pm) in Shikoku and 15 from Uno (宇野) in Okayama-ken (¥280, 20 minutes, 6.10am to 8.25pm). Uno is at the end of the JR Uno line, about an hour from Okayama (¥570). You may have to change trains at Chaya-machi (茶屋町). Travelling via Naoshima is a good way to get from Honshū to Shikoku, or vice versa.

IZUMO 出雲

☎ 0853 / pop 148,000

Izumo has one major attraction – the great Izumo Taisha shrine, which ranks with Ise-jingū (p160) as one of the most important shrines in Japan.

ORIENTATION & INFORMATION

Izumo Taisha is 8km northwest of central Izumo. The shrine area, basically one sleepy street, is accessible from the Ichibata Line Taisha Ekimae Station and runs right up the shrine gates. Izumo Taisha can be visited easily as a day trip from Matsue. The **tourist information office** (☎ 53-2298; 1346-9 Kizuki Minami Shinmondōri Taisha-chō; ⏱ 9am-5.30pm) is located in the station building, and has pamphlets and maps.

SIGHTS

IZUMO TAISHA 出雲大社

Perhaps the oldest Shintō shrine of all, **Izumo Taisha shrine** (出雲大社; ☎ 53-3100; 195 Kizuki Higashi Taisha-chō; ⏱ 6am-8pm) is second in importance only to Ise-jingū, the home of the sun goddess Amaterasu. The shrine is as old as Japanese history – there are references to Izumo in the *Kojiki*, Japan's oldest book – and its origins stretch back into the age of the gods. Impressive as the structure is today, it was once even bigger. Records dating from AD 970 describe the shrine as the tallest building in the country; there is evidence that the shrine towered as high as 48m above the ground during the Heian period. It may well have been too high for its own good – the structure collapsed five times between 1061 and 1225, and the roofs today are a more modest 24m.

The current appearance of the main shrine dates from 1744. The main hall is currently undergoing one of its periodic rebuildings, and from April 2008 to May 2013 the deity will take up residence in a temporary shrine in front of the main hall.

The shrine is dedicated to Ōkuninushi who, according to tradition, ceded control over Izumo to the sun goddess' line – he did this on the condition that a huge temple would be built in his honour, one that would reach as high as the heavens. Long revered as a bringer of good fortune, Ōkuninushi is worshipped as he god of marriage, and visitors to the hrine summon the deity by clapping our times rather than the usual two.

Just to the right of the shrine's front gate is **Shimane Museum of Ancient zumo** (島根県立古代出雲歴史博物館; ☎ 53-8600; 99-4 Kizuki Higashi Taisha-chō; admission ¥600, foreigners with ID ¥300; ✆ 9am-6pm, to pm Nov-Feb, closed 3rd Tue of month; Ⓟ), containing exhibits on local history. These nclude reconstructions of the shrine in ts pomp, and recordings of the annual ceremonies held to welcome the gods to Izumo. The museum also houses a superb collection of bronze from the ancient Yayoi period, excavated nearby n 1996.

To get an idea of the original size of Izumo Taisha, check out the **Kodai zumo Ōyashiro Mokei Tenjikan** (古代出雲大社模型展示館; **Ancient Izumo Shrine Model Hall**; ☎ 53-3100; admission free; ✆ 8.30am-4.30pm), where there is a scale model of the shrine as it was about 800 years ago.

GETTING THERE & AWAY
The private Ichibata line starts from Matsue Shinjiko-onsen Station in Matsue and runs along the northern side of Shinji-ko (Lake Shinsji) to Taisha Ekimae Station (¥790, one hour, with a transfer at Kawato, 川跡). The JR line runs from JR Matsue Station to JR Izumo-shi Station (¥570, 42 minutes), where you can transfer to an Ichibata train to Izumo Taisha (¥480). There are also buses to the shrine from Izumo-shi Station (¥490, 25 minutes).

SHIKOKU 四国
KŌCHI 高知
☎ 088 / pop 335,000

The prefectural capital is a pleasant city with excellent nightlife, and has one of Japan's few castles to have survived with most of its original buildings intact. The city played an important role in the Meiji Restoration, when a young samurai named Sakamoto Ryōma was instrumental in bringing down the feudal government. He's the

OLIVER STREWE

Meal break for a farming family in rural Shikoku

serious-looking young man in samurai garb whose picture is all over town.

ORIENTATION & INFORMATION

Harimayabashi-dōri is the main road that leads straight ahead from the station. Trams travel along this road, passing the Obiyamachi arcade before intersecting with the main east–west road tram line at Harimaya-bashi.

Tourist information office (☎ 826-3337; ⏰ 9am-5pm) This helpful office is inside JR Kōchi Station.

SIGHTS & ACTIVITIES

KŌCHI-JŌ 高知城

Unlike many of Japan's modern concrete reconstructions, **Kōchi-jō** (Kōchi Castle; ☎ 824-5701; 1-2-1 Marunouchi; admission ¥400; ⏰ 9am-5pm) is the real thing – one of just a dozen in Japan to have survived with its original *tenshu-kaku* (keep) intact. The castle was originally built during the first decade of the 17th century by Yamanouchi Katsutoyo, who was appointed *daimyō* (domain lord) by Tokugawa Ieyasu after he fought on the victorious Tokugawa side in the Battle of Sekigahara in 1600. A major fire destroyed much of the original structure in 1727, and the castle was largely rebuilt between 1748 and 1753.

SUNDAY MARKET 日曜市

If you're in Kōchi on a Sunday, don't miss the colourful **street market** (⏰ 5am-6pm Sun Apr-Sep, 6am-5pm Sun Oct-Mar) along Ōte-suji, the main road leading to the castle. The market, which has been going for some 300 years, has everything from fruit, vegetables and goldfish to antiques, knives and large garden stones.

SLEEPING

Hotel No 1 Kōchi (☎ 873-3333; fax 875-9999; www.hotelno1.jp/kochi/, in Japanese; 16-8

Nijūdai-machi; s/tw ¥5140/7870; P ⌧ 🖳 📶) This business hotel is in a quiet area between the station and the castle. Western style rooms are on the small side, but the rooftop onsen is a nice touch. There is LAN access in all rooms, and there are internet consoles in the lobby.

Richmond Hotel (☎ 820-1122; www.richmondhotel.jp/e/kochi/index.htm; 9-4 Obiyamachi; s ¥11,000, d ¥16,000-20,000; P ⌧ 🖳 📶) This elegant hotel with immaculate rooms and professional service is a cut above most other places in this price range and is just off the main shopping arcade in the heart of the city. There are public consoles with free internet access; rental laptops are also available and LAN access is in all rooms.

EATING

Tokugetsurō (☎ 882-0101; 1-17-3 Minami-harimaya-chō; ⏰ lunch & dinner) Open since 1870, this traditional restaurant is an elegant place to try local *Tosa-ryōri* (Tosa cuisine) in tatami rooms overlooking a garden. The menu consists of a short list of set courses featuring local fish such as bonito and sea bream, according to what's in season. If the thought of eating whale meat is offensive to you, keep away from menu items featuring *kujira* (鯨), which is the Japanese word for whale. The restaurant is in a building with an imposing wooden facade across from the Dentetsu Tāminaru-biru Mae tram stop. If you're on a budget, *bentō* (boxed-meal) specials start at ¥2625; expect to pay at least twice as much in the evening.

GETTING THERE & AWAY

Kōchi's Ryōma airport, 10km east of the city, is accessible by bus (¥700, 35 minutes) from the station. There are flights to/from Tokyo (¥31,500, one hour and 20 minutes, eight daily), Nagoya (¥25,800,

WESTERN HONSHŪ, SHIKOKU & KYŪSHŪ

SHIKOKU

OLIVER STREWE

Izakaya (pub-eatery) in Kōchi

one hour, two daily), Osaka (¥17,500, 45 minutes, six daily) and Fukuoka (¥23,700, 45 minutes, three daily).

Kōchi is on the JR Dosan line, and is connected by *tokkyū* (limited express) to Takamatsu (¥4760, two hours and 10 minutes) via Awa Ikeda (*tokkyū*, ¥2730, one hour and nine minutes), a jumping-off point for the Iya Valley in Tokushima-ken. Trains also run west to Kubokawa (*tokkyū*, ¥2560, one hour), where you can change for Nakamura (for the Shimanto-gawa) and Uwajima on the west coast.

GETTING AROUND

Kōchi's colourful tram service (¥190 per trip) has been running since 1904. There are two lines: the north–south line from the station intersects with the east–west tram route at the Harimaya-bashi junction. Pay when you get off, and ask for a *norikae-ken* (transfer ticket) if you have to change lines.

The My-Yū circular bus runs to Godaisan and Katsurahama from Kōchi Station.

MATSUYAMA 松山

☎ 089 / pop 513,000

Shikoku's largest city is a major transportation hub that rivals anything on the 'mainland'. Matsuyama has several first-rate attractions, most notably its immaculately preserved castle and Dōgo Onsen Honkan, a luxurious 19th-century public bath house built over one of the most ancient hot springs in Japan. Matsuyama is also home to seven of the 88 Temples in the Shikoku Pilgrimage, including Ishite-ji, one of the most famous stops on the pilgrimage.

ORIENTATION & INFORMATION

Most visitors arrive at JR Matsuyama Station, which is about 500m west of the castle's outer moat. The city centre is south of the castle, closer to the Matsuyama-shi Station on the private Iyo-tetsudō line. Dōgo Onsen is 2km east of the city centre, while the ferry port is north of Matsuyama in the city of Takahama.

Tourist information office JR Matsuyama Station (☎ 931-3914; ☾ 8.30am-

8.30pm); Dōgo Onsen-mae (☎ 921-3708; ◷ 8am-4.45pm) The main office is located inside JR Matsuyama Station, while a branch office is near the tram terminus for Dōgo Onsen.

SIGHTS

MATSUYAMA-JŌ 松山城
Perched on top of Mt Katsuyama in the centre of town, the castle dominates the city, as it has for centuries. Matsuyama-jō (☎ 921-4873; admission ¥500; ◷ 9am-5pm, to 5.30pm Aug, to 4.30pm Dec & Jan) is one of Japan's finest surviving castles, and one of the very few with anything interesting to look at inside: there are excellent displays on the history of the city and the castle from which it was ruled (much of the information has been translated uncommonly well into English).

A ropeway (one-way/return ¥260/500) is on hand to whisk you up the hill, though there is a pleasant pathway if you prefer to walk. It's worth walking down via the back slopes of the castle and stopping off at Ninomaru Shiseki Tei-en (admission

¥100; ◷ 9am-5pm, to 5.30pm Aug, to 4.30pm Dec & Jan) in the outer citadel of the fort, consisting of old gardens and modern water features. From here it's a short wander to underwhelming Ehime Museum of Art (☎ 932-0010; Horinouchi; admission ¥3; ◷ 9.40am-6.30pm, closed Mon), which features a solitary Monet and lots of European-style work by local painters.

DŌGO ONSEN 道後温泉
According to legend, Dōgo Onsen was discovered during the age of the gods when a white heron was found healing itself in the spring. Since then, Dōgo has featured prominently in a number of literary classics, and won itself a reputation for the curative powers of its waters. The mono-alkaline spring contains sulphur and is believed to be particularly effective at treating rheumatism, neuralgia and hysteria.

The main building, Dōgo Onsen Honkan (道後温泉本館; ☎ 089-921-5141; 5-6 Dōgo-yunomachi; ◷ 6am-11pm), was constructed in 1894, and designated a

Matsuyama-jō

MASON FLORENCE

⚐ AN INSIDER'S GUIDE TO DŌGO ONSEN

Even if you're well versed in onsen (hot springs) culture, Dōgo can be a bit confusing as there are two separate baths (and four pricing options) from which to choose. The larger and more popular of the two baths is *kami-no-yu* (神の 湯; water of the gods), which is separated by gender and adorned with heron mosaics. A basic bath costs ¥400, while a bath followed by tea and *senbei* (rice crackers) in the 2nd-floor tatami room costs ¥800, and includes a rental *yukata* (light cotton kimono). A rental towel and soap will set you back a further ¥50. The smaller and more private of the two baths is the *tama-no-yu* (魂の湯; water of the spirit), which is also separated by gender and adorned with simple tiles. A bath followed by tea and *dango* (sweet dumplings) in the 2nd-floor tatami room costs ¥1200, while the top price of ¥1500 allows you to enjoy your snack in a private tatami room on the 3rd floor.

Although there are English-language pamphlets on hand to clarify the correct sequence of steps, Dōgo Onsen can be a bit intimidating if you don't speak Japanese. After paying your money outside, you should enter the building and leave your shoes in a locker. If you've paid ¥400, go to the *kami-no-yu* changing room (signposted in English), where you can use the free lockers for your clothing. If you've paid ¥800 or ¥1200, first go upstairs to receive your *yukata,* and then return to either the *kami-no-yu* or *tama-no-yu* (also signposted in English) changing room.

After your bath, you should don your *yukata* and retire to the 2nd-floor tatami room to sip your tea and gaze down on the bath-hoppers clip-clopping by in *geta* (traditional wooden sandals). If you've paid top whack, head directly to the 3rd floor, where you will be escorted to your private tatami room. Here, you can change into your *yukata* before heading to the *tama-no-yu* changing room, and also return after your bath to sip tea in complete isolation.

---

an important cultural site in 1994. The three-storey, castle-style building incorporates traditional design elements, and is crowned by a statue of a white heron to commemorate its legendary origins. Although countless famous people have passed through its doors, Dōgo Onsen Honkan is perhaps best known for its inclusion in the famous 1906 novel *Botchan* by Natsume Sōseki, the greatest literary figure of Japan's modern age, who based his novel on his time as a schoolteacher in Matsuyama in the early 20th century.

Dōgo Onsen is 2km east of the city centre, and can be reached by the regular tram service, which terminates at the start of the spa's shopping arcade. This arcade is lined with small restaurants and souvenir stores, and leads directly to the front of the Honkan.

Dōgo can get quite crowded, especially on weekends and holidays, although at dinner time it's usually empty, because most Japanese tourists will be having dinner in their inns. If you want to escape the crowds, one minute on foot from the Honkan (through the shopping arcade) is Tsubaki-no-yu (椿の湯; admission ¥360; ⊙ 6am-11pm), Dōgo Onsen's hot-spring annexe, frequented primarily by locals.

ISHITE-JI 石手寺

East of Dōgo Onsen is Ishite-ji, 51st of the 88 Temples, and one of the largest and most impressive in the circuit. *Ishite* means 'stone hand' and comes from a legend associated with Kōbō Daishi. A statue of the famous religious figure overlooks the temple from the hillside.

SLEEPING

Check Inn Matsuyama (☎ 998-7000; fax 998-7801; www.checkin.co.jp/matsuyama, in Japanese; 2-7-3 Sanban-chō; s/tw from ¥4380/7700; **P** ✖ 🖳) This swish hotel is excellent value for money, with well-equipped modern rooms, chandeliers in the lobby, and an onsen on the roof. A short walk from the Ōkaidō arcade, the hotel is convenient to the city's nightlife and restaurants. LAN internet is in all rooms and there are consoles in the lobby.

Millennia Hotel Matsuyama (☎ 943-1011; fax 921-4111; 2-5-5 Honmachi; s/tw ¥6800/10,900) Spacious and comfortable rooms, along with satellite TV and a dim-sum restaurant,

make this hotel near the castle moat a goo option. It's directly opposite the Honmach 3-chōme tram stop.

Funaya (☎ 947-0278; fax 943-2139; ww .dogo-fu naya.co.jp, in Japanese; 1-33 Dōg Yunomachi; per person with meals from ¥22,05 **P**) A short walk from the Dōgo Onse tram station along the road that leads u to Isaniwa-jinja, this luxurious hotel ha been in business for more than 350 year Natsume Sōseki and various members c the royal family are among the famou people who have stayed here. Despite it unpromising exterior, Funaya is centre on an exquisite garden and features el egant tatami rooms (and a few Western style rooms) and private onsen that dra their water from the famous spring.

EATING

Tengu no Kakurega (☎ 931-1009; 2-5-1 Sanban-chō; ⏰ 5pm-midnight, to 1am Fri & Sat This chic young people's *izakaya* (pub eatery) serves *yakitori* (skewers of grille chicken) and other dishes in a pleasan

OLIVER STRE

Cooking homemade udon

273

etting. Paper screens give onto a little garden at the back. There is no English menu; options include *uzura* (quail's eggs; ¥150), *tsukune* (chicken meat balls; ¥150), *supara-maki* (chicken with asparagus; ¥200) and *nira-maki* (chicken with shallots; ¥150). It has 100 different types of sake and *shōchū* (distilled grain liquor). It's tucked away and a little hard to find – heading away from the post office, look for the small sign on the right in the second block after the Ōkaidō arcade.

GETTING THERE & AWAY

Matsuyama's airport, 6km west of the city, is easily reached by bus (¥330, 20 minutes, hourly) from the front of the JR Matsuyama Station. There are direct flights to/from Tokyo (¥32,000, one hour and 25 minutes, 10 daily), Nagoya (¥23,700, one hour, three daily), Osaka (¥17,000, 50 minutes, 15 daily) and Fukuoka (¥28,000, 50 minutes, three daily).

The JR Yosan line connects Matsuyama with Takamatsu (*tokkyū*, ¥5500, 2½ hours), and there are also services across the Seto-ōhashi to Okayama (*tokkyū*, ¥6120, 2¾ hours) on Honshū.

JR Highway buses run to/from Osaka (¥6700, 5½ hours, five daily) and Tokyo (¥12,200, 12 hours, one daily). There are frequent buses to major cities in Shikoku.

The superjet hydrofoil, run by the **Setonaikai Kisen ferry** (☎ 082-253-1212, Matsuyama booking office 089-953-1003; ☉ 9am-9pm), has regular hydrofoil connections between Matsuyama and Hiroshima (¥6300, 1¼ hours, 14 daily). The Hiroshima-to-Matsuyama ferry (¥2900, 2¾ hours, 10 daily) is also a popular way of getting to/from Shikoku.

GETTING AROUND

Matsuyama has an excellent tram service that costs a flat ¥150 for each trip (pay when you get off). A day pass costs ¥300. Trams to the terminus at Dōgo Onsen leave from outside both JR Matsuyama and Matsuyama-shi Stations. The Ōkaidō stop outside the Mitsukoshi department store is a good central stopping point.

Lines 1 and 2 are loop lines, running clockwise and anticlockwise around Katsuyama (the castle mountain). Line 3 runs from Matsuyama-shi Station to Dōgo Onsen, line 5 goes from JR Matsuyama Station to Dōgo Onsen, and line 6 from Kiya-chō to Dōgo Onsen.

Bike rental (per day ¥300; ☉ 9am-6pm Mon-Sat) is available at the large bicycle park to the right as you exit the JR station.

KYŪSHŪ 九州

NAGASAKI 長崎
☎ 095 / pop 451,740

The tragedy of Nagasaki's atomic devastation overshadows the story of its colourful trading history. Today Nagasaki has plenty to offer visitors – an array of museums with content ranging from the fascinating to the profound. There are churches, shrines and temples, culinary delights and a landscape that rivals far more visited parts of Japan. Schedule at least a few days here to meet the people and get a sense of the spirit of this unique and embracing place.

ORIENTATION & INFORMATION

About 2km southeast of JR Nagasaki Station, the Hamano-machi arcade and Shianbashi entertainment district are where the locals go to shop and eat. Nagasaki's sights are scattered over a broad area, but it's feasible to walk from Shianbashi through Chinatown, all the way south to the Dutch slopes and Glover Garden. The atomic bomb hypocentre is in the opposite direction in the suburb

Omikuji (paper fortunes) at a shrine in Matsuyama

SALLY DILLON

➘ IF YOU LIKE...

If you like Matsuyama (p269), we think you'll like these other less visited but interesting sights in Western Honshū and Kyūshū:

- Okayama This Western Honshū castle city is home to one of Japan's most famous gardens and a nice collection of art museums.
- Kurashiki Not far from Okayama, this Western Honshū city has a fine historic district with canals lined with old *kura* (storehouses).
- Onomichi Between Okayama and Hiroshima, this port town on the Inland Sea has a fine temple walk with great views.
- Kagoshima At the southern end of Kyūshū, this friendly city makes a great stop en route to Japan's southwest islands.

of Urakami, about 2.5km north of JR Nagasaki Station.

Nagasaki Prefectural Convention & Visitors Bureau (Map p275; ☎ 828-7875; 8th fl,14-10 Motofuna-machi; ☷ 9am-5.30pm, closed 27 Dec-3 Jan) Has detailed information on the city and prefecture and helpful English-speaking staff.

Nagasaki Tourist Information Centre (Map p275; www.at-nagasaki.jp/foreign/english; ☎ 823-3631; 1st fl, JR Nagasaki Station; ☷ 8am-

8pm) Can assist with finding accommodation and has a swag of brochures and maps in English.

SIGHTS

URAKAMI 浦上

Urakami, the hypocentre of the atomic explosion, is a prosperous, peaceful suburb with shops, eateries and even a couple of love hotels just a few steps from the hypocentre. Nuclear ruin seems comfortably far away.

The Atomic Bomb Hypocentre Park (Map p275) has a smooth, black stone column marking the point above which the bomb exploded. Nearby are bomb-blasted relics, including a section of the wall of the Urakami Cathedral. The nearest tram stop is Matsuyama-cho.

An essential experience for visitors to Nagasaki, the sombre Nagasaki Atomic Bomb Museum (Map p275; ☎ 844-1231; www1.city.nagasaki.nagasaki.jp/na-bomb-museum/museume01.html; 7-8 Hirano-machi; admission ¥200, audioguide rental ¥150; ☷ 8.30am-5pm; closed 29-31 Dec) graphically recounts the city's destruction and loss of human life. The exhibits also cover Japan's 15 years of military prewar aggression, chronicle the postbombing struggle for nuclear disarmament and conclude with a frightening illustration of which nations still bear nuclear arms.

Adjacent to the Atomic Bomb Museum and completed in 2003, the deeply symbolic Nagasaki National Peace Memorial Hall for the Atomic Bomb Victims (Map p275; ☎ 814-0055; www.peace-nagasaki.go.jp; 7-8 Hirano-machi; admission free; ☷ 8.30am-5.30pm Sep-Apr, to 6.30pm May-Aug, to 8pm 7-9 Aug, closed 29-31 Dec) is a profoundly moving place. It is best approached by quietly reading the carved inscriptions and walking around the sculpted water

NAGASAKI

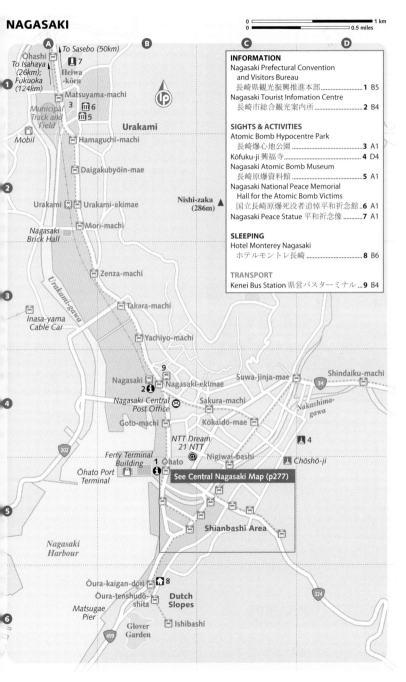

0 ———————————— 1 km
0 ———————————— 0.5 miles

INFORMATION

Nagasaki Prefectural Convention
  and Visitors Bureau
長崎県観光振興推進本部........................**1** B5
Nagasaki Tourist Infomation Centre
長崎市総合観光案内所........................**2** B4

SIGHTS & ACTIVITIES

Atomic Bomb Hypocentre Park
長崎爆心地公園 **3** A1
Kōfuku-ji 興福寺.......................................**4** D4
Nagasaki Atomic Bomb Museum
長崎原爆資料館 **5** A1
Nagasaki National Peace Memorial
  Hall for the Atomic Bomb Victims
国立長崎原爆死没者追悼平和祈念館..**6** A1
Nagasaki Peace Statue 平和祈念像...........**7** A1

SLEEPING

Hotel Monterey Nagasaki
ホテルモントレ長崎 **8** B6

TRANSPORT

Kenei Bus Station 県営バスターミナル ...**9** B4

RICHARD CUMMINS

Nagasaki Peace Statue

temples, Sōfuku-ji and Kōfuku-ji, both Chinese in origin. The path connecting them is home to several smaller temples and famous gravesites and makes for a relaxing and fascinating stroll. Despite the Chinese influences, it feels thoroughly Japanese here.

An Ōbaku (the third-largest Zen sect after Rinzai and Sōtō) temple, Sōfuku-ji (Map p277; ☎ 823-2645; 7-5 Kajiya-machi; admission ¥300; ☼ 8am-5pm) was built in 1629 by Chinese monk Chaonian. Its red entrance gate (Daiippo-mon) exemplifies Ming dynasty architecture. Inside the temple is a huge cauldron that was used to prepare food for famine victims in 1681, and a statue of Maso, goddess of the sea.

SLEEPING

Hotel Monterey Nagasaki (Map p275; ☎ 827-7111; www.hotelmonterey.co.jp/nagasaki, in Japanese; 1-22 Ōura-machi; s/d from ¥9000/18,000; ✗ ▯) Excellent rates for this lovely Portuguese-themed hotel near the Dutch Slopes and Glover Garden can be found online. Rooms are spacious and light filled, the beds are comfy and there's free internet via LAN cable. The staff is courteous and used to the vagaries of foreign guests.

Richmond Hotel Nagasaki Shianbashi (Map p277; ☎ 832-2525; fax 832-2526; www.richmondhotel.jp/e/nagasaki/index.htm; 6-38 Motoshikkui-chō; d from ¥11,000; ✗ ▯) You can't be closer to the heart of Shianbashi than here. Completed in 2007, rooms are ultramodern with dark tones, flat-screen TVs and LAN internet connectivity. Deluxe rooms are large by Japanese standards and have feature walls.

EATING

Hyōuntei (Map p277; ☎ 821-9333; 1-1 Motoshikkui-machi; plate of gyōza ¥300; ☼ dinner) This tidy *izakaya* near Shianbashi

basin above before entering the hall below. Be prepared for tears.

Heiwa-kōen (平和公園; Peace Park), north of the hypocentre, is presided over by the Nagasaki Peace Statue (Map p275) and includes the Peace Symbol Zone, an unusual sculpture garden with contributions from around the world. On 9 August, a rowdy antinuclear protest is held within earshot of the more respectful official memorial ceremony for those lost to the bomb.

TERA-MACHI (TEMPLE ROW) 寺町
Between Shianbashi and Nakajima-gawa, the smaller of the city's two rivers, justly famous Tera-machi is anchored at either end by Nagasaki's two best-known

WESTERN HONSHŪ, SHIKOKU & KYŪSHŪ

KYŪSHŪ

CENTRAL NAGASAKI

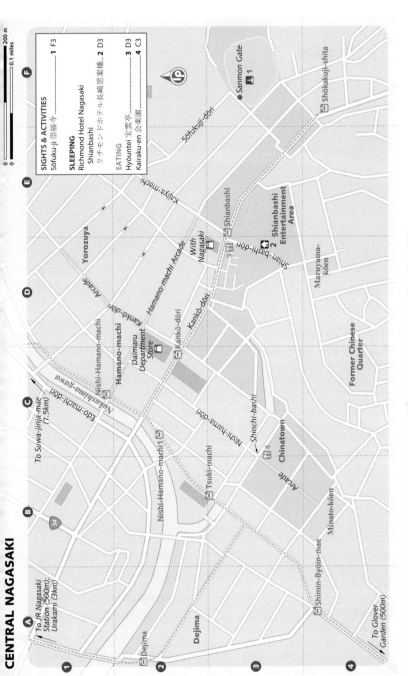

SIGHTS & ACTIVITIES
Sōfuku-ji 崇福寺 **1** F3

SLEEPING
Richmond Hotel Nagasaki
Shianbashi
リッチモンドホテル長崎思案橋..**2** D3

EATING
Hyōuntei 宝雲亭 **3** D3
Kairaku-en 会楽園 **4** C3

Sanmon Gate ● ■ 1

Shōkakuji-shita

Sōfukuji-dōri

Shianbashi

Shianbashi
Entertainment
Area

Shian-bashi-dōri

Maruyama-
kōen

Former Chinese
Quarter

Yorozuya

Kajiya-machi

Hamano-machi Arcade

With
Nagasaki

Arcade

Kankō-dōri

Kankō-dōri

Hamano-machi

Nishi-Hamano-machi

Daimaru
Department
Store

Shinchi-bashi

Chinatown

Arcade

Nishi-hama-dōri

Nakashima-gawa

Edo-machi-dōri

To Suwa-jinja-mae
(1.5km)

Tsuki-machi

Nishi-Hamano-machi

Minato-kōen

To JR Nagasaki
Station (500m);
Urakami (3km)

Dejima

Dejima

Shimin-Byōin-mae

To Glover
Garden (500m)

0   200 m
0   0.1 miles

Interior of the Nagasaki Atomic Bomb Museum (p274)

tram stop is noticeable for its rustic wooden facade. Inside, there's more of the same styling, mouth-watering *gyōza* (dumplings) and cold beer. Also try the *butaniratoji* (pork and shallots cooked omelette style) for ¥520. There's an English menu if you ask.

Kairaku-en (Map p277; ☎ 822-4261; 10-16 Shinchi-chō; dishes ¥700-1000) This restuarant has been serving southern Chinese cuisine since 1950 and there's a distinct possibility that some of the wonderful black-dressed, starchedwhite-aproned servers have been there since. Expect to pay ¥1500 to ¥3000 for a few dishes or splurge on the Peking duck with miso for ¥5000. Most dishes are displayed in the window. It's just inside the Chinatown North gate.

GETTING THERE & AWAY

There are flights between Nagasaki and Tokyo (Haneda airport; ¥38,900), Osaka (Itami airport; ¥25,700), Okinawa (¥28,500) and Nagoya (¥31,900).

From the Kenei bus station oppo site JR Nagasaki Station, buses depar for Unzen (¥1900, 1¾ hours), Sasebo (¥1450, 1½ hours), Fukuoka (¥2500, 2¾ hours), Kumamoto (¥3600, three hours and Beppu (¥4500, 3½ hours). Night buse for Osaka (¥11,000, 10 hours) leave fron both the Kenei bus station and the high way bus station next to the Irie-mach tram stop.

JR lines from Nagasaki head for Sasebo (*kaisoku;* ¥1600, 1¾ hours) or Fukuoka (*tokkyū;* ¥4410, two hours).

GETTING AROUND
TO/FROM THE AIRPORT

Nagasaki's airport is about 40km from the city. Airport buses (¥800, 45 minutes) op erate from stand 4 of the Kenei bus station opposite JR Nagasaki Station (Map p275) A taxi costs about ¥9000.

BICYCLE

Bicycles can be rented (40% discount for JR Pass holders) from JR Nagasaki

Station (Map p275; ☎ 826-0480) at the Eki Rent-a-Car. Some are even electric powered. Rates are reasonable (per two hours/day ¥500/1500).

TRAM

The best way of getting around Nagasaki is by tram. There are four colour-coded routes numbered 1, 3, 4 and 5 (tram 2 is for special events) and stops are signposted in English. It costs ¥100 to travel anywhere in town, but you can only transfer for free at the Tsuki-machi stop if you have a ¥500 all-day pass for unlimited travel, available from the Nagasaki Tourist Information Centre (p274) and many hotels. Most trams stop running before 11.30pm.

ASO-SAN AREA 阿蘇山

☎ 0967 / pop 29,370

In the centre of Kyūshū, halfway between Kumamoto and Beppu, lies the gigantic and very beautiful Aso-san volcano caldera. There has been a series of eruptions over the past 300,000 years, but the explosion that formed the outer crater about 90,000 years ago was monstrous. The resultant crater has a 128km circumference and now accommodates towns, villages and train lines.

Aso-san is the largest active caldera in the world. A 1979 eruption of Naka-dake killed a woman on her honeymoon. The last major blast was back in 1993, but the summit is frequently off-limits due to toxic gas emissions. Check with the Tourist Information Centre (right) for updates. The summit may close for a day or just an hour, depending on wind conditions.

ORIENTATION & INFORMATION

It's hard at first to get a sense of the crater's shape and scale. Best explored by car, the area offers some fabulous drives, diverse scenery and peaceful retreats. Routes 57, 265 and 325 make a circuit of the outer caldera, and the JR Hōhi line runs across the northern section. If you're driving, Daikanbō Lookout is one of the best places to take it all in, but it's often crowded with tour buses. Shiroyama Tembōdai on the Yamanami Hwy is a nice alternative. Aso is the main town, but there are others, including Takamori, to the south.

Next to JR Aso Station, the helpful **Tourist Information Centre** (☎ 34-0751; ⏰ 9am-6pm) offers free road and hiking maps and local information. Coin lockers are available. A postal ATM is 100m south, across Hwy 57.

SIGHTS

ASO-GOGAKU 阿蘇五岳

The Five Mountains of Aso are the five smaller mountains within the outer rim. They are Eboshi-dake (1337m), Kijima-dake (1321m), Naka-dake (1506m), Neko-dake (1408m) and Taka-dake (1592m). Naka-dake is currently the active volcano in this group. Neko-dake, furthest to the east, is instantly recognisable by its craggy peak but Taka-dake is highest.

ASO VOLCANIC MUSEUM
阿蘇火山博物館

This unique museum (☎ 34-2111; www .asomuse.jp, in Japanese; admission with/without cable-car return ¥1480/840; ⏰ 9am-5pm) has a real-time video feed from a camera mounted inside the active crater wall, which you can direct from inside the museum. There are English-language brochures and a video presentation of Aso friends showing off.

NAKA-DAKE 中岳

Naka-dake (1506m) has been very active in recent years. The cable car to the

ASO-SAN

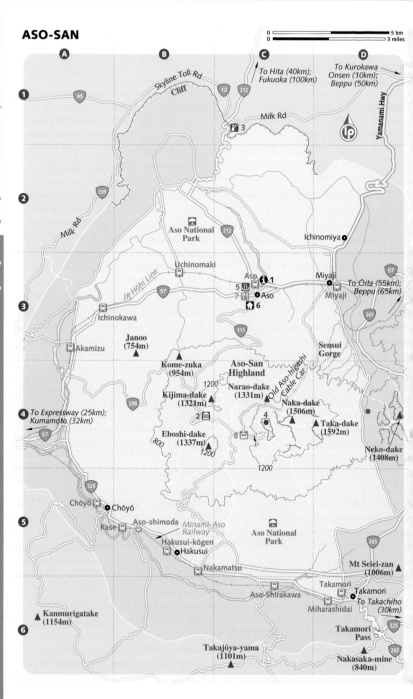

0 ____ 5 km
0 ____ 3 miles

Skyline Toll Rd

Cliff

To Hita (40km);
Fukuoka (100km)

To Kurokawa
Onsen (10km);
Beppu (50km)

Milk Rd

Milk Rd

Aso National
Park

Uchinomaki

JR Hōhi Line

Ichinokawa

Akamizu

Janoo
(754m)

Kome-zuka
(954m)

Kijima-dake
(1321m)

Eboshi-dake
(1337m)

Ichinomiya

Aso 1
5
7   Aso
6

Miyaji
Miyaji

To Ōita (55km);
Beppu (65km)

Sensui
Gorge

Aso-San
Highland

Narao-dake
(1331m)

Old Aso-higashi
Cable Car

Naka-dake
(1506m)

Taka-dake
(1592m)

Neko-dake
(1408m)

To Expressway (25km);
Kumamoto (32km)

Chōyō   Chōyō

Kase

Aso-shimoda

Minami-Aso
Railway

Hakusui-kōgen
Hakusui

Nakamatsu

Aso National
Park

Aso-Shirakawa

Mt Seiei-zan
(1006m)

Takamori
Takamori

To Takachiho
(30km)

Miharashidai

Kanmurigatake
(1154m)

Takamori
Pass

Takajōya-yama
(1101m)

Nakasaka-mine
(840m)

ummit was closed from August 1989 to March 1990 due to eruptions, and it had only been opened for a few weeks when the volcano erupted again in April 1990, pewing ash over a large area.

In 1958, after an eruption killed 12 onlookers, concrete bunkers were built around the rim to protect sightseers from such events. Nevertheless, an eruption in 1979 killed three visitors over 1km from the cone, in an area that was thought to be safe.

From the Aso Volcanic Museum (p279), it's 3km up to the cable-car station. If Naka-dake is behaving, the **cable car** (ropeway; each way ¥410; 9am-5pm) whisks you up to the summit in just four minutes, or it's ¥560 in tolls and parking if driving yourself. From there, the walk to the top takes less than 30 minutes. The 100m-deep crater varies in width from 400m to 1100m and there's a walk around the southern edge of the crater rim. Arrive early in the morning to glimpse a sea of clouds hovering inside the crater, with Kujū-san (1787m) on the horizon.

ACTIVITIES

From the top of the cable-car run you can walk around the crater rim to the peak of Naka-dake, on to the top of Taka-dake and then descend to Sensui Gorge (Sensui-kyō), which blooms with azaleas in mid-May, or to the road that runs between Taka-dake and Neko-dake. Either way will lead you to Miyaji, the next train station east of Aso. The direct descent to Sensui Gorge is steep, so it's easier to continue back from Taka-dake to the Naka-dake rim and then follow the old Aso-higashi cable-car route down to Sensui Gorge. Allow four to five hours from the Aso-nishi cable-car station walking uphill to Sensui Gorge, then another 1½ hours for the descent.

Shorter walks include the easy ascent of Kijima-dake from the Aso Volcanic Museum, about 25 minutes to the top. You can then return to the museum or take the branch trail to the Naka-dake ropeway in about 30 minutes. You can also climb to the top of Eboshi-dake in about 50 minutes.

Perfect after a long hike, **Yume-no-yu Onsen** (35-5777; admission ¥400; 10am-10pm), just in front of JR Aso Station, has wonderful indoor and outdoor pools and a large sauna. Family baths are available (¥1000 per hour).

SLEEPING & EATING

Finding a bed in the area is easy, with most accommodation in Aso, Akamizu or Takamori. Away from the towns, restaurants and lodgings are scattered and hard to reach by public transport. Stocking up on snacks is a good idea and there's a cluster of eateries on Hwy 57 near JR Aso Station.

ASO TOWN

Shukubou Aso (34-0194; fax 34-1342; r per person with/without 2 meals from ¥11,000/5000; P) This lovely rustic *minshuku* (Japanese guesthouse) with modern touches is set in the trees, less than 500m from Aso Station, offering excellent value.

Sanzoku-Tabiji (☎ 34-2011; set meals from ¥950; ✆11am-7pm; ♿ Ⓥ) Known for its *dangojiru* (miso soup with dumplings) and healthy mountain-vegetable *teishoku* (set-course meal). It's on Hwy 57, opposite the Villa Park Hotel, 10 minutes' walk from JR Aso Station and has an English menu.

GETTING THERE & AROUND

Aso is on the JR Hōhi line between Kumamoto (*tokkyū*; ¥1980, 70 minutes) and Ōita (*tokkyū*; ¥3290, 1¾ hours). Some buses from Beppu (¥3080, 2¾ hours) continue to the Aso-nishi cable-car station (an extra ¥1130).

To get to Takamori on the southern side of the crater, transfer from the JR Hōhi line at Tateno (¥360, 30 minutes) to the scenic Minami-Aso private line, which terminates at Takamori (¥470, 30 minutes). Buses from Takamori continue southeast to Takachiho (¥1280, 70 minutes, three daily).

Buses operate approximately every 90 minutes from JR Aso Station via the volcano museum to Aso-nishi cable-car station (¥470, 35 minutes). The first bus up leaves at 8.37am, with the last return trip down from the cable-car station at 5pm.

Bike rentals are available at JR Aso Station (¥300, two hours). Cars can be rented for the day at **Eki Rent-a-Car** (☎ 34-1001 www.ekiren.co.jp, in Japanese), opposite the tourist information office adjacent to the train station, from ¥6000.

If driving, a toll (¥560) is required on a portion of the road skirting the crater from Aso-nishi to Kato-nishi.

KUROKAWA ONSEN
黒川温泉

☎ 0967 / pop 400

A few dozen ryokan lie along a steep valley beside the Kurokawa (Black River), some 6km west of the Yamanami Hwy. Considered one of the best onsen villages in Japan, Kurokawa is everything a resort town should be. Although well known in

Farmer planting rice in rural Shikoku (p267)

apan, this idyllic village is safely secluded from the rest of the world and maintains its tranquillity. It's the perfect spot to experience a ryokan.

For day trippers, an 'onsen passport' ¥1200) from the **tourist information desk** (☎ 44-0076; ☽ 9am-6pm) allows access to three baths of your choice (8.30am o 9pm). Kurokawa is especially famous for its 23 *rotemburo* (outdoor baths). Among local favourites are Yamamizuki, Kurokawa-sō and Shimmei-kan, with its cave baths and riverside *rotemburo*. Many places offer *konyoku* (mixed bathing).

SLEEPING
Sanga Ryokan (山河旅館; ☎ 44-0906; www .sanga-ryokan.com, in Japanese; r per person with 2 meals from ¥14,300; **P**) Several of the 15 delightful rooms at this romantic ryokan have private onsen attached. Exquisite *kaiseki* (Japanese haute cuisine) meals, attention to detail and heartfelt service make this a place to treat yourself to the Japanese art of hospitality.

GETTING THERE & AWAY
Experiencing this area is most enjoyable by car. But there are also five daily buses between JR Aso Station and Kurokawa Onsen (¥960, one hour). The last bus back to Aso departs at 5.55pm, to Kumamoto at 8.30pm (¥1430, one hour) or Beppu at 7pm (¥2350, two hours).

KIRISHIMA-YAKU NATIONAL PARK
霧島屋久国立公園
The day walk from Ebino-kōgen (not to be confused with the town of Ebino down on the plains) to the summits of a string of volcanoes is one of the finest hikes in Japan. It's 15km from the summit of Karakuni-dake (1700m) to the summit of Takachiho-no-mine (1574m). If the peaks

aren't being lashed by thunderstorms or shrouded in fog, common during the rainy season (mid-May through June), the vistas are superb. Shorter walks include a lake stroll on the plateau, and if hiking isn't an option, the windy mountain highways are great to drive. The area is known for its wild azaleas, hot springs and the impressive 75m waterfall, **Senriga-taki**, unimpressively dammed and shrouded by concrete reinforcements.

INFORMATION
Ebino-kōgen Eco Museum Centre (☎ 0984-33-3002; ☽ 9am-5pm) Has free information on local sleeping and eating options with topographic hiking maps for sale. There's an indoor rest area with vending machines and displays on wildlife and geology.
Takachiho-gawara Visitors Centre (☎ 0995-57-2505; ☽ 9am-5pm) Established to provide information on the local environment and wildlife.

SIGHTS & ACTIVITIES
EBINO PLATEAU WALKS
The Ebino-kōgen lake circuit is a relaxed 4km stroll around a series of volcanic lakes – **Rokkannon Mi-ike** is intensely cyan in colour. Across the road from the lake, **Fudō-ike**, at the base of Karakuni-dake, is a steaming *jigoku* (boiling mineral hot springs) . The stiffer climb to the 1700m summit of **Karakuni-dake** skirts the edge of the volcano's deep crater before arriving at the high point on the eastern side. The panoramic view to the south is outstanding, taking in the perfectly circular caldera lake of **Ōnami-ike**, rounded **Shinmoe-dake** and the perfect cone of **Takachiho-no-mine**. On a clear day, you can see Kagoshima and the smoking cone of Sakurajima. Naka-dake is another nice half-day walk, and in May and

MARTIN MOC

Hiking up Takachiho-no-mine

June it offers good views of the Miyama-Kirishima azaleas. Friendly wild deer roam freely through the town of Ebino-kōgen and are happy to be photographed.

LONGER WALKS

The long views across the lunarlike terrain of volcano summits are truly otherworldly. If you are in good shape and have six or seven hours, you can continue from Karakuni-dake to Shishiko-dake, Shinmoe-dake, Naka-dake and Takachiho-gawara, from where you can make the ascent of Takachiho-no-mine. Close up, Takachiho is a formidable volcano with a huge, gaping crater. The whole trek goes above and below the treeline on a trail that can be muddy or dry, clear or foggy; some Kagoshima monks-in-training do this route daily!

If you miss the afternoon bus (3.49pm) from Takachiho-gawara to Kirishima-jingū, it's a 7km walk down to the village shrine area, or a ¥1200 taxi ride. A taxi up to Ebino-kōgen is about ¥3750.

SLEEPING & EATING

Ebino-kōgen Onsen Hotel (☎ 0984-33 0161; www.ebinokogenso.jp, in Japanese; s/tw per person with 2 meals from ¥9200/10,800; P ⊠ ▣ The friendly front-desk staff of this large 'people's hotel' communicate well in English. The facilities are excellent, the location superb and the restaurant makes tasty affordable meals. The lovely *rotem buro* is open to the public from 11.30am to 7.30pm (¥500).

GETTING THERE & AWAY

The main train junctions are JR Kobayash Station, northeast of Ebino Plateau, and Kirishima-jingū Station to the south, but a direct bus from Kagoshima to Ebino-kōgen (¥1570, 1¾ hours) is the best method of public transport. Schedules change often.

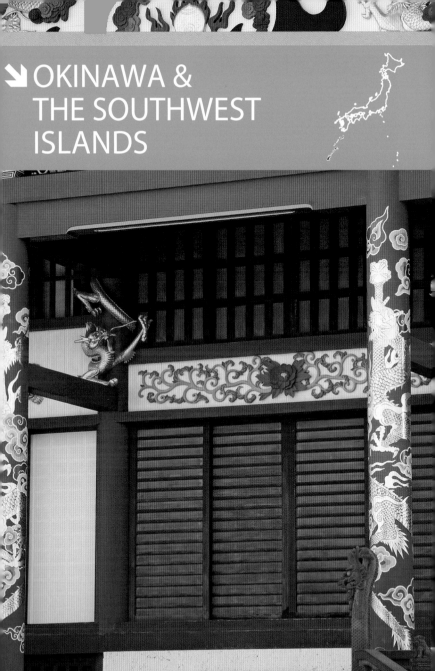

OKINAWA &
THE SOUTHWEST
ISLANDS

JAMES MARSHAL

An artist uses stencils and dyes to make *bingata*, a traditional Okinawan fabric

OKINAWA & THE SOUTHWEST ISLANDS

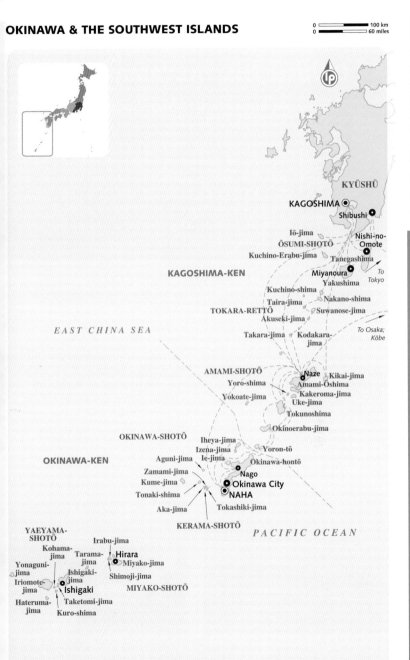

0 ——— 100 km
0 ——— 60 miles

KYŪSHŪ

KAGOSHIMA ◉

Shibushi ◉

Iō-jima

ŌSUMI-SHOTŌ

Nishi-no-
Omote ◉

Kuchino-Erabu-jima

Tanegashima

KAGOSHIMA-KEN

Miyanoura ◉
Yakushima

To
Tokyo

Kuchino-shima

Taira-jima

Nakano-shima

TOKARA-RETTŌ

Suwanose-jima

Akuseki-jima

EAST CHINA SEA

Takara-jima

Kodakara-
jima

To Osaka;
Kōbe

AMAMI-SHOTŌ

Yoro-shima

Naze ◉

Kikai-jima

Amami-Ōshima

Yokoate-jima

Kakeroma-jima

Uke-jima

Tokunoshima

Okinoerabu-jima

OKINAWA-SHOTŌ

Iheya-jima

Izena-jima

Yoron-tō

Aguni-jima

Ie-jima

Okinawa-hontō

OKINAWA-KEN

Zamami-jima

Nago

Kume-jima

Okinawa City

Tonaki-shima

◉ NAHA

Aka-jima

Tokashiki-jima

KERAMA-SHOTŌ

PACIFIC OCEAN

YAEYAMA-
SHOTŌ

Irabu-jima

Kohama-
jima

Tarama-
jima

Hirara

Yonaguni-
jima

◉ Miyako-jima

Ishigaki-
jima

Iriomote-
jima

Shimoji-jima

◉ Ishigaki

MIYAKO-SHOTŌ

Haterumi-
jima

Taketomi-jima

Kuro-shima

HIGHLIGHTS

1 DIVING THE YAEYAMA-SHOTŌ

BY SONODA MAKOTO, OWNER OF DIVING SCHOOL UMICOZA

The seas around the Yaeyama-shotō islands are full of well-developed coral reefs and tropical fish and there are many mantas around Ishigaki-jima that are friendly to divers. Diving is great around here because there is still a lot of pristine nature in these islands. Also, the local people are all warm-hearted and welcoming.

⇖ SONODA MAKOTO'S DON'T MISS LIST

❶ KABIRA ISHIZAKI MANTA SCRAMBLE

Located a few hundred metres offshore from Ishizaki cape on the west coast of Ishigaki-jima is the main gathering point for the Yaeyama's famous manta rays (p314). If you dive here in between April and November, you can usually count on seeing mantas, sometimes several mantas in one dive. The clear water and healthy coral in the area adds to the enjoyment.

❷ IRIZAKI HAMMERHEAD ROCK

Yonaguni-jima is the furthest wes point in the Japan archipelago – yo can even make out the island of Taiwa on a really clear day. Off Irizaki (p320 the western tip of the island, larg schools of hammerheads gather dur ing the winter months (December t March). This is one of the few place on earth where divers can count o fairly reliable sightings of hammerhea sharks.

Clockwise from top: Kaitei Iseki (Underwater Ruins; p320) off Yonaguni-jima; Hammerhead sharks (p320); Kabira-wan (p314); Diving with manta rays (p314)

NAKANOUGAN-JIMA

Nakanougan-jima is a small islet about 5km southwest of Iriomote-jima. It's surrounded by perfect healthy coral and a variety of fish, including dog-tooth tuna. The best time to dive around this island is from April to August, when the winds are mild. This diving spot is certainly not for beginners due to it's rather fast current; however, for the advanced diver, this is a great spot for viewing fish and underwater photography.

KABIRA-WAN

On the west coast of Ishigaki-jima, Kabira-wan (p314) isn't a dive site, just a brilliant beach to relax on after a day spent diving around the islands. It may be the most photographed site in the

Yaeyama-shotō, and if you visit on a clear day, you'll see why: the clear turquoise water dotted with green islets seems custom-designed for postcards. Fairly heavy boat traffic close to shore means that this isn't really a swimming beach (for swimming, head across the point to Yonehara Beach).

⬎ THINGS YOU NEED TO KNOW

English-speaking dive shop Umicoza (☎ 88-2434; www.umicoza.com/english/; 827-15 Kabira, Ishigaki-shi) Be warned Typhoons can strike these islands between July and October See our author's review on p311

HIGHLIGHTS

2

◈ IRIOMOTE-JIMA

Iriomote-jima (p316) is Japan's greatest natural wonder. Both above and below the water, it's a storehouse of incredible biodiversity. Iriomote-jima is almost completely covered in natural jungle or mangrove swamps. Around its shores you will find healthy and colourful coral reefs swarming with tropical fish. If you're looking for white-sand beaches to laze away on, however, head for the Kerama-shotō.

3

◈ YAKUSHIMA

You won't forget your first sighting of Yakushima (p297): covered with towering peaks wreathed in clouds, it's the sort of island where King Kong might spend his vacations. Yakushima is one of Japan's great outdoor sports destinations: you can hike to see the ancient *yaku-sugi* cedar trees; swim and snorkel offshore; cycle the scenic road network and soak in wonderful seaside onsen (hot springs).

OKINAWA & THE SOUTHWEST ISLANDS

HIGHLIGHTS

⬊ KERAMA-SHOTŌ BEACHES

For the classic Okinawan combination of white-sand beaches and crystal-clear aquamarine water, make a beeline for the Kerama-shotō (p310). Lying 30km west of the Naha, this collection of tiny islands boasts the best beaches in the entire Southwest Island chain and the visibility in the surrounding ocean averages about 30m.

⬊ NAHA

The largest city in the Southwest Island chain, Naha (p304) is a place where cultures collide: Ryūkyū, Japanese, American, Chinese and a growing number of Korean, Taiwanese and Hong Kong tourists. It is a place of delicious contrasts and juxtapositions, and the better you know Japan, the more you'll find yourself wondering, 'Where the heck am I?'

⬊ TAKETOMI-JIMA

Taking a ferry from the port of Ishigaki to the tiny island of Taketomi-jima (p318) is like taking a journey back in time. Here, buffalo-drawn carts ply sandy roads lined with stone fences, and the pace of life seems, well, to have ground to a halt. You won't believe you're still in the same country as Tokyo.

2 Mangroves at Iriomote-jima (p316); 3 *Yaku-sugi* cedar tree in Yakushima (p297); 4 Kerama-shotō (p310); 5 Pottery near Naha (p304); 6 Transport in Taketomi-jima (p318)

OKINAWA & THE SOUTHWEST ISLANDS

THE BEST...

THE BEST...

⤵ PLACES TO SWIM

- **Nishibama Beach** (p310) One kilometre of sandy perfection.
- **Furuzamami Beach** (p310) A classic Kerama beach.
- **Nagata Inaka-hama** (p300) A favourite of both sea turtles and people.
- **Yonehara Beach** (p314) One of the best beaches in the Yaeyama-shotō.

⤵ EXPERIENCES

- **Climbing Miyanoura-dake** (p300) Climb through Yaku-sugi forests to Yakushima's highest point.
- **Diving off Iriomote** (p317) Explore Japan's healthiest coral reefs.
- **Exploring the backstreets of Naha** (p304) Delve into the funky lanes in the old Ryūkyū capital.
- **Soaking in an onsen on Yakushima** (p298) Relieve those sore hiking muscles while gazing over the Pacific.

⤵ LOCAL SPECIALITIES

- **Gōya-champurū** A stir-fry of bitter melon, pork and *shima-dōfu* (island tōfu).
- **Sōki-soba** *Rāmen* done the Okinawan way: lots of noodles and a pork spare rib.
- **Umi budō** Literally 'sea grapes', this seaweed is sometimes translated as 'green caviar'.

⤵ ONSEN

- **Hirauchi Kaichū Onsen** (p298) Literally 'Hirauchi's Onsen in the Sea', this onsen is right in the rocks on the southern coast of Yakushima.
- **Yudomari Onsen** (p299) Soak beside the Pacific in this tiny Yakushima onsen.
- **Onoaida Onsen** (p299) A quaint local onsen in the village of Onoaida on the island of Yakushima.

獅子のコーナー

LEFT: RICHARD CUMMINS; RIGHT: MARTIN MOO

Left: Dragon statues in a shop window on Kokusai-dōri (p304), Naha; Right: Butterfly, Iriomote-jima (p316)

THINGS YOU NEED TO KNOW

⬎ VITAL STATISTICS

- **Populations** Yakushima 14,000, Naha 320,000, Ishigaki 48,000
- **Area codes** Yakushima ☎ 0997, Okinawa-hontō and nearby islands ☎ 098, Yaeyama-shotō ☎ 0980
- **Best time to visit** Any time outside of the July to October typhoon season

⬎ ISLANDS IN A NUTSHELL

- **Yakushima** (p297) A mountainous hikers paradise with fine seaside onsen.
- **Okinawa-hontō** (p303) A well-developed resort island centred on the sprawling city of Naha.
- **Kerama-shotō** (p310) A handful of pristine beach-fringed gems within easy ferry distance of Naha.
- **Ishigaki-jima** (p311) A mountainous island that occasionally calls to mind Hawaii.
- **Iriomote-jima** (p316) With intact jungle and healthy coral reefs, this is one of Japan's great natural wonders.
- **Taketomi-jima** (p318) A living museum of Okinawan traditional culture.
- **Yonaguni-jima** (p320) A diving destination famous for its winter hammerhead sightings.

⬎ RESOURCES

- **Naha Airport Tourist Information Counter** This is the most useful TIC in the Southwest Islands.

- **Yama-to-Kougen-no-Chizu-Yakushima Map** (山と高原の地図屋久島) This Japanese-language map is a must for those planning serious hikes on Yakushima. Pick up a copy in a major bookstore on the mainland or after arriving on the island.

⬎ EMERGENCY NUMBERS

- **Ambulance & Fire** ☎ 119
- **Police** ☎ 110

⬎ GETTING AROUND

- **Walk** around Naha.
- **Rent a car** to explore Yakushima, Okinawa-hontō, Ishigaki and Iriomote.
- **Ferry** between Okinawa-hontō. and the Keramas, and around the Yaeyamas.
- **Fly** between Naha and Ishigaki.

⬎ BE FOREWARNED

- **Typhoons** can wreak havoc with your Southwest Island travel plans any time between July and October.
- **Summer** (June to September) can be quite hot in the Southwest Islands.
- **Flights** are the only way to get to the Yaeyama-shotō.
- **Crowds** can be thick on the hiking trails on Yakushima during Japanese holiday periods.

OKINAWA & THE SOUTHWEST ISLANDS ITINERARIES

YAKUSHIMA: ANCIENT TREES & SEASIDE ONSEN Three Days

A mere two hours by ferry and 35 minutes by plane from **(1) Kagoshima** (Kyūshū), **(2) Yakushima** (p297) is a good destination for those who want to experience the Southwest Islands but don't have a lot of time on their hands. Keep in mind that while Yakushima has some good beaches, it's more of a hiker's destination; those seeking sun, sand and snorkelling should head south to the islands of Okinawa-ken.

Start your Yakushima adventure in Miyanoura (p297), the island's main settlement, where you will find accommodation and shops, as well as rental-car agencies (a rental car is the best way to explore the island).

The next day, try one of the island's main hikes, the hike up the 1935m summit of Miyanoura-dake (p300) or the hike to Jōmon-sugi (p299), then follow it up with a dip in one of the onsens on the southern coast: Hirauchi Kaichū Onsen (p298) or Yudomari Onsen (p299).

The following day, consider a swim at Nagata Inaka-hama (p300) or a hike around Yaku-sugi Land (p300).

BIG CITY, BEAUTIFUL BEACHES: NAHA & THE KERAMAS Five Days

If you'd like a side dish of the tropics to go with your main course of temples and big cities in mainland Japan, why not grab a plane down to Okinawa? It's less than three hours from Tokyo but it feels like another world.

Base yourself in **(1) Naha** (p304), which has a wealth of accommodation in all budget ranges. Highlights here include the castle of Shuri-jō (p305) and market streets (p304) that feel more Southeast Asian than Japanese.

Next, rent a car and explore the WWII sites and the Memorial Peace Park (p309) in the south of the island, or the beaches and bays to the north of the city.

Finally, to sample the crystal-clear water and white-sand beaches you've seen in all the tourist brochures of Okinawa, take a ferry from Naha to Aka-jima (p310) or Zamami-jima (p310) in the **(2) Kerama-shotō.**

YAEYAMA ADVENTURE: ISHIGAKI & IRIOMOTE One Week

The Yaeyama-shotō, Japan's southernmost island group, has it all: great beaches, vibrant coral reefs, mangrove swamps and virgin jungle. If you're a nature lover, this one is for you.

There are few direct flights to the group: most flights from the mainland go via Naha. Take advantage of this fact and spend a day or two in (1) Naha (p304) on the way down. Then, fly from Naha to (2) Ishigaki-jima (p311), where Ishigaki City is the main centre and transport hub of the Yaeyamas. If you're a diver and you're there between June and October, you'll want to head out to Manta Scramble (p314) to see the mantas who gather here each summer. If not, rent a car and drive around the island, stopping at the excellent beaches on the west coast.

Next, grab a ferry over to the nearby island of (3) Iriomote-jima (p316) and rent another car. Spend the next few days snorkelling off Hoshizuka-no-hama (p316), taking river trips into the interior of the island (p316), and, if you're really adventurous, hiking across the island in the company of a guide (don't try it alone as the trails are hard to follow).

OKINAWA & THE SOUTHWEST ISLANDS

DISCOVER OKINAWA & THE SOUTHWEST ISLANDS

Japan's Southwest Islands, or Nansei-shotō, are *the other Japan:* a chain of semitropical islands that feels more like Hawaii or Southeast Asia than the main islands of Japan. Stretching from Kyūshū in the north to within sight of Taiwan in the south, these coral-fringed islands are sure to be a revelation to those who make the journey.

First and foremost, the islands are a nature lover's paradise: starting with the islands of Kagoshima-ken in the north, you'll find lush primeval forests hidden among the craggy peaks of Yakushima.

Heading south, the first stop is Okinawa-hontō, the bustling main island of Japan's southernmost prefecture, Okinawa-ken. While the main island is great, the offshore islands are even better, including the spectacular Kerama-shotō, a group of tiny gems with white-sand beaches and crystal-clear waters. And, finally, there is brilliant Yaeyama-shotō, with Japan's best coral reefs, subtropical jungles and extensive mangrove swamps.

Of course, spectacular nature is only the half of it: the southern islands also boast a fascinating and peculiarly 'un-Japanese' culture.

GETTING THERE & AWAY

There are flights between major cities in mainland Japan and Amami-Ōshima, Okinawa-hontō (Naha), Miyako-jima and Ishigaki-jima (Map p375). Kagoshima, in Kyūshū, has flights to/from all these islands and many of the smaller islands as well. Other outer islands such as Yonaguni-jima, Kume-jima and Zamami-jima can be reached by air with a change of flight in Naha (or, Ishigaki, in some cases).

There are ferries between Tokyo, Osaka/Kōbe and Kagoshima to the islands of Amami-shotō and Okinawa-hontō, as well as plentiful ferries between Kagoshima and Yakushima and Tanegashima. Once you arrive in a major port such as Naze on Amami-Ōshima or Naha on Okinawa-hontō, there are plenty of local ferry services to nearby islands. Unfortunately, the Arimura Sangyō ferry service that used to ply the length of the Southwest Islands between Kyūshū and Taiwan is now defunct.

Thus, you cannot reach Miyako-shotō or Yaeyama-shotō by ferry from mainland Japan. A new service might start at any time, so you can always check with tourist information offices for the latest details.

If you are arriving in Japan by air, it is worth noting that Japan Airlines (JAL) and All Nippon Airlines (ANA) both offer 'visit Japan'–type airfares for domestic flights within Japan – as long as they are bought outside Japan in conjunction with a ticket to Japan. Such tickets, if used to Okinawa, are an incredible saving from standard domestic airfares bought within Japan.

GETTING AROUND

Once you arrive in a major hub such as Naha on Okinawa-hontō or Ishigaki on Ishigaki-jima, you will find plenty of ferry services to the surrounding islands. Services are plentiful and you can use cities such as these as bases for island-hopping vacations. There are also easonable air networks in Amami-shotō, Okinawa-shotō and Yaeyama-shotō, with airfields on most (but not all) islands.

Getting around the islands themselves is a little less convenient. While most islands have public bus networks, there are usually not more than a few buses per day on each route. Thus, if at all possible, we recommend bringing an International Driving Permit and renting a car or scooter, particularly on Yakushima, Ishigaki, Iriomote and Okinawa-hontō. Another solution is renting a bicycle, but rental bikes are often old creakers, so if you're serious about cycling, you may want to bring your own touring bicycle.

KAGOSHIMA-KEN
鹿児島県

YAKUSHIMA 屋久島

☎ 0997 / pop 14,000

Designated a Unesco World Heritage Site in 1993, Yakushima is one of the most rewarding islands in the Southwest Islands. The craggy mountain peaks of the island's interior are home to the world-famous *yaku-sugi* (屋久杉; *Cryptomeria japonica*), ancient cedar trees that are said to have been the inspiration for some of the scenes in Miyazaki Hayao's animation classic *Princess Mononoke*.

Hiking among the high peaks and mossy forests is the main activity on Yakushima, but the island is also home to some excellent coastal onsen and a few sandy beaches.

Keep in mind that Yakushima is a place of extremes: the mountains wring every last drop of moisture from the passing clouds and the interior of the island is one of the wettest places in Japan. In the winter, the peaks may be covered

RICHARD CUMMINS
Toy dragons for sale in Naha (p304), Okinawa-hontō

in snow, while the coast is still relatively balmy. Whatever you do, come prepared and don't set off on a hike without a good map and the proper gear. An International Driving Permit will also vastly increase your enjoyment here, as buses are few and far between.

INFORMATION

Miyanoura's ferry terminal has a useful **tourist information centre** (TIC; ☎ 42-1019; ⏰ 8.30am-5pm) in the white building on your right as you emerge from the Toppy and Rocket ferry offices. It can help you find lodgings and can answer all your questions about the island. In Anbō there's a smaller **tourist office** (☎ 46-2333; ⏰ 9am-5.30pm) on the main road just north of the river.

YAKUSHIMA

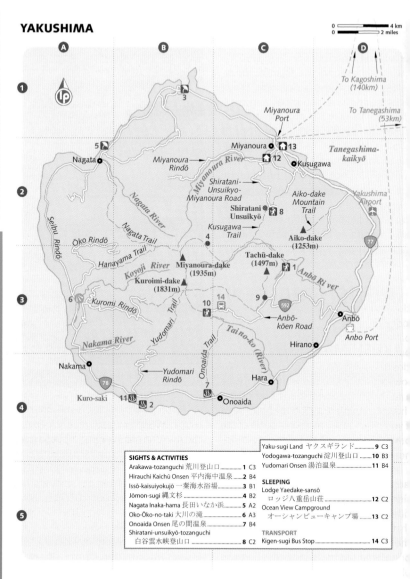

SIGHTS & ACTIVITIES	
Arakawa-tozanguchi 荒川登山口	1 C3
Hirauchi Kaichū Onsen 平内海中温泉	2 B4
Issō-kaisuiyokujō 一秦海水浴場	3 B1
Jōmon-sugi 縄文杉	4 B2
Nagata Inaka-hama 長田いなか浜	5 A2
Oko-Ōko-no-taki 大川の滝	6 A3
Onoaida Onsen 尾の間温泉	7 B4
Shiratani-unsuikyō-tozanguchi 白谷雲水峡登山口	8 C2

Yaku-sugi Land ヤクスギランド	9 C3
Yodogawa-tozanguchi 淀川登山口	10 B3
Yudomari Onsen 湯泊温泉	11 B4
SLEEPING	
Lodge Yaedake-sansō ロッジ八重岳山荘	12 C2
Ocean View Campground オーシャンビューキャンプ場	13 C2
TRANSPORT	
Kigen-sugi Bus Stop	14 C3

SIGHTS & ACTIVITIES

ONSEN

There are several onsen to be found around the island, the best of which are located near the village of **Onoaida**, on the southern coast of the island, accessible by southbound buses from Miyanoura or Anbō.

Onsen lovers will be in heaven at the **Hirauchi Kaichū Onsen** (admission ¥100; 24hr). The outdoor baths are in the rock by the sea and can only be entered at o

Moss-covered *yaku-sugi* cedar tree

FABIAN GONZALES COMMERCIAL/ALAMY

close to low tide (ask at the TIC or at your lodgings for times). You can walk to the baths from the Kaichū Onsen bus stop, but the next stop, Nishikaikon, is actually closer. From Nishikaikon, walk downhill towards the sea for about 200m and take a right at the bottom of the hill. Note that this is a *konyoku* onsen (mixed bath), so if you're shy, you'll just have to wait until other bathers clear off, as swimsuits are not allowed.

About 600m west is **Yudomari Onsen** (admission ¥100; 🕑 24hr), another great seaside onsen that can be entered at any tide. The small bath here has a divider that affords a bit more privacy. Get off at the Yudomari bus stop and take the road opposite the post office in the direction of the sea. Once you enter the village, the way is marked. It's a 300m walk and you pass a great banyan tree en route.

In the village of Onoaida is **Onoaida Onsen** (admission ¥200; 🕑 7am-9.30pm May-Oct, to 9pm Nov-Apr, from noon Mon), a rustic indoor bathhouse that is divided by gender. This is a great local bath and you're likely to be

bathing with the village elders here. It's at the top (mountain side) of the village, a few minutes' walk uphill (about 350m) from the Onoaida Onsen bus stop.

HIKING

Hiking is the best way to experience Yakushima's beauty. If you're planning anything more than a short stroll around Yaku-sugi Land (see p300), pick up a copy of the Japanese-language *Yama-to-Kougen-no-Chizu-Yakushima* (山と高原の地図屋久島; ¥840), available at major bookshops in Japan. You'll also need proper hiking gear, including rain gear and warm clothing, especially in winter, as well as a sleeping bag and sufficient food if you intend to overnight in the *yama-goya* (mountain huts).

Before heading up into the hills, be sure to alert someone at your accommodation of your intended route and fill in a *tōzan todokede* (route plan) at the trailhead.

The most popular hiking destination on the island is the **Jōmon-sugi**, a monster

Jars of pickled foods at a market in Naha (p304), Okinawa-hontō

of a *yaku-sugi* that is estimated to be at least 3000 years old. There are two ways to reach the tree: the 19.5km, eight- to 10-hour round-trip from the **Arakawa-tozanguchi** trailhead (604m), which is served by two daily buses to/from Miyanoura (¥1380, 85 minutes, March to November), and the round-trip from the **Shiratani-unsuikyō-tozanguchi** trailhead (622m), which is served by up to eight daily buses to/from Miyanoura (¥530, 35 minutes, March to November).

The granddaddy of hikes on Yakushima is the day-long outing to the 1935m summit of **Miyanoura-dake**, the highest point in southern Japan. Fit climbers should allow about seven hours return from **Yodogawa-tozanguchi** trailhead (1370m). Yodogawa-tozanguchi is about 1.5km (about 30 minutes) beyond the Kigen-sugi bus stop, which is served by two buses a day to/from Anbō (¥910, one hour). Note that the buses do not give you sufficient time to complete the round-trip in a day – an early-morning taxi from Miyanoura (around ¥10,000)

will give you time to make the second bus back to Anbō.

If you're feeling a little less adventurous, consider a visit to **Yaku-sugi Land** (admission ¥300; ☺ 9am-5pm). The name screams tourist trap, but this forest preserve amid the island's peaks is well worth a trip and it's a great way to see some *yaku-sugi* without a long trek into the forest. It offers shorter hiking courses over wooden boardwalks and longer treks deep into the ancient cedar forest. There are four walking courses here, the two shorter ones being mostly over boardwalks. There are four buses (¥720, 40 minutes) a day to/from Anbō.

OTHER ATTRACTIONS

On the northwest coast of the island in the village of Nagata is **Nagata Inaka-hama**, a beautiful stretch of yellow sand where sea turtles come to lay their eggs from May to July. It's beside the Inaka-hama bus stop, which is served by Nagata-bound buses from Miyanoura.

The **Issō-kaisuiyokujō** is another fine beach, located on the north coast of the sland, about midway between Miyanoura nd Nagata. It's a short walk from the ʼahazu bus stop (served by any Nagata-ʼound bus from Miyanoura).

On the west coast is Ōko-no-taki, which s Yakushima's highest waterfall at 88m. t's a five-minute walk from Ōko-no-taki ʼus stop, which is the last stop on some ʼf the buses running south and west from Miyano-ura and Anbō (note that only two ʼuses a day run all the way out here).

SLEEPING

The most convenient place to be based is Miyanoura, which has two hotels and lots ʼf *minshuku* (Japanese guest houses), as vell as some riverside cabins. You'll find ʼdditional lodgings in each of the island's villages and several barebones *yama-goya* n the mountains.

In July and August and the spring Golden Week holiday, it's best to try to eserve ahead, since places fill up early. And if you're staying outside Miyanoura, ʼou'll want to phone ahead anyway in the ʼope that the lodge owner will meet you ʼt the ferry pier.

MIYANOURA

Ocean View Campground (Yakushima Youth ʼampground; ☎ 47-3751; www.yakushima-yh.net; ʼer person ¥840) This basic camping ground s pretty much just a field for tents and a ʼouple of showers and bathrooms, with ʼ bit of rocky beach down the hill. It's just vest of the Eneos petrol station. There ʼre a few other camping grounds on the sland, including one in Anbō and another n Yahazu.

Miyanoura Portside Youth Hostel ☎ 49-1316; www.yakushima-yh.net; dm HI ʼmember/nonmember ¥3200/3800; P 💻) About 10 minutes' walk from the pier in Miyanoura is this simple and clean youth ʼostel. The place doesn't offer meals, but

there are several good restaurants close by. To get there from the pier, walk into the village, then follow the first main shoreline road on the left.

Lodge Yaedake-sansō (☎ 42-1551; r per person with meals ¥7800; P) This secluded accommodation features Japanese-style rooms in rustic riverside cabins connected by wooden walkways. There's a private bath where you can soak up the beauty of your surroundings and children will enjoy splashing in the river. The lodge is located inland upriver on the Miyanoura-gawa; if you make a booking, staff will pick you up in Miyanoura. There are no cooking facilities but meals are served. You'll probably need a vehicle if you're staying here.

Seaside Hotel (☎ 42-0175; www.ssh -yakushima.co.jp, in Japanese; r with 2 meals from ¥12,600; P 💻) Overlooking the ferry port in Miyanoura, this popular resort hotel is extremely convenient and quite appealing. The mostly Western-style rooms are spacious and the seaside rooms have great ocean views. There's a very nice pool and meals are available. It's a five-minute walk from the Miyanoura ferry pier (look for the access road on your right as you walk towards town).

EATING

There are a few restaurants in each of the island's villages, with the best selection in Miyanoura. If you're staying anywhere but Miyanoura, you should ask for the set two-meal plan at your lodgings, since it's troublesome to have to eat out. If you're going hiking, you can ask your lodging to prepare a *bentō* (boxed meal) the night before you set out.

Resutoran Yakushima (☎ 42-0091; Miyanoura; ⏱ 9.30am-4.30pm) On the 2nd floor of the Yakushima Kankō Sentaa (look for the green two-storey building on the main road, near the road to the pier), this

CHRISTOPHER GROENHOUT
Bentō (boxed meal)

simple restaurant serves a ¥500 morning set breakfast with eggs, toast and coffee and a tasty *tobi uo sashimi teishoku* (flying fish sashimi set meal, ¥900) for lunch. You can also access the internet on two Japanese laptops here.

Oshokuji-dokoro Shiosai (☎ 42-2721; 🕙 11.30am-2pm & 5.30-10pm, closed Thu) On the main road in the middle of Miyanoura, this fine restaurant offers counter, table and tatami (woven floor matting) seating and a full range of Japanese standard dishes and great local seafood. There is no English menu, so if you're at a loss, try the *sashimi teishoku* (sashimi full set, ¥1700) or the wonderful *ebi-furai teishoku* (fried shrimp full set, ¥1400). Look for the blue-and-whitish building and the automatic glass doors.

GETTING THERE & AWAY
BOAT
Three ferry services operate between Kagoshima (Kyūshū) and Yakushima, some of which stop at Tanegashima en route. **Kagoshima Shōsen/Toppy** (☎ 099-226-0128) and **Cosmo Line/Rocket** (☎ 099-223-1011) each run at least three hydrofoils a day between Kagoshima and Miyanoura (¥5000, one hour 50 minutes for direct sailings, two hours 50 minutes with a stop in Tanegashima).

Keep in mind that the hydrofoils stop running at the slightest hint of inclement weather. During the summer and Golden Week high seasons, you should reserve in advance by telephone or in person at the ferry offices the day before your intended departure from Kagoshima. In other seasons, you can usually just turn up and board the next sailing.

Orita Kisen (☎ 099-226-0731) runs the normal *Ferry Yakushima 2* between Kagoshima and Miyanoura (one-way/return ¥5200/8500, four hours, once daily). The ferry departs from Kagoshima at 8.30am, and leaves Miyanoura at 1.30pm. Reservations aren't usually necessary for this ferry.

GETTING AROUND
Local buses travel the coastal road part way around Yakushima roughly every hour or two, though only a few head up into the interior. Buses are expensive and you'll save a lot of money by purchasing a *Furii Jōsha Kippu*, which is good for unlimited travel on island buses. One-/two-day passes cost ¥2000/3000 and are available at the Toppy Ferry Office in Miyanoura.

Hitching is also possible, but the best way to get around the island is to rent a car. **Toyota Rent-a-Car** (☎ 43-5180; up to 12hr from ¥5775; 🕙 8am-8pm) is located near the terminal in Miyanoura.

OKINAWA-KEN
沖縄県

pop 1.35 million

apan's southernmost prefecture of Okinawa-ken makes up the southern half of the Southwest Islands. The prefecture stretches from the southern islands n Kagoshima-ken to within 110km of Taiwan. Three island groups make up the prefecture: Okinawa-shotō, Miyako-shotō and Yaeyama-shotō.

The northernmost island group is Okinawa-shotō, which contains Okinawa-hontō (meaning 'Okinawa Main Island' n Japanese). The largest island in the chain, Okinawa-hontō is home to the prefectural capital, Naha. This bustling city is Okinawa-ken's transport hub, and s easily accessed by flights and ferries to/from the mainland. Plentiful ferries run between Naha and Kerama-shotō, which lie about 30km west of Okinawa-hontō. The Kerama islands offer excellent beaches and brilliantly clear water.

The southernmost island group is Yaeyama-shotō, a further 100km southwest. This island group includes the coral-ringed island of Ishigaki and the nearby jungle-clad Iriomote-jima. Like Miyako-hontō, there are no ferries to this group; only flights from the mainland, Naha or Miyako-jima.

OKINAWA-HONTŌ
沖縄本島

☎ 098

Okinawa-hontō is the largest island in the Southwest Islands, and the historical seat of power of the Ryūkyū dynasty. Although its cultural differences with mainland Japan were once evident in its architecture, almost all traces were completely obliterated in WWII. Fortunately, Allied bombing wasn't powerful enough to completely stamp out other remnants of Okinawan culture, and today the island is home to a unique culinary, artistic and musical tradition.

It's worth noting that Okinawa-hontō has been somewhat overdeveloped for domestic tourism. If you seek Southeast Asian-style beaches and fewer big resorts, we suggest that you explore the cultural and historical sights of Okinawa-hontō for a few days and then head elsewhere in Okinawa-ken for your tropical beach holiday.

JTB PHOTO/PHOTOLIBRARY
Amami-Ōshima

⬊ IF YOU LIKE…

If you like Okinawa-hontō, we think you'll like these other less visited but wonderful southwestern Japanese islands:

- **Tanegashima** This laid-back island in Kagoshima-ken is popular with Japanese surfers.
- **Iō-jima** A tiny volcanic island with some fine seaside onsen. It's in Kagoshima-ken.
- **Amami-Ōshima** Between Yakushima and Okinawa-hontō, this large island has great beaches, drives and some decent diving.
- **Yoron-tō** The southernmost island in Kagoshima-ken, this island is almost nothing but beaches.

NAHA 那覇
pop 320,000

Although it was flattened during WWII, the prefectural capital of Naha has been completely rebuilt and is now a thriving urban centre. The city sports a convenient elevated monorail and a rapidly expanding skyline of modern high-rise apartments, as well as the inevitable traffic jams.

At first glance, Naha looks like the archetypal tourist trap, but a little poking around reveals a city with soul. The shopping arcades off Kokusai-dōri seem transplanted straight from Malaysia or Thailand, and the Tsuboya pottery area and nearby neighbourhoods have oodles of *aji* (a Japanese word meaning flavour or character). Oh, and let's not forget that Naha is the world capital of the cool short-sleeve shirt.

ORIENTATION
Naha is fairly easy to navigate, especially since the main sights and attractions are located in the city centre. The main drag is Kokusai-dōri, while the Tsuboya pottery area is to the southeast via a series of covered arcades. The Shuri district is located about 3km to the east of the city centre. For information on public transport, see p308.

INFORMATION
Tourist information counter (☎ 857-6884; Arrivals Terminal, Naha airport; ☷ 9am-9pm) At this helpful prefectural counter, we suggest picking up a copy of the *Naha City Guide Map* before heading into town. If you plan to explore outside Naha, also grab a copy of the *Okinawa Guide Map*.

Tourist information office (☎ 868-4887; ☷ 8.30am-8pm Mon-Fri, 10am-8pm Sat & Sun) The city office also has free maps. It's just off Kokusai-dōri (turn at Starbucks).

SIGHTS & ACTIVITIES
CENTRAL NAHA 那覇中心街
The city's main artery, **Kokusai-dōri** (国際通り), is a riot of neon, noise, souvenir shops, bustling restaurants and Japanese young things out strutting their stuff. It's a festival of tat and tackiness, but it's a good time if you're in the mood for it.

Many people prefer the atmosphere of the three shopping arcades that run south off Kokusai-dōri roughly opposite Mitsukoshi Department Store: **Ichibahon-dōri** (市場本道り), **Mutsumibashi-dōri** (むつみ橋通り) and **Heiwa-dōri** (平和通り). Prepare for some serious cognitive dissonance as you explore these places; you may think you somehow stepped through a secret passageway to the Chinatown district of Bangkok.

Our favourite stop in this area is the **Daichi Makishi Kōsetsu Ichiba** (2-10-2 Matsuo; ☷ 10am-8pm), a covered food market just off Ichibahon-dōri, about 200m south of Kokusai-dōri. The colourful variety of fish and produce on offer here is amazing, and don't miss the wonderful local restaurants upstairs. Keep in mind, however, that this is a working market, so please don't get in the way of shopkeepers and consider buying something as a souvenir.

Another highlight is the **Tsuboya pottery area** (壺屋). More than a dozen traditional kilns still operate in this neighbourhood, which has served as a centre of ceramic production since 1682, when Ryūkyū kilns were consolidated here by royal decree. Most shops sell all the popular Okinawan ceramics, including *shiisā* (lion-dog roof guardians) and containers for serving *awamori,* the local firewater. To get here from Kokusai-dōri, walk south through the Heiwa-dōri arcade for about 350m.

In Tsuboya, you will find the excellent **Tsuboya Pottery Museum** (☎ 862-3761

RICHARD CUMMINS

Shuri-jō

↘ SHURI-JŌ 首里城

The reconstructed castle of Shuri-jō sits atop a hilltop in the centre of Shuri, overlooking the urban sprawl of modern-day Naha. It was originally built in the 14th century and served as the administrative centre and royal residence of the Ryūkyū kingdom until the 19th century.

Enter through the Kankai-mon (歓会門) and proceed up to the Hōshin-mon (奉神門), which forms the entryway to the inner sanctum of the castle, dominated by the impressive Seiden (正殿). Visitors can enter the Seiden, which contains exhibits on the castle and the Okinawan royals. There is also a small collection of displays in the nearby Hokuden.

While you're at the castle, be sure to visit the Irino-Azana (西のアザナ), a viewpoint about 200m west of the Seiden that affords great views over Naha and as far as Kerama-shotō.

To reach the complex, take the Yui-rail monorail to its eastern terminal, Shuri station. Exit to the west, go down the steps, walk straight, cross one big street, then a smaller one and go right on the opposite side, then walk about 350m and look for the signs on the left.

Things you need to know: ☎ 886-2020; admission ¥800; ⏰ 9am-5.30pm

-9-32 Tsuboya; admission ¥315; ⏰ 10am-6pm, losed Mon), which contains some fine examples of traditional Okinawan pottery. Here you can also inspect potters' wheels nd see *arayachi* (unglazed) and *jōyachi* glazed) pieces.

After visiting the museum, we recommend strolling down the incredibly at-

mospheric Tsuboya-yachimun-dōri (壺屋やちむん通り), which is lined with pottery shops. The lanes off the main street here contain some classic crumbling old Okinawan houses.

About 15 minutes' walk northwest of the Omuromachi monorail station, you will find the Okinawa Prefectural

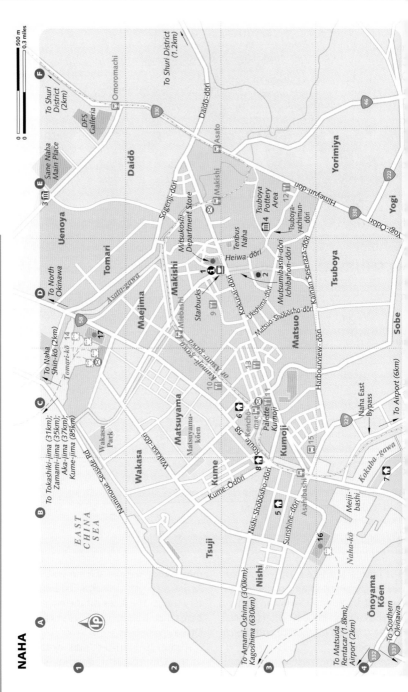

NAHA

500 m
0.3 miles

EAST
CHINA
SEA

To Tokashiki-jima (31km);
Zamami-jima (35km);
Aka-jima (37km);
Kume-jima (85km)

To Amami-Oshima (300km);
Kagoshima (630km)

To Matsuda
Rentacar (1.8km);
Airport (2km)

To Southern
Okinawa

To Naha
Shin-kō (2km)

To North
Okinawa

To Airport (6km)

To Shuri
District
(2km)

To Shuri District
(1.2km)

To Shuri
District
(2km)

Ōnoyama
Kōen

Naha-kō

Tsuji

Nishi

Kume

Wakasa

Matsuyama

Matsuyama-
kōen

Wakasa
Park

Kumoji

Matsuo

Tsuboya

Sobe

Yorimiya

Yogi

Tsuboya
Pottery
Area

Tsuboya-
yachimun-
dōri

Daidō

Uenoya

Tomari

Maejima

Makishi

Daidō

Omoromachi

DFS
Galleria

Sane Naha
Main Place

Makishi

Asato

Tenbus
Naha

Mitsukoshi
Department Store

Starbucks

Miebashi

Naha East
Bypass

Meiji-
bashi

Asahibashi

Kenchō-
mae

Palette
Kumoji

Naminoue Seaside Rd

Tomari-kō

Wakasa-dōri

Kume-Ōdori

Nishi-Shobōsho-dōri

Sunshine-dōri

Matsuo-Shobōsho-dōri

Harbourview-dōri

Kokusai-dōri

Heiwa-dōri

Sōgenji-dōri

Asato-gawa

Kumoji-gawa

Kumoji-gawa

Kokaba-gawa

Daidō-dōri

Himeyuri-dōri

Yogi-Ōdori

Mutsumibashi-dōri
Ichibanhon-dōri

Ukishima-dōri

Kainan Seseraza-dōri

Tsuboya-
dōri

330

330

329

331

332

46

222

1

2

3

5

6

7

8

9

10

11

12

13

14

15

16

17

58

58

Museum (☎ 941-8200; 3-1-1 Omuromachi; admission ¥400; ☉ 9am-5.30pm, closed Mon). Opened in 2007, this museum of Okinawa's history, culture and natural history is easily one of the best museums in Japan. Displays are well laid out, easy to understand and attractively presented. The art museum section holds interesting special exhibits with an emphasis on local artists.

SHURI DISTRICT 首里

Shuri was the original capital of Okinawa, though the title was surrendered to Naha in 1879 just prior to the Meiji Restoration. Shuri's temples, shrines, tombs and castle were all destroyed in WWII, but the castle and surrounding structures were rebuilt in 1992.

SLEEPING

Okinawa International Youth Hostel
(☎ 857-0073; www.jyh.gr.jp/okinawa/english
.htm; 51 Ōnoyama; dm HI member/nonmember
¥3360/3960; ⓟ 🖳) This excellent youth
hostel is located in Ōnoyama-kōen, a
five-minute walk from Asahibashi station (cross to the far side of Meiji-bashi).
If you're walking from Asahibashi station,
turn left at the torii (shrine gate).

Tōyoko Inn Naha Asahibashi-eki-mae (☎ 951-1045; www.toyoko-inn.com/
e_hotel/00076/; 2-1-20 Kume; s/d from ¥5460/8190;
ⓟ 🖳) Just a short walk north of Kokusai-
dōri, the Tōyoko is a good-value business
hotel with small but serviceable rooms
and useful features such as free internet
and washing machines. It's one of the better values in this price range.

Hotel Marine West Naha (☎ 863-0055;
www.marine-west.jp, in Japanese; 2-5-1 Kumoji;
s/tw from ¥5040/9450; ⓟ 🖳) A short walk
west of Kokusai-dōri, this converted apartment building has comfortable rooms, a
pleasant breakfast nook and free internet,
as well as helpful staff. It's popular with
divers and there's a gear storage and drying room on the ground floor.

Hotel Sun Palace (☎ 863-4181; www
.palace-okinawa.com/sunpalace, in Japanese; 2-5-
1 Kumoji; per person with breakfast from ¥6500;
ⓟ 🖳) About 10 minutes' walk from
Kokusai-dōri, the Sun Palace is a step up
from a standard business hotel. The fairly
spacious rooms have interesting design
touches and some have balconies.

EATING

Daitō Soba (☎ 867-3889; 1-4-59 Makishi;
☉ 11am-9pm) This little noodle house is the
perfect spot for sampling your first bowl
of okinawa-soba (¥500, ask for daitō-soba).
It's one block north of Kokusai-dōri; look
for the yellow banner and lantern. Last
order 8.30pm.

Minoya (☎ 869-4955; 9th fl, Palette Kumoji Shopping Mall; ❧ 11am-10pm) This restaurant has zero ambience, but it serves tasty versions of all the local favourites. There's a picture menu with such standards as sōki-soba (¥650) and gōya-teishoku (set-course meal with bitter melon; ¥850). You'll see the restaurant as you emerge from the elevators; look for the black-and-yellow sign.

Gen (☎ 861-0429; 2-6-23 Kumoji; ❧ 11.30am-2pm & 5pm-midnight) This atmospheric ya-kiniku (grillled meat) place is one of our favourite places in Naha for a good meal. If you're a carnivore and want some excellent grilled meat washed down with great awamori, this is the place. Look for the English sign at the bottom of the steps. If you can't speak Japanese, ask your accommodation owner to call and order the yakiniku course (¥3500 per person) as it must be ordered in advance.

Yūnangi (☎ 867-3765; 3-3-3 Kumoji; ❧ noon-3pm & 5.30-10pm, closed Sun & national holidays) You'll be lucky to get a seat here, but if you do, you'll be treated to some of the best Okinawan food around, served in atmospheric traditional surroundings. Try the okinawa-soba set (¥1400). Look for the wooden sign with white letters in Japanese and the plants.

Uchina Chaya Buku Buku (☎ 861-2950; 1-28-3 Tsuboya; ❧ 10am-4.30pm, closed Wed) This incredibly atmospheric tea house near the east end of the Tsuboya pottery area is worth a special trip. It takes its name from the traditional frothy Okinawan tea served here: buku buku cha. It's up a small lane just north of Tsuboya-yachimun-dōri.

Daichi Makishi Kōsetsu Ichiba (2-10-1 Matsuo; meals from ¥800; ❧ 10am-8pm) We highly recommend a meal at one of the eateries on the 2nd floor of this food market. It's pointless to make a recommendation; have a look at what the locals are eating and grab a seat.

GETTING THERE & AWAY

AIR

Naha International Airport (OKA) ha international air connections wit Seoul, Taipei, Hong Kong and Shangha Connections with mainland Japan in clude Kagoshima (¥24,100, one hou 25 minutes), Hiroshima (¥29,400, tw hours), Osaka (¥31,400, two hours 1. minutes), Nagoya (¥35,600, two hour 25 minutes), Tokyo (¥37,500, two hour 45 minutes) and Sapporo (¥54,400, thre hours 40 minutes).

FERRY

Maruei Ferry/A Line (☎ in Naha 861-188 in Tokyo 03-5643-6170; www.aline-ferry.com, i Japanese) operates four or five ferries month running to/from Tokyo (¥24,50 46 hours) and Osaka/Kōbe (¥19,600, 4 hours), as well as daily ferries to/from Kagoshima (¥14,600, 25 hours).

There are three ports in Naha, and this ca be confusing: Kagoshima/Amami-shot ferries operate from Naha-kō (Nah Port); Tokyo/Osaka/Kōbe ferries oper ate from Naha Shin-kō; and Kume-jim and Kerama-shotō ferries operate from Tomari-kō (Tomari Port).

GETTING AROUND

The Yui-rail monorail is perfect for ex ploring Naha. The line runs from Nah International Airport in the south to Shu in the north. Prices range from ¥200 t ¥290. Kenchō-mae station is at the wes ern end of Kokusai-dōri, while Makish station is at its eastern end.

A rental car makes everything easie when exploring Okinawa-hontō (onc you escape the traffic of Naha). There a rental-car counter in the arrivals hall c Naha International Airport, where staff ca arrange for you to be taken to the office of the main rental agencies. Normally, w

Menu board in Naha's Shuri district (p307)

RICHARD CUMMINS

ke Toyota Rent-a-Car, but its Naha office can be very crowded since it's a favourte of domestic tourists. You'll get more attentive service at **Matsuda Rentacar** (☎ 857-0802; 2-13-10 Akamine), which is near Akamine station and has a courtesy bus o/from the airport.

SOUTHERN OKINAWA-HONTŌ
沖縄本島の南部

During the closing days of the Battle of Okinawa, the southern part of Okinawa-hontō served as one of the last holdouts of the Japanese military and an evacuation point for wounded Japanese soldiers. Although southern Okinawa-hontō is now a residential area, there are some striking reminders of those terrible days. A visit to the area is highly recommended for those with an interest in the wartime history of Okinawa. The area can easily be visited as a day or half-day trip from Naha.

Okinawa's most important war memorials are clustered in the **Memorial Peace Park** (◷ dawn-dusk), located in the city of Itoman on the southern coast of the island. The centrepiece of the park is the **Okinawa Prefectural Peace Memorial Museum** (☎ 997-3844; admission ¥300; ◷ 9am-5pm, closed Mon), which focuses on the suffering of the Okinawan people during the invasion of the island and under the subsequent American occupation. The main exhibits are on the 2nd floor. The museum strives to present a balanced picture of the Pacific War and the history that led to the invasion, but there is plenty here to stir debate.

Outside the peace museum is the **Cornerstone of Peace** (◷ dawn-dusk), which is inscribed with the names of everyone – foreign, Okinawan, Japanese, military and civilian – who died in the Battle of Okinawa. To reach the park, take bus 89 from Naha bus terminal to the Itoman bus terminal (¥500, one hour, every 20 minutes), then transfer to bus 82, which goes to Heiwa Kinen-kōen (¥400, 25 minutes, hourly).

ISLANDS NEAR OKINAWA-HONTŌ

If you've had enough of the crowds and resorts of Okinawa-hontō, hop on a ferry to one of the nearby islands. The best of the lot are the three main islands of Kerama-shotō, which lie a mere 30km offshore from Naha. These islands are among the most attractive in the entire Southwest Islands, with crystal-clear water and excellent white-sand beaches. A little further out is the rarely visited island of Kume-jima. For those with a sense of adventure, there are several other islands that we don't cover in this guide: Ie-jima, Iheya-jima, Izena-jima, Aguni-jima, Kita-daitō-jima and Tonaki-jima.

KERAMA-SHOTŌ 慶良間諸島

The islands of Kerama-shotō are a world away from the hustle and bustle of Okinawa-hontō, though even these islands can get crowded during the summer holiday season. The three main islands here are Zamami-jima, Aka-jima and Tokashiki-jima. You can easily visit any of these as a day trip from Naha, but we recommend a few days in a *minshuku* on one of the islands to really savour the experience.

AKA-JIMA 阿嘉島

☎ 098 / pop 310

A mere 2km in diameter, tiny Aka-jima makes up for in beauty what it lacks in size. With some of the best beaches in the Keramas and an extremely peaceful atmosphere, it's easy to get stuck here for several days. There's also some great snorkelling and diving nearby.

There are great beaches on every side of the island, but for sheer postcard-perfect beauty, it's hard to beat the 1km stretch of white sand on the northeast coast known as **Nishibama Beach** (ニシバマビーチ). This beach can be crowded in summer;

if you want privacy, there are quieter beaches on the other sides of the island.

Dive shop–hotel **Marine House Seasir** (ペンションシーサー; ☎ 0120-10-2737; www.seasir.com, in Japanese; r per person with meals ¥7350) at the west end of the main village has good, clean Western-style and Japanese rooms with attached bathrooms. Most of the guests are divers.

Air Dolphin (☎ 858-3363) has two daily flights between Naha and Kerama airport (¥6500, 20 minutes). **Zamami Sonei Ferry** (☎ 868-4567) has two or three fast ferries a day (¥2750, 50 minutes) and one regular ferry (¥1860, 1½ hours) to/from Naha's Tomari-kō. A motorboat also makes four trips a day between Aka-jima and Zamami-jima (¥300, 15 minutes).

ZAMAMI-JIMA 座間味島

☎ 098 / pop 610

A stone's throw from Aka-jima, Zamami-jima is *slightly* more developed, but also has some great beaches and a few rocky vistas. It's got some brilliant offshore islands and great diving and snorkelling in the surrounding waters. There is a **tourist information office** (☎ 987-2277; ⏰ 9am–5pm) at the port.

Furuzamami Beach (古座間味ビーチ), approximately 1km southeast from the port (over the hill), is a stunning 700m stretch of white sand that is fronted by clear, shallow water and a bit of coral. The beach is well developed for day-trippers and has toilets, showers and food stalls. You can also rent snorkelling gear here (¥1000).

If you fancy a little solitude, you'll find picturesque empty beaches in several of the coves on the other sides of the island. The best beaches, however, are on **Gahi-jima** (嘉比島) and **Agenashiku-jima** (安慶名敷島), which are located about a kilometre south of the port. Ringed by delightful white-sand beaches, they are perfect for a half-day *Robinson Crusoe* experience. One boat operator who can take you to these islands and arrange snorkelling trips is **Zamami Tour Operation** (☎ 987-3586). The TIC can also help arrange boat tours (pick-up/drop-off ¥1500 per person round trip).

Zamami-jima makes a great day trip from Naha, but an overnight stay will be more relaxing. A good spot to call home for the night is **Joy Joy** (ジョイジョイ; ☎ 0120-10-2445; http://keramajoyjoy.com/index.html; r per person with breakfast from ¥5250) in the northwest corner of the village. Accommodation is in a variety of rooms that surround a small garden. This pension also runs a dive shop.

Minshuku Summer House Yū Yū (民宿 サマーハウス遊遊; ☎ 987-3055; www.yuyu okinawa.jp/index.html, in Japanese; r per person with/without meals from ¥6000/3500) is a friendly *minshuku* that is just up the street from Joy Joy in the main village. Both places are an easy walk from the pier.

Zamami Sonei (☎ 868-4567) has two or three fast ferries a day (¥2750, 50 minutes) and one regular ferry (¥1860, two hours) to/from Naha's Tomari-kō. The ferries usually stop at Aka-jima en route from Naha to Zamami. A motorboat also makes four trips a day between Aka-jima and Zamami-jima (¥300, 15 minutes).

YAEYAMA-SHOTŌ
八重山諸島

At the far southwestern end of the Southwest Islands are the islands of Yaeyama-shotō, which include the main islands of Ishigaki-jima and Iriomote-jima as well as a spread of 17 isles. Located near the Tropic of Cancer, the isles of Yaeyama-shotō are renowned for their lovely beaches, superb diving and lush landscapes.

FRANK'N'FOCUS/ALAMY
View from Zamami-jima

Yaeyama-shotō is arguably the top destination in the Southwest Islands. These islands offer Japan's best snorkelling and diving, and some of Japan's last intact subtropical jungles and mangrove swamps (both on Iriomote-jima). Perhaps the best feature of the Yaeyamas is their variety and the ease with which you can explore them: plentiful ferry services run between Ishigaki City and nearby islands such as Iriomote-jima and Taketomi-jima, and you can easily explore three or four islands in one trip.

ISHIGAKI-JIMA 石垣島
☎ 0980 / pop 48,420

Located 100km southwest of Miyako-jima, Ishigaki-jima is the most populated and developed island in Yaeyama-shotō. Ishigaki-jima has some excellent beaches around its coastline, and there are some

YAEYAMA-SHOTŌ

A   **B**   **C**   **D**

1

SIGHTS & ACTIVITIES

Hoshisuna-no-hama 星砂の浜............................**1** B3
Kabira-wan 川平湾..**2** F3
Kambirē-no-taki カンビレーの滝........................**3** B4
Manta Scramble...**4** E2
Mariyudō-no-taki マリユドゥの滝.......................**5** B4
Sukuji Beach 底地ビーチ...................................**6** F3
Sunset Beach サンセットビーチ.........................**7** H2
Tsuki-ga-hama 月が浜.......................................**8** B3
Umicoza..**9** F3
Urauchi-gawa River Trip Pier
　浦川観光遊覧船乗り場
....**10** B4
Yonehara Beach 米原ビーチ............................**11** G3

SLEEPING

Irumote-sō Youth Hostel いるもて荘ＹＨ........**12** B4
Pension Hoshi-no-Suna ペンシォン星の砂......**13** B3

EATING

Shinpachi Shokudo 新八食堂...........................**14** B4

TRANSPORT

Funauki Port 船浮港.......................................**15** A4
Oha-Ōhara Port 大原港...................................**16** C5
Shirahama Port 白浜港....................................**17** B4
Uehara Port 上原港...**18** B3

2

3

EAST
CHINA
SEA

Hatoma-jima

Uehara

Funaura

EAST
CHINA
SEA

Kayama-jima

4

Sonai

Shirahama
wan

Shirahama

Komi-dake
(469m)

Tedō-yama
(441m)

Cape Nobaru

Funauki
wan

Gorilla
Rock

Ida-no-
hama

Funauki

Sakiyama-wan

Iriomote-jima

Nakara-gawa

Kohama
-jima

Cape Kasa

5

Cape Pai

Nakama-dake
(307m)

Haemi-dake
(425m)

Naka ma-gawa

Ōhara

Cape Nakama

Cape Hai

6

To Yonaguni-jima
(75km)

Aragusuku
-jima

PACIFIC
OCEAN

To Hateruma-jima
(45km)

0   10 km
0   6 miles

Cape
Hirakubo-saki

Ara-dake
(366m)

206

7

Kuura-dake
(255m)

Akaishi

*Ibaruma-
wan*

Cape Nosoko

Hanna-dake
(239m)

*EAST
CHINA
SEA*

79

4

Nosoko-dake
(282m)

390

Kabira Ishizaki

6

Sakieda-wan

207

11

Mae-dake
(263m)

9   2

Kabira

79

Cape Ogan

Omoto-dake
(526m)

Hōra-dake
(351m)

Ishigaki-jima

209

Yarebu-dake
(217m)

87

Nagura-wan

211

211

208

Banna-dake
(230m)

209

390

79

87

*Ishigaki
Airport*

Shiraho

Ishigaki

*Miyara
wan*

Shiraho Reef

See Ishigaki
City Map
(p315)

**Taketomi-
jima**

Kuroshima

*PACIFIC

OCEAN*

brilliant diving and snorkelling spots offshore. The rugged geography of the island is also extremely attractive, both for long drives and day hikes, and there are times when you might think you're in Hawaii instead of southern Japan. Oh, and let's not forget the great food and lively nightlife to be found in Ishigaki City.

SIGHTS & ACTIVITIES

ISHIGAKI CITY 石垣市

Before you hit the beaches, you might want to spend a half-day exploring some of the sights around Ishigaki City. Located 100m southeast of the post office is the modest **Ishigaki City Yaeyama Museum** (Map p315; ☎ 82-4712; admission ¥200; ☒ 9am-5pm, closed Mon), which has exhibits on the culture and history of the island, and displays coffin palanquins, dugout canoes, island textiles and festival photographs. Enter by 4.30pm.

BEACHES

Some of the best beaches on the island are found on the west coast. North of Ishigaki City along Rte 79 is **Yonehara Beach** (Map pp312–13), a nice sand beach with a good bit of reef offshore. You can rent snorkel gear (¥1000) at any of the shops along the main road.

Just west of Yonehara is the equally famous **Kabira-wan** (Map pp312–13), a sheltered bay with white-sand shores and a couple of interesting clumplike islands offshore. This is more of a wading beach than a swimming beach and it's usually busy with boat traffic, which detracts somewhat from its beauty. On the opposite side of the peninsula is **Sukuji Beach** (Map pp312–13), a shallow beach that is good for families with children.

At the north end of the island, on the west coast, you will find **Sunset Beach** (Map pp312–13), another long strip of sand with a bit of offshore reef. As the

name implies, this is a good spot to watch the sun set into the East China Sea.

DIVING

The sea around Ishigaki-jima is famous among the Japanese diving community for its large schools of manta rays, particularly from June to October. The most popular place is **Manta Scramble** (Map pp312–13) off the coast of Kabira Ishizaki. Although it's likely that you'll be sharing with a fair number of dive boats, you're almost guaranteed to see a manta (or four).

There are several dive shops on Ishigaki-jima. Two shops with English-speaking dive guides are **Umicoza** (Map pp312–13; ☎ 88-2434; 827-15 Kabira, Ishigaki-shi; 1/2 dives ¥9450/12,600, equipment rental ¥5250; ☒ 8am-6pm) and **Sea Friends** (off Map p315; ☎ 82-0863; 349 Ishigaki, Ishigaki-shi Aza; 1/2 dives ¥11,550/15,750, equipment rental ¥3150; ☒ 8am-8pm).

SLEEPING

Hotel Harbor Ishigakijima (Map p315; ☎ 88-8383; s from ¥5250; P) You can't beat the location of this small, friendly three-storey business hotel: it looks right over the harbour and it's a one-minute walk to the ferry terminal. Rooms are fairly spacious and include massage chairs.

Super Hotel Ishigaki (Map p315; ☎ 83-9000; www.infinix.co.jp/sh, in Japanese; s with light breakfast ¥5800; P ☐) Four blocks northeast of the city hall is this efficient business hotel. The rooms are what you'd expect of a business hotel and will suit if you prefer more privacy than a guest house affords.

EATING & DRINKING

Asian Kitchen KAPI (Map p315; ☎ 82-2026; lunch/dinner about ¥1000/3000; ☒ 11.30am-3pm & 6.30-11pm; closed Thu) Next door to Mori-no-Kokage (look for the English sign), this trendy Pan-Asian bistro is a good choice if your Japanese is limited. In addition to the

OKINAWA & THE SOUTHWEST ISLANDS

OKINAWA-KEN

ISHIGAKI CITY

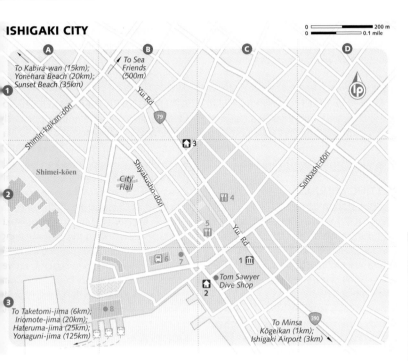

local cuisine, KAPI also offers an impressive range of Asian favourites, from Korean-style hotpots to fiery Indonesian curries.

Paikaji (Map p315; ☎ 82-6027; ⏰ 5pm-midnight) It's worth the wait to get into this deservedly popular local restaurant that serves all the Okinawan and Yaeyama standards. Both the atmosphere and kitchen get top marks. Try the *ikasumi chahan* (squid ink fried rice; ¥650), the *gōya-champurū* (butter-melon stir-fry; ¥700) or the *sashimi moriawase* (sashimi assortment; ¥750/1300/1800 depending on size). There's no English sign or menu. Look for the traditional front, coral around the entryway and a red-and-white sign.

GETTING THERE & AWAY

AIR

Ishigaki-jima has direct flights to/from Tokyo's Haneda airport (Japan Transocean

Air – JTA, ¥54,000, 3½ hours, two daily), Osaka's Kansai International Airport (JTA; ¥44,400, two hours 50 minutes, one daily), Kōbe (JTA; ¥44,400, 2¼ hours, one daily), Naha (JTA/ANA; ¥21,100, one hour, 20 daily), Miyako-jima (JTA/RAC; ¥10,900, 35 minutes, three daily), Yonaguni-jima (JTA/

RAC; ¥29,100, 30 minutes, one or two daily) and Hateruma-jima (Air Dolphin; ¥8500, 25 minutes, four weekly, more in summer).

BOAT

Ishigaki-jima Rittō Ferry Terminal (Map p315) is located on Ishigaki-wan, a short walk southwest of the city centre. Countless daily ferries operate between here and outlying islands in Yaeyama-shotō each day.

GETTING AROUND

The bus station is across the road from the ferry terminal in Ishigaki City. There are hourly buses to the airport (¥200, 20 minutes), as well as a few daily buses to Kabira-wan (¥700, 50 minutes), Yonehara Beach (¥800, one hour) and Shiraho (¥400, 30 minutes).

Rental cars, scooters and bicycles are readily available at shops throughout the city centre. If you're comfortable on a scooter, it's a scenic four- to five-hour cruise around the island, though you should plan for longer if you want to spend some time relaxing on the island's beaches. **Ishigaki Rentacar** (Map p315; ☎ 82-8840) is located in the city centre and has reasonable rates.

IRIOMOTE-JIMA 西表島

☎ 0980 / pop 2290

Although it's just 20km west of Ishigaki-jima, Iriomote-jima could easily qualify as Japan's last frontier. Dense jungles and mangrove forest blanket more than 90% of the island, and it's fringed by some of the most beautiful coral reefs in all Japan. If you're superlucky, you may even spot one of the island's rare *yamaneko,* a nocturnal and rarely seen wildcat.

Needless to say, Iriomote-jima is the perfect destination for outdoor enthusiasts. Several rivers penetrate far into the lush interior of the island and these can be explored by riverboat or kayak. Add to the mix sun-drenched beaches and spectacular diving and snorkelling, and it's easy to see why Iriomote-jima is one of the best destinations in Japan for nature lovers.

ORIENTATION & INFORMATION

Iriomote-jima has a 58km-long perimeter road that runs about halfway around the coast. No roads run into the interior, which is virtually untouched. Boats from Ishigaki-jima either dock at Uehara on the north coast, which is closer to the main points of interest, or at Ōhara on the southeast coast. Ōhara is the closest thing to a population centre on the island. At the western terminus of the main road, you will find the hamlet of Shirahama. The best beaches on the island are around its northern end, while river trips take place on the Urauchi-gawa in the central/north part of the island.

SIGHTS & ACTIVITIES
BEACHES

The majority of the Iriomote-jima's beaches are shallow due to the extensive coral reef that surrounds the island. The best swimming beach on the island is **Tsuki-ga-hama** (Moon Beach; Map pp312–13), a crescent-shaped yellow-sand beach at the mouth of the Urauchi-gawa on the north coast.

If you're looking to snorkel, head to **Hoshisuna-no-hama** (Star Sand Beach; Map pp312–13) on the northwestern tip of the island. The beach is named after its star sand, which actually consists of the dried skeletons of tiny sea creatures. If you are a competent swimmer and the sea is calm, make your way with mask and snorkel to the outside of the reef – the coral and tropical fish here are spectacular.

RIVER TRIPS

Iriomote's number-one attraction is a boat trip up the **Urauchi-gawa** (浦内川)

River-kayaking in Iriomote-jima

MASON FLORENCE

winding brown river that is reminiscent of a tiny stretch of the Amazon. From the mouth of the river, **Urauchi-gawa Kankō** (☎ 85-6154) runs boat tours 8km up the river (round-trip ¥1500, 30 minutes each way, multiple departures daily between 8.30am and 5pm). At the 8km point, the boat docks and you can walk a further 2km to reach the scenic waterfalls known as the **Mariyudō-no-taki** (マリユドウの滝; Map pp312–13), from where another 200m brings you to the **Kambiray-no-taki** (カンビレーの滝; Map pp312–13). The walk from the dock to Kambiray-no-taki and back takes around two hours. Of course, if you want, you can just take the boat trip to the dock and back. The pier for these boat trips is about 6km west of Uehara.

DIVING

Iriomote has some brilliant coral around its shores, much of which is accessible to proficient snorkellers. Most of the offshore dive sites around Iriomote are served by dive operators based on Ishigaki; see p314 for details.

SLEEPING

Irumote-sō Youth Hostel (Map pp312-13; ☎ 85-6255; www.ishigaki.com/irumote, in Japanese; dm from ¥3600; ℗ 🖳) If you're on a budget, a good choice is this well-run youth hostel, which is located fairly close to Uehara Port. Accommodation is in comfortable dorms and simple Japanese-style private rooms. Meals are served in the large communal dining room (breakfast/dinner ¥500/1000). It's inland and up the hill a little south from Uehara Port; we recommend calling for a pick-up before you arrive the first time, since it's not easy to find on your own.

Pension Hoshi-no-Suna (Map pp312-13; ☎ 85-6448; www.hoshinosuna.ne.jp; r per person from ¥7500; ℗) Located right above Hoshinosuna-hama, this popular pension is a great choice in terms of location. Accommodation is in Western- and Japanese-style rooms with ocean views and small verandahs. There is also a small on-site bar and restaurant, as well as a dive shop.

Japanese liquor

EATING

Shinpachi Shokudō (Map pp312-13; ☎ 85-6078; ⊙ lunch & dinner) Just 200m south of the port in Uehara, this no-frills noodle shop is the perfect spot for a hot bowl of *sōki-soba* (¥700) or a *gōya-champuru* (¥800), washed down with a nice draught beer. Look for the blue front and the banners outside.

For those who want to self-cater, there is a supermarket in the middle of Uehara, just north of Eneos petrol station.

GETTING THERE & AROUND

Yaeyama Kankō Ferry (☎ 82-5010), **Ishigaki Dream Kankō** (☎ 84-3178) and **Anei Kankō** (☎ 83-0055) operate ferries between Ishigaki City (on Ishigaki-jima) and Iriomote-jima. Ferries from Ishigaki

sail to/from two main ports on Iriomote Uehara Port (¥2000, 40 minutes, up to 2 daily) and Ōhara Port (¥1540, 35 minutes up to 27 daily). Note that Uehara Port i more convenient for most destination on Iriomote.

Six buses each day ply the island's mai coastal road between Ōhara and Shiraham (¥1200, 1½ hours). Due to the relative sca city of buses, it's a good idea to rent a car c scooter if you have an International Drivin Permit. **Yamaneko Rentacar** (☎ 85-5111 has offices in both Uehara and Ōhara (th Uehara office is on the main road a littl south of the ferry pier).

TAKETOMI-JIMA 竹富島
☎ 0980 / pop 350

A mere 10-minute boat ride from Ishigaki jima, the tiny islet of Taketomi-jima is living museum of Ryūkyū culture. Centre on a flower-bedecked village of tradi tional houses complete with red *kawar* (tiled) roofs, coral walls and *shiisā* statue Taketomi is a breath of fresh air if you'r suffering from an overdose of moder Japan.

While Taketomi is besieged by Japanes day-trippers in the busy summer months the island is blissfully quiet at night, eve in summer. If you have the chance, it' worth spending a night here as Taketom truly weaves its spell after the sun dip below the horizon.

ORIENTATION & INFORMATION

Ferries arrive at the small port (竹富東港) on the northeast corner of the island while Taketomi village is located in th centre of the island. Since the island i only 3km long and 2km wide, it is easil explored on foot or by bicycle.

There's a small **information desk** (☎ 84 5633; ⊙ 7.30am-6pm) in the port building, bu for the full scoop on Taketomi-jima, hea next door to the **Taketomi-jima Yugafu-kan** (竹富島ゆがふ館; ☎ 85-2488; 🕑 8am-6pm) visitors centre, which has excellent displays and exhibits on the island.

SIGHTS & ACTIVITIES

Roughly in the centre of the village, the modest lookout tower of **Nagomi-no-tō** (admission free; 🕑 24hr) has good views over the red-tiled roofs of the pancake-flat island. Nearby, **Nishitō Utaki** is a shrine dedicated to a 16th-century ruler of Yaeyama-shotō who was born on Taketomi-jima. **Kihōin Shūshūkan** (☎ 85-2202; admission ¥300; 🕑 9am-5pm) is a private museum with a diverse collection of folk artefacts. **Taketomi Mingei-kan** (☎ 85-2302; admission free; 🕑 9am-5pm) is where the island's woven *minsā* (narrow) belts and other textiles are produced.

Taketomi-jima also has some decent beaches. At **Kondoi Beach** on the west coast you'll find the best swimming on the island. Just south is **Gaiji-hama**, which is the main *hoshi-suna* (star sand) hunting ground.

SLEEPING & EATING

Takana Ryokan (高那旅館; ☎ 85-2151; www.kit.hi-ho.ne.jp/hayasaka-my, in Japanese; dm with/without meals ¥4390/2990, r per person with meals from ¥8500) Opposite the tiny post office, Takana actually consists of a basic youth hostel and an attached up-market ryokan. Basic Western-style dorms in the youth hostel are a great option if you're on a budget, though the charming Japanese-style tatami rooms in the ryokan are a romantic choice if you're travelling with a loved one.

Ōhama-sō (大浜荘; ☎ 85-2226; fax 85-2226; r per person with/without meals ¥5500/3500) Beside the post office, this *minshuku* has a light and jovial atmosphere, especially when the owner starts to entertain on the *sanshin* (Okinawan three-stringed lute) after dinner. Accommodation is in simple yet comfortable Japanese-style tatami rooms with shared facilities.

Soba Dokoro Takenoko (☎ 85-2251; 🕑 10.30am-4pm & 6.30-10pm) This tiny restaurant on the northwest side of the village (look for the blue banner and the

Coral bed on Kondoi Beach

MASON FLORENCE

umbrellas) serves *sōki-soba* (¥700) and *yaki-soba* (fried buckwheat noodles; ¥700), as well as Orion beer to wash it down with.

GETTING THERE & AROUND

Yaeyama Kankō Ferry (☎ 82-5010), **Ishigaki Dream Kankō** (☎ 84-3178) and **Anei Kankō** (☎ 83-0055) operate ferries between Ishigaki City (on Ishigaki-jima) and Taketomi-jima (¥590, 10 minutes, up to 45 daily).

YONAGUNI-JIMA 与-那国島
☎ 0980 / pop 1630

About 125km west of Ishigaki and 110km east of Taiwan is the islet of Yonaguni-jima, Japan's westernmost inhabited island. Renowned for its strong sake, small horses and marlin fishing, the island is also home to the jumbo-sized Yonaguni atlas moth, the largest moth in the world.

In addition, the waters off the west coast are frequented by large schools of hammerhead sharks. Needless to say, this makes the island perhaps the most famous single diving destination in Japa and it would make a good counterpoint t the coral reefs and mantas around Ishigal and Iriomote.

ACTIVITIES
DIVING

Local divers have long known about th thrills that await at **Irizaki Point** (西岬 ポイント), off the coast of Cape Irizak In the winter months (January, Februar and March), the deep waters here ar frequented by large schools of ham merhead sharks. Local dive operators sa that if you dive here two days in a ro during one of the winter months, yo have a good chance of seeing a ham merhead school.

Even more popular than the sharks ar the famous **Kaitei Iseki** (Underwater Ruin 海底遺跡), which were discovered b chance in 1985 by the Japanese marine ex plorer Kihachirou Aratake. Some claim tha these ruins, which look like giant blocks o steps of a sunken pyramid, are the remain of a Pacific Atlantis, although there ar

Sign identifying local flora and fauna, Iriomote-jima (p316)

qually compelling arguments that they re just the random result of geological rocesses. We suggest that you judge for ourself. If you don't dive, Jack's Dolphin lass-bottomed boat (☎ 87-2311; per person 6000; ⏰ sailings at 9am & noon) does two daily rips to the ruins, provided a minimum of hree people are present.

There are numerous dive operators on he island. SaWest (☎ 87-2311; 59-6 Yonaguni, onaguni-chō Aza, Yaeyama-gun; 1/2 dives 8000/12,000, equipment rental ¥5000; ⏰ 8am-pm) has English-speaking guides.

LEEPING & EATING

lthough there are several sleeping op-ons around the island, it's best to phone head as Yonaguni is quite a distance to ravel without a reservation. The following laces will pick you up at either the airport r the ferry terminal.

Hotel Irifune (ホテル入船; ☎ 87-2311; ww.yonaguni.jp, in Japanese; r per person with eals ¥6000) If you want to be based in onai, this simple business hotel is located ear the main post office. Irifune offers airly standard Japanese- and Western-tyle rooms, though it's a good option if ou're looking for a little bit of privacy.

Minshuku Yoshimarusō (民宿よし る荘; ☎ 87-2658; r per person with meals 6825) Near the ferry terminal in Kubura, oshimarusō is ideal for divers, as the riendly owners also operate the on-ite Yonaguni Diving Service. Simple apanese-style tatami rooms with shared acilities have nice views of the nearby ort, though the real appeal of this min-huku is the owners' local diving expertise. .'s up the hill, overlooking the port.

Ailand Resort (アイランドリゾート 与那国; ☎ 87-2300; www.ailand-resort.co.jp; tw per person with 2 meals from ¥13,000; Ⓟ ⌨) This spiffy new hotel-resort is located on the north side of the island, between the airport and Sonai. It's got spacious, light, comfortable Western-style rooms and an on-site restaurant.

Adan (阿壇; ☎ 87-2140; ⏰ lunch & dinner, closed Sun or Mon) In the centre of Sonai, about 100m northeast of the only traffic light in town, you'll find this delightful lit-tle Okinawan-style restaurant that serves soba, yaki-soba and gyūdon (cooked beef over noodles), all for around ¥600. Three nights a week, it has have live music in the evenings. Look for the English sign outside.

GETTING THERE & AROUND

RAC has flights between Yonaguni and Naha (¥29,100, one hour 40 minutes, four daily). RAC or JTA operate flights between Yonaguni and Ishigaki-jima (¥18,000, 30 minutes, one or two daily).

Fukuyama Kaiun (☎ 87-2555) op-erates one or two ferries a week be-tween Ishigaki-jima and Kubura Port on Yonaguni (¥3460, 4½ hours).

There are public buses operating on Yonaguni-jima, but they make only four trips around the island per day, so the best way to get around the island is by rental car or scooter. Yonaguni Honda (☎ 87-2376) in central Sonai will send a car to meet you at the airport or the ferry ter-minal if you phone ahead. Another good car-rental operation that will also pick you up at the airport is Ailand Rentacar (☎ 87-2300).

FAMILY TRAVEL

DOMINIC BONUCE

Children in Ginza, Tokyo

Japan is a great place to travel with kids: it's safe, clean and illness is not much of a concern. In addition, Japanese positively fawn over children, particularly young children, and you will soon grow used to the constant chorus of *'kawaii!'* (cute!). Perhaps more importantly for parents, most children actually like travelling in Japan, particularly once they are old enough to make some sense of what they are seeing. The novelty and oddness of Japan, not to mention the delights of trains, electronics and abundance of cute things, tend to keep children amused.

COSTS & CARE

Travelling with children can be costly, particularly the plane tickets, but you may be pleasantly surprised to find that, once you arrive, Japan is actually cheaper than North America, Australia, New Zealand and most countries in Western Europe (although fluctuations in the exchange rate can change this). There are plenty of discounts for children, nutritious meals can be had for a reasonable price, and ryokan (traditional Japanese inns) will often let you spread out extra futons on the floor and sleep together in one room.

The one major problem concerns child seats for cars and taxis: these are generally not available. Child-care agencies are available in most larger cities. The only problem is the language barrier: outside Tokyo, there are few, if any, agencies with English speaking staff.

THE NITTY GRITTY

- **Breastfeeding** Not usual in public; department stores have feeding rooms
- **Change facilities** In department stores, airports, large train stations and some public buildings
- **Cots** Available in many hotels (try to book in advance) but not usually ryokan
- **Health** Neither food-borne nor infectious diseases are a big problem in Japan
- **Highchairs** Available in many restaurants
- **Nappies (diapers)** Widely available
- **Strollers** Available in Japan, but consider bringing your own
- **Transport** Comfortable and safe

EATING WITH KIDS

Japan offers such a variety of food that even the most particular eaters can find something to their liking, and if noodles and rice begins to pale there are always Japanese fast-food chains in almost every city. At most budget restaurants during the day, you can find *okosama-setto* (children's set meal), which is often Western style and actually rather good, though the minihamburgers and wiener sausages won't appeal to non-meat-eaters.

See p334 for a few phrases that will come in handy when dining out with children in tow.

THINGS TO SEE & DO

In terms of activities, you won't win any prizes for guessing that most children will get bored with art museums and temples pretty quickly. In large cities, you'll find lots of places specifically for children: parks, playgrounds, zoos, children's museums, and (though you may not like these) game centres. Language is sometimes an issue at museums and game centres, but children are often less bothered by this than their parents.

Tokyo has the most child-friendly attractions in Japan, including Tokyo Disneyland (p73). In Kansai, popular attractions for the young 'uns include the Osaka Aquarium (p148) and Nara-kōen (p153) in Nara, with its resident deer population.

Children who enjoy the beach and activities such as snorkelling will also adore the islands of Okinawa (p285).

JAPAN IN FOCUS

FOOD

FOOD

OLIVER STREY

Restaurant kitchen, Tokyo

Those familiar with *nihon ryōri* (Japanese cuisine) know that eating is half the fun of travelling in Japan. Even if you've already tried some of Japan's better-known specialities in Japanese restaurants in your own country, you're likely to be surprised by how delicious the original is when served on its home turf. More importantly, the adventurous eater will be delighted to find that Japanese food is far more than just sushi, tempura or sukiyaki. Indeed, it is possible to spend a month in Japan and dine in a different speciality restaurant each night.

Of course, you may baulk at charging into a restaurant where both the language and the menu are likely to be incomprehensible. The best way to get over this fear is to familiarise yourself with the main types of Japanese restaurants so that you have some idea of what's on offer and how to order it. Those timid of heart should take solace in the fact that the Japanese will go to extraordinary lengths to understand what you want and will help you to order.

With the exception of *shokudō* (all-round restaurants) and *izakaya* (pub-style restaurants), most Japanese restaurants concentrate on a speciality cuisine. This naturally makes for delicious eating, but does limit your choice. To help you choose the right place for your taste, we've compiled the main types of Japanese restaurants, along with a menu sample of some of the most common dishes served.

EATING IN A JAPANESE RESTAURANT

When you enter a restaurant in Japan, you'll be greeted with a hearty 'irasshaimase' (Welcome!). In all but the most casual places the waiter will next ask you 'nan-mei sama' (How many people?). Answer with your fingers, which is what the Japanese do. You will then be led to a table, a place at the counter or a tatami room.

At this point you will be given an *oshibori* (hot towel), a cup of tea and a menu. The *oshibori* is for wiping your hands and face. When you're done with it, just roll it up and leave it next to your place.

MENUS & ORDERING

Now comes the hard part: ordering. If you don't read Japanese, you can use the roman-ised translations in this book to help you, or direct the waiter's attention to the Japanese script. If this doesn't work, there are two phrases that may help: 'o-susume wa nan des ka' (What do you recommend?) and 'o-makase shimas' (Please decide for me). If you're still having problems, you can try pointing at other diners' food or, if the restaurant has them, at the plastic food models in the window.

PAYING THE BILL

When you've finished eating, you can signal for the bill by crossing one index finger over the other to form the sign of an 'x'. This is the standard sign for 'bill please'. You can also say 'o-kanjō kudasai'. Remember there is no tipping in Japan and tea is free of charge. Usually you will be given a bill to take to the cashier at the front of the restaurant. At more upmarket places, the host of the party will discreetly excuse themselves to pay before the group leaves. Unlike some places in the West, one doesn't usually leave cash on the table by way of payment. Only the bigger and more international places take credit cards, so cash is always the surer option.

When leaving, it is polite to say to the restaurant staff, 'gochisō-sama deshita', which means 'It was a real feast'. See p332 for more restaurant words and phrases.

RESTAURANTS & SAMPLE MENUS

SHOKUDŌ

A *shokudō* is the most common type of restaurant in Japan, and is found near train stations, tourist spots and just about any other place where people congregate. Easily distinguished by the presence of plastic food displays in the window, these inexpensive places usually serve a variety of *washoku* (Japanese dishes) and *yōshoku* (Western dishes).

EATING ETIQUETTE

- **Chopsticks in rice** Do not stick your *hashi* (chopsticks) upright in a bowl of rice.
- **Polite expressions** When eating with other people, especially when you're a guest, it is polite to say 'itadakimas' (literally 'I will receive') before digging in. At the end of the meal, you should thank your host by saying 'gochisō-sama deshita' which means, 'It was a real feast'.
- **Kampai** It is bad form to fill your own glass with beer or sake.
- **Slurp** When you eat noodles in Japan, it's perfectly OK, even expected, to slurp them.

JAPAN IN FOCUS

FOOD

Soba (buckwheat noodles) dish

GREG ELM

At lunch, and sometimes dinner, the easiest meal to order at a *shokudō* is a *teishoku* (set-course meal), which is sometimes also called *ranchi setto* (lunch set) or *kōsu*. This usually includes a main dish of meat or fish, a bowl of rice, miso soup, shredded cabbage and some *tsukemono* (Japanese pickles). In addition, most *shokudō* serve a fairly standard selection of *donburi-mono* (rice dishes) and *menrui* (noodle dishes). When you order noodles, you can choose between *soba* (buckwheat noodles) and udon, both of which are served with a variety of toppings. If you're at a loss as to what to order, simply say *kyō-no-ranchi* (today's lunch), and they'll do the rest. Expect to spend from ¥800 to ¥1000 for a *shokudō* meal.

RICE DISHES

katsu-don	かつ丼	rice topped with a fried pork cutlet
niku-don	牛丼	rice topped with thin slices of cooked beef
oyako-don	親子丼	rice topped with egg and chicken
ten-don	天丼	rice topped with tempura shrimp and vegetables

NOODLE DISHES

soba	そば	buckwheat noodles
udon	うどん	thick, white wheat noodles
kake soba/udon	かけそば/うどん	*soba*/udon noodles in broth
kitsune soba/udon	きつねそば/うどん	*soba*/udon noodles with fried tofu
tempura soba/udon	天ぷらそば/うどん	*soba*/udon noodles with tempura shrimp
tsukimi soba/udon	月見そば/うどん	*soba*/udon noodles with raw egg on top

IZAKAYA

An *izakaya* is the Japanese equivalent of a pub. It's a good place to visit when you want a casual meal, a wide selection of food, a hearty atmosphere and, of course, plenty of beer and sake. When you enter an *izakaya,* you are given the choice of sitting around the counter, at a table or on a tatami floor. You usually order a bit at a time, choosing from a selection of typical Japanese foods such as *yakitori* (skewers of grilled chicken), sashimi and grilled fish, as well as Japanese interpretations of Western foods like french fries and beef stew.

agedashi-dōfu	揚げだし豆腐	deep-fried tofu in a dashi broth
chiizu-age	チーズ揚げ	deep-fried cheese
hiya-yakko	冷奴	a cold block of tofu with soya sauce and spring onions
jaga-batā	ジャガバター	baked potatoes with butter
kata yaki-soba	固焼きそば	hard fried noodles with meat and vegetables
niku-jaga	肉ジャガ	beef and potato stew
poteto furai	ポテトフライ	french fries
sashimi mori-awase	刺身盛り合わせ	a selection of sliced sashimi
shio-yaki-zakana	塩焼魚	a whole fish grilled with salt
tsuna sarada	ツナサラダ	tuna salad over cabbage
yaki-onigiri	焼きおにぎり	a triangle of grilled rice with *yakitori* sauce
yaki-soba	焼きそば	fried noodles with meat and vegetables

YAKITORI

Yakitori is a popular after-work meal. *Yakitori* is not so much a full meal as an accompaniment for beer and sake. At a *yakitori-ya* (*yakitori* restaurant) you sit around a counter with the other patrons and watch the chef grill your selections over charcoal. The best way to eat here is to order several varieties, then order seconds of the ones you really like. Ordering can be a little confusing since one serving often means two or three skewers be careful – the price listed on the menu is usually that of a single skewer).

gyū-niku	牛肉	pieces of beef
hasami/negima	はさみ/ねぎま	pieces of white meat alternating with leek
kawa	皮	chicken skin
piiman	ピーマン	small green peppers
rebā	レバー	chicken livers
sasami	ささみ	skinless chicken-breast pieces
shiitake	しいたけ	Japanese mushrooms
tama-negi	玉ねぎ	round, white onions
tebasaki	手羽先	chicken wings
tsukune	つくね	chicken meat balls
yaki-onigiri	焼きおにぎり	a triangle of rice grilled with *yakitori* sauce
yakitori	焼き鳥	plain, grilled white meat

JAPAN IN FOCUS

FOOD

SUSHI & SASHIMI

Like *yakitori,* sushi is considered an accompaniment for beer and sake. Nonetheless, both Japanese and foreigners often make a meal of it, and it's one of the healthiest meals around. All proper sushi restaurants serve their fish over rice, in which case it's called sushi, or without rice, in which case it's called sashimi or *tsukuri* (or, politely, *o-tsukuri*). There are two main types of sushi: *nigiri-zushi* (served on a small bed of rice – the most common variety) and *maki-zushi* (served in a seaweed roll).

ama-ebi	甘海老	sweet shrimp
awabi	あわび	abalone
ebi	海老	prawn or shrimp
hamachi	はまち	yellowtail
ika	いか	squid
ikura	イクラ	salmon roe
kai-bashira	貝柱	scallop
kani	かに	crab
katsuo	かつお	bonito
maguro	まぐろ	tuna
tai	鯛	sea bream
tamago	たまご	sweetened egg
toro	とろ	the choicest cut of fatty tuna belly
unagi	うなぎ	eel with a sweet sauce
uni	うに	sea urchin roe

SUKIYAKI & SHABU-SHABU

Restaurants usually specialise in both these dishes. Popular in the West, sukiyaki is a favourite of most foreign visitors to Japan. Sukiyaki consists of thin slices of beef cooked in a broth of *shōyu* (soy sauce), sugar and sake, and is accompanied by a variety of vegetables and tofu. After cooking, all the ingredients are dipped in raw egg before being eaten. When made with high-quality beef, like Kōbe beef, it is a sublime experience.

Shabu-shabu consists of thin slices of beef and vegetables cooked by swirling the ingredients in a light broth, then dipping them in a variety of special sesame seed and citrus-based sauces. Both of these dishes are prepared in a pot over a fire at your private table; don't fret about preparation – the waiter will usually help you get started, and keep a close watch as you proceed. The key is to take your time, add the ingredients a little at a time and savour the flavours as you go.

THE BEST

GLENN BEANLAND

PLACES TO EAT SUSHI & SASHIMI

- Kyūbei (p77)
- Ganko Zushi (p137)
- Tsukiji Fish Market (p66)
- Nijō Fish Market (p230)

Sukiyaki and *shabu-shabu* restaurants usually have traditional Japanese decor and sometimes a picture of a cow to help you identify them. Ordering is not difficult. Simply say sukiyaki or *shabu-shabu* and indicate how many people are dining. Expect to pay from ¥3000 to ¥10,000 per person.

TEMPURA

Tempura consists of portions of fish, prawns and vegetables cooked in fluffy, nongreasy batter. When you sit down at a tempura restaurant, you will be given a small bowl of *ten-tsuyu* (a light brown sauce), and a plate of grated daikon to mix into the sauce. Dip each piece of tempura into this sauce before eating it. Tempura is best when it's hot, so don't wait too long – use the sauce to cool each piece, and dig in.

VEGETARIANS & VEGANS

Vegetarians who eat fish should have almost no trouble dining in Japan: almost all *shokudō, izakaya* and other common restaurants offer a set meal with fish as the main dish. Vegans and vegetarians who don't eat fish will have to get their protein from tofu and other bean products. Note that most *miso-shiru* (miso soup) is made with dashi (stock) that contains fish, so if you want to avoid fish, you'll also have to avoid *miso-shiru*. Most big cities in Japan have vegetarian and/or organic restaurants. See p334 for some handy phrases.

While it's possible to order à la carte, most diners choose to order *teishoku* (full set), which includes rice, *miso-shiru* (miso soup) and Japanese pickles. Some tempura restaurants offer tempura courses that include different numbers of tempura pieces. Expect to pay between ¥2000 and ¥10,000 for a full tempura meal.

kaki-age	かき揚げ	tempura with shredded vegetables or fish
shōjin-age	精進揚げ	vegetarian tempura
tempura mori-awase	天ぷら盛り合わせ	a selection of tempura

RĀMEN

The Japanese imported this dish from China and put their own spin on it to make what is one of the world's most delicious fast foods. *Rāmen* dishes are big bowls of noodles in a meat broth, served with a variety of toppings, such as sliced pork, bean sprouts and leeks. In some restaurants, particularly in Kansai, you may be asked if you'd prefer *kotteri* (thick) or *assari* (thin) soup. Other than this, ordering is simple: just sidle up to the counter and say *rāmen*, or ask for any of the other choices usually on offer.

rāmen	ラーメン	soup and noodles with a sprinkling of meat and vegetables
chānpon-men	ちゃんぽん麺	Nagasaki-style *rāmen*
chāshū-men	チャーシュー麺	*rāmen* topped with slices of roasted pork
miso-rāmen	みそラーメン	*rāmen* with miso-flavoured broth
wantan-men	ワンタン麺	*rāmen* with meat dumplings

SOBA & UDON

Soba and udon are Japan's answer to Chinese-style *rāmen*. *Soba* are thin, brown buckwheat noodles; udon are thick, white wheat noodles. Most Japanese noodle shops serve both *soba* and udon in a variety of ways. Noodles are usually served in a bowl containing a light, bonito-flavoured broth, but you can also order them served cold and piled on a bamboo screen with a cold broth for dipping. See p328 for some *soba* and udon dishes.

OKONOMIYAKI

The name means 'cook what you like', and an *okonomiyaki* restaurant provides you with an inexpensive opportunity to do just that. Sometimes described as

> **THE BEST**

GREG ELMS

PLACES TO EAT SOBA & UDON

- **Omen** (p139)
- **Misoka-an Kawamichi-ya** (p137)
- **Honke Tagoto** (p137)
- **Mimiu** (p76)

Japanese pizza or pancake, the resemblance is in form only. At an *okonomiyaki* restaurant you sit around a *teppan* (iron hotplate), armed with a spatula and chopsticks to cook your choice of meat, seafood and vegetables in a cabbage and vegetable batter to form a pancake-style patty.

gyū okonomiyaki	牛お好み焼き	beef *okonomiyaki*
ika okonomiyaki	いかお好み焼き	squid *okonomiyaki*
mikkusu	ミックスお好み焼き	*okonomiyaki* with mixed fillings of seafood, meat and vegetables
modan-yaki	モダン焼き	*okonomiyaki* with *yaki soba* and a fried egg
negi okonomiyaki	ネギお好み焼き	thin *okonomiyaki* with spring onions

USEFUL WORDS & PHRASES
EATING OUT

A table for (one/two/three/...), please.
(一人/二人/三人/...人)、　　　　(hitori/futari/san-nin/...-nin)
お願いします。　　　　　　　　　onegai shimas

I'd like to reserve a table for eight o'clock (tonight/tomorrow night).
(今晩/明日の晩)　　　　　　　　(konban/ashita no ban)
八時に予約したいのですが。　　hachi-ji ni yoyaku shitai no des ga

We have a reservation.
予約しました。　　　　　　　　　yoyaku shimashita

We don't have a reservation.
予約していません。　　　　　　　yoyaku shiteimasen

What's that?
あれは何ですか？　　　　　　　　are wa nan des ka

What's the speciality here?
ここの特別料理は何ですか？　　　*koko no tokubetsu ryōri wa nan des ka*

What do you recommend?
おすすめは何ですか？　　　　　*o-susume wa nan des ka*

Do you have...?
...がありますか？　　　　　　　*... ga arimas ka*

Can I see the menu, please?
メニューを見せてください。　　*menyū o misete kudasai*

Do you have a menu in English?
英語のメニューはありますか？　*eigo no menyū wa arimas ka*

I'd like...	...をください。	*... o kudasai*
Please bring me...	...をお願いします。	*... o onegai shimas*
some/more bread	パン	*pan*
some pepper	コショウ	*koshō*
a plate	お皿	*o-sara*
some salt	塩	*shio*
soy sauce	お醤油	*o-shōyu*
a spoon	スプーン	*supūn*
a beer	ビール	*beeru*
some water	お水	*o-mizu*
some wine	ワイン	*wain*

The bill/check, please.
お勘定をお願いします。　　　　*o-kanjō o onegai shimas*

OLIVER STREWE

A waiter seves a bowl of udon

JAPANESE TEA & COFFEE

bancha	番茶	ordinary-grade green tea, has a brownish colour
kōcha	紅茶	black, British-style tea
matcha	抹茶	powdered green tea used in the tea ceremony
mugicha	麦茶	roasted barley tea
o-cha	お茶	green tea
sencha	煎茶	medium-grade green tea
american kōhii	アメリカンコーヒー	weak coffee
burendo kōhii	ブレンドコーヒー	blended coffee, fairly strong
kafe ōre	カフェオレ	café au lait, hot or cold
kōhii	コーヒー	regular coffee

CHILDREN

Are children allowed?
子供連れでもいいですか？   *kodomo-zure demo ii des ka*

Is there a children's menu?
子供用のメニューはありますか？   *kodomo-yō no menyū wa arimas ka*

Do you have a highchair for the baby?
ベビー用の椅子はありますか？   *bebii-yō no isu wa arimas ka*

VEGANS & VEGETARIANS

I'm a vegetarian.
私はベジタリアンです。   *watashi wa bejitarian des*

I'm a vegan, I don't eat meat or dairy products.
私は菜食主義者ですから、   *watashi wa saishoku-shugisha des kara,*
肉や乳製品は食べません。   *niku ya nyūseihin wa tabemasen*

Do you have any vegetarian dishes?
ベジタリアン料理がありますか？   *bejitarian-ryōri ga arimas ka*

Is it cooked with pork lard or chicken stock?
これはラードか鶏の   *kore wa rādo ka tori no*
だしを使っていますか？   *dashi o tsukatte imas ka*

I'm allergic to (peanuts).
私は(ピーナッツ)アレルギーです。   *watashi wa (pīnattsu) arerugii des*

I don't eat...	...は食べません。	*... wa tabemasen*
meat	肉	*niku*
pork	豚肉	*buta-niku*
seafood	シーフード/海産物	*shiifūdo*

HISTORY

FRANK CARTER

Ukiyo-e (wood-block print)

The origin of Japan's earliest inhabitants is obscure. There was certainly emigration via land bridges that once connected Japan with Siberia and Korea, but it is also thought that seafaring migrants from Polynesia may have landed on Kyūshū and Okinawa. It is likely that the Japanese people are a result of emigration from Siberia in the north, China and Korea to the west and, perhaps, Polynesian stock from the south.

PREHISTORY

The first signs of civilisation in Japan are from around 13,000 BC. This is called the Jōmon (Rope Mark) period after the discovery of pottery fragments with rope marks. The people at this time lived as fishers, hunters and food-gatherers.

This period was superseded by the Yayoi era, which dates from around 400 BC and is named after the site near Tokyo where pottery fragments were found. The Yayoi people are thought to have had a strong connection with Korea and their most important developments were the wet cultivation of rice and the use of bronze and iron implements.

c 13,000 BC	c 400 BC	3rd century AD
First evidence of the hunter-gatherer Jōmon people.	The Yayoi people appear in southwest Japan (probably via Korea).	Queen Himiko reigns over the Yamato clan.

☇ KOFUN BURIAL MOUNDS

The origins of the Japanese imperial line and the Japanese people in general are shrouded in mystery. Much of what we do know comes from large, earthen burial mounds scattered around the islands of Honshū, Kyūshū and Shikoku. These burial mounds, which are known as *kofun*, served as tombs for members of Japan's early nobility. The practice of building these mounds started quite suddenly during the 3rd century AD and died out gradually by the end of the 7th century. It was during this period that the forerunners of the present imperial family, the Yamato clan, were consolidating their power as rulers of Japan.

The period following the Yayoi era has been called the Kofun (Burial Mound) period by archaeologists who discovered thousands of grave mounds concentrated mostly in central and western Japan.

As more and more settlements banded together to defend their land, groups became larger until, by AD 300, the Yamato clan had loosely unified the nation through either conquest or alliance. With the ascendancy of the Yamato emperors, Japan for the first time became a true nation, stretching from the islands south of Kyūshū to the northern wilds of Honshū.

BUDDHISM & EARLY CHINESE INFLUENCE

In the mid-6th century, Buddhism was introduced from China via the Korean kingdom of Paekche. From the earliest days of the Yamato court, it was the custom to relocate the capital following the death of an emperor (presumably to free the capital from the taint of death). However, after the shift of the capital to Nara in 710, this long-held custom was altered as the capital remained there for the next 74 years, before moving to Nagaoka-kyō in 784.

ESTABLISHMENT OF A NATIVE CULTURE

By the end of the 8th century, the Buddhist clergy in Nara had become so politically meddlesome that Emperor Kammu decided to relocate the capital to insulate it against their growing influence. The site eventually chosen was Heian-kyō (modern-day Kyoto).

The Heian period (794–1185) saw a great flourishing in the arts and important developments in religious thinking as Chinese ideas and institutions were imported and adapted to the needs of the Japanese.

During the late Heian period, emperors began to devote more time to leisure and scholarly pursuit and less time to government. This created an opening for the Fujiwara

c 300	Mid-5th century	604
Suijin is the first verifiable emperor of Japan.	Writing, in the form of Chinese characters, is introduced into Japan.	Japan tries to emulate China, drawing up a basic constitution.

FRANK CARTER

Buddhist monks at Kongōbu-ji (p158), Kōya-san

noble family, to capture important court posts and become the chief power brokers, role the clan was able to maintain for several centuries.

The Heian period is considered the apogee of Japanese courtly elegance, but out n the provinces a new power was on the rise, that of the samurai, or 'warrior class', which built up its own armed forces and readily turned to arms to defend its autonomy. Samurai families soon moved into the capital Heian-kyō, where they muscled n on the court.

The corrupt Fujiwara were eventually eclipsed by the Taira clan, who ruled briefly before being ousted by the Minamoto family (also known as the Genji) at the battle of Dan-no-ura (modern-day Shimonoseki) in 1185.

DOMINATION THROUGH MILITARY RULE

The Kamakura period (1185–1333) followed on from the Heian period. In 1192 Minamoto oritomo conquered the inhabitants of what is now Aomori-ken, thereby extending his rule to the tip of northern Honshū. For the first time in its history, all of Japan proper was now under unified rule. After assuming the title of shōgun (military leader), Minamoto set up his headquarters in Kamakura (p92), while the emperor remained the nominal ruler in Kyoto. It was the beginning of a long period of feudal rule by successive samurai

712 & 720	9th–12th centuries	1156
Writing of the major works *Kojiki* (Record of Old Things; 712) and *Nihon Shoki* (Record of Japan; 720).	Real power shifts from the imperial family to regional military chieftains.	Two major provincial families, the Taira and the Minamoto, engage in bitter warfare.

JAPAN IN FOCUS

HISTORY

HISTORICAL PERIODS

Period	Date
Jōmon	c 13,000– c 400 BC
Yayoi	c 400 BC–c AD 250
Kofun	250–710
Nara	710–94
Heian	794–1185
Kamakura	1185–1333
Muromachi	1333–1568
Azuchi-Momoyama	1568–1600
Edo/Tokugawa	1600–1868
Meiji	1868–1912
Taishō	1912–26
Shōwa	1926–89
Heisei	1989–present

families. In fact, this feudal system was t
linger on, in one form or another, unt
imperial power was restored in 1868.

The Kamakura government emerge
victorious in battles with the Mongo
(who attacked twice in the 13th century
but it was unable to pay its soldiers an
lost the support of the samurai class.
an attempt to take advantage of popula
discontent, Emperor Go-Daigo led an un
successful rebellion against the govern
ment and was exiled to Oki-shotō, th
islands near Matsue in western Honshū
where he waited a year before tryin
again. The second attempt successful
toppled the government.

COUNTRY AT WAR

This heralded the start of the Muromach
period (1333–1568). Emperor Go-Daig
refused to reward his warriors, favouring the aristocracy and priesthood instead. Thi
led to the revolt of Ashikaga Takauji, who had previously changed sides to suppor
Emperor Go-Daigo. Ashikaga defeated Go-Daigo at Kyoto, then installed a new em
peror and appointed himself shōgun; the Ashikaga family later settled at Muromach
an area of Kyoto.

The Ashikaga ruled with gradually diminishing effectiveness in a land slipping stead
ily into civil war and chaos. The Ōnin War, which broke out in 1467, developed into
full-scale civil war and marked the rapid decline of the Ashikaga family. *Daimyō* (domai
lords) and local leaders fought for power in bitter territorial disputes that were to las
for a century. This period, from 1467 to around the start of the Azuchi-Momoyam
period in 1568, is known as the Sengoku (Warring States) era.

RETURN TO UNITY

In 1568 Oda Nobunaga, the son of a *daimyō,* seized power from the imperial cou
in Kyoto and used his military genius to initiate a process of pacification and unifica
tion in central Japan. Oda was succeeded by his most able commander, Toyotom
Hideyoshi, who extended unification so that by 1590 the whole country was unde
his rule.

1185	1192	13th century
The Taira are toppled by Minamoto Yoritomo, who becomes the most powerful man in the land.	Yoritomo takes the title shōgun from a largely puppet emperor and establishes his headquarters in Kamakura.	Zen Buddhism becomes established in Japan.

↘ SAMURAI

The samurai were members of Japan's warrior class who were active in Japan from around the 12th century. The samurai's best-known weapon was the *katana* sword, though in earlier days the bow was also prominent. Arguably the world's finest swordsmen, samurai were formidable opponents in single combat. During modernisation in the late 19th century, the government – itself comprising samurai – realised that a conscript army was more efficient as a unified fighting force, and disestablished the samurai class. However, samurai ideals such as endurance and fighting to the death were revived through propaganda prior to the Pacific War.

JAPAN IN FOCUS

THE CHRISTIAN CENTURY

In the mid-16th century, when the Europeans first made their appearance, foreign trade was little regulated by Japan's central government. The first Portuguese to be shipwrecked off southern Kyūshū in 1543 found an appreciative reception for their skills in firearm manufacture, skills which were soon adopted by the Japanese. The Jesuit missionary Francis Xavier arrived in Kagoshima in 1549 and was followed by more missionaries, who quickly converted local lords keen to profit from foreign trade and assistance with military supplies. The new religion spread rapidly, gaining several hundred thousand converts, particularly in Nagasaki.

At first Oda Nobunaga saw the advantages of trading with Europeans and tolerated the arrival of Christianity as a counterbalance to Buddhism. Once Toyotomi Hideyoshi had assumed power, however, this tolerance gradually gave way to a suspicion that an alien religion would subvert his rule. Edicts against Christianity were followed in 1597 by the crucifixion of 26 people, including foreign priests and Japanese converts.

HISTORY

PEACE & SECLUSION

The supporters of Toyotomi Hideyoshi's young heir, Toyotomi Hideyori, were defeated in 1600 by Toyotomi's former ally, Tokugawa Ieyasu, at the battle of Sekigahara. Tokugawa set up his *bakufu* (field headquarters) at Edo (modern-day Tokyo) and assumed the title of shōgun. This marked the beginning of the Edo or Tokugawa period (1600–1868). The emperor and court continued to exercise purely nominal authority in Kyoto.

Under Tokugawa rule, Japan entered a period of *sakoku* (national seclusion). Japanese were forbidden on pain of death to travel abroad or engage in trade with foreign countries. Only the Dutch, Chinese and Koreans were allowed to remain in

1274 & 1281	15th & 16th centuries	1543
■	■	■
Under Kublai Khan the Mongols twice attempt and fail to invade Japan.	Japan is in almost constant internal warfare, including the particularly fierce Ōnin War (1467–77).	The first Westerners, Portuguese, arrive (by chance) in Japan, heralding the advent of firearms and Christianity.

JAPAN IN FOCUS

HISTORY

FRANK CARTER

Monks at Tōdai-ji (p154), Nara

PLACES TO LEARN ABOUT JAPANESE HISTORY

- Nara (p151)
- Kyoto (p110)
- Hiroshima (p256)
- Okinawa-hontō (p303)

Japan, and they were placed under strict supervision. The Dutch were confined to the island of Dejima, near Nagasaki, and their contacts restricted to merchants and prostitutes.

By the turn of the 19th century, the Tokugawa government was falling into stagnation and corruption. Famines and poverty among the peasants and samurai further weakened the system. Foreign ships started to challenge Japan's isolation with increasing insistence, and the Japanese soon realised that their outmoded defences were ineffectual. Russian contact in the north were followed by British and American visits. In 1853 Commodore Matthew Perry of the US Navy arrived with a squadron of 'black ships' to demand the opening up of Japan to trade.

The arrival of foreigners proved to be the decisive blow to an already shaky Tokugawa regime. Upset by the shōgunate's handling of the foreign incursion, two large *daimyō* areas in western Japan, the Satsuma and the Chōshū, allied themselves with disenchanted samurai. They succeeded in capturing the emperor in 1868, declaring a restoration of imperial rule and an end to the power of the shōgun. The ruling shōgun, Tokugawa Yoshinobu, resigned, and Emperor Meiji assumed control of state affairs.

EMERGENCE FROM ISOLATION

The initial stages of the Meiji Restoration (1868–1912) were resisted in a state of virtual civil war. The abolition of the shōgunate was followed by the surrender of the *daimyō* whose lands were divided into the prefectures that exist today. Edo became Japan's new capital and was renamed Tokyo (Eastern Capital).

Under the slogan *fukoku kyōhei* (rich country; strong military), the economy underwent a crash course in Westernisation and industrialisation. An influx of Western experts was encouraged and Japanese students were sent abroad to acquire expertise in modern technologies.

Japan's growing confidence was demonstrated by the abolition of foreign treaty rights and by the ease with which it trounced China in the Sino-Japanese War (1894–95).

1568	1582	1592 & 1597–98
The warlord Oda Nobunaga seizes Kyoto and soon becomes the supreme power in the land.	Nobunaga is forced to commit suicide and is replaced by one of his generals, Toyotomi Hideyoshi.	Hideyoshi twice tries unsuccessfully to conquer Korea as part of a grand plan to control Asia.

JAPAN IN FOCUS

HISTORY

FRANK CARTER

Man wearing a traditional soldier costume at a festival in Kyoto

The subsequent treaty recognised Korean independence and ceded Taiwan to Japan. Friction with Russia eventually led to the Russo-Japanese War (1904–05), in which the Japanese army attacked the Russians in Manchuria and Korea. The Japanese Navy stunned the Russians by inflicting a crushing defeat on their Baltic fleet at the battle of Tsushima.

INDUSTRIALISATION & ASIAN DOMINANCE

On his death in 1912, Emperor Meiji was succeeded by his son, Yoshihito, who chose the name Taishō for his reign. His period of rule was named the Taishō era (1912–26). The later stages of his life were dogged by ill health that was probably attributable to meningitis.

When WWI broke out, Japan sided against Germany but did not become deeply involved in the conflict. While the Allies were occupied with war, Japan took the opportunity, through shipping and trade, to expand its economy at top speed. At the same time Japan gained a strong foothold in China, thereby gaining the dominant position in Asia.

1600	1603	Early 19th century
The warlord Tokugawa Ieyasu seizes power at the Battle of Sekigahara.	Ieyasu formally becomes shōgun.	The shōgunate's policy of national isolation is challenged by foreign sailing vessels.

The Divine Gate in front of Yasukuni-jinja, a Shinto shrine dedicated to Japan's war dead

KRZYSZTOF DYDYN

NATIONALISM & THE PURSUIT OF EMPIRE

The Shōwa era (1926–89) commenced when Emperor Hirohito acceded the throne in 1926. He had toured extensively in Europe, mixed with European nobility and developed quite a liking for the British lifestyle.

A rising tide of nationalism was quickened by the world economic depression that began in 1930. Popular unrest was marked by plots to overthrow the government and political assassinations. This led to a strong increase in the power of the militarists, who approved the invasion of Manchuria in 1931 and the installation there of a puppet regime controlled by the Japanese. In 1933 Japan withdrew from the League of Nations and in 1937 entered into full-scale hostilities against China.

As the leader of a new order for Asia, Japan signed a tripartite pact with Germany and Italy in 1940. The Japanese military leaders saw their main opponents to this new order for Asia, the so-called Greater East Asia Co-prosperity Sphere, in the USA.

WORLD WAR II

When diplomatic attempts to gain US neutrality failed, Japan launched itself into WWII with a surprise attack on Pearl Harbor on 7 December 1941.

1853–54	1867–68	1870s–early 1890s
US Commodore Matthew Perry uses 'gunboat diplomacy' to force Japan to open up for trade.	The samurai coup known as the Meiji Restoration topples the shōgunate.	Japan's new rulers implement policies of modernisation and Westernisation.

At first, Japan scored rapid successes, pushing its battle fronts across to India, down to the fringes of Australia and out into the mid-Pacific. The Battle of Midway opened the US counterattack, puncturing Japanese naval superiority and turning the tide of the war against Japan. By 1945, exhausted by submarine blockades and aerial bombing, Japan had been driven back on all fronts. In August of the same year, the declaration of war by the Soviet Union and the atomic bombs dropped by the USA on Hiroshima and Nagasaki proved to be the final straw: Emperor Hirohito announced Japan's unconditional surrender.

POSTWAR RECONSTRUCTION

At the end of the war, the Japanese economy was in ruins and inflation was rampant. A program of recovery provided loans, restricted imports and encouraged capital investment and personal saving.

> ## A NARROW ESCAPE FOR THE OLD CAPITALS
>
> Kyoto's good fortune in escaping US bombing during WWII is a well-publicised fact. Historians have suggested that in fact both Kyoto and Nara were on a list of some 180 cities earmarked for air raids. Kyoto, with a population of over one million people, was also a prime target for atomic annihilation and many avow the choice could easily have been Kyoto. Nara, it has been suggested, escaped merely due to having a population under 60,000, which kept it far down enough on the list not to be reached before the unconditional surrender of Japan in September 1945.

By the late 1950s trade was again flourishing, and the economy continued to expand rapidly. From textiles and the manufacture of labour-intensive goods, such as cameras, the Japanese 'economic miracle' spread into virtually every sector of economic activity. Economic recession and inflation surfaced in 1974 and again in 1980, mostly as a result of steep increases in the price of imported oil, on which Japan is dependent. But despite these setbacks, Japan became the world's most successful export economy, generating massive trade surpluses and dominating such fields as electronics, robotics, computer technology, car manufacturing and banking.

THE BUBBLE BURSTS

By the late 1980s Japan was by some criteria the richest nation on the planet, of which it occupied a mere 0.3% in terms of area but 16% in terms of economic might and an incredible 60% in terms of real-estate value. Some major Japanese companies had more wealth than many nations' entire GNP.

1894–95	1902	1941
Japan defeats China in the Sino-Japanese War (1895).	Japan signs the Anglo-Japanese Alliance, the first-ever equal alliance between a Western and non-Western nation.	Japan enters WWII by striking Pearl Harbor on 7 December.

BRENT WINEBRENNE

Neon-lit passageway in Namba Station, Osaka

The so-called 'Bubble Economy' may have seemed unstoppable, but the laws of economics eventually prevailed and in the late 1980s the bubble burst. Though Japan was to remain an economic superpower, the consequences were nevertheless severe. Economically, Japan entered a recession of some 10 years, which saw almost zero growth in real terms, plummeting land prices, increased unemployment, and even dismissal of managers who had believed they were guaranteed 'lifetime' employment. Socially, the impact was even greater. The public, whose lives were often based around corporations and assumed economic growth, were disoriented by the effective collapse of corporatism and the economy.

RECENT HISTORY

The economy started to recover from around 2002, in part thanks to increased demand from China, and steadied around the 2% to 3% per annum growth mark. The year 2002 was also marked by a successful co-hosting of the Soccer World Cup with rivals Korea. However, relations with Asian nations are still far from fully harmonious, with the continued appearance of history textbooks that downplay atrocities

1945	1945–52	1970s & 1980s
On 6 August Hiroshima becomes the first-ever victim of an atomic bombing.	Japan experiences a US-led occupation.	Japan is widely seen as having achieved an economic miracle.

GREG ELMS

Baseball game at Tokyo Dome

such as Nanjing, and with controversial visits by Prime Minister Koizumi Junichirō (in office 2001–2006) to Yasukuni Shrine to honour Japanese war dead, including war criminals.

There are other worries for Japan. It is the world's most rapidly aging society, with the birth rate declining to a mere 1.3 per woman; its elderly (65 years plus) comprise 21% of the population while its children (up to 15 years) comprise just 13%. This has serious ramifications economically as well as socially, with a growing ratio of supported to supporter, and increased pension and health costs.

Japan was hit by the global financial collapse that started in 2008. Exports plunged by 50% in the early part of 2009 and unemployment surged. In August 2009, perhaps as a reaction to the economic turmoil of the preceding months, the Liberal Democratic Party of Japan was replaced by the Democratic Party of Japan in a landslide election result. Japan's new prime minister, the foreign-educated Hotayama Yukio, has promised to clean up corruption, revisit the America–Japan relationship and strengthen ties with mainland Asia.

1990s–early 2000s	1995	2008–09
After its 'Bubble Economy' bursts in the early 1990s, Japan enters a decade of recession.	On 17 January an earthquake with a magnitude of 7.2 hits Kōbe, killing more than 5000 people.	Japan is hit by the global recession and exports drop by 50% in early 2009.

KYOTO'S GEISHA

FRANK CARTE

A geisha kneels during a dance performance

Catching a glimpse of a geisha scurrying to an appointment in the narrow streets of Kyoto's Gion entertainment district is a moment of pure magic. With their startling white faces and brilliant kimono, they seem equal parts alien and apparition. If you're like most travellers, you may find it hard to believe your own eyes, for these exquisite beings seem out of place in the modern world.

According to most estimates, there are about 1000 geisha in Japan, and many of them live and work in Kyoto, where they are properly known as *geiko*. Kyoto is also home to about 90 *maiko* (apprentice *geiko*), who are girls between the ages of 16 and 20 who are in the process of completing the four or five years of study it takes to become a fully fledged *geiko*. It's easy to tell the difference between the two: *maiko* wear elaborate hairpins in their own hair and elaborate kimono, while *geiko* wear wigs with only the simplest ornamentation (usually just a boxwood comb) and simpler kimono.

A LIVING TRADITION

The origins of today's geisha (*geiko* and *maiko*) can be traced back to the Edo Period (1600–1868), although they became most popular during the Taishō Period (1912–1926). To answer the most common question regarding geisha: they are most definitely *not* prostitutes. Rather, geisha are highly skilled entertainers, who entertain guests at private parties and dinners. In many ways, geisha are living embodiments of Japanese traditional culture: each one is well versed in traditional dancing, singing, musical instruments and occasionally other arts such as tea ceremony and ikebana.

An evening of geisha entertainment often begins with an exquisite meal of *kaiseki* (Japanese haute-cuisine). During the meal, the geisha will chat with guests, pour drinks and light cigarettes. Following dinner, the geisha may dance to music provided by a *jikata*, who plays the traditional, three-stringed *shamisen*. Geisha may also engage the guests in a variety of drinking games, at which they excel, almost always resulting in guests getting progressively sozzled.

GEISHA EVENTS

Considering the cost of a geisha's training and kimono, it's hardly surprising that geisha entertainment is quite expensive: dinner for two guests with one geisha runs about US$700 and parties with a *jikata* and two or more geisha easily tops US$1000

THE BEST

FRANK CARTER

GEISHA DANCES

- **Gion Odori** (p140)
- **Kamogawa Odori** (p140)
- **Kitano Odori** (p140)
- **Kyô Odori** (p140)
- **Miyako Odori** (p141)

(making geisha entertainment a better idea for groups of travellers than individuals).

These days, some hotels and ryokan in Kyoto offer regular geisha events for guests. If you happen to be in Kyoto in the spring or fall, the geisha dances put on by the city's five geisha districts should be considered must-sees. For those who want to arrange private geisha entertainment, it can be done through private tour companies and high-end ryokan and hotels. Finally, if you spot a woman who looks like a geisha wandering through the tourist districts of Kyoto during the daytime trailed by a photographer, you can be pretty sure she's a tourist who's paid to be maid up as a geisha, and not a real *maiko* or *geiko*!

JAPAN IN FOCUS

ONSEN

ONSEN

GREG ELM

Funaoka Onsen (p127), Kyoto

Japan is in hot water. Literally. The stuff percolates up out of the ground from one end of the country to the other. The Japanese word for a hot spring is onsen, and there are more than 3000 of them in the country, more than anywhere else on earth – it's like Iceland on steroids. So if your idea of relaxation involves spending a few hours soaking away your aches and cares in a tub of bubbling hot water, then you've definitely come to the right place.

With so many onsen, it's hardly surprising that they come in every size, shape and colour. There is an onsen on an artificial island in Tokyo Bay. There are onsen high up in the Japan Alps that you can only get to by walking for a full day over high mountain peaks. There are onsen bubbling up among the rocks on the coast that only exist when the tide is just right.

THE ONSEN PILGRIMAGE

Some Japanese will tell you that the only distinctively Japanese aspect of their culture – that is, something that didn't ultimately originate in mainland Asia – is the bath. There are accounts of onsen bathing in Japan's earliest historical records, and it's pretty certain that the Japanese have been bathing in onsen as long as there have been Japanese.

Over the millennia, they have turned the simple act of bathing in an onsen into something like a religion. And, for the average modern Japanese, making a pilgrimage to a famous onsen is the closest he or she will come to a religious pilgrimage.

⚓ TATTOOS & JEWELLERY

Be warned that if you have tattoos, you may not be allowed to enter some Japanese onsen or *sentō* (public baths). The reason for this is that *yakuza* (Japanese mafia) almost always sport tattoos. If your tattoo is small enough to cover with some adhesive bandages, then cover it up. Otherwise, ask if you can go in despite your tattoos. The phrase to use is: '*irezumi wa daijōbu desu ka*' (are tattoos okay?).

The minerals in certain onsen can discolour jewellery, particularly anything made of silver. Fortunately, after a few hours, the discolouration usually fades.

Today, the ultimate way to experience an onsen is to visit an onsen ryokan, a traditional Japanese inn with its own private hot-spring bath on the premises. Here you spend all day enjoying the bath, relaxing in your room and eating sumptuous Japanese food.

Like many of the best things in life, some of the finest onsen in Japan are free. Just show up with a towel and your birthday suit, splash a little water on yourself and plunge in. No communication hassles, no expenses and no worries. And even if you must pay to enter, it's usually just a minor snip – averaging about ¥700 per person.

ONSEN ETIQUETTE

First: relax. That's what onsen are all about. You'll be relieved to hear that there really is nothing tricky about taking an onsen bath. If you remember just one basic point, you won't go too far wrong. This is the point: the water in the pools and tubs is for soaking in, not washing in, and it should only be entered after you've washed or rinsed your body.

This is the drill. Pay your entry fee, if there is one. Rent a hand towel if you don't have one. Take off your shoes and put them in the lockers or shelves provided. Find the correct changing room/bath for your gender (man: 男; woman: 女). Grab a basket, strip down and put your clothes in the basket. Put the basket in a locker and bring the hand towel in with you.

Once in the bathing area, find a place around the wall (if there is one) to put down your toiletries (if you have them) and wash your body, or, at least, rinse your body. You'll note that some scofflaws dispense with this step and just stride over to the tubs and grab a bucket (there are usually some around) and splash a few scoops over their privates. Some miscreants can't even be bothered with this step and plunge right into the tubs unwashed and unrinsed. Frankly, we like to think that these people will be reincarnated into a world where there are only cold-water showers for their bathing needs.

⚓ THE BEST

NOBORU KOMINE

Nishimuraya Honkan (p145), Kinosaki

ONSEN IN JAPAN

- Takaragawa Onsen (p87)
- Kinosaki (p145)
- Hirauchi Kaichū Onsen (p298)
- Dōgo Onsen (p270)

RYOKAN

GREG EL

Hiiragiya (p133), Kyoto

Let's face it: a hotel is a hotel wherever you go. Just as you want to try local food when you're on the road, you probably also want to try a night in traditional local accommodation. Ryokan (written with the Japanese characters for 'travel' and 'hall') are often fine old Japanese wooden buildings, with tatami mats, futons, gardens, deep bathtubs, traditional service and kitchens that turn out classic Japanese cuisine.

Of course much simpler ryokan also exist, and some even resemble hotels in every respect but the Japanese-style rooms. Due to language difficulties and unfamiliarity, staying in a ryokan is not as straightforward as staying in a Western-style hotel. However, with a little education, it can be a breeze, even if you don't speak a word of Japanese.

BEFORE YOU ARRIVE

There are a few simple steps that can make finding and booking a ryokan (or other form of accommodation) much easier. Whenever possible, book ahead: giving some notice, even if it's just a quick call a few hours before arriving, vastly increases your chances of getting a room. Faxing a room request and including all your details is another good idea, as many Japanese are much more comfortable with written, rather than spoken English – you can always follow up with a call once you're on the same page. Another option is to ask your present accommodation to call ahead and reserve your next night's accommodation for you. And remember, staff at tourist information offices can usually help you find a place to stay.

THE RYOKAN EXPERIENCE

Here's the basic drill. When you arrive, leave your shoes in the *genkan* (foyer area) and step up into the reception area. Here, you'll be asked to sign in and perhaps show your passport (you pay when you check out). You'll be shown around the place and then to your room where you will be served a cup of tea, or shown a hot-water flask and some tea cups so you can make your own. You'll note that there is no bedding to be seen in your room – your futon is in the closet and will be laid out later. You can leave your luggage anywhere except the *tokonoma* (sacred alcove), which will usually contain some flowers or a hanging scroll. If it's early enough, you can then go out to do some sightseeing.

GREG ELMS

▶ THE BEST

RYOKAN IN JAPAN

- Tawaraya (p134)
- Hiiragiya (p133)
- Nishimuraya Honkan (p145)
- Hōshi Onsen Chōjūkan (p87)

When you return, you can change into your *yukata* (lightweight cotton Japanese robe or kimono) and be served dinner in your room or in a dining room. In a ryokan, dinner is often a multicourse feast of the finest local delicacies. After dinner, you can take a bath. If it's a big place, you can generally bathe anytime in the evening until around 11pm. If it's a small place, you'll be given a time slot. While you're in the bath, some mysterious elves will go into your room and lay out your futon so that it will be waiting for you when you return all toasty from the bath.

In the morning, you'll be served a Japanese-style breakfast (some places these days serve a simple Western-style breakfast for those who can't stomach rice and fish in the morning). You pay on check out, which is usually around 11am.

SAKE

JOHN BANAG

Sake bottles outside a restaurant in Osaka

Brewed from rice, sake has been enjoyed for centuries in Japan, and although it's been overtaken in terms of consumption by beer and *shōchū* (distilled grain liquor) in recent years, it is still regarded by most Japanese people as the national drink. Indeed, what is called 'sake' in the West is more commonly known in Japan as *nihonshu* – the 'drink of Japan'.

Sake has traditionally been associated with Shintō and other traditional ceremonies and you will still see huge barrels of sake (known as *o-miki*) on display at almost every shrine you visit. Although consumption has been on the wane in recent years, it is generally agreed that the quality of sake available is better now than ever, and many of the best have a complexity of flavours and aromas comparable to the fine wines and beers of Europe.

Not surprisingly, sake makes the perfect accompaniment to traditional Japanese food, and *izakaya* (dining pubs) generally also serve excellent seasonal fish and other foods to go with the booze. Sake is drunk *reishu* (chilled), *jō-on* (at room temperature), *nuru-kan* (warmed), or *atsu-kan* (piping hot), according to the season and personal preference. The top-drawer stuff is normally served well chilled.

Sake is traditionally served in a ceramic jug known as a *tokkuri,* and poured into tiny cups known as *o-choko* or *sakazuki*. A traditional measure of sake is one *gō* (一合), a little over 180mL, or 6 fluid oz. In speciality bars, you'll have the option of ordering by the glass, which will often be filled to overflowing and brought to you in a wooden container to catch the overspill. If you're in company, the tradition is to pour for your neighbour first, and then be waited on by them in turn.

⌁ SAKE-SPEAK

ama-kuchi	甘口	sweet flavour
dai-ginjō	大吟醸	sake brewed from rice polished down to at least 50% of its original size
ginjō	吟醸	sake brewed from rice polished down to at least 60% of its original size
jizake	地酒	'local sake', often from small, traditional breweries
junmai-shu	純米酒	pure rice sake, made from only rice, *kōji* (a benign mould) and water
kara-kuchi	辛口	dry, sharp flavour
nihonshu	日本酒	Japanese word for sake
o-choko	お猪口	small cups traditionally used for sake
tokkuri	徳利	traditional ceramic serving vessel

SAKE BREWING

Sake is brewed during the winter, in the cold months that follow the rice harvest in September. The main ingredients are rice and yeast, together with a benign mould known as *kōji* that helps to convert the starch in the rice into fermentable sugars.

Brewing takes place in every prefecture in Japan, with the single exception of Kagoshima in southern Kyūshū, the traditional stronghold of the distilled drink known as *shōchū*, and there are more than 1500 breweries in operation today. Niigata and other parts of Northern Honshū are particularly famous for the quality of their sake, with Hiroshima and Nada-ku (in Kōbe) also major centres of the brewing industry. Almost everywhere you go in Japan you will have an opportunity to drink sake brewed just a few miles from where you are staying. A foreign visitor who shows an interest in the *jizake* (local brew) is likely to be treated to enthusiastic recommendations and the kind of hospitality that has been known to lead to sore heads the next morning.

TYPES OF SAKE

Sake is categorised by law into two main classes: *futsū-shu* (ordinary sake, which makes up the bulk of what's produced), and premium sake known as *tokutei-meishōshu*, further classified by the extent to which the rice is refined before fermentation to remove proteins and oils that interfere with the flavour of the final product. This is generally shown on the label as the *seimai buai*, expressed as the percentage of the original size to which the grain is reduced by polishing before the brewing process starts. As a general rule, the lower this number, the better (or at least, the more expensive) the sake will be. Sake made from rice polished to 60% or less of its original size is known as *ginjō*; rice polished to 50% or less of its original size produces the finest sake of all, known as *dai-ginjō*. Sake made only with rice and *kōji* (without the use of added alcohol) is known as *junmai-shu,* or 'pure rice' sake.

JAPAN IN FOCUS

SKIING & SNOWBOARDING

SKIING & SNOWBOARDING

FELIX RIO

Skiing on powder in Central Honshū

With more than 600 ski resorts and some of the most reliable snow anywhere, Japan might just be the skiing world's best-kept secret – the perfect place to combine some world-class skiing with an exotic vacation. Japan offers stunning mountain vistas, great runs at all levels of difficulty, kilometres of groomed runs along with ripping mogul runs, snowboard parks, friendly locals and good food. And let's not forget the incredible variety of onsen (hot springs) for that all-important après-ski soak.

With so many ski resorts, you're spoiled for choice in Japan. Powder hounds flock to Hokkaidō's Niseko, which offers the world's most reliable lift-served powder snow. Others head to the sprawling Shiga Kōgen resort in Central Honshū, which, by some estimations, is the largest ski resort in the world. Those who want a little European atmosphere head for nearby Nozawa Onsen, which, as its name suggests, offers great hot springs as well as excellent skiing. In addition to headlining places such as these, you'll also find plenty of small local areas near the big areas, and these are often great for families.

PRACTICALITIES

Skiing in Japan is remarkably reasonable: it actually costs less to ski here than in comparable areas in North America and Europe, with a one-day lift ticket costing around ¥4800. At most major areas you can find plenty of accommodation in the ¥8000-per person range, and this will often include one or two meals. On-slope meals average around ¥1000.

It's also quite easy to get to the slopes from gateways such as Tokyo's Narita International Airport and Osaka's Kansai International Airport.

Almost everything you need for skiing is available in Japan, with the most notable exception being large boots. Rental places at most resorts only have boots up to 30cm (equivalent to size 12 in the USA, UK or Australia), so bring your own boots if you've large feet. It's also worth bring a small 'around the arm' type case to hold your ski lift chip, which you need to scan at every lift.

Many of Japan's ski areas are covered by one or more mobile-phone networks, so bring your phone or consider hiring one, as they are a great way to keep in touch with others in your party.

JOHN BORTHWICK

THE BEST

Hakuba

PLACES TO SKI IN JAPAN

- Niseko (p236)
- Hakuba (p189)
- Nozawa Onsen (p188)
- Shiga Kōgen (p188)

JAPAN IN FOCUS

SKIING & SNOWBOARDING

GETTING TO THE SLOPES

Japan's brilliant public transport system makes getting to the slopes a breeze. Take Japan's premier resort, Niseko in Hokkaidō. If you're coming from abroad and want to go straight to the resort, you'll find the journey painless and efficient. First, you fly

JOHN BORTHWICK

Rotemburo (outdoor bath) in Nagano

JAPAN IN FOCUS

SKIING & SNOWBOARDING

JOHN BORTHWI

Snowboarding at Shiga Kōgen (p188)

into Tokyo's Narita International Airport, then change to a domestic flight to Sapporo'
New Chitose Airport. Buses to Niseko depart from right outside the arrivals hall here
take a mere 2½ hours and cost only ¥2300 to reach the resort. If you arrive in Sappor
in the morning, you can be skiing that afternoon. Likewise, the journey by train fron
Tokyo to Nagano, the heart of Japan's Central Honshū ski country, takes only 1¾ hour
and costs only ¥7970. And the best part is this: you get to ride on one of the country'
ultramodern *shinkansen* (bullet trains). You could literally start the day with a look a
Tokyo's incredible Tsukiji Fish Market and be skiing in Nagano that afternoon.

DIRECTORY & TRANSPORT

DIRECTORY

ACCOMMODATION

Japan offers a wide range of accommodation, from cheap guesthouses to first-class hotels. In addition to the Western-style accommodation, you'll also find distinctive Japanese-style places such as ryokan (traditional Japanese inns; p350) and *minshuku* (inexpensive Japanese guesthouses).

In this guide, accommodation listings have been organised by neighbourhood and price. Budget options cost ¥6000 or less; midrange rooms cost between ¥6000 and ¥15,000; and top-end rooms will cost more than ¥15,000 (per double). Room rates listed in this book include tax (ie the national 5% consumption tax is figured into the rates).

Since air-conditioning is basically ubiquitous in Japan (due to its hot summers), we do not list air-con icons for accommodation options in this guide. We only note places that do not have air-con. If nothing is mentioned about air-con, you can assume a place has it.

RESERVATIONS

It can be hard to find accommodation during the following holiday periods: Shōgatsu (New Year) – 31 December to 3 January; Golden Week – 29 April to 5 May; and O-Bon – mid-August. If you plan to be in Japan during these periods, you should make reservations as far in advance as possible.

Tourist information offices at main train stations can usually help with reservations, and are often open until about 6.30pm or later. Even if you are travelling by car, the train station is a good first stop in town for information, reservations and cheap car parking.

Making phone reservations in English is usually possible at larger hotels and foreigner-friendly ryokan. Providing you speak clearly and simply, there will usually be someone around who can get the gist of what you want. For more information on making accommodation reservations in Japan, see p350.

The International Tourism Center of Japan (formerly Welcome Inn Reservation Center; www.itcj.jp/) operates five Welcome Inn Reservation Centers in Japan as well as an online booking system. It's free service includes hundreds of *minshuku*, ryokan, inns and pensions in Japan. It operates counters in the main tourist information offices in Tokyo (see p62) and Kyoto (see p114), and at the main tourist information counters in Narita and Kansai airports. You can also make reservations online through its website (which is also an excellent source of information on member hotels and inns).

HOTELS

You'll find a range of Western-style hotels in most Japanese cities and resort areas. Rates at standard midrange hotels average ¥9000 for a single and ¥12,000 for a double or twin. Rates at first-class hotels average ¥15,000 for a single and ¥20,000 for a double or twin. In addition to the 5% consumption tax that is levied on all

---

⚓ BOOK YOUR STAY ONLINE

For more accommodation reviews and recommendations by Lonely Planet authors, check out the online booking service at www.lonelyplanet.com. You'll find the true, insider lowdown on the best places to stay. Reviews are thorough and independent. Best of all, you can book online.

accommodation in Japan, you may have to pay an additional 10% or more as a service charge at luxury hotels. Note that the rooms rates listed in this book include the consumption tax.

BUSINESS HOTELS

These are economical and practical places geared to the single traveller, usually local businessmen who want to stay somewhere close to the station. Rooms are clean, Western style, just big enough for you to turn around in and include a 'unit bath' (ie a bath/shower and toilet). Vending machines replace room service.

Cheap single rooms can sometimes be found for as low as ¥4500, though the average rate is around ¥8000. Most business hotels also have twin and double rooms, and usually do not have a service charge.

RYOKAN

Ryokan are traditional Japanese lodgings. They are often interesting wooden buildings with traditional tatami rooms and futons for bedding. Ryokan range from ultra-exclusive establishments to reasonably priced places with a homey atmosphere. Prices start at around ¥4000 (per person per night) for a no-frills ryokan without meals and climb right up to ¥100,000 for the best establishments. For around ¥10,000 per person, you can usually find a very good place that will serve you two excellent Japanese meals to complement your stay.

See the websites of the **International Tourism Center of Japan** (formerly Welcome Inn Reservation Center; www.itcj.jp/) and the **Japanese Inn Group** (www.jpinn.com/index .html) for information about the ryokan booking services they offer. For information on staying in a ryokan, see p350.

ACTIVITIES

Japan may be best known for its cultural attractions, but it's also a great place to ski, climb, trek, dive, snorkel and cycle. And, needless to say, it's an ideal destination to pursue martial arts, such as judo, aikido and karate.

CYCLING

Bicycle touring is fairly popular in Japan, despite the fact that most of the country is quite mountainous. See p375 for more information on cycling in Japan.

DIVING & SNORKELLING

The great diving and snorkelling to be had around Japan's southern islands is one of the world's best kept underwater secrets. How many people even know that you can dive with mantas or hammerheads in the Land of the Rising Sun? Popular diving destinations include the Okinawan islands (p303), in the far southwest of Japan, and the chain of islands south of Tokyo, known as Izu-shotō (Izu Seven Islands). Other dive sites in Japan include the waters around Tobi-shima, off northern Honshū, and the Ogasawara-shotō (p95).

Diving in Japan can be expensive in comparison with other parts of Asia. Typical rates are ¥12,000 per day for two boat dives and lunch. Courses for beginners are available in places such as Ishigaki-jima (p314) and Iriomote-jima (p317) in Okinawa, but starting costs are around ¥80,000. Instruction will usually be in Japanese.

If your plans include a trip to Okinawa or the Ogasawa-shotō, consider bringing your own mask, snorkel and fins (large-sized fins can be hard to find at dive shops). Serious divers may want to go further and bring their own regulars and even buoyancy control devices (BCDs), although these are available for rent at dive shops in country.

HIKING

The Japanese are keen hikers, and many national parks in Japan have hiking routes. The popular hiking areas near Tokyo are around Nikkō (p82) and Izu-shotō. In the Kansai region, Nara (p151), Shiga-ken and Kyoto (p110) all have pleasant hikes.

Japan comes into its own as a hiking destination in the Japan Alps National Park, particularly in Kamikōchi (p183) in central Honshū; the Bandai plateau in northern Honshū; and Hokkaidō's national parks (p241).

While rudimentary English-language hiking maps may be available from local tourism authorities, it's better to seek out proper Japanese maps and decipher the kanji. Shobunsha's *Yama-to-Kōgen No Chizu* series covers all of Japan's most popular hiking areas in exquisite detail. The maps are available in all major bookshops in Japan.

Serious hikers will also want to pick up a copy of Lonely Planet's *Hiking in Japan,* which covers convenient one-day hikes near major cities and extended hikes in more remote areas.

SKIING

Japan is the best place to ski in Asia and it boasts some of the most reliable snow in the world. For more information see p354.

CLIMATE

The combination of Japan's mountainous territory and the length of the archipelago (covering about 20° of latitude) makes for a complex climate. Most of the country is located in the northern temperate zone, which yields four distinct seasons. In addition, there are significant climatic differences between Hokkaidō in the north, which has short summers and lengthy winters with heavy snowfalls, and the southern islands, such as Okinawa in Nansei-shotō (Southwest Archipelago), which enjoy a subtropical climate.

In the winter months (December to February), cold, dry air-masses from Siberia move down over Japan, where they meet warmer, moister air-masses from the Pacific. The resulting precipitation causes huge snowfalls on the side of the country that faces the Sea of Japan. The Pacific Ocean side of Japan receives less snow but can still be quite cold, while the big cities of Honshū such as Tokyo, Osaka, Nagoya and Kyoto have winters with highs in the single digits or low teens and lows temps a few degrees above zero (celsius). The odd January or February day will be colder, but these cold snaps usually don't last.

The summer months (June to August) are dominated by warm, moist air currents from the Pacific, and produce high temperatures and humidity throughout most of Japan (with the blissful exception of Hokkaidō). In the early part of summer, usually mid-May to June, there is a rainy season lasting a few weeks that starts in the south and gradually works its way northward.

Although it can be inconvenient, this rainy season is not usually a significant barrier to travel. August, September and October is typhoon season, which can make travel in Okinawa, the Izu-shotō and Ogasawara-shotō difficult.

In contrast to the extremes of summer and winter, spring (March to May) and autumn (September to November) in Japan are comparatively mild. Rainfall is relatively low and the days are often clear. These are, without a doubt, the very best times to visit the country.

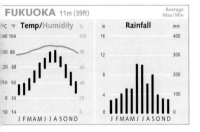

FUKUOKA 11m (39ft)

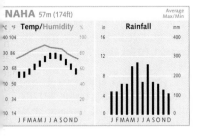

NAHA 57m (174ft)

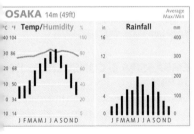

OSAKA 14m (49ft)

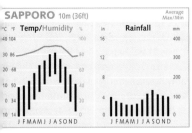

SAPPORO 10m (36ft)

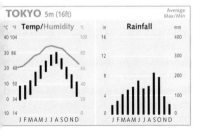

TOKYO 5m (16ft)

CUSTOMS

Customs allowances include the usual tobacco products plus three 760mL bottles of alcoholic beverages, 56mL of perfume, and gifts and souvenirs up to a value of ¥200,000 or its equivalent. You must be over the age of 20 to qualify for these allowances. Customs officers will confiscate any pornographic materials in which pubic hair is visible.

There are no limits on the importation of foreign or Japanese currency. The export of foreign currency is also unlimited but there is a ¥5 million export limit for Japanese currency.

Visit Japan Customs (www.customs.go.jp/english/index.htm) for more information on Japan's customs regulations.

DANGERS & ANNOYANCES
EARTHQUAKES

Japan is an earthquake-prone country, although most earthquakes can only be detected by sensitive instruments.

If you experience a strong earthquake, head for a doorway or supporting pillar. Small rooms, such as a bathroom or cupboard, are often stronger than large rooms, but even a table or desk can provide some protection from falling debris. If you are in an urban area, do not run outside as this could expose you to falling debris.

All Japanese hotels have maps indicating the location of emergency exits, and local wards have emergency evacuation areas (fires frequently follow in the wake of a major earthquake).

In the event of a major earthquake, try to stay calm and to follow the locals, who should be heading for a designated safe area.

DIRECTORY

CUSTOMS

NOISE

In Japanese cities the assault on the auditory senses can be somewhat overwhelming: you'll hear announcements on buses, escalators, elevators, on footpaths, in shopping malls, even at popular beaches and ski resorts. Earplugs can help, particularly when you're trying to sleep.

SIZE

Even medium-sized foreigners need to mind their heads in Japanese dwellings. The Western frame may make it hard to fit into some seats and those with long legs will often find themselves wedged tight. Toilets in cramped accommodation necessitate contortions and careful aim (be warned!). Bathtubs are also sometimes on the small side and may require considerable flexibility on the part of the bather.

EMBASSIES & CONSULATES

JAPANESE EMBASSIES & CONSULATES

Diplomatic representation abroad:

Australia Canberra (embassy; ☎ 02-6273 3244; www.au.emb-japan.go.jp; 112 Empire Circuit, Yarralumla, Canberra, ACT 2600); Brisbane (consulate; ☎ 07-3221 5188); Melbourne (consulate; ☎ 03-9639 3244); Perth (consulate; ☎ 08-9480 1800); Sydney (consulate; ☎ 02-9231 3455)

Canada Ontario (embassy; ☎ 613-241 8541; www.ca.emb-japan.go.jp; 255 Sussex Dr, Ottawa, Ontario K1N 9E6); Calgary (consulate; ☎ 403-294 0782); Montreal (consulate; ☎ 514-866 3429); Toronto (consulate; ☎ 416-363 7038); Vancouver (consulate; ☎ 604-684 5868)

France (☎ 01 48 88 62 00; www.fr.emb-japan .go.jp; 7 ave Hoche, 75008 Paris)

Germany (☎ 493-021 09 40; www.de.emb -japan.go.jp; Hiroshimastr.6, 10785 Berlin, Bun desrepublik Deutschland)

Ireland (☎ 01-202 8300; www.ie.emb-japan .go.jp; Nutley Bldg, Merrion Centre, Nutley Lane Dublin 4)

Netherlands (☎ 70-346-95-44; www.n .emb-japan.go.jp; Tobias Asserlaan 2 2517 KC, De Haag)

New Zealand Wellington (embassy ☎ 04-473 1540; www.nz.emb-japan.go.jp Level 18, Majestic Centre, 100 Willis St, We lington 1, PO Box 6340); Auckland (consulate ☎ 09-303 4106)

UK (☎ 020-7465 6500; www.uk.emb-japan .go.jp; 101-104 Piccadilly, London, W1J 7JT)

USA Washington DC (embassy; ☎ 202-23 6700; www.us.emb-japan.go.jp; 2520 Massachu setts Ave NW, Washington DC, 20008-2869); Los Angeles (consulate; ☎ 213-617 6700); New York (consulate; ☎ 212-371 8222)

EMBASSIES & CONSULATES IN JAPAN

Diplomatic representation in Japan:

Australia Tokyo (embassy; ☎ 03-5232 4111; www.australia.or.jp/english; 2-1-14 Mita Minato-ku); Fukuoka (consulate; ☎ 092-734 5055; 7th fl, Tenjin Twin Bldg, 1-6-8 Tenjin, Chūō ku); Osaka (consulate; ☎ 06-6941-9271; 16t fl, Twin 21 MID Tower, 2-1-61 Shiromi, Chūō-ku)

Canada Tokyo (embassy; ☎ 03-5412-6200 www.canadanet.or.jp/english.shtml; 7-3-38 Akasaka, Minato-ku); Hiroshima (consulate ☎ 082-211-0505; No 709, 5-44 Motomachi Naka-ku); Nagoya (consulate; ☎ 052-972 0450; Nakatō Marunouchi Bldg, 6F, 3-17-6 Marunouchi, Naka-ku); Sapporo (consulate ☎ 011-281-6565; Nikko Bldg, 5F, 1, Kita 4 Nish 4, Chūō-ku)

France Tokyo (embassy; ☎ 03-5798-6000 www.ambafrance-jp.org; 4-11-44 Minami Azabu Minato-ku); Osaka (consulate; ☎ 06-4790-1505 10th fl, Crystal Tower, 1-2-27 Shiromi, Chūō-ku)

Germany Tokyo (☎ 03-5791-7700; www
tokyo.diplo.de/Vertretung/tokyo/de/Startseite
html; 4-5-10 Minami Azabu, Minato-ku); Osaka
(consulate; ☎ 06-6440-5070; 35th fl, Umeda Sky
Bldg Tower East, 1-1-88-3501 Ōyodonaka, Kita-ku)

Ireland Tokyo (embassy; ☎ 03-3263-0695;
www.irishembassy.jp; Ireland House, 2-10-7 Kōji-
machi, Chiyoda-ku); Osaka (honorary consulate;
☎ 06-6204-2024; c/o Takeda Pharmaceutical
ompany Ltd, 4-1-1, Doshō-machi, Chūō-ku)

Netherlands Tokyo (embassy; ☎ 03-5401-
5411; www.mfa.nl/tok-en/; 3-6-3 Shiba-kōen,
Minato-ku); Osaka (consulate; ☎ 06-6944-
7272; 33rd fl, Twin 21 MID Tower, 2-1-61 Shiromi,
Chūō-ku)

New Zealand Tokyo (embassy; ☎ 03-
3467-2271; www.nzembassy.com/home
.cfm?c=17; 20-40 Kamiyama-chō, Shibuya-ku);
Osaka (consulate; ☎ 06-6373-4583; Umeda
Centre Bldg, 2-4-12 Nakazaki-nishi Kita-ku,
Osaka 530-8323)

UK Tokyo (embassy; ☎ 03-5211-1100; www
.uknow.or.jp/index_e.htm; 1 Ichiban-chō, Chiyoda-ku); Osaka (consulate; ☎ 06-6120-5600;
19th fl, Epson Osaka Bldg, 3-5-1 Bakuromachi,
Chūō-ku)

USA Tokyo (embassy; ☎ 03-3224-5000;
http://japan.usembassy.gov/t-main.html; 1-10-
5 Akasaka, Minato-ku); Fukuoka (consulate;
☎ 092-751-9331; 2-5-26 Ōhori, Chūō-ku); Osaka
(consulate; ☎ 06-6315-5900; 2-11-5 Nishitenma,
Kita-ku)

FESTIVALS & EVENTS

A *matsuri* (festival) is often the highlight
of a trip to Japan. It is a chance to see
the Japanese at their most uninhibited,
and get some insight into the ancient
traditions and beliefs of the country.
In addition to *matsuri,* there are several important annual events, including Buddhist imports from China, and
more recent imports from the West (eg
Christmas).

For a list of Japan's most interesting
matsuri and other yearly events, see the
Calendar (p46).

GAY & LESBIAN TRAVELLERS

With the possible exception of Thailand,
Japan is Asia's most enlightened nation
with regard to the sexual preferences of
foreigners. Shinjuku-nichōme in Tokyo is an
established scene where English is spoken
and meeting men is fairly straightforward.

There are no legal restraints to same-sex
sexual activities of either gender in Japan.
Public displays of affection are likely to be
the only cause for concern for all visitors –
gay, straight or otherwise.

HEALTH

Japan is a wealthy industrialised country
with a high standard of medical care, although quality can vary, depending on
where you go. Food and water sanitation
is generally good, though there is a slight
risk of disease transmission through eating
certain raw or undercooked foods. There
is a low risk of catching an insect-borne
disease such as Japanese encephalitis,
Lyme disease and tick-borne encephalitis
in specific areas at certain times of the
year. Medical care is reasonably priced,
but ensure you have adequate travel
insurance.

BEFORE YOU GO

Prevention is the key to staying healthy
while abroad. Planning before departure,
particularly for pre-existing illnesses, will
save trouble later. See your dentist before
a long trip, carry a spare pair of contact
lenses and glasses, and take your optical
prescription with you. Bring medications
in their original, clearly labelled containers. A signed and dated letter from
your physician describing your medical

conditions and medications, including generic names, is also a good idea. If carrying syringes or needles, be sure to have a physician's letter documenting their medical necessity. If you have a heart condition, bring a copy of a recent electrocardiogram (ECG/EKG). If you take any regular medication, carry extra supplies in case of loss or theft – it may be difficult to get exactly the same medications in Japan. In particular it can be difficult to get oral contraceptives.

RECOMMENDED VACCINATIONS

No vaccinations are required for Japan. However, Japan scrupulously checks visitors who arrive from countries where there is a risk of yellow fever and other similar diseases. Consult a doctor and ensure you receive an International Certificate of Vaccination (the yellow booklet), which lists the vaccines you have received.

Under certain circumstances, or for those at special risk, the following vaccinations are recommended: hepatitis A, hepatitis B, influenza, Japanese B encephalitis, pneumonia (pneumococcal) and tick-borne encephalitis. These should be discussed with a doctor specialised in travel medicine.

IN JAPAN

AVAILABILITY & COST OF HEALTH CARE

Japan has a national health-insurance system, but this is only available to foreigners if they have long-term visas in Japan. Be aware that medical facilities will require full payment at the time of treatment, or proof that your travel insurance will pay for any treatment that you receive.

Tourist offices operated by Japan National Tourism Organization (JNTO) have lists of English-speaking doctors and dentists, and hospitals where English is spoken. You can contact your insurance company or embassy to locate the nearest English-speaking facility.

ENVIRONMENTAL HAZARDS

AIR POLLUTION

If you have an underlying lung condition air pollution can be a problem in major centres such as Tokyo. Speak with your doctor to ensure you have adequate medications to treat an exacerbation.

ALTITUDE SICKNESS

Altitude sickness could develop in some people when climbing Mt Fuji or on some

🐌 JAPANESE B ENCEPHALITIS

Japanese B encephalitis is a viral disease transmitted by mosquitoes. It is a rare disease in travellers and the vaccine is part of the routine childhood vaccination schedule in Japan. Risk exists in rural areas of all islands, but is highest in the western part of the country. In western Japan the risk season is from July to October. In the Nansei-shotō (the islands of Kagoshima-ken and Okinawa-ken) the risk season runs from April to December. Vaccination is recommended for travellers spending more than a month in rural areas during the transmission season. Other precautions include general insect avoidance measures such as using repellents and sleeping under nets (if not in screened rooms). Although this is a rare disease, it is very serious – there is no specific treatment and a third of people infected will die and a third will suffer permanent brain damage.

of the higher mountains in the Japan Alps. Altitude sickness is best avoided by slowly acclimatising to higher altitudes.

HYPOTHERMIA

Hypothermia is possible when hiking in the Japan Alps, swimming in cold water or simply being outside in winter (December to March). It is best to dress in layers; silk, wool and some of the new artificial fibres are all good insulating materials. A hat is important, as a lot of heat is lost through the head. A strong, waterproof outer layer and a space blanket for emergencies) is essential. Carry basic supplies, including food that contains simple sugars to generate heat quickly, and fluid to drink.

INSECT BITES & STINGS

Insect bites and stings are not a common problem in Japan. You should, however, follow general insect avoidance measures if you are hiking in the woods or are in rural areas during the summer months.

WATER

The water in Japan is generally safe to drink.

WOMEN'S HEALTH

Supplies of sanitary products are readily available in Japan. It can be very difficult to get the oral contraceptive pill so ensure you bring adequate supplies of your own pill from home.

Pregnant women should receive specialised advice before travelling.

HOLIDAYS

Japan has 15 national holidays. When a public holiday falls on a Sunday, the following Monday is taken as a holiday. If that Monday is already a holiday, the following day becomes a holiday as well. And, if two weekdays (say, Tuesday and Thursday) are holidays, the day in between (Wednesday) will also become a holiday.

You can expect travel and accommodation options to be fully booked during the New Year festivities (29 December to 6 January), Golden Week (29 April to 5 May) and the mid-August O-Bon festival. See p46 for more details of these festivals and events.

Japan's national holidays:

Ganjitsu (New Year's Day) 1 January

Seijin-no-hi (Coming-of-Age Day) Second Monday in January

Kenkoku Kinem-bi (National Foundation Day) 11 February

Shumbun-no-hi (Spring Equinox) 20 or 21 March

Shōwa-no-hi (Shōwa Emperor's Day) 29 April

Kempō Kinem-bi (Constitution Day) 3 May

Midori-no-hi (Green Day) 4 May

Kodomo-no-hi (Children's Day) 5 May

Umi-no-hi (Marine Day) Third Monday in July

Keirō-no-hi (Respect-for-the-Aged Day) Third Monday in September

Shūbun-no-hi (Autumn Equinox) 23 or 24 September

Taiiku-no-hi (Health-Sports Day) Second Monday in October

Bunka-no-hi (Culture Day) 3 November

Kinrō Kansha-no-hi (Labour Thanksgiving Day) 23 November

Tennō Tanjōbi (Emperor's Birthday) 23 December

INSURANCE

A travel insurance policy to cover theft, loss and medical problems is a good idea. Some policies will specifically exclude 'dangerous activities', which can include scuba diving, motorcycling and even trekking; if you plan to engage in such activities, you'll want a policy that covers them.

You may prefer a policy that pays doctors or hospitals directly rather than have you pay on the spot and claim later. If you have to claim later, make sure you keep all documentation. Some policies ask you to call (reverse charge) a centre in your home country where an immediate assessment of your problem is made. Check that the policy covers ambulances or an emergency flight home.

Some insurance policies offer lower and higher medical-expense options; choose the high-cost option for Japan. Be sure to bring your insurance card or other certificate of insurance to Japan; Japanese hospitals have been known to refuse treatment to foreign patients who cannot provide proof of medical insurance.

INTERNET ACCESS

If you plan on bringing your laptop to Japan, first make sure that it is compatible with the Japanese current (100V AC; 50Hz in eastern Japan and 60Hz in western Japan). Most makes of laptop function just fine on Japanese current. Second, check to see if your plug will fit Japanese wall sockets (Japanese plugs are flat two pin, identical to most ungrounded North American plugs). Both transformers and plug adaptors are readily available in electronics districts, such as Tokyo's Akihabara (p63), Osaka's Den Den Town or Kyoto's Teramachi-dōri (Map p116).

Modems and phone jacks used in Japan are similar to those used in the USA (RJ11 phone jacks). Many of the grey international direct dialling (IDD) pay phones in Japan have a standard phone jack and an infrared port, so you can log on to the internet just about anywhere in the country if your computer has an infrared port.

In this book, an internet symbol (☐) indicates that the accommodation option has at least one computer with interne for guests' use. We also note where wi-fi (�) is available. Note that wi-fi is fa less common in Japanese hotels than in their Western counterparts. It is much more common to find local area network (LAN) cable internet access points in hote rooms (the hotels can usually provide LAN cables, but you may want to bring you own to avoid having to ask for one every where you stay). These LAN connections usually work fine, but you may occasion ally find it hard to log on due to software or hardware compatibility issues or con figuration problems.

You'll find internet cafes and other ac cess points in most major Japanese cities Rates vary, usually ranging from ¥200 to ¥700 per hour. As a rule, internet connec tions are fast (DSL or ADSL) and reliable in Japan. Most accommodation options also have some way of getting online, with ter minals in the lobby, wi-fi or LAN access.

LEFT LUGGAGE

Only major train stations have left luggage facilities, but almost all stations have coin-operated storage lockers (¥100 to ¥500 per day, depending on size). The lockers are rented until midnight (not fo 24 hours). After that time you have to insert more money before your key wil work. If your bag is simply too large to fit in the locker, ask someone, 'Tenimotsu azukai wa doko desu ka?' (Where is the left-luggage office?).

LEGAL MATTERS

Japanese police have extraordinary powers. They can detain a suspect without charging them for up to three days, after which a prosecutor can decide to extend this period for another 20 days. Police can so choose whether to allow a suspect to phone their embassy or lawyer, though if you find yourself in police custody you should insist that you will not cooperate in any way until allowed to make such a call. Your embassy is the first place you should call if given the chance.

Police will speak almost no English; insist that a *tsuyakusha* (interpreter) be summoned. Police are legally bound to provide one before proceeding with any questioning. Even if you do speak Japanese, it's best to deny it and stay with your native language.

If you have a problem, call the Japan Helpline (☎ 0120-46-1997), a nationwide emergency number that operates 24 hours a day, seven days a week.

MAPS

If you'd like to buy a map of Japan before arriving, both Nelles and Periplus produce reasonable maps of Japan. If you want something more detailed, wait until you get to Tokyo or Kyoto, where you'll find lots of detailed maps in both English and Japanese.

The JNTO's free *Tourist Map of Japan,* available at JNTO-operated tourist information centres inside the country and JNTO offices abroad, is a reasonable English-language map that is suitable for general route planning.

The *Japan Road Atlas* (Shobunsha) is a good choice for those planning to drive around the country. Those looking for something less bulky should pick up a copy of the *Bilingual Atlas of Japan* (Kodansha).

MONEY

The currency in Japan is the yen (¥) and banknotes and coins are easily identifiable. There are ¥1, ¥5, ¥10, ¥50, ¥100 and ¥500 coins; and ¥1000, ¥2000, ¥5000 and ¥10,000

banknotes (the ¥2000 notes are very rarely seen). The ¥1 coin is an aluminium lightweight coin, the ¥5 and ¥50 coins have a punched hole in the middle (the former is coloured bronze and the latter silver). Note that some vending machines do not accept older ¥500 coins (a South Korean coin of much less value was often used in its place to rip off vending machines). The Japanese pronounce yen as 'en', with no 'y' sound. The kanji for yen is: 円.

The Japanese postal system has recently linked its ATMs to the international Cirrus and Plus networks, and 7-Eleven convenience stores have followed suit, so getting money is no longer the issue it once was for travellers to Japan. Of course, it always makes sense to carry some foreign cash and some credit cards just to be on the safe side. For those without credit cards, it would be a good idea to bring some travellers cheques as a back-up.

◢ WARNING: JAPAN IS A CASH SOCIETY!

Be warned that cold hard yen (¥) is the way to pay in Japan. While credit cards are becoming more common, cash is still much more widely used, and travellers cheques are rarely accepted. Do not assume that you can pay for things with a credit card; always carry sufficient cash. The only places where you can count on paying by credit card are department stores and large hotels.

For those without credit cards, it would be a good idea to bring some travellers cheques as a back-up. As in most other countries, the US dollar is still the currency of choice in terms of exchanging cash and cashing travellers cheques.

For exchange rates, see the inside front cover of this guide.

ATMS

Automated teller machines (ATMs) are almost as common as vending machines in Japan. Unfortunately, most of these do not accept foreign-issued cards. Even if they display Visa and MasterCard logos, most accept only Japan-issued versions of these cards.

Fortunately, Japanese postal ATMs accept cards that belong to the following international networks: Visa, Plus, MasterCard, Maestro, Cirrus American Express and Diners Club cards. Check the sticker(s) on the back of your card to see which network(s) your card belongs to. You'll find postal ATMs in almost all post offices, and you'll find post offices in even the smallest Japanese village.

Note that postal ATMs work with bank or cash cards – you cannot use credit cards, even with a pin number, in postal ATMs. That is to say, you cannot use postal ATMs to perform a cash advance.

Most postal ATMs are open 9am to 5pm on weekdays, 9am to noon on Saturday, and are closed on Sunday and holidays. Some postal ATMs in very large central post offices are open longer hours.

Postal ATMs are relatively easy to use. Here's the drill: press 'English Guide', select 'Withdrawal', then insert your card, press 'Visitor Withdrawal', input your pin number, then hit the button marked 'Kakunin' (確認 in Japanese), then enter the amount, hit 'Yen' and 'Confirm' and you should hear the delightful sound of bills being dispensed.

In addition to postal ATMs, you will find a few international ATMs in big cities such as Tokyo, Osaka and Kyoto, as well as major airports like Narita and Kansai International Airport. International cards also work in Citibank Japan ATMs. Visit www.citibank.co.jp/en/branch/index.html for a useful branch index.

Finally, 7-11 convenience stores across Japan have recently linked their ATMs to international cash networks, and these often seem to accept cards that for one reason or other will not work with postal ATMs. They are also open 24 hours. So, if you can't find an open post office or your card won't work with postal ATMs, don't give up: ask around for a 7-Eleven (pronounced 'sebun erebun' in Japanese).

CREDIT CARDS

Except for making cash withdrawals at banks and ATMs, it is best not to rely on credit cards in Japan (see also the boxed text, p367). While department stores, top-end hotels and some restaurants do accept cards, most businesses in Japan do not. Cash and carry is still very much the rule. If you do decide to bring a credit card, you'll find Visa the most useful, followed by MasterCard, Amex and Diners Club.

The main credit-card offices are in Tokyo.

Amex (☎ 0120-02-0120; 4-30-16 Ogikubo, Suginami-ku; ⊗ 24hr)
MasterCard (☎ 03-5728-5200; 16th fl, Cerulean Tower, 26-1 Sakuragaoka-chō, Shibuya-ku)
Visa (☎ 03-5275-7604; 7th fl, Hitotsubashi Bldg, 2-6-3 Hitotsubashi, Chiyoda-ku)

EXCHANGING MONEY

Banks, post offices and discount ticket shops will change all major currencies and travellers cheques. As with most other countries, you'll find that US dollars are the easiest to change, although you should have no problems with other major currencies. Note, however, that the currencies of neighbouring Taiwan (New Taiwan dollar) and Korea (won) are not easy to change, so you should change these into yen or US dollars before arriving in Japan.

You can change cash or travellers cheques at most banks, major post offices, discount ticket shops, some travel agents, some large hotels and most big department stores. Note that discount ticket shops (known as *kakuyasu kippu uriba* in Japanese) often have the best rates. These can be found around major train stations.

TAXES

Japan has a 5% *shōhizei* (consumption tax). If you eat at expensive restaurants and stay in top-end accommodation, you will encounter a service charge that varies from 10% to 15%.

TIPPING

There is little tipping in Japan. If you want to show your gratitude to someone, give them a gift rather than a tip. If you do choose to give someone a cash gift (a staff member in a ryokan, for instance), place the money in an envelope first.

TELEPHONE

Japanese telephone codes consist of an area code plus the number. You do not dial the area code when making a call in that area. When dialling Japan from abroad, dial the country code ☎ 81, followed by the area code (drop the '0') and the number. Numbers that begin with the digits ☎ 0120, ☎ 0070, ☎ 0077, ☎ 0088 and ☎ 0800 are toll-free.

DIRECTORY ASSISTANCE

For local directory assistance dial ☎ 104 (the call costs ¥105), or for assistance in English ring ☎ 0120-36-4463 from 9am to 5pm weekdays. For international directory assistance dial ☎ 0057.

INTERNATIONAL CALLS

The best way to make an international phone call from within Japan is to use a prepaid international phone card (see below).

Paid overseas calls can be made from grey international ISDN phones. These are usually found in phone booths marked 'International & Domestic Card/Coin Phone'. Unfortunately, these phones are very rare; try looking for them in the lobbies of top-end hotels and at airports. Some new green phones also allow international calls: look for them in phone booths.

Calls are charged by the unit, each of which is six seconds, so if you don't have much to say you could phone home for just ¥100. Reverse-charge (collect) overseas calls can be made from any pay phone.

You can save money by dialling late at night. Economy rates are available from 11pm to 8am. Note that it is also cheaper to make domestic calls by dialling outside the standard hours.

To place an international call through the operator, dial ☎ 0051 (KDDI operator; most international operators speak English). To make the call yourself, dial ☎ 001-010 (KDDI), ☎ 0041-010 (SoftBank Telecom) or ☎ 0033-010 (NTT) – there's very little difference in their rates – then the international country code, the local code and the number.

PREPAID INTERNATIONAL PHONECARDS

Because of the lack of pay phones from which you can make international phone calls in Japan, the easiest way to make an international phone call is to buy a prepaid international phone card. Most convenience stores carry at least one of the following types of phone cards. These cards can be used with any regular pay phone in Japan.

- KDDI Superworld Card
- NTT Communications World Card
- SoftBank Telecom Comica Card

LOCAL CALLS

The Japanese public phone system is extremely reliable and efficient., but the number of pay phones is decreasing fast as more and more Japanese buy mobile (cell) phones. Local calls from pay phones cost ¥10 per minute; unused ¥10 coins are returned after the call is completed but no change is given on ¥100 coins.

In general it's much easier to buy a *terefon kādo* (telephone card) when you arrive rather than worry about always having coins on hand. Phone cards are sold in ¥500 and ¥1000 denominations (the latter earns you an extra ¥50 in calls) and can be used in most green or grey pay phones. They are available from vending machines (some of which can be found in public phone booths) and convenience stores. They come in a myriad of designs and are also a collectable item.

MOBILE PHONES

Japan's mobile-phone networks use 3G (third generation) mobile-phone technology on a variety of frequencies. Thus, non-3G mobile phones cannot be used in Japan. This means that most foreign mobile phones *will not work* in Japan. Furthermore, SIM cards are not commonly available in Japan. Thus, for most people who want to use a mobile phone while in Japan, the only solution is to rent a mobile phone.

Several telecommunications companies in Japan specialise in short-term mobile-phone rentals, a good option for travellers whose own phones won't work in Japan, or whose own phones would be prohibitively expensive to use here.

The following companies provide this service:

Mobile Phone Japan (☎ 090-8523-2053; www.mobilephonejp.com) This company offers basic mobile-phone rental for as low as ¥2900 per week. Incoming calls, whether international or domestic, are free, and outgoing domestic calls are ¥90 per minute (outgoing domestic calls vary according to country and time of day). Free delivery anywhere in Japan is included and a free prepaid return envelope is also included.

Rentafone Japan (☎ 0120-74-6487; www.rentafonejapan.com) This company rents out mobile phones for ¥3900 per week and offers free delivery of the phone to your accommodation. Domestic rates are ¥35 per minute and overseas calls are ¥45 per minute.

TIME

Despite the distance between Japan's east and west coasts, the country is all on the same time: nine hours ahead of Greenwich Mean Time (GMT). Sydney and Wellington are ahead of Japan (+1 and +3 hours, respectively), and most of the world's other big cities are behind Japan (New York -14, Los Angeles -17 and London -9). Japan does not have daylight saving time (also known as summer time).

TOILETS

In Japan you will come across both Western-style toilets and Asian squat toilets. When you are compelled to squat, the correct position is facing the hood, away from the door. Make sure the contents of your pockets don't spill out! Toilet paper isn't always provided, so it is best to carry tissues with you. You may be given small packets of tissue on the street in Japan, common form of advertising.

In many bathrooms in Japan, separate toilet slippers are often provided just inside the toilet door. These are for use in the toilet only, so remember to change out of them when you leave.

It's quite common to see men urinating in public – the unspoken rule is that it's acceptable at night time if you happen to be drunk. Public toilets are free in Japan. The katakana script for 'toilet' is トイレ, and the kanji script is お手洗い.

You'll often also see these kanji:

- Female 女
- Male 男

TOURIST INFORMATION

Japan's tourist information services are first-rate. You will find information offices in most cities, towns and even some small villages. They are almost always located inside or in front of the main train station in a town or city.

A note on language difficulties: English speakers are usually available at tourist information offices in larger cities. Away from the big cities, you'll find varying degrees of English-language ability. In rural areas and small towns you may find yourself relying more on one-word communication and hand signals. Nonetheless, with a little patience and a smile you will usually get the information you need from even the smallest local tourist information office.

JAPAN NATIONAL TOURISM ORGANIZATION (JNTO)

The **Japan National Tourism Organization** (JNTO; www.jnto.go.jp, www.japantravelinfo.com) is the main English-language information service for foreign travellers to Japan. JNTO produces a great deal of useful literature, which is available from both its overseas offices and its Tourist Information Center (p62) in Tokyo.

Most publications are available in English and, in some cases, other European and Asian languages. JNTO's website is very useful in planning your journey.

Unfortunately for foreign travellers, JNTO is pulling out of the business of operating tourist information centres inside Japan. The sole remaining domestic office is the Tokyo office.

JNTO has a number of overseas offices:
Australia (☎ 02-9279 2177; Level 7, 36-38 Clarence St, Sydney, NSW Australia 2000)
Canada (☎ 416-366 7140; 481 University Avenue, Suite 306, Toronto, ON M5G 2E9)
France (☎ 01 42 96 20 29; 4 rue de Ventadour, 75001 Paris)
Germany (☎ 069-20353; Kaiserstrasse 11, 60311 Frankfurt am Main)
UK (☎ 020-7398-5670; 5th fl, 12/13 Nicholas Lane, London, EC4N 7BN)
USA Los Angeles (☎ 213-623 1952; 340 E 2nd St, Little Tokyo Plaza, Suite 302, Los Angeles, CA 90012); New York (☎ 212-757 5640; 1 Rockefeller Plaza, Suite 1250, New York, NY 10020)

OTHER INFORMATION OFFICES

There are tourist information offices (kankō annai-sho; 観光案内所) in or near almost all major train stations, but the further you venture into outlying regions, the less chance you have of finding English-speaking staff.

TRAVELLERS WITH DISABILITIES

Japan gets mixed marks in terms of ease of travel for those with disabilities. On the plus side, many new buildings in Japan have access ramps, traffic lights have speakers playing melodies when it is safe to cross, train platforms have raised dots and lines to provide guidance, and some ticket machines in Tokyo have Braille. Some attractions also offer free entry to disabled persons and one companion. On the negative side, many of Japan's cities are still rather difficult for disabled persons to negotiate, often due to the relative lack of normal footpaths on narrow streets.

If you are going to travel by train and need assistance, ask one of the station workers as you enter the station. Try asking: *'karada no fujiyuū no kata no sharyō wa arimasu ka?'* (Are there train carriages for disabled travellers?).

There are carriages on most lines that have areas set aside for people in wheelchairs. Those with other physical disabilities can use the seats set near the train exits, called *yūsen-zaseki*. You will also find these seats near the front of buses; usually they're a different colour from the regular seats.

The most useful information for disabled visitors is provided by the **Japanese Red Cross Language Service Volunteers** (c/o Volunteers Division, Japanese Red Cross Society, 1-1-3 Shiba Daimon, Minato-ku, Tokyo 105-8521, Japan). It can provide useful information for disabled travellers, particularly for the cities of Tokyo, Kyoto and Kamakura.

For information on negotiating Japan in a wheelchair, see the website for **Accessible Japan** (www.tesco-premium.co.jp/aj/index.htm). Also, listings throughout this book indicate with the icon ♿ if a place has wheelchair-access.

VISAS

Generally, visitors who are not planning to engage in income-producing activities while in Japan are exempt from obtaining visas and will be issued a *tanki-taizai* (temporary visitor) visa on arrival in Japan.

Stays of up to six months are permitted for citizens of Austria, Germany, Ireland, Mexico, Switzerland and the UK. Citizens of these countries will almost always be given a 90-day temporary visitor visa upon arrival, which can usually be extended for another 90 days at immigration bureaus inside Japan.

Citizens of the USA, Australia and New Zealand are granted 90-day temporary visitor visas, while stays of up to three months are permitted for citizens of Argentina, Belgium, Canada, Denmark, Finland, France, Iceland, Israel, Italy, the Netherlands, Norway, Singapore, Spain, Sweden and a number of other countries.

Japanese law requires that visitors to the country entering on a temporary visitor visa possess an ongoing air or sea ticket or evidence thereof. In practice, few travellers are asked to produce such documents, but to avoid surprises it pays to be on the safe side.

For additional information on visas and regulations, contact your nearest Japanese embassy or consulate, or visit the website of the **Ministry of Foreign Affairs of Japan** (www.mofa.go.jp). Here you can find out about the different types of visas available, read about working-holiday visas and find details on the Japan Exchange & Teaching (JET) program, which sponsors native English speakers to teach in the Japanese public school system.

Note that on entering Japan, all short-term foreign visitors are required to be photographed and fingerprinted. This happens when you show your passport on arrival.

WOMEN TRAVELLERS

Japan is a relatively safe country for women travellers, though perhaps not quite as safe as some might think. Women travellers are occasionally subjected to some forms of verbal harassment or pry ing questions. Physical attacks are very rare, but have occurred.

The best advice is to avoid being lulled into a false sense of security by Japan's image as one of the world's safest countries and to take the normal precautions you would in your home country. If a neighbourhood or establishment looks unsafe, then treat it that way. As long as you use your common sense, you will most likely find that Japan is a pleasant and rewarding place to travel as a woman.

Several train companies in Japan have recently introduced women-only cars to protect female passengers from *chikan* (men who feel up women and girls on packed trains). These cars are usually available during rush-hour periods on weekdays on busy urban lines. There are signs (usually pink in colour) on the platform indicating where to board these cars, and the cars themselves are usually labelled in both Japanese and English (again, these are often marked in pink).

If you have a problem and find the local police unhelpful, you can call the Japan Helpline (☎ 0120-46-1997), a nationwide emergency number that operates 24 hours a day, seven days a week.

TRANSPORT

GETTING THERE & AWAY
ENTERING THE COUNTRY
While most travellers to Japan fly via Tokyo, there are several other ways of getting into and out of the country. For a start, there are many other airports in Japan, which can make better entry points than Tokyo's somewhat inconvenient Narita International Airport.

PASSPORT
A passport is essential. If your passport is within a few months of expiry, get a new one – you will not be issued a visa if your passport is due to expire before the visa. For information on visas, see opposite.

AIR
There are flights to Japan from all over the world, usually to Tokyo, but also to a number of other Japanese airports. Although Tokyo may seem the obvious arrival and departure point in Japan, for many visitors this may not be the case. For example, if you plan on exploring western Japan or the Kansai region, it might be more convenient to fly into Kansai International Airport near Osaka.

TRANSPORT

GETTING THERE & AWAY

◥ CLIMATE CHANGE & TRAVEL

Travel – especially air travel – is a significant contributor to global climate change. At Lonely Planet, we believe that all who travel have a responsibility to limit their personal impact. As a result, we have teamed with Rough Guides and other concerned industry partners to support Climate Care, which allows people to offset the greenhouse gases they are responsible for with contributions to energy-saving projects and other climate-friendly initiatives in the developing world. Lonely Planet offsets all staff and author travel.

For more information, turn to the responsible travel pages on www.lonely planet.com. For details on offsetting your carbon emissions and a carbon calculator, go to www.climatecare.org.

AIRPORTS & AIRLINES

Japan has many international airports. On the main island of Honshū they are located at Nagoya, Niigata, Osaka/Kansai and Tokyo Narita; on Kyūshū at Fukuoka, Kagoshima, Kumamoto and Nagasaki; in Okinawa at Naha; and on Hokkaidō at Sapporo.

GETTING AROUND

Japan is justifiably famous for its extensive, well-organised and efficient transport network. Schedules are strictly adhered to and late or cancelled services are almost unheard of. All this convenience comes at a price, however, and you'd be well advised to look into money-saving deals whenever possible (see Passes & Discount Tickets, p379).

AIR

Air services in Japan are extensive, reliable and safe. In many cases, flying is much faster than even *shinkansen* (bullet trains) and not that much more expensive. Flying is also an efficient way to travel from the main islands to the many small islands around Japan, particularly the Nansei-shotō (the southern islands of Kagoshima-ken and Okinawa-ken).

In most of Japan's major cities there are travel agencies where English is spoken. To get an idea of the latest prices in Tokyo check the travel ads in the various local English-language publications, and in Kansai check *Kansai Time Out*. In other parts of Japan check the ads in the *Japan Times*.

AIRLINES IN JAPAN

Japan Airlines (JAL; ☎ 03-5460-0522, 0120-255-971; www.jal.co.jp/en) is the major international carrier and also has a domestic network linking the major cities. **All Nippon Airways** (ANA; ☎ 0570-029-709, 03-6741-1120, 0120-029-709; www.ana.co.jp/eng) is the second-largest international carrier and operates a more extensive domestic system. **Japan Trans Ocean Air** (JTA; ☎ 03-5460-0522, 0120-255-971; www.jal.co.jp/jta, in Japanese) is a smaller domestic carrier that mostly services routes in the Nansei-shotō.

In addition to these, **Skymark Airlines** (SKY; ☎ 050-3116-7370; www.skymark.co.jp/en) is a recent start-up budget airline, and **Shinchūō Kōkū** (☎ 0422-31-4191; www.central-air.co.jp, in Japanese) has light-plane flights between Chōfu airport, outside Tokyo, and the islands of Izu-shotō.

🛄 BAGGAGE FORWARDING

If you have too much luggage to carry comfortably or just can't be bothered, you can do what many Japanese travellers do: send it to your next stop by *takkyūbin* (express shipping companies). Prices are surprisingly reasonable and overnight service is the norm. Perhaps the most convenient service is Yamato Takkyūbin, which operates from most convenience stores. Simply pack your luggage and take it to the nearest convenience store; staff will help with the paperwork and arrange for pick-up. Note that you'll need the full address of your next destination in Japanese, along with the phone number of the place. Alternatively, ask the owner of your accommodation to come and pick it up (this is usually possible but might cost extra).

DOMESTIC AIRFARES

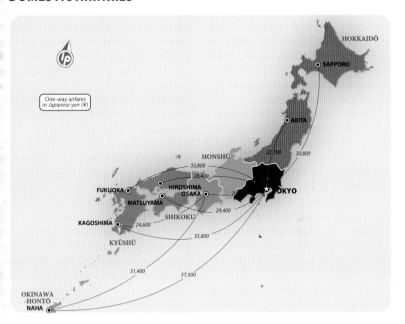

One-way airfares in Japanese yen (¥)

The Domestic Airfares map (above) shows some of the major connections and one-way fares. Note that return fares are usually around 10% cheaper than buying two one-way tickets. The airlines also have some weird and wonderful discounts if you know what to ask for. The most useful of these are the advance-purchase reductions: both ANA and JAL offer discounts of up to 50% if you purchase your ticket a month or more in advance, with smaller discounts for purchases made one to three weeks in advance. Seniors over 65 also qualify for discounts on most Japanese airlines, but these are sometimes only available if you fly on weekdays.

ANA also offers the Star Alliance Japan Airpass for foreign travellers on ANA or Star Alliance network airlines. Provided you reside outside Japan, purchase your tickets outside Japan and carry a valid in-ternational ticket on any airline, you can fly up to five times within 60 days on any ANA domestic route for only ¥11,550 per flight (a huge saving on some routes). Visit www.ana.co.jp/wws/us/e/travelservice/reservations/special/airpass.html for more details.

BICYCLE

Japan is a good country for bicycle touring and several thousand cyclists, both Japanese and foreign, traverse the country every year. Favourite bike touring areas include Kyūshū, Shikoku, the Japan Alps (if you like steep hills!), Noto-hantō and Hokkaidō.

There's no point in fighting your way out of big cities by bicycle. Put your bike on the train or bus and get out to the country before you start pedalling. To take a bicycle on a train you may need to use a bicycle carrying bag, available from good bicycle shops.

See opposite for information on road maps of Japan. In addition to the maps mentioned in that section, a useful series of maps is the *Touring Mapple* (Shobunsha) series, which is aimed at motorcyclists, but is also very useful for cyclists.

For more information on cycling in Japan, you can check out the excellent website of KANcycling (www.kancycling.com).

GUIDED BICYCLE TOURS

For information about guided bicycle tours in Kyoto, see p144. There is talk of a similar service being offered in Tokyo in the future – a web search should turn up the operator once it's up and running.

HIRE

You will find bicycle rental shops out-side the train or bus stations in most of Japan's popular tourist areas, as well as near the ferry piers on many of the country's smaller islands. Typical charges are around ¥200/1000 per hour/day. Kyoto, for example, is ideally suited to bicycle ex-ploration and there are plenty of cheap hire shops to choose from.

Note that the bicycles for rent are not usually performance vehicles. More commonly they're what the Japanese call *mama chari* (literally 'mama's bicycles'): one- or three-speed shopping bikes that are murder on hills of any size. They're also usually too small for anyone over 180cm in height.

BUS

Japan has a comprehensive network of long-distance buses. These 'highway buses' are nowhere near as fast as the *shinkansen* but the fares are comparable with those of normal *futsū* (local) trains. The trip between Tokyo and Sendai

(Northern Honshū), for example, takes about two hours by *shinkansen,* four hours by *tokkyū* (limited express) train and nearly eight hours by bus. Of course, there are many places in Japan where trains do not run and bus travel is the only public transport option.

Bookings can be made through any travel agency in Japan or at the *midori-no-madoguchi* (green counters – look for the counter displaying a green band across the glass) in large Japan Rail (JR) stations. The Japan Rail Pass is valid on some highway buses, but in most cases the *shinkansen* would be far preferable (it's much faster and more comfortable). Note that the storage racks on most buses are generally too small for large backpacks, but you can usually stow them in the lug-gage compartment underneath the bus.

CAR & MOTORCYCLE

Driving in Japan is quite feasible, even for just the mildly adventurous. The major roads are signposted in English; road rules are generally adhered to and driving is safer than in other Asian coun-tries; and petrol, while expensive, is not prohibitively so. Indeed, in some areas of the country it can prove much more convenient than other forms of travel and, between a group of people, it can also prove quite economical.

AUTOMOBILE ASSOCIATIONS

If you're a member of an automobile as-sociation in your home country, you're eli-gible for reciprocal rights with the Japan Automobile Federation (JAF; ☎ 03-6833-9000, 0570-00-2811; www.jaf.or.jp/e/index_e.htm; 2-2-17 Shiba, Minato-ku, Tokyo 105-0014). Its of-fice is near Onarimon Station on the Tōei Mita line. JAF produces a variety of pub-lications, and will make up strip maps for its members.

DRIVING LICENCE

Travellers from most nations are able to drive in Japan with an International Driving Permit backed up by their own regular licence. The international permit is issued by your national automobile association and costs around US$5 in most countries. Make sure it's endorsed for cars and motorcycles if you're licensed for both.

Travellers from Switzerland, France and Germany (and others whose countries are not signatories to the Geneva Convention of 1949 concerning international drivers' licences) are not allowed to drive in Japan on a regular international permit. Rather, travellers from these countries must have their own licence backed by an authorised translation of the same licence. These translations can be made by their country's embassy or consulate in Japan or by the JAF. If you are unsure which category your country falls into, contact the nearest JNTO office (see p371 for more information).

Foreign licences and International Driving Permits are only valid in Japan for six months. If you are staying longer, you will have to get a Japanese licence from the local department of motor vehicles. To do this, you will need to provide your own licence, passport photos, Alien Registration Card and the fee, and also take a simple eye test.

HIRE

You'll usually find car-rental agencies clustered around train stations and ferry piers in Japan. Typical rental rates for a small car are ¥5000 to ¥7000 per day, with reductions for rentals of more than one day. On top of the rental charge, there's about a ¥1000 per day insurance cost.

It's also worth bearing in mind that car rental costs go up during high seasons (28 April to 6 May, 20 July to 31 August and 28 December to 5 January). The increase can make quite a difference to costs.

Communication can sometimes be a major problem when hiring a car. Some of the offices will have a rent-a-car phrasebook, with questions you might need to ask in English. Otherwise, just speak as slowly as possible and hope for the best. A good way to open the conversation is to say 'kokusai menkyō wo motteimasu' (I have an international licence).

Two of the main Japanese car-rental companies and their Tokyo phone numbers are Hertz (☎ 0120-489-882) and Toyota Rent-a-Lease (☎ 0070-8000-10000).

MAPS & NAVIGATION

Get yourself a copy of the *Road Atlas Japan* (Shōbunsha). It's all in romaji with enough names in kanji to make navigation possible even off the major roads. If you're really intent on making your way through the back blocks, a Japanese map will prove useful even if your knowledge of kanji is nil. By far the best Japanese road atlases are the *Super Mapple* series (Shōbunsha), which are available in bookshops and also at some convenience stores.

There is a reasonable amount of signposting in romaji, so getting around isn't all that difficult, especially in developed areas. If you are attempting tricky navigation, use your maps imaginatively – watch out for the railway line, the rivers, the landmarks. They're all useful ways of locating yourself when you can't read the signs. A compass will also come in handy when navigating.

These days, many rental cars come equipped with satellite car navigation systems, which can make navigation a snap, provided you can figure out how to work the system (ask the person at the rental agency to explain it and be sure to take notes). With most of these systems, you can input the phone number of your destination, which is easy, or its address, which is just about impossible if you don't read Japanese (although you can always ask for help here, too). Even without programming in your destination, with the device on the default 'genzai-chi' (present location) setting, you will find it very useful.

LOCAL TRANSPORT

All the major cities offer a wide variety of public transport. In many cities you can get day passes for unlimited travel on bus, tram or subway systems. Such passes are usually called an ichi-nichi-jōsha-ken. If you're staying for an extended period in one city, commuter passes are available for regular travel.

TRAIN

Japanese rail services are among the best in the world: they are fast, frequent, clean and comfortable. The services range from small local lines to the shinkansen super-expresses or 'bullet trains', which have become a symbol of modern Japan.

The 'national' railway is **Japan Railways** (**JR; www.japanrail.com**), which is actually a number of separate private rail systems providing one linked service. The JR system covers the country from one end to the other and provides local services around major cities such as Tokyo and Osaka. There is more than 20,000km of railway line and about 20,000 services daily. JR operates the shinkansen network throughout Japan. Shinkansen lines operate on separate tracks from regular trains, and, in some places, the shinkansen stations are a fair distance from the main JR station (as is the case in Osaka). JR also operates buses and ferries, and conven-

ient ticketing can combine more than one form of transport.

In addition to JR services, there is a huge network of private railways in Japan. Each large city usually has at least one private train line that services that city and the surrounding area, or connects that city to nearby cities.

TYPES OF TRAINS

The slowest trains stopping at all stations are called futsū or kaku-eki-teisha. A step up from this is the kyūkō (ordinary express), which stops at only a limited number of stations. A variation on the kyūkō train is the kaisoku (rapid) service (usually operating on JR lines). Finally, the fastest regular (non-shinkansen) trains are the tokkyū (limited express) services, which are sometimes known as shin-kaisoku (again usually operating on JR lines).

TRAIN TYPES

shinkansen	新幹線	**bullet train**
tokkyū	特急	**limited express**
shin-kaisoku	新快速	**JR special rapid train**
kyūkō	急行	**ordinary express**
kaisoku	快速	**JR rapid or express**
futsū	普通	**local**
kaku-eki-teisha	各駅停車	**local**

OTHER USEFUL WORDS

jiyū-seki	自由席	**unreserved seat**
shitei-seki	指定席	**reserved seat**
green-sha	グリーン車	**1st-class carriage**
ōfuku	往復	**round trip**
katamichi	片道	**one-way**
kinen-sha	禁煙車	**nonsmoking carriage**
kitsuen-sha	喫煙車	**smoking carriage**

SHINKANSEN

The fastest and best-known train services are JR's shinkansen, Japan's famed 'bullet trains'. Shinkansen reach speeds of up to 300km/h and some experimental modls have gone significantly faster. In addition to being incredibly fast, *shinkansen* re also incredibly safe: in more than 30 ears of operation, there has never been a fatality.

The service efficiency starts even before you board the train. Your ticket indicates your carriage and seat number, and platform signs indicate where you should stand for that carriage entrance. The train pulls in precisely to the scheduled minute and, sure enough, the carriage door you want is right beside where you're standing.

On most *shinkansen* routes, there are two or three types of service: faster express services stopping at a limited number of stations, and slower local services stopping at more stations. There is no difference in fare, except for the Green Car 1st-class) carriages, which cost slightly more.

There are a limited number of *kin'en-ha* (nonsmoking carriages); request one when booking or ask on the platform for the *kin'en-sha-jiyū-seki* (unreserved nonsmoking carriages). Unreserved carriages are available on all trains, but at peak holiday periods they can be very crowded and you may have to stand.

CLASSES

Most long-distance JR trains, including *shinkansen,* have regular and Green Car carriages. The seating is slightly more spacious in Green Car carriages, but most people will find the regular carriages perfectly acceptable.

PASSES & DISCOUNT TICKETS

JAPAN RAIL PASS

The Japan Rail Pass is a must for anyone planning to do extensive train travel within Japan. The most important thing to note about the pass is this: the Japan Rail Pass

must be purchased outside Japan. It is available to foreign tourists and Japanese overseas residents (but not foreign residents of Japan). The pass lets you use any JR service for seven days for ¥28,300, 14 days for ¥45,100 or 21 days for ¥57,700. Green Car passes are ¥37,800, ¥61,200 and ¥79,600, respectively. The pass cannot be used for the superexpress Nozomi *shinkansen* service, but is OK for everything else (including other *shinkansen* services).

Since a one-way reserved seat Tokyo–Kyoto *shinkansen* ticket costs ¥13,220, you only have to travel Tokyo–Kyoto–Tokyo to make a seven-day pass come close to paying off. The only surcharge levied on the Japan Rail Pass is for overnight sleepers. Note that the pass is valid only on JR services; you will still have to pay for private train services.

In order to get a pass, you must first purchase an 'exchange order' outside Japan at JAL and ANA offices or major travel agencies. Once you arrive in Japan, you must bring this order to a JR Travel Service Centre (found in most major JR stations and at Narita and Kansai international airports). When you validate your pass, you'll have to show your passport. The pass can only be used by those with a temporary visitor visa, which means it cannot be used by foreign residents of Japan (those on any visa other than the temporary visitor visa).

The clock starts to tick on the pass as soon as you validate it, so don't validate it if you're just going into Tokyo or Kyoto and intend to hang around for a few days. Instead, wait and validate when you leave those cities to explore the rest of the country.

For more information on the pass and overseas purchase locations, visit the JR website's Japan Rail Pass (www.japanrailpass.net/eng/en001.html) section.

TICKETS & RESERVATIONS

Tickets for most journeys can be bought from train station vending machines or ticket counters/reservation offices. For reservations of complicated tickets, larger train stations have *midori-no-madoguchi*. Major travel agencies in Japan also sell reserved-seat tickets, and you can buy *shinkansen* tickets through JAL offices overseas if you will be flying JAL to Japan.

On *futsū* services, there are no reserved seats. On the faster *tokkyū* and *shinkansen* services you can choose to travel reserved or unreserved. However, if you travel unreserved, there's always the risk of not getting a seat and having to stand, possibly for the entire trip. This is a particular danger at weekends, high-travel seasons and on holidays. Reserved-seat tickets can be bought any time from a month in advance to the day of departure.

Information and tickets can be obtained from travel agencies, of which there are a great number in Japan. Nearly every train station of any size will have at least one travel agency in the station building to handle all sorts of bookings in addition to train services. Japan Travel Bureau (JTB) is the big daddy of Japanese travel agencies. However, for most train tickets and long-distance bus reservations, you don't need to go through a travel agency – just go to the ticket counters or *midori-no-madoguchi* of any major train station.

GLOSSARY

or a list of culinary terms, see p332.

Ainu – indigenous people of Hokkaidō and parts of Northern Honshū
ANA – All Nippon Airlines
annai-sho – information office

basho – sumō tournament

chōme – subarea

daibutsu – Great Buddha
daimyō – regional lords under the shōgun
daira/taira – plain
dake/take – peak
dani/tani – valley
dera/tera – temple

eki – train station

fu – urban prefecture
fusuma – sliding screen door
futsū – a local train; literally 'ordinary'

gaijin – foreigners; literally 'outside people'
gasoreen sutando – petrol station
gasshō-zukuri – an architectural style (usually thatch-roofed); literally 'hands in prayer'
gawa/kawa – river
genkan – foyer area where shoes are removed or replaced when entering or leaving a building
gū – shrine

hama/bama – beach
hanami – blossom viewing (usually cherry blossoms)

hantō – peninsula
hatsu-mōde – first shrine visit of the new year
Hikari – the second-fastest type of *shinkansen*
hiragana – phonetic syllabary used to write Japanese words

JAC – Japan Air Commuter
JAF – Japan Automobile Federation
JAL – Japan Airlines
JAS – Japan Air System
ji – temple
jikokuhyō – timetable or book of timetables
jima/shima – island
jingū/jinja – shrine
jizō – small stone statues of the Buddhist protector of travellers and children
JNTO – Japan National Tourism Organization
jō – castle
JR – Japan Railways

kaikyō – channel/strait
kaisoku – rapid train
kaisū-ken – a book of transport tickets
kami – *Shintō* gods; spirits of natural phenomena
kana – the two phonetic syllabaries, *hiragana* and *katakana*
kanji – Chinese ideographic script used for writing Japanese; literally 'Chinese script'
Kannon – Bodhisattva of Compassion (commonly referred to as the Buddhist Goddess of Mercy)
katakana – phonetic syllabary used to write foreign words
katamichi – one-way transport ticket

ken – prefecture
kinen-sha – nonsmoking train carriage
kissaten – coffee shop
ko – lake
kō – port
kōban – police box
kōen – park
ku – ward
kūkō – airport
kura – earth-walled storehouses
kyō – gorge
kyūkō – ordinary express train (faster than a *futsū*, only stopping at certain stations)

machi – city area (for large cities) between a *ku* and *chōme* in size; also street or area
machiya – traditional Japanese town house or city house
maiko – apprentice geisha
manga – Japanese comics
matsuri – festival
minato – harbour
minshuku – the Japanese equivalent of a B&B; family-run budget accommodation
misaki – cape
mon – gate
mura – village

N'EX – Narita Express

ōfuku – return ticket
o-furo – traditional Japanese bath
onsen – hot spring; hot mineral-spa area, usually with accommodation
oshibori – hot towels provided in restaurants

rettō – island group
romaji – Japanese roman script

ropeway – Japanese word for a cabl car, tramway or funicular railway
rotemburo – open-air or outdoor bath
ryokan – traditional Japanese inn

saki – cape
sakura – cherry blossoms
san – mountain
sentō – public baths
shi – city
shinkaisoku – express trains or specia rapid train (usually on JR lines)
shinkansen – superexpress trains known in the West as 'bullet trains'
Shintō – the indigenous religion o Japan; literally 'the way of the gods'
shōji – sliding rice-paper screens
shotō – archipelago or island group
shukubō – temple lodgings

taiko – drum
taisha – great shrine
taki – waterfall
teien – garden
TIC – tourist information center
to – metropolis, eg Tokyo-to
tō – island
tokkyū – limited express; faster than a *kyūkō* train
torii – entrance gate to a *Shintō* shrine

wan – bay
washi – Japanese handmade paper

yama – mountain
yama-goya – mountain huts
yatai – festival floats/hawker stalls
yukata – light cotton summer kimono worn for lounging or casual use; stand ard issue when staying at a *ryokan*

zaki – cape
zan – mountain

◥ BEHIND THE SCENES

THE AUTHORS
CHRIS ROWTHORN
Coordinating Author, This is Japan, Japan's Top Itineraries, Planning Your Trip, Kyoto & Kansai, Okinawa & the Southwest Islands, Japan in Focus, Directory & Transport

Born in England and raised in the USA, Chris has lived in Kyoto since 1992. Soon after his arrival in Kyoto, Chris started studying the Japanese language and culture. In 1995 he became a regional correspondent for the *Japan Times*. He joined Lonely Planet in 1996 and has worked on guides to Kyoto, Tokyo, Japan and hiking in Japan. When not on the road, he spends his time seeking out Kyoto's best restaurants, temples, hiking trails and gardens. He also conducts walking tours of Kyoto, Nara and Tokyo. For more on Chris, check out his website at www.chrisrowthorn.com.

Author thanks
Thanks to the following people: Emily Wolman, David Carroll, David Connolly, Anita Banh, Sam Trafford, Lauren Hunt, Eoin Dunlevy, Ijuin Koko, Kono Kiyomi, Takahashi Michiko, Shibata Sumie, Taga Kazuo, Sonoda Makoto, Ohno Jiro, Matt Cooper, Maruyama Chiyuki, Nakanishi Norio, Aoki Takashi, Hagiwara Keiko, Wendy Yanagihara, Matthew Firestone, Andrew Bender, Paul Warham, Ben Walker, Timothy Hornyak and all the readers who were kind enough to send us emails about Japan.

ANDREW BENDER
Central Honshū

France was closed, so after college Andy left his native New England to work in Tokyo. It ended up being a life-changing journey, as visits to Japan often are. He's since mastered chopsticks, the language, karaoke and taking his shoes off at the door, and he's worked with Japanese companies on both sides of the Pacific, from his current base of Los Angeles. His writing has appeared in *Travel + Leisure*, *Forbes*, the *Los Angeles Times* and many airline magazines, plus over a dozen Lonely Planet titles. In an effort toward even greater transoceanic harmony, Andy does cross-cultural consulting with businesses and sometimes takes tour groups to Japan. Find out more at www.andrewbender.com.

MATTHEW D FIRESTONE   Northern Honshū, Hokkaidō

Matt is a trained anthropologist and epidemiologist who should probably be in the midst of a successful academic career by now, though somehow he can't seem to pry himself away from Japan. A resident of the massive megalopolis that is Tokyo, Matt works primarily as a freelance journalist and writer, though he took a break from his urban trappings to research Japan's far north. Matt has also written more than a dozen guidebooks for Lonely Planet covering Asia, Africa and Latin America.

TIMOTHY N HORNYAK   North, South & West of Tokyo, Ogaswara-shotō

A native of Montreal, Tim moved to Japan in 1999 and has written on Japanese culture, technology and history for publications including *Scientific American*, *Wired News* and the *Far Eastern Economic Review*. He has lectured on Japanese robots at the Kennedy Center in Washington, DC; travelled to the heart of Hokkaidō to find the remains of a forgotten theme park called Canadian World; and retraced the steps of haiku poet Matsuo Bashō in Akita-ken. He firmly believes that the greatest Japanese invention of all time is the onsen (hot spring). Having visited all 47 of Japan's prefectures, his next goal is to go to the hot springs officially listed as 'secret' by an industry group.

BENEDICT WALKER   Kyūshū

Inspired by a primary school teacher, Ben's love of Japan blossomed early and by 17 he was runner-up in the Australian finals of the Japan Foundation Japanese Speech Contest and had made two solo trips to Japan. In 1998, with a degree in Communications under his belt, Ben hit the road in earnest. After long stints in Canada and Europe, he found himself teaching English in Osaka until his tattered Lonely Planet guide led him to the mountains of Matsumoto, where he found work as a translator and lived like a local. Currently based in Melbourne, Ben manages travel for rock stars and dreams about his next trip.

PAUL WARHAM   Western Honshū, Shikoku

Paul grew up in Lancashire, and got out as soon as he could. He came to Japan as a teenager and after waiting tables at golf clubs in Osaka and Kōbe went on to have an undistinguished career as a student of Japanese literature at Oxford and Harvard. He is based in Tokyo, where his current research interests include drinking in old sake pubs and translating Japanese novels set in supermarkets. Paul also wrote the Sake text for Japan in Focus.

WENDY YANAGIHARA   Tokyo

Wendy first toured Tokyo on her mother's hip at age two and was raised on white rice and wanderlust. Between and beyond childhood summers spent in Japan, she has woven travels through her stints as psychology and art student, bread peddler, jewellery pusher, espresso puller, graphic designer, English teacher and more recently as author for titles including *Tokyo Encounter, Costa Rica, Indonesia* and *Grand Canyon National Park*. She has spent months over the last several years eating, drinking and dancing her way across Tokyo in the name of research. She's currently based in beautiful Boulder, Colorado.

CONTRIBUTING AUTHORS

The Health section was based on text written by Dr Trish Batchelor, who is a travel medicine specialist and a medical advisor to the Travel Doctor New Zealand clinics. She teaches travel medicine through the University of Otago and is interested in underwater and high-altitude medicine, and in the impact of tourism on host countries.

THIS BOOK

This 1st edition of *Discover Japan* was coordinated by Chris Rowthorn, and researched and written by Andrew Bender, Matthew D Firestone, Timothy N Hornyak, Benedict Walker, Paul Warham and Wendy Yanagihara. This guidebook was commissioned in Lonely Planet's Oakland office, and produced by the following:

Commissioning Editor Emily K Wolman
Coordinating Editor David Carroll
Coordinating Cartographer Anita Banh
Coordinating Layout Designer Jessica Rose
Managing Editor Brigitte Ellemor
Managing Cartographers David Connolly, Herman So
Managing Layout Designer Sally Darmody
Assisting Editor Kate Evans
Assisting Cartographers Hunor Csutoros, Birgit Jordan, Alison Lyall, Ross Macaw, Amanda Sierp
Cover Naomi Parker, lonelyplanetimages.com
Internal Image Research Jane Hart, lonelyplanetimages.com
Project Manager Eoin Dunlevy

Thanks to Shahara Ahmed, Sasha Baskett, Glenn Beanland, Yvonne Bischofberger, Adrian Blackburn, Jessica Boland, Nicholas Colicchia, Laura Crawford, Melanie Dankel, Ryan Evans, Jane Hart, Suki Gear, Joshua Geoghegan, Mark Germanchis, Chris Girdler, Michelle Glynn, Brice Gosnell, Imogen Hall, James Hardy, Steve Henderson, Lauren Hunt, Laura Jane, Chris Lee Ack, Nic Lehman, John Mazzocchi, Annelies Mertens, Jennifer Mullins, Wayne Murphy, Darren O'Connell, Naomi Parker, Piers Pickard, Howard Ralley, Raphael Richards, Lachlan Ross, Julie Sheridan, Jason Shugg, Caroline Sieg, Naomi

Stephens, Geoff Stringer, John Taufa, Jane Thompson, Sam Trafford, Stefanie Di Trocchio, Tashi Wheeler, Clifton Wilkinson, Juan Winata, Nick Wood

Internal photographs

p4 *Ukiyo-e* (wood-block prints), Frank Carter; p10 Sushi restaurant on Sanjo-dōri, downtown Kyoto, Brent Winebrenner; p12 Himeji-jō, Himeji, John Banagan; p31 Kimono on display, Kyoto, Phil Weymouth; p39 Waterspout, pool and maple leaves at Zennoji, Takayama, Brent Winebrenner; p50 Pedestrian crossing at dusk, Shinjuku, Tokyo, Rachel Lewis; p97 Stepping stones at Heian-jingū, Kyoto, Christopher Groenhout; p163 Japanese macaque in onsen, Jigokudani, John Borthwick; p205 Young girls read *omikuji* (paper fortunes) at a festival in Sapporo, Paul Dymond; p245 Decorations above a boat on the Yoshino-gawa, Shikoku, Mason Florence; p285 Detail of Shuri-jo, Naha, Richard Cummins; p322 Tea ceremony, Kyoto, Greg Elms; p357 Tokyo subway train, Rachel Lewis.

NOTES

NOTES

↘ INDEX

INDEX

H-K

INDEX

S-T

INDEX

T-U

INDEX

V-Z

MAP LEGEND

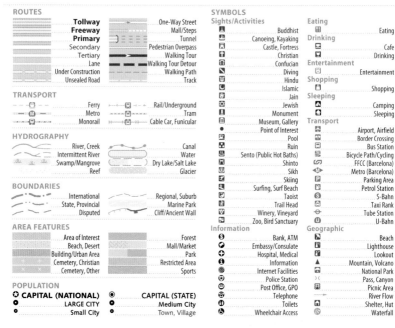

LONELY PLANET OFFICES

Australia

Head Office
Locked Bag 1, Footscray, Victoria 3011
☎ 03 8379 8000, fax 03 8379 8111
talk2us@lonelyplanet.com.au

USA

150 Linden St, Oakland, CA 94607
☎ 510 250 6400, toll free 800 275 8555,
fax 510 893 8572
info@lonelyplanet.com

UK

2nd fl, 186 City Rd,
London EC1V 2NT
☎ 020 7106 2100, fax 020 7106 2101
go@lonelyplanet.co.uk

Published by Lonely Planet
ABN 36 005 607 983

Printed by Hang Tai Printing Company, Hong Kong
Printed in China.